# The Creative Imagination

# The Creative Imagination

## ENLIGHTENMENT TO ROMANTICISM

### JAMES ENGELL

43494
HARVARD UNIVERSITY PRESS
Cambridge, Massachusetts
&
London, England
1981

Publication of this book has been aided by a grant
from the Hyder Edward Rollins Fund.

Library of Congress Cataloging in Publication Data
Engell, James, 1951–
  The creative imagination.

  Bibliography: p.
  Includes index.
  1. Imagination—History.   2. Enlightenment—History.
3. Romanticism—Great Britain.   4. Romanticism—Germany.
5. Empiricism—History.   6. Creation (Literary, artistic, ect.)   I. Title.
B105.I49E53          128'.3          80-20265
ISBN 0-674-17572-7

TO RUTH ENGELL
AND THE MEMORY OF
FREDERICK ENGELL

# PREFACE

This book shows how the idea of the imagination, as understood in the Romantic period and as we still understand it today, was actually the creation of the eighteenth century. During the eighteenth century the effort to define—to create—an idea of the imagination permitted and encouraged a critical survey of the entire creative process and of the history of literature and the arts. Such an opportunity was unprecedented. The immediate result was that the creative imagination emerged as the central value of the late eighteenth century and of Romanticism.

The idea of the imagination developed simultaneously in literature and criticism, philosophy, religion, and even science. In an atmosphere of discovery that was cosmopolitan and genial, individuals in all fields strongly hoped, they felt it their duty, to communicate with and to learn from others whose specialties differed. Major figures like Hobbes, Addison, Hume, Gerard, Goethe, Kant, and Coleridge combined several interests in their search for the nature of the imagination. As it was discussed, the idea, like an ore being processed, was enriched. The more it was analyzed, the more it was joined and synthesized with a number of concerns—poetry, psychology, and metaphysics, the interest of genius and originality, the relatively new areas of anthropology and literary history, theology and the moral life. As an idea, the imagination grew by constant additions; each important figure in the adventure of this idea read scores of other writers. Yet there was a continual sense of affirmation, of preserving and not denying what had been stated before, and then enlarging on it.

By 1775 or 1780 "imagination" meant far more, and was a distinctly more popular idea, than at the beginning of the century. With a few exceptions, mostly in German philosophical writing, the idea had matured. The phrase "the creative imagination" appears as early as the

1730s. Each romantic poet and critic, finding a particular emphasis or distinct angle of vision for his own concept and exercise of the imagination, drew that angle of vision from ones that had originated in the eighteenth century and had reached a level of completeness before 1800. Throughout the Enlightenment the idea had been undergoing a continuum of development. It followed a sort of *Lex Continui* that Leibniz perceived in nature and that we see in intellectual and literary history as well. This continuity of development produced all the significant concepts of the imagination that are now identified with the years from the 1780s to the 1830s. Of the major Romantics, such as Coleridge, Hazlitt, Blake, Shelley, Wordsworth, and Keats, each had several ideas of the creative imagination at hand. Their poetry and criticism represented the great practical application and achievement of their ready trust in the imagination, and this confidence, with its resulting productivity, could have existed only if these writers had been exposed to and been given the chance to apply concepts of the imaginative power that were already specific and refined.

The idea of the imagination dramatized and made articulate a great dialectic between matter and spirit, nature and the inner psyche, materialism and transcendentalism, as well as between the concrete sensuous images of poetry and the "fading coal" of its inspiration. The imagination had already become, in a phrase used by Sir Joshua Reynolds in 1786, "the residence of truth." It laid the groundwork for an organic view of mind and nature together. The creative imagination had also become, by 1780, an ideal to believe in wholeheartedly, a goal, a state of mind or being toward which to aspire—something it had never been before. This aspiration and growth toward the ideal is the frequent subject of much of the greatest romantic poetry. As an ideal, too, the imagination provided a flexible and resonant critical approach and fostered a new critical vocabulary.

As the imagination became the popular and dominant subject of literature and even philosophy, its connotations multiplied. The progress of the idea is, to some degree, semantic. The "heat" and fervor, the enthusiasm, "fire," and "divine inspiration" of the poet—all terms originating in classical times and used widely by neoclassical critics—now came under the arch of one term. "Imagination" acquired several meanings, and critics and philosophers began to differentiate among its levels or degrees. By 1780 there was a growing and often painstaking effort to distinguish "fancy" from "imagination" and to see imagination itself as governing the interrelated activities of perception, experience, aesthetic appreciation, and the crown of all, artistic creativity. Imagination was also viewed as a cosmic power, responsible for bringing forth and organizing the unity of all creation and for implanting the divine in man.

The philosophical and psychological terms used to describe imagination as it involves sensations, memory, and intuition blended together with the literary and critical vocabulary developed to convey a poet's feelings and passions, his vision and creative insight, and his gift of prophecy. It is a tribute to the tolerance, sympathy, and open nature of those who treated the imagination that, while not always in conformity, they avoided bitter controversy. On the subject of the imagination, no matter their disputes elsewhere, their attitude was basically cooperative and affirmative.

This book also shows how the eighteenth century, especially after 1750, participated in a self-transformation of its values and tastes, how it argued itself from an age of reason into an age of what Wordsworth defines as imagination, "reason in her most exalted mood." There is no quarrel with the view that the eighteenth century closed with an age of sentiment or sensibility that differed from the Enlightenment, and indeed in Germany was in rebellion against some of what the Enlightenment stood for. Yet this wonderful period of the later eighteenth century is here seen—and can best be seen in its handling of the idea of the imagination—as the process of the Enlightenment's transforming itself. The last thirty or forty years of the century constitute that time when the Enlightenment was creating Romanticism, primarily by developing the idea of the imagination.

This book is not a critical analysis of poetry and imaginative literature, though such analyses naturally enter. Nor is it an attempt simply to infer from such literature what particular views about the imagination were held by individual authors. Rather it examines the growth of the idea as it was directly and critically expressed, which in turn promoted and encouraged imaginative literature, and without which that literature could hardly have been written. Most of the chapters deal with one or two individuals and are not, as a rule, devised according to topics or concepts. This is because the idea matured as writers and thinkers extended the work of their predecessors and contemporaries. The idea lived in a community of minds more than in a bundle of abstractions. Topics related to the imagination—such as genius, the sublime, myth, symbolism, poetical suggestiveness, the cult of primitivism, beauty, and taste—emerged in a dramatic way as they were animated and considered together by individual writers.

It is inevitable that this book center on Britain and Germany, including exchanges between poets and critics of these countries. An effort is also made to understand important repercussions in America before 1825. France, as several distinguished scholars of the period have pointed out, faced a different set of circumstances. Its literature and criticism, while in the highest sense imaginative, did not originate or develop the idea of the imagination in the same fashion nor to the same extent as that of England, Scotland, and Germany.

Having reached maturity in the later eighteenth century, the idea of the imagination then enjoyed its brilliant romantic expression. But by the early nineteeenth century, before 1820, the development of the idea had slowed. The idea has since been rediscovered a number of times, and each time it has been given even greater value and hope, until imagination is now considered, without question, the supreme value of art and literature. Yet this supremacy was established before the end of the eighteenth century.

For help in the publication of this book I express special thanks to the Hyder Rollins Fund. Unless otherwise noted, all translations are my own.

Inevitably, a work of this sort, attempting to discuss the thought and writings of over a century and a half, owes a heavy debt to the insights and researches of many scholars. I hope these obligations are recorded in my notes. Especially influential in the conception and writing of the book have been the works of M. H. Abrams, W. J. Bate, Sir Isaiah Berlin, John Boyd, Douglas Bush, Ernst Cassirer, Richard Fogle, Lilian R. Furst, W. J. Hipple, Arthur Lovejoy, Thomas McFarland, John Mahoney, Frank Manuel, Emerson Marks, I. A. Richards, Clarence Thorpe, Mary Warnock, and René Wellek. Several friends and colleagues, among those who have read the manuscript, have preserved me from blunders and given fresh suggestions. I particularly wish to thank Herschel Baker, W. J. Bate, Kathleen Coburn, Jerome Buckley, Alan Heimert, Walter Kaiser, Gwin Kolb, Harry Levin, Emerson Marks, and David Perkins. My greatest debt is expressed in the dedication.

# CONTENTS

## Part One. Probing the Source

### 1/The Essential Idea   3

Nature of the idea, a product of the eighteenth century; how it
unifies related concerns; the idea of the imagination creates the Romantic movement and becomes its key concept.

### 2/Empiricism in Earnest: Hobbes and Locke   11

The British empirical tradition.
Hobbes: inclusiveness at the beginning; "decaying sense," the
"compounded imagination," and "mental discourse";
imagination and will; imagination as the distinguishing
mark of civilization.
Locke: "The mind has a power"; a new view of reason; the *tabula rasa* an oversimplification; imagination active as well
as passive; Lee, Norris, Law, Harte.

### 3/Claims of the Spirit: Shaftesbury and Leibniz   22

The ideal or spiritual philosophers; Cambridge Platonists;
Shaftesbury's curious personal relationship to Locke;
"harmony" in Shaftesbury; the intuitive and productive
power.
Leibniz and the wonder of force; admiration of Shaftesbury
and answers to Locke in the *Nouveaux essais; "la puissance active"* or *"vis activa."*
Leibniz and romantic anticipations; an organic view of mind
and cosmos.

of emotion and thought. Extensions and refinements; Hartley's system abridged and modified by Priestley; imagination as an organizing power; relation to beliefs and feelings.

Associationism and the creative process; Gerard and Whiter.

## 7/Investigators of Genius: Gerard and Duff  78

"It is imagination that produces genius"; Gerard's exhaustive and incisive analysis; individuals differ in imagination and hence in genius; originality and invention.

Duff's plastic power; scope of imagination in poetry is "absolute and unconfined"; it assimilates judgment; imagination in early societies and primitive art; German reaction to British associationists; Hissmann and Maass.

## Part Three. The German Foundation

## 8/Shadows a Century Long  91

Intellectual climate of Germany; differences from Britain. First principles; the philosophical establishment; Leibniz and Shaftesbury.

The next generation; Wolff and the *facultas fingendi;* Baumgarten; the "Swiss Critics" Bodmer and Breitinger, their success and debt to Addison; Klopstock vindicates their position.

Stirrings of a grand synthesis, the empirical tradition transformed.

The quick response to associationism; Hissmann's thorough knowledge of the British; Maass's history of associationism.

The psychology of the imagination enters artistic theory: Platner.

## 9/The New Focus of Literature and Myth  102

Meister's suggestive work from 1770 through the 1790s.

Sulzer's essential analysis; its clarity and importance for art theory and literature.

In the critical whirlwind; Blankenberg's research and compilations reveal extensive and learned interest; his work a source book.

## 12/The Psyche Reaches Out: Coalescence and the
## Chemistry of the Mind    161

## 13/Distinctions Between Fancy and
## Imagination    172

## 14/A Plateau in Britain and Developments in America    184

## 15/Organic Sensibility: Hazlitt    197

Levels of the imagination; Coleridge draws on many thinkers
    and poets.
Imagination's image of imagination.
Art and symbol.
Criticism; principles and practice.
The critical ideal of unity.
Beauty and the ideal.
The moral imperative and friendly heart.
Religion, the alpha and omega of imagination; Coleridge culmi-
    nates the study; the idea remains open.

# PART ONE

## Probing the Source

# 1

# THE ESSENTIAL IDEA

*T*he Enlightenment created the idea of the imagination. As the idea evolved in the eighteenth century, it became the vital principle for an expanding network of concepts and values. The understanding of genius, poetic power, and originality, of sympathy, individuality, knowledge, and even of ethics grew and took lifeblood from the idea of imagination.

The imagination, as a rising element in thought, propelled literature, aesthetics, philosophy, criticism, religion, and psychology into new regions. Values and beliefs changed but did not splinter and fly apart. By influencing each of these branches of art and thought, the idea of the imagination tended to mix and draw them into one body, a "university" in the original sense, an awareness, an atmosphere of knowledge and creativity reflecting the interconnected nature of human life and the universe itself. The dream of unity in Friedrich Schelling's ideal system (where human endeavor is organized by philosophy, and philosophy is crowned by art), the faith that Coleridge placed in imagination, and the value of poetry not as decoration but as new truth, which Wordsworth called "the first and last of all knowledge"—none of this would have been possible without the aggregate steps taken by men like Mark Akenside, Nicolaus Tetens, Joseph Priestley, and Dugald Stewart.

Giants of the Enlightenment too—Locke and Shaftesbury, Hume, Kant, and Leibniz—all extended the idea of imagination from a different starting point. Like a coral reef, the idea spread from various centers, then merged to cover a vast area. The Romantics soon had, as a foundation, an idea whose power both to assimilate and to foster other ideas seemed virtually limitless; it was an idea "to show . . . the very age and body of the time his form and pressure." A captivating metaphor of mid-eighteenth century thought—one used by Edward Young, Samuel

Johnson, and German writers, later expanded by Goethe, Shelley, Coleridge, and other Romantics—holds that an original poem or idea develops from a seed or germ.[1] Out of this almost spiritually compact beginning emerges, by degrees, an integrated whole. This is how the idea of imagination evolved, and its embryonic phase, its youth—everything except its fullest maturity—occurred in the eighteenth century.

In order to grasp this growth of the idea, we must, as Coleridge said, "interpret and understand the symbol, that the wings of the air-sylph are forming within the skin of the caterpillar." As we study the individuals participating in the history of this idea, we can "know and feel, that the *potential* works *in* them, even as the *actual* works on them!"[2] The history of the creative imagination from 1660 to 1820 was a human drama, unfolding by stages. Seldom in Western culture has one idea excited so many leading minds for such a stretch of time. It became the impelling force in artistic and intellectual life, in literature and philosophy, even in much political and social thought, especially from 1750 on. The creative imagination, Wordsworth's "mild creative breeze," rustled through and animated a forest of individuals, stirring each to participate in it and to add his own force until it turned into a *Zeitgeist.* The new idea of creative imagination, at its best, was not conceived as an abstract puzzle or impersonal theory. Poetic reputations, misgivings, fame, livelihoods, the hope and apprehension of human achievement were gambled on the effort to define as well as to exercise it. Individuals handed down, imported, and amplified the idea.

There is really nothing with which to compare it. Humble rhymers and home-spun philosophers, great poets and philosophers, level-headed and half-mad men brought it to ripeness in the Enlightenment. Its literary expression assured the birth of Romanticism. More than vague "inspiration," the imagination became the way to grasp truth.

By the later years of the eighteenth century, a penetrating, articulate philosophy of the imagination existed. It became the core and *sine qua non* of Romanticism and the key to romantic art, literature, and thought. Though the concept of the imagination is the quintessence of Romanticism, that brilliant phase in art and thought did not itself create the idea of imagination. The reverse happened. Far more than any other one thing, this idea shaped and sustained Romanticism, which itself might be described as the mingled achievements of a number of individuals who in their own characteristic ways, shared a faith in imaginative power. Romanticism grew around the imagination in the manner that a storm masses around a vortex, a central area that differs in pressure from the surrounding space. If that area vanishes—if the idea is taken away—there will be only light and aimless winds. The attracting and unifying force of the imagination made Romanticism in the first place.[3] Without that force the period would have become something radically different, its poetry and thought fragmented and disappointing.

The idea of imagination, and with it Romanticism, was not only an outgrowth of the eighteenth century but a reaction to other tendencies and ideas in the century as well. This reaction was hardly directed at the open and inquiring spirit of the Enlightenment, and usually not at the last three or four decades of the century. Coleridge loved Akenside and would hardly revolt against or condemn men like Francis Hutcheson, Hugh Blair, or Archibald Alison. William Hazlitt thought Hobbes a great philosopher, and Hazlitt's second book was an abridgment of Abraham Tucker's *Light of Nature Pursued* (1768-1777). Wordsworth read widely in eighteenth-century aesthetics, psychology, and moral philosophy. Keats dedicated *Endymion* to the memory of Chatterton. The German Romantics often took issue with Kant but rarely, if ever, regarded him as a sworn enemy. Shaftesbury, Spinoza, and Leibniz were "discovered," debated, and revered.

The Romantics were not denouncing the whole eighteenth century; they wanted to repudiate certain aspects of thought and literary practice, especially those associated with neoclassic formalism, materialistic theories of mind and body, and atomistic philosophy. The bugbears of the Romantics, figures against whom the concept of the imagination was used as a weapon, hardly included Adam Smith with his belief in sympathy, William Duff on original genius, or Tetens on the qualities of poetic power. Rather the reaction was against the narrowly sterile and mechanistic side of previous generations. The Germans were especially concerned with casting off France's cultural imperialism. But more than an indictment of particular men, Romanticism was a reaction against a popular and social condition, an intellectual atmosphere in which large numbers of second and third-rate minds held power. In simplifying Locke, popularizers had made him more rigidly mechanistic. The reaction to Pope was real enough. But although it was directed at him in name, much of the underlying cause was that the very kind of scribblers satirized and abhorred by Pope and Swift had, by 1760, become no less common. They walked the streets in flesh and blood. They clogged Grub Street. They got poetry and books published. Johnson, who virtually dismissed the unities of time and place on the basis of the audience's capacity for imaginative response, lampooned mechanical critics and thinkers in his series on Dick Minim in the *Idler* (Nos. 60–61). Yet thirty to fifty years later, the tendency in reacting to a popular ethos and in attacking a vested interest of thought and a literary establishment that seemed crusty was to select figures like Pope, Johnson, and Locke. They became symbols—often erroneously—of a pervading and undistinguished mass of ideas and conventions that were more formal and mechanistic than any they had ever believed in themselves. The Colley Cibbers and Thomas Rymers and Soame Jenynses were not scathed in the Romantic period because they had already been reduced to size by the Johnsons, Popes, and Swifts.

The leading writers and minds of the late eighteenth and early nineteenth century recognized this fact most of the time. They knew that the history of letters and thought is diverse. There is not one important thinker on the imagination who did not owe a debt to several writers in the period from 1660 to 1760. When the Romantics leapt back to a love of the Elizabethan, or of Longinus, or of the imagination found in Homer and Shakespeare, they continued a trend in taste fostered for a century before them.

Reaction, then, was part of the growth of the idea of imagination, but in a special way. The reaction was, in substance if not in polemics, more a case of the later decades of the eighteenth century overturning an abstract and mechanistic formalism found in the first half of the century, than a case of Romanticism throwing off the weight of the previous hundred years as a whole.[4]

The idea of the imagination forms a hinge connecting the Enlightenment and Romanticism. It pivots and swings from one period to the other in a fashion that tells more about both of them than does any other point of contact. In a larger perspective, the medieval and Renaissance world-views end and the classical tradition in literature wanes as the idea of the imagination becomes dominant. It introduces the modern era. During the century and a half from 1660 to 1810, the Great Chain of Being enjoyed its last viable influence. The concept of imagination replaced it. The two ideas are not antithetical; they have some common ground, especially in their more Platonic interpretations. Shaftesbury, Leibniz, Addison, Akenside, Schelling, and Coleridge all combine the two ideas. But the Great Chain of Being could no longer take the full brunt of philosophical inquiry, nor support a view of man and nature, or of God, that squared with empiricism, psychology, and the new sciences of chemistry, astronomy, geology, and biology. The imagination offers the dynamic and active. It is a force, an energy, not a state of being. It more easily explains the interchange of state and the transforming, organic qualities of psyche and nature. The imagination better solved the problem why God would create the boundless diversity of nature if He were self-sufficient unto Himself. In the Western tradition the idea of imagination, developed in the Enlightenment and triumphant in Romanticism, marks the end of an epoch stretching back 2500 years and introduces a new stage of thought and letters, now two hundred years in progress.

One reason for this key place in what Coleridge calls the history of the collective human mind is that so many gifted individuals saw in the imagination a power that could bridge the gulf between man and nature and knit the two together again. Since the seventeenth century when the new philosophy called "all in doubt," a haunting and almost sinister dualism had thrust its way into prominence. This split, a bifurcation of man and nature, upset the pattern of Western thought and overturned one of its most cherished goals of unity. The popular optimism associated with Newton's work and with the new science and its methods of proof could not heal this split. A mechanistic outlook simply strengthened the barrier between man and nature. Reason was popularly viewed less as an intuitional power with direct apprehension of nature and truth, and more as a method of deduction. Mystical and Platonic writers, on the other side, were drawn onto a tactically dangerous terrain. They were being forced to prove, empirically, that the empiricists and mechanists were wrong.

The world and the cosmos seemed to operate according to principles that were either alien to or beyond common understanding. The principles could be learned only as the senses received them piecemeal from the external world or as the mind intuited them from an internal sensibility and store of innate ideas. The imagination held out hope and promised a reconciliation of this dualism. It could overcome the alienation between man and nature by establishing a power of knowledge and creation common to nature and the mind, a power Coleridge might call "connatural."

By the mid 1700s a rapid movement was under way to show that the idea of imagination, with one foot in the empirical and one foot in the ideal or transcendental, could bestride those two peninsulas of thought and, like a colossus, protect and unify the harbor between. The imagination could, in its dialectic, synthesize soul and body; it could unite man's spirit and affections with the concrete reality of nature. The imagination would solve the dilemma of dualism. Each thinker who treated the idea of the imagination with any perspicacity soon realized that this grand synthesis promised fulfillment in the art of creative genius.

But the creative imagination was not a new system of thought, though several systems were built on it. Since it was a moving force, creative and active itself, it could express in art the aesthetic play or balance, and the final unity, between ideal and real, sensuous and transcendental, subjective and objective, the magic by which we perceive and create, and even the miracle by which the cosmos first took and is continuing to take shape. As an idea, it invigorated several "systems" and tended to erode the barriers separating them.

The creative imagination therefore promised to the arts a crowning role in philosophical thought, in knowledge, power, and even in religion.

It could lead to grace and salvation. It could recapture the ideal of unity. Literature and art were elevated to a height and popularity they had never before enjoyed and from which they have yet to descend. The increasing confidence in the creative imagination from about 1740 on led poets and critics to trust and to believe in it, to sense that they had a mission not only to fabricate a new world-view, a reappraisal of man and nature, but even more to swaddle this thought and energy around human feelings in the forms, colors, and sounds of a rediscovered natural world.

The creative imagination became the way to unify man's psyche and, by extension, to reunify man with nature, to return by the paths of self-consciousness to a state of higher nature, a state of the sublime where senses, mind, and spirit elevate the world around them even as they elevate themselves. The new concept of the imagination enlarged the humanities and increased the expectations placed on secular art, and the promise and burden of those expectations continue today.

As the "high Romantics" receive and develop the concept of the imagination, it becomes the resolving and unifying force of all antitheses and contradictions. It reconciles and identifies man with nature, the subjective with the objective, the internal mind with the external world, time with eternity, matter with spirit, the finite with the infinite, the conscious with the unconscious, and self-consciousness with the absence of self-consciousness. It relates the static to the dynamic, passive to active, ideal to real, and universal to particular. The Homeric catalogue of polar opposites that make up man and the universe becomes a list of unities. Imagination becomes the process to understand and to view both the world and the self. The imaginative poet obtains a power that is the essence of inspiration (the Greek *enthousiasmos*). He is the voice of knowledge, wisdom, and beauty, the creator of a metaphorical language that identifies one thing or spirit with another and expresses man's harmony with nature.

Late eighteenth-century and romantic writers used the figure of Proteus to invoke the power of imagination, to personify what was called its "lively" force, and sometimes to give it a religious and Hellenic flavor. Coleridge and August Schlegel refer to Shakespeare as a Proteus, as does Hazlitt, but as early as 1774 William Richardson describes Shakespeare as "the Proteus of the drama; he changes himself into every character, and enters easily into every condition of human nature."[5] To modify imagination with the word "protean" may seem a tautology. But the use suggests at least three important ways to look at the complex story we face. First, the imagination was an idea that operated through and changed numerous areas of thought. It generated other ideas. It touched the arts and literature profoundly, and with them philosophy. Aesthetics, morality, and religion shared it, though it was never interpreted in quite the same way. In poetry the imagination became responsible for overall poetic "genius" and for the gift of particular and striking characterizations. It could organize a composition, whether lyric, epic, or dramatic, into a whole whose patterns emerge from an internal *Geist* and not from an externally predetermined form.

Second, although an idea may have a life of its own, ideas that remain aloof from fresh and individual treatment are, as Alfred North Whitehead said, inert. They become moribund and die. After everyone agrees about an idea for a long enough period of time, they kill it. The imagination luckily never acquired a monolithic profile. As it is touched and used by each individual, it obtains a separate life, and all the interacting, inheriting, disowning, and reconciling of these separate lives form the idea at large, which is what we see on the gross canvas of history and literature. The story of an idea is a story about people, many related stories of many men and women. What Keats thought about the imagination differs, though not utterly, from Hobbes's view. Blake and Locke were not yoked together by W. S. Landor in his *Imaginary Conversations*. Perhaps Landor lacked the imagination for it. But the distance between those men is not one of years and natural conviction alone. It is also a distance created by the thoughts of other men who are intermediaries direct and indirect. The progress of the imagination is like a long play. It is dramatic over decades and will get nowhere unless the characters are different, and unless they themselves change with the news and action brought by others who exit early or enter late. The imagination is also protean, then, in the diverse and personal identities of individual agents who are its real life.

Last, as we enter the culmination of the Enlightenment from 1740 to 1760 and then pass into Romanticism, we discover a haunting and wonderful phenomenon. Many of the individuals who fall in love with the concept of the imagination—Coleridge, Blake, Schelling, Shelley, Tetens—have such capacious identities of their own, or at least offer such new and expansive views of the world, that each one of them is transformed and elevated. They are men of force and energy. They exemplify, as Shakespeare exemplified to them, that imagination can free us from a self-centered world. Each mind, as it exercises and acts out its particular faith in the imaginative power, becomes protean. Just as individuals change the nature of the idea by their own interpretation and use, so the idea changes the individual. The imaginative poet or thinker seems to feel and know, from the inside, the experience of other lives. And he touches us because he is touched by humanity.

This large subject of the imagination involves us in *Geistesgeschichte*, or the history of an intellectual or cultural spirit, but it also introduces us to a series of personal dramas. Literature and thought are the product, after all, of people writing and not of a sky-sent blast forcing every pen to the same slant. On the one hand, we should be able to see the forces of the *Zeitgeist,* history, trends, periods, tradition, and reaction. On the other hand, we draw these abstractions from many unique attempts and personal hopes. Intellectual history is a species of multiple biography. We must also add the glue of anonymous and collective achievements. We wrestle with the problem of diversity and unity, a challenge that Whitehead calls the greatest one confronting modern thought. The concept of the imagination was, and perhaps remains, the boldest reply to that challenge.

## 2

# EMPIRICISM IN EARNEST:
# HOBBES AND LOCKE

*T*he Middle Ages and the Renaissance had largely been concerned with the question how and why God had created man, the universe, and all links in the chain of being that makes up nature. There was comparatively little psychological penetration into exactly how the mind recreates and builds within itself a picture of the world, or why genius in art is more than technical superiority.[1] In this simplified overview exceptions come to mind, such as the character of Imaginatif in *Piers Plowman*, the battle between the nominalists and realists, Ficino's and Sidney's speculations, and the idea of the poet as a "second Maker" or Promethean figure. It was these exceptions, which in a rough way tried to explain the inner working of perceptions and of the creative impulse, that were revived and greatly expanded in the seventeenth and eighteenth centuries. The scholastic terms "subjective" and "objective" gained new currency and new meaning, as did *natura naturata* versus *natura naturans*.[2]. The poet or artist was seen once again, though not in the same Renaissance way, to participate in a divine and formative power.

But on the whole, the pre-1600 world was more interested in man's relationship to external nature and to God than it was in internal processes of thought and feeling that sustain a comprehensive and aesthetic view of the world. Whenever the mind's inner life and experiences were probed, the tendency was either to present them in an allegorical or archetypical framework that used the trappings of the external world, as in Spenser's *Faerie Queene*, or to link them with fatally imprecise, if not preposterous, physiological and medical theories. These solutions, however, were often enchanting and full of sanity, for in choosing between either looking outward to nature and to the why of creation, or peering inward at the self and how it operates, only the egomaniac or charlatan could suffer the incredible boredom of the latter choice. But the late Enlightenment and the Romantics wanted both—a unity of external with internal, of the subjective and objective, where the mind and soul feel an intrinsic connection with nature, where the individual life grows into one with everything around it, and, by doing so, realizes its own identity.

In the seventeenth century, British empirical psychology revived a perspective on the world that had been relatively ignored. It was based on questions and discoveries about the formation of passions, thoughts, perceptions, and knowledge within the mind. This empirical psychology soon combined with at least two other elements. One was a Platonic strain, represented by the Cambridge Platonists, Shaftesbury, and a revived interest in ancient philosophy. The other was the eighteenth-century "return to nature," a new interest in the external and the cult of the natural. By the middle of the Enlightenment, the empirical systems had become more flexible and, except in France, were shedding their far-fetched physiological and mechanistic notions. The Platonic strain had picked up, from Leibniz and even from Locke, the idea of an active force or power in the mind paralleled by one working in nature. The cult of nature embraced aesthetic and artistic values, such as the picturesque, the pathetic, and the sublime, which in turn had their roots in the way the mind perceives and orders external reality. Kant and the transcendental philosophers delved into the self, into the mind's gauge of its own knowledge and the modes by which it gathers that knowledge. Soon all these strains and ways of approaching man, nature, and art began to converge.

### HOBBES: INCLUSIVENESS AT THE BEGINNING

Thomas Hobbes was born the year that Drake defeated the Spanish Armada (1588). As he grew to be one of the seventeenth century's foremost thinkers, he combined the sweep and scope of Renaissance philosophy with the new interest in empiricism and scientific method. Although he can be called a materialist, as did Coleridge, his first subject was always man and human nature, which he embraced with gargantuan-sized intellectual arms. He avoided the queer systems and idiotic schemes of the projectors and enthusiasts whom Swift later satirized. He drew the whole level of philosophical discussion—and with it the question of artistic creation—onto a psychological plane, where the inner workings of the mind and the passions gain paramount importance. He opened a

Northwest passage in the world of ideas, a route that, among other places, led to a direct and deep inquiry about the imagination.

In his *Leviathan* (1651) and *Elements of Philosophy* (1655–1658), Hobbes starts to discuss the imagination on an elementary level, but then he quickly builds up a rich and varied faculty that is responsible, in whole or in part, for *everything* that goes on in the mind. At its highest level—a quantum leap beyond simple images, dreams, and memory— the imagination is man's profoundly constructive power. With thought and emotion, desire and knowledge, it makes the connections and pro- duces the works that constitute the arts of civilization. "Fancy" is the ordering and creative force of the world. Hobbes lacks the debonair and gracious flair of Sidney in the *Apology* (he was seven when Sidney's *Apology* was published), and he falls short of Shelley's impassioned conviction in the *Defence;* but his point is essentially the same. Imagina- tion, which gives us our picture of complex experience, is also the wisest interpreter of experience. Literature and the arts are wrought from a feeling acquaintance with life so rich that it must burst out and create new experiences, putting them in striking images and novel metaphors.[3]

Hobbes lays the ground rules for a century-long empirical study of the imagination. His influence resounds through Locke, Hume, and Burke. Hazlitt, who later tried to refute Hobbes's view that the imagina- tion produces basically selfish desires and appetites, nevertheless called him "the father of modern philosophy." For Hobbes, the key to philoso- phy and understanding is the mind itself. Part One of *Leviathan* is sim- ply titled "Of Man." Divorced from the mind, reality is nothing more than a moving, material present. It is limited and evanescent. "Things *past* have a being in the memory only," and "things *to come* have no being at all; the *future* being but a fiction of the mind, applying the se- quels of actions past, to the actions that are present." Hazlitt's sense that the future is essentially  a construct of the imagination probably came from Hobbes; Johnson, Goethe, and Hume also stressed the importance of the imagination as a temporal power governing all that is optative in human nature. Our sense of reality, understanding, and continuity of experience, according to Hobbes, are formed when the mind pieces to- gether and combines images, accruing them and seeking meanings for "trains of imaginations." Order and reality emerge from the "contex- ture" of imagination that connects separate experiences into units large and comprehensive enough to be intelligent or meaningful. Language, for example, consists of "signs" we use to order and transmit the con- tents of our imagination.[4]

As maker and arbiter of experience, the imagination offers tremen- dously vivid results. It generates desires, hopes, and fears. On its strength rests the intensity of human passion as well as the completeness of understanding. The world, life, reality—all assume form and meaning according to patterns built up by the imagination and colored by pleasure and pain, equally products of the imagination.[5] If a thing or a desire is "imaginary," it is not therefore false or mirage-like. On the contrary, the term means that, true or not, the mind is convinced of a thing or desires it with vivid intensity.

Hobbes slides back and forth in his terminology, but his thrust and intent are clear.[6] The first few pages of *Leviathan* explain the difference between the Latin *imaginatio* and the Greek *phantasia* (Ludovico Vives, perhaps read by Hobbes while he was on the Continent, also distinguished between *imaginatio* and *phantasia*).* The Latin word, according to Hobbes, essentially means the representation of an object no longer present. Imagination, in this respect, is "decaying sense," which Hobbes believes should strictly apply to the visual sense only, even though the Romans themselves were not so precise.  The Greek *phantasia* is more flexible. Hobbes sees it as encompassing all sense impressions, and suggesting an ability to rearrange these impressions. But having made this distinction, Hobbes goes ahead and uses imagination in the broader sense of *phantasia.* The result, despite his initial care in differentiating *imaginatio* from *phantasia*, is that he uses imagination and fancy as synonyms. "This *decaying sense* . . . I mean *fancy* itself, we call imagination."[7]

After this shuffle at the start of *Leviathan*, Hobbes makes two points. He is breaking ground carefully and trying to make himself clear at every step. First, he says "that imagination and memory are but one thing," but then immediately qualifies this; memory is a "simple" kind of imagination or fancy. There is also a "compounded" function of imagination that connects, reorders, fuses, and arranges experience and images.[8] This compound process is essential both to analysis and to artistic creation. Second, Hobbes takes pains not to deceive readers with his own expressions "decaying" and "weakening sense." A manner of speech, they mean only that the objects of sense are no longer present. Actually, imagination can produce sharper, more fortified effects than sense impressions.[9] Dreams are an example. We may wake from them screaming, or in the most pleasant reverie. Our appetites and desires, formed by the imagination, are strong enough to drive us to extreme actions in order to attain a specific object or experience. What we imagine is not a weak sister of what is real. It is the tangy fabric of reality itself.

The "compounded imagination," working with images and desires, builds "trains" of them—a concept important to later theories about the

* For a complete discussion of fancy and imagination, see below, Ch. 13.

"association of ideas" and artistic creativity (Locke may have gleaned from Hobbes his fundamental distinction between simple and complex ideas). The compounded imagination, according to Hobbes, especially if it is "regulated," or directed to a certain end, deals in consequences, in causes and effects. Its intricacy and constant operation form "mental discourse," in which the mind passes from one object to another, connecting them into larger trains and comprehensive schemata. Experience is the sum total of all mental discourse, especially as we recall, sift, and apply it to present or to anticipated situations. Hobbes adds a moral slant here. In considering the future, we attempt to be prudent and wise, but our only guide is an imaginative extrapolation of previous experience. A lively and far-ranging imagination becomes indispensable for moral judgment.[10]

Mental discourse, when properly judged and arranged, leads to *sagacitas* or *solertia*, a ready and perceptive view of the world that handles situations and circumstances by calling on a ready stock of "trains of imaginations." In the arts, *sagacitas* is important because with it the creative mind establishes the end and aim of its work. "In sum, the discourse of the mind, when it is governed by design, is . . . the faculty of invention." Thus, the literal meaning of "invention"—to find things out and their causes, to be knowing and wise—Hobbes relates to the artistic meaning of "invention," the ability to plan and execute a new work.[11]

In this way, Hobbes is expanding his original meaning of fancy or imagination. It is not, as first seemed, a passive register of the world. It actively forms our conception of the world and, compounded and regulated to form an end or design governing its function, it becomes the process of artistic creation. In Hobbes we see a fundamental distinction between two powers of imagination, a distinction that was to pervade English and German thought for at least 175 years. The imagination is responsible for perceptions and ideas, for our "experience" and picture of reality. On a "higher" second level, it produces new pictures and ideas, it fashions new experiences; it adorns and creates; it is the force behind art. By placing emphasis on this second role of imagination, Hobbes "brought the whole creative process indoors."[12] And there it has stayed ever since.

Imagination is not "mechanical" but a live and active power. Adding to its vitality and range, Hobbes concludes that emotions, "appetites," desires, and even the human will all depend on the imagination.[13] Mental discourse, that silent voice of thought and feeling within us, is often led toward a specific end by some overwhelming desire or emotional urge. Art and every production of the mind become more complete and forceful if desire and "passionate thought" control their creation. Hume and others later observed what Hobbes first recognized, that there is a reciprocal relationship between desire and the imagination. Desire and feelings originally stem from the imagination, but then they may turn about-face and, once solidly formed and entrenched in the mind, direct the imagination to a new end and cause it to form new trains, even new works of art.[14]

Hobbes ventures into an area of tricky footing—the question of the will. In a religious context, it had long been important. But he makes it part of all experience. Will is appetite or desire approved and reinforced by conscious, voluntary deliberation. In the productions of fancy, such as art, the will thus seems necessary to motivate and keep creative inertia going until a work is completed. The creative imagination owes a debt to conscious and deliberate choice, but especially as that choice magnifies a strong and perhaps involuntary *desire*. The drive behind art has a dimension of desiring and caring. The artist becomes inwardly obsessed (in the positive sense of the word) by an emotional feeling. Hobbes, by implication, is delving into the real psychological sense of ancient clichés that the artist is "inspired," or possessed with "divine fire." In the late Enlightenment and Romanticism the question of will and art resurfaces. Burke, Tetens, Schelling, Coleridge, and others speak of will, or something very like it, as indispensable to the creative act. But Hobbes first introduced it as connected to the web of the mind's imagination, and he suggested, more acutely than many after him, that the will not only is deliberate and chosen but carries the urgency of desire, which lifts an artist to the level of genius.[15]

Bacon, with whom Hobbes was friendly as a young man, also believed that imagination is the source of art and poetry. But in consequence Bacon distrusted it and thought it was dangerous to reason. Hobbes, who was also personally acquainted with Ben Jonson, claims that reason itself is a kind of imagination, refined with judgment and the desire for a specific end. He goes a step farther (a step Schelling would take 150 years later) to say that a rich and well-formed imagination, where feelings and images are in abundant harmony, is the essence of philosophy as well as art. The "wonderful celerity" of fancy consists not "so much in motion as in copious imagery discretely ordered and perfectly registered in the memory; which most men, under the name of philosophy, have a glimpse of."[16] In the philosophical *Advancement of Learning* Bacon admitted, "I find not any science that doth properly or fitly pertain to the imagination," a sentence Hobbes's eye might have crossed in Bacon's own manuscript. Hobbes is attempting to fill the gap, to establish the "science" that Bacon found, and left, wanting.

Hobbes's "Answer to Davenant's *Preface before* Gondibert" (1650) shows that finally, in its complete exercise, the imagination—or "fancy," as Hobbes calls it here—is to the modern world everything that Apollo was to ancient societies:

> All that is beautiful or defensible in building, or marvellous in engines and instruments of motion, whatsoever commodity[advantage] men receive from the observations of the heavens, from the description of the earth, from the account of time . . . and whatsoever distinguisheth the civility of Europe from the barbarity of the American savages, is the workmanship of fancy.

In an astonishingly quick odyssey, Hobbes carries the imagination from a seemingly mechanical faculty not much above rudimentary sensation to the driving force of man's intellectual, moral, and emotional being, the dynamo of creative energies and wisdom. There is much he does not dwell on or expand, and much he does not consider. The question of morality is knotty, and he cannot, even with the concept of the imagination, reduce it with the precision he desires. The idea of Hobbes discussing imaginative identification or sympathy sounds comic. He gives short shrift to metaphysical, religious, or transcendental speculation. Whatever seems ideal is, for his flinty and tactile mind, rooted ultimately in the real. Although he provides imagination with an Aristotelian bent, particularly from the *De Anima*, not until Shaftesbury is it enriched with a Platonic strain. But Hobbes gave to the imagination a great deal that afterward could never be excluded. The man whom Leibniz called "among the deepest minds of the century" pulled knowledge, perception, memory, desire, the passions, thought, judgment, wit, will, the creative arts, and philosophy all within the sphere of imagination.

In criticism, the effect of Hobbes was to challenge authoritarian rules and a heavy reliance on form. Fundamental truth to nature and to experience, including the emotional side of experience, was valued as much or more than any convention. Every later writer and critic who examined how the mind combines images to form a new artistic whole without first being enslaved to a formula had in Hobbes an original source and ally. He broadened the English neoclassical movement at its start.

### LOCKE: "THE MIND HAS A POWER"

Locke's critique of knowledge, and the resulting strengthened tide of British empiricism, eroded faith in reason as it had been traditionally conceived.[17] Largely because of him, as well as Descartes and the late seventeenth-century spirit of experimental science, the Enlightenment often thought of "reason" as something mechanical, a step-by-step deduction or logic. But the irony and the importance of Locke's position is that when he cast out reason as an intuitive power of knowledge, he actually cleared the ground for its substitute, the imagination.

Redefining the problem of knowledge, he concluded that the mind receives simple ideas passively, but then it actively fuses, compares, and assembles them into complex ideas, which are "made voluntarily": "But as the mind is wholly passive in the reception of all its simple ideas, so it exerts several acts of its own, whereby out of its simple ideas, as the materials and foundations of the rest, the other are formed."[18] No matter how much Locke denigrates "imagination" as something largely illusory, fit for little more than recreative "entertainment," his stress on the mind's active and free manipulation of simple ideas encouraged other thinkers to develop interest and confidence in the imagination. Ironically, this interest would endow imagination with some of those intuitive and innate characteristics once assigned to reason.

In the chapter entitled "Of Complex Ideas" in his *Essay Concerning Human Understanding* (1690), the concept of productive, as opposed to reproductive, imagination appears in primordial form. Locke assumes that the mind begins life as a *tabula rasa*. How far too much of a stock notion about Locke this is, because he also states that the mind rapidly loses its mental virginity; in fact, in Book Four of the *Essay* Locke affirms that we have a rational insight that can be immediate and intuitive. The psyche, from its first experiences after birth, becomes marked, scored, impressed, and indented. It is able "to repeat" simple ideas. But more important, it has an almost innate power—something quite different from an innate idea—to rearrange, to alter, and to fuse the separate elements it receives in "an almost infinite variety":

> As simple ideas ... exist in several combinations united together, so the mind has a power to consider several of them united together as one idea; *and that not only as they are united in external objects, but as itself [the mind] has joined them.* Ideas thus made up of several simple ones put together I call 'complex.'[19]

These crucial phrases are explicit and clear. Locke, like Hobbes, believes that the mind is both passive and active, and he anticipates Leibniz's and Coleridge's views that imagination is an active and a passive power. Locke affirms that "the mind ... can, by its own power, put together those ideas it has, and make new complex ones which it never received so united."[20] Presumably the mind has always had this power. His point, the mind's joining and amalgamating capacity, became a mainstay to thinkers who identified this power with "imagination." British associationists soon explored the nature of this power. In Germany, Tetens paid such detailed attention to Locke that he even repeated Locke's comment that whereas the productive power creates unified ideas not already in nature, it cannot create matter itself. Kant relied heavily on the distinction between reproductive and productive imagination.

Locke expresses, too, the mind's formation of many ideas and elements into one integrated whole, a notion that became central for theories of poetic imagination and symbolism. It played an important part in mid-century and romantic concepts of the way genius designs the overall plan of a system or an art work, and also in the German approach to *Einbildungskraft*, which Tetens, Kant, Schelling and others envisioned as a power of complete synthesis, as in Schelling's *"In-Eins-Bildung,"* where he takes *eins* to mean "one." Locke's own phrasing is terse but unmistakable. The mind "unites" many ideas and associations into one. Some ideas are "complicated of various simple ideas or complex ideas made up of simple ones, yet are, when the mind pleases, considered each by itself as one entire thing, and signified by one name."[21] The phrase "when the mind pleases" implies a voluntary or conscious control of the productive power, another qualification that recalls Hobbes but also foreshadows later investigators of the imagination and the role of the will.

Despite their importance, these comments of Locke's should not be stretched too far. He does not stress the creative and artistic side of the mind's productive power. He does not use the words "original" or, what was then more common, "inventive." He does not talk about genius, nor does he pause to ask how the productive power operates, to give examples, or to delve into psychological particulars. For him, it is enough to state that "the mind has a power."

Critics of Locke exposed these weaknesses. Henry Lee in his *Anti-Scepticism* (1702) and John Broughton in *Psychologia* (1703) represent the ideal and mystical strain also present in English thought. Rooted in a Platonic tradition, these thinkers were soon championed by the third Earl of Shaftesbury, Anthony Ashley Cooper. John Norris, one of Locke's antagonists and author of the *Theory of the Ideal or Intelligible World* (1701–1704), protests that it is hard to tell from reading Locke by what specific process ideas "come to be united" in the mind. This kind of perceptive attack and Locke's own haziness on the point prompted Addison and Akenside to explain more fully Locke's "power," which they called imagination.

The influence of Locke and his skepticism concerning innate ideas—which helped to turn the meaning of reason topsy-turvy from a largely immediate and intuitive power to one of deduction, logic, and effort—left a substantial vacuum. Yet into that vacuum he threw a handful of particles. What he describes as the mind's innate *power* to produce complex ideas, similar to the German sense of *Kraft*, would crystallize in later authors as the "imagination." Locke believed the mind to be both active and passive. From simple ideas it forms unified, complex ideas that may be completely new, and this formation works through voluntary control or will. As the Enlightenment explored the relationship of mind to nature, and of mind and nature to spiritual and ideal forces, the attributes ascribed by Locke to the mind's interplay with external reality became dimensions of a "power" that, more and more, went under the name of "imagination."

Because of a stress on the five senses and on concrete reality, the empirical school might seem the natural enemy of imagination. But British empiricism escapes the prevailing rationalistic method of Continental thought in the late seventeenth century. This rationalism, found to varying degrees in Descartes, Malebranche, Spinoza, and Leibniz, identifies reason as the highest faculty in the mind and generally discredits the imagination. The empiricists, on the contrary, view the imagination as a power that might replace or compliment "reason." A. S. P. Woodhouse gives the pith of the matter when he comments that, "A philosophy which grounded all knowledge in sense experience had less reason to distrust imagination than had rationalism in its Cartesian or any other form."[22]

In English thought the imagination becomes less diametrically opposed to reason and more the working partner of reason, the act of reasoning itself, a process so complex that it cannot be broken down into the logical or "rational" steps of "method." From the start many thinkers denied a rigid faculty psychology in which the mind operates like a machine with interlocking but distinct parts. William Law, divine and mystic, in *Case of Reason, or Natural Religion, Fairly and Fully Stated* (1732), states simply that "the imagination signifies no distinct faculty from our reason, but only reason acting upon our own ideas."[23] Three years later the poet Walter Harte wrote *An Essay on Reason,* in which he describes the complete operation of the mind from its earliest state to the point where it creates on its own. Harte's approach is empirical and recognizes an important empirical fact: the mind, shaping new things and ideas, appears to function in a way that cannot be reduced to a set of propositions or to the mere receptivity of sense information. The mind has a capacity to "work" and to "dare"; it has a potential ("seeds") that can be tapped:

> Yet in this infant state, by stealth, by chance,
> Th'increasing mind still feels a slow advance,
> Thro' the dark void ev'n gleams of truth can shoot,
> Nor more the tender seeds unquicken'd lie,
> But stretch their form and wait for wings to fly.

Sensation first, the ground-work of the whole,
Deals ray by ray each image to the soul:
Perception true to every nerve, receives
The various impulse, now exults, now grieves:
Thought works and ends, and dares afresh begin:
So whirlpools pour out streams, and suck them in;
That thought romantic Memory detains
In unknown cells, and in aerial chains:
Imagination thence her flow'rs translates;
And Fancy, emulous of God, creates.

(234–248)

By mentioning "seeds unquicken'd" and a process in which "Thought works," "Imagination . . . translates," and "Fancy . . . creates," Harte presents a concept of mind free from the mechanical simplicities of empiricism. Reductionistic elements nevertheless persisted. Hartley's work does not appear until the middle of the century. But many empiricists avoided the naive and narrow application of theory, and the rationalists absorbed empirical observations about the mind that were too plain to deny. This confluence of thought included another strain favoring neither reason nor the senses, but a harmony of matter and spirit, a bond between nature and man's whole self.

# 3

# CLAIMS OF THE SPIRIT:
# SHAFTESBURY AND LEIBNIZ

*P*rompted by Hobbes and Locke, the British virtually created and developed empirical psychology. Yet in their approach to art and literature, while applying empirical psychology more thoroughly than had ever been done before, they broke the empirical spell and extricated themselves from a hide-bound approach. They were able to do so because they also found different inspiration in a doctrine formed outside the predominance of empirical thinking.[1]

In early eighteenth-century England, this doctrine is best represented by Shaftesbury. He harmonized many elements and, instead of formulating a philosophical system, established a unified sensibility that bears many similarities to later, more "romantic" ideas of experience and imagination. He revived Platonism, not only by keeping alive the work of the Cambridge Platonists, among them Ralph Cudworth, John Smith, Henry More, and Nathanael Culverwel, but also by turning directly to Plato and the earlier neo-Platonists. Shaftesbury's first publication (1698) was a *Preface to the Sermons of Dr. Whichcote*, one of the Cambridge Platonists. Shaftesbury tried to steer a course between rigid empiricism and rampant rationalism.

Plurality of thought usually creates irony. Shaftesbury himself owed his own life in a sense to one of the greatest empiricists, Locke. In this case the irony is rewarding rather than undercutting or tragic. According to a story told by Shaftesbury, Locke, who at Oxford had met and become a close friend of the first earl of Shaftesbury, the third earl's grandfather and the Achitophel of Dryden's *Absalom and Achitophel* (1681), had acted as an agent for the family in negotiating and arranging the marriage of his parents. Furthermore, Locke was medical attendant to the family and reportedly aided at the birth of Shaftesbury. Locke became responsible for the early education of the boy, who was enriched by travel on the Continent starting at the age of fifteen, and Shaftesbury was schooled according to Locke's own *Some Thoughts Concerning Education* (1693).

Arching over Shaftesbury's work is the concept of a complete association of sensibilities, a combination and harmony not only of aesthetic, intellectual, and moral impulses but also of emotion and epistemology. This attitude is approximated by that highly prized and ancient Greek virtue of *sophrosyne,* a state where life and life's engagement with nature are kept in timely order through the balanced interpenetration of all sides of human behavior, thought, and feeling.

This harmony between man and the world—and between the various parts of man's inner self—when attained, is a trinity of the good, true, and beautiful. This trinity is, at bottom, one. It is grasped immediately and understood intuitively. Its visible or material symbol is beauty, which Ernst Cassirer explains as having profound significance:

> The purest harmony between man and the world is available only through the medium of the beautiful. For here man not only understands but experiences and knows that all order and regularity, all unity and law, depend on one and the same original form . . . The truth of the universe speaks, as it were, through the phenomenon of beauty; it is no longer inaccessible, but acquires a means of expression, a language, in which the meaning of this truth, its real logos, is first completely revealed.[2]

The later Enlightenment and the Romantic period's rediscovery of this Shaftesburian temper combined with a broadening empirical strain to enrich the idea of imagination from all sides. Wordsworth, Keats, Shelley, and Coleridge—in their ideas of beauty, truth, and the intuitive imagination seizing on truth—all pick up threads of Shaftesbury and continue his legacy, even though indirectly. The legacy never passed into obscurity. The Scottish Common Sense School drew from Shaftesbury as well as from Locke. For example, Francis Hutcheson's *Inquiry into the Original of Our Ideas of Beauty and Virtue* (1725) combined both empirical and intuitional strains. If poets like John Pomfret, Akenside, and William Collins did not give Shaftesbury's attitudes a forceful and dramatic expression, at least they kept those attitudes simmering. Shaftesbury himself, in a marked difference from the common ideas of poetry, genius, and creativity in his own time, ascribed the creative power not to an especially large dose of reason or to an ability to see and discover more, but to a productive function in the mind. Genius perceives and recreates in a new form the process and harmony of the world.[3] It participates in nature, drawing out and sharing nature's truth and secrets by what Keats, a century later, called a "greeting of the spirit." Where Locke and his followers kept alive the empirical quality of the imaginative mind, Shaftesbury explored the ideal and spiritual side. Shaftesbury's major work, the *Characteristics of Men, Manners, Opinions, Times* (1711), was popular for decades.

The two approaches represented by Locke and Shaftesbury merged and cross-pollinated, as in Akenside's *Pleasures of Imagination* (1744). The unity in man's sensibilities and thought was being found not as the excrescence of reason or understanding, or of ideas or things, but as the child of the combining force of imagination. Shaftesbury introduced into British psychology and moral thought what had been a favorite religious and philosophical topic of the seventeenth century. He stressed the disinterestedness of the heart, the need for "affections" to make virtue and philosophy complete. This developed into the investigation of sympathy as an instrument of virtue and as an act of the imagination permitting the self to identify with others. Shaftesbury's important work here, besides the *Characteristics*, is his *Investigation Concerning Virtue and Merit* (1699). At a time when Newtonian mathematics and geometry were exerting a strong hold not only on world-views but also on the nature of man and man's morality, Shaftesbury provided an important alternative.

He perceived physical entities and separate ideas in infinite and imaginative relations. An organicism of sorts, his approch can be summarized in the word "interconnectedness." So in *The Moralists* the character of Theocles exclaims:

> All things in this world are united . . . as the branch is united with the tree, so is the tree as immediately with the earth, air, and water which feed it . . . so much are the leaves, the seeds, and fruits of these trees fitted to the various animals; these again to one another and to the elements where they of necessity view all in one . . . Thus too in the system of the bigger world. See there the mutual dependency of things! the relations of one to another . . . of the earth and other planets to the sun! . . . and know, my ingenious friend, that by this survey you will be obliged to own the universal system and coherent scheme of things to be established . . . capable of convincing any fair and just contemplator of the work of nature.[4]

This mode of "contemplating" nature implies a constitutive bond between nature and the individual mind; the mind, at least in part, *is* nature. Charles Gildon in 1718 affirmed that "Fancy is what we generally call *Nature*, or a *Genius*."[5] Further, a brotherhood or community of mind is anchored in nature, a "natural sympathy" (the phrase was to become common) exists among members of society. At the heart of this morally formative view rests the individual's imaginative perception, a major theme of Cowper's *Task* (1785) and of *The Prelude*, especially Book Eight, "Retrospect—Love of Nature Leading to Love of Man."[6]

If we understand that Shaftesbury intends the imaginative mind to extrapolate from the senses an order and relation behind experience that is deeper than the senses alone can supply, we also have a Platonic basis of the kind Collins and Shelley will employ. The senses become a veil behind which moves or "hides" a paradoxically more solid existence.

Shaftesbury was widely read on the Continent as well as in England, especially in Germany, and Leibniz, discovering Shaftesbury's *The Moralists, A Philosophical Rhapsody*, wrote: "I perceived that I had been in the forechamber only and was not entirely surprised to find myself in the . . . sanctuary of the most sublime philosophy . . . I found in it almost all of my *Theodicy* before it saw the light of day. The universe all of a piece, its beauty, its universal harmony, the disappearance of real evil."[7]

Through Leibniz, Shaftesbury entered the mainstream of German thought in the Enlightenment. He served as a velvet shoehorn for the revival of Spinoza and later influenced Herder, Kant, and Schiller. Thus, not only did Shaftesbury go to Germany, but through Leibniz and later German Romantics, with their interest in Plotinus, he was given a new cast and exported back into the English-speaking world. Shaftesbury encouraged an exchange of ideas between England and Germany throughout the transition from the Enlightenment to Romanticism. Most of his impact can be seen in the slow but steadily expanding curiosity in imagination as a power that unifies man's disparate experiences.[8]

## LEIBNIZ AND THE WONDER OF FORCE

Gottfried Wilhelm Leibniz was, in a manner of speaking, the Shaftesbury of the Continent. The *Nouveaux essais* (1765)—which he generously withdrew from publication when Locke died in 1704, because they were largely a commentary and refutation of Locke's *Essay Concerning Human Understanding*—offer an organic view of nature and argue for the presence of a force in nature and in the mind, *"la puissance active"* or *"vis activa,"* that can be seen as a full-fledged concept of imagination. Leibniz was a charming and urbane man; like Alfred North Whitehead and Bertrand Russell, he was a cosmologist and philosopher as well as a superb mathematician. His work encouraged a unified view of man and nature in which imagination links the two. Coleridge and Schelling looked on him and Spinoza as oases relieving the materialistic plain and "scientific" wasteland of the late seventeenth and early eighteenth centuries.

*"L'Harmonie Préétablie"* and *"la matière organique partout"* of Leibniz's universe depend upon an imaginative power that connects the soul with the external world and reflects the divine plan itself. Those

thinkers whom Leibniz considered incomplete, either too dualistic, doc-
trinaire, or materialistic, such as Descartes, Locke, Pascal, and Hobbes,
indicate the affinity of his own position with the high Romantics whom
he was to attract, philosophers and poets who grew up and wrote after
1765 when the *Nouveaux essais* were finally published. Leibniz even
made an unusual and rather intricate distinction between fancy (*les
idées phantastiques ou chimériques*) and imagination (*la combinaison
des idées unifiées*).

Part of Leibniz's view is sustained by religious faith, his belief that
God creates and is the source of all things, that all things connect and
relate to each other, and that to be aware of His reason, man must exercise not only human reason but sensibility and imaginative vision as
well. Leibniz attracted thinkers whose own religious concerns were reflected in their ideas of the imagination, such as Abraham Tucker,
Schelling, Coleridge, and Friedrich Jacobi. He avoided the pantheism of
Spinoza that, aside from scaring the orthodox, sabotaged the imagination because it assumed a more static identity of all things as God. No
interconnection was urgently needed. Spinoza does not stress the active
revealing and discovering force of imagination. Leibniz's philosophy
takes the form of active present participles, but Spinoza's is more of an
all-embracing "is." The individual is constantly looking outward and
not, as in Leibniz, both inward and outward.

Leibniz ushers in an intellectual sensibility uniquely conducive to romantic views of nature and human consciousness. His thought transcends routine labels affixed to the late seventeenth century and provides an architectonic scheme, a dynamic universe open to all kinds of
phenomena—material, unconscious, spiritual, metaphysical, mathematical, speculative, and aesthetic. An enemy of what he called the sectarian
spirit of philosophy, he affirms parts of what others have thought rather
than rejecting their whole systems out of hand. His own "system"—and
in this he is like Coleridge and Schelling—holds that the universe itself
is the only true "system," and that it contains mysteries open to experience but incapable of being pinned down by either purely experimental
or purely contemplative and aesthetic approaches. Leibniz may be
called antimechanistic or antimystical only in the sense that he is not
wholly either one. Hamlet would have listened to him with fascination
rather than contempt. That there is more in heaven and earth than is
dreamt of in any one philosophy becomes a central message of Leibniz.

The *Nouveaux essais* open with a respectful but firm attack on the
*tabula rasa* of Locke. As a marble has veins and cleavages favorable to
sculpting certain figures, so each mind, argues Leibniz, has internal pre-
dispositions compatible to particular throughts and feelings.[9] How else

can we explain the diversity in human intellect and character? Leibniz also calls on a theological argument with scholastic flavor. How could God create souls as blanks to be informed only by images from the senses, thus leaving us mere automatons of the environment? Here Leibniz resorts to an ingenious ploy. As soon as the senses receive anything, the *tabula rasa* is lost. Yet the mind can never verify that it actually enjoyed such a state in the first place, because the only way to verify, according to Locke, is empirically, and the *tabula rasa* is the complete absence of empirical data. When the mind crosses the border and leaves the alleged *tabula rasa*, there is no trace of it left, no compelling reason to believe it was ever there.

The mind, believes Leibniz, has innate ideas and an intrinsic power to act upon these ideas as well as upon sensations, to group them together or to separate them by analysis. This force in the mind, the essence of invention, Locke himself touches on, as does Coleridge, and Leibniz suggests that this force has a connection with the entelechy of Aristotle. But Leibniz makes *"la puissance active"* absolutely central. Not only does it form "complex ideas," but it is the one creative, building, and productive power of the mind—the imagination. This force is the cause of all cause and effect in the mind, the agent of all its creativity. Images molded by this force are not the result of conscious and voluntary experience alone. Leibniz contends that the psyche also receives constant salvos of *"perceptions insensibles,"* sensations to which we pay little or no attention, but which actually form an internal reservoir of images and feelings. We discover things not only from nature but also as they come from the mixed activities of our minds. We have a *"sens interne"* and experience things and certainly feelings internally. The *"perceptions insensibles"* or *"petites perceptions"* within us are infinite in number and range. Their values and impressions form a calculus of the psyche. They establish a continuous bridge of awareness between the mind and physical reality. They are the stuff of the "pre-established Harmony."

Added to this welter of sub- and unconscious content, which breaks into consciousness, are habits and dispositions, intellectual ideas, sentiments, instincts, passions, and customs.[10] We feel or realize all of these with the force of truths; the mind is predisposed to them. They, or at least their potential, are in the mind from birth or before. With these and the "inner sense" in view, Leibniz makes his refutation of radical empiricism:

> One will oppose me with the axiom, received among the philosophers, that nothing is in the soul that does not come from the senses. But it is necessary to except the soul itself and its inclinations. Nothing is in the mind that was not in the senses, except the mind itself.[11]

But Leibniz does not reject empiricism itself. Rather, he achieves what few thinkers from 1650 to 1775 were able to do. He strikes a balance between active force and passive receptivity of the mind. This concept of a dual nature in the mind itself, the active and the passive, crops up increasingly during the Enlightenment and becomes a fundamental attribute of the imagination. Locke had strongly hinted at it. Coleridge affirms it repeatedly in the *Biographia*. Explored by Hobbes, Addison, Akenside, Tetens, and Kant—to name the major figures—the theme of imagination as active and passive is put by Leibniz particularly well because he stresses the mutual effects and tension between action and experience. To witness and to create through action become a single and coordinated function.

Leibniz's picture of the mind and world is complex, full, and varying. The *"perceptions insensibles,"* a series of perpetual tugs at creating, interpreting, discerning, and sensing, all respond to a changing universe. There are no discrete intervals; all is flowing and evolves. Nature and the mind are nowhere fixed, but their motions are not random. They are truly relevant to each other. The organization and interaction of objects and life—even of all atoms—follow certain causes.[12] They are created and governed by a cosmic force. There is a chemistry as well as a mechanics to life and the universal order. The mind follows and recreates nature by an imaginative process that registers and unites what it senses and perceives. Then, with its own elective affinities, it fashions a new picture of reality to correspond with each new moment. This concept parallels the primary imagination of Coleridge.

Leibniz presents an organic view of nature and, in addition, an organic view of the relationship between mind and nature. This awareness becomes a cornerstone of all Romanticism that goes beyond the purely subjective and sentimental:

> I see all things regulated and embellished beyond everything that was conceived up to now; the organic material everywhere, nothing empty, sterile, or neglected; nothing too uniform, everything varied but with order and—what passes the imagination—all the universe in abridgment, but from a different frame of reference in each of its parts, and even in each of its unities of substance.[13]

Yet Leibniz does not idolize *"la matière organique."* The imagination itself is a force, and the existence of spirit must be as certain as that of objects.[14] Schelling and Coleridge later shared this conviction. Schelling began his brilliant philosophy from the material side in *Die Naturphilosophie* then worked through ideal stages until he reached *Die Philosophie der Kunst*, a view based on the formative and self-conscious power of individual spirit and intelligence. Coleridge, though on the surface not as systematic, argued for the coexistence and interpenetration of matter and spirit, with the beginning of all creation found in the self-affirming intelligence, "I am that I am."

## LEIBNIZ AND ROMANTIC ANTICIPATIONS

The idea of force in Leibniz foreshadows a major development in the late eighteenth century. Especially in German thought, though also in English figures like Tucker, Blake, Keats, Shelley, Coleridge, and even Wordsworth, the imagination reconciles antitheses and polarities. It joins or envisions opposites with such energy or beauty that, as Keats says, "disagreeables evaporate." Matter and spirit, mortality and the eternal, man's tenement of clay and the empyrean realms, the self and nature or society, are revealed as part of one pattern and dialectic. But this deeper unity and understanding of human life and nature can appear only if there is a way to connect opposites by describing and re-creating them with the images of each other and, through metaphor, suggesting how they resemble one another and, in the psyche and in nature, become transformed into their "opposite." No entity or thing can provide this connection and transformation. It would dissolve into the mass of polarities and acquire its own opposite. Any entity, spiritual or material, is too limited. Even the consideration of God throws open the question of evil and the Devil. Reason has a powerful opposite in the irrational or insane. A force, a power to create and to act, is required. This is one of Leibniz's great insights. Only through the idea of force, and not through an entity or a fixed body of truths, can the strife of opposites be raised to harmony and interplay. Leibniz explains the need for this force and argues for its existence. In the decades that follow, the Enlightenment gives this force a local habitation and a name (though not a completely new one), the "imagination."

With stunning directness the *Nouveaux essais* present the basic premises of Romanticism. Leibniz endows nature and the mind with a feeling spirit and with ideas both from and beyond the senses. He gives the imagination an active and creating force as well as an open receptivity. A continuum of awareness, a kind of intuition, flows from the collision of inner events, resources, and "dispositions" with external circumstance, reality, and the creative power.

Leibniz himself does not actually speak of "imagination" as directly controlling or even participating in this drama of mind and nature. At the beginning of the eighteenth century the common usage of the word had not gained such scope. Especially on the Continent he would have been thought rash to base so much on what would normally be conveyed by the word. Hobbes had been revolutionary in speaking of all psychological and creative processes as resting largely on imagination, but Leibniz would have had to say even more about imagination, had he chosen to use the term, simply because his own philosophy had greater range. Neither French, Latin, nor German yet gave the breadth of meaning to imagination that was found in English writers like Hobbes and Dryden. Leibniz favors *"vis activa"* or *"la puissance active."* But the real point is that everything he discusses in relation to this force or power becomes vital to romantic theories of imagination. In fact, he furnishes the essentials for those theories. What he said in the 1690s and early 1700s was necessary to and, with some extensions, sufficient for the high Romantics' faith in imagination.

Even with the dawning of this new power, Leibniz never abandons trust in reason. To him it is not a scientific, experimental method or a step-by-step logic. He gives reason the general meaning it has in Plato and in medieval and Renaissance philosophy. Yet he does this without denying or opposing science, warning only that empirical science and Cartesian method are not the last word on reality. The answer lies in mind and nature, in reason, internal sense, fact, feeling, intuition—in all that the psyche can command and call its own. When Coleridge, Renolds, Hazlitt, Wordsworth, and Keats protest the debasement of reason into what Keats calls "consequitive reasoning," they are echoing Leibniz's challenge to the mechanistic systems even as they usurped the field.[15] Reason, he says, ought to be allied with truth, not "proof." Leibniz first solves the problem of what to do with reason as a value if greater stock were placed in the imagination. Imagination becomes the process, the dynamic or the dialectic, through which truths of reason may be obtained and understood. Reason is thus more static; it is a "higher" power than imagination but one fulfilled only through the active working and forms of imagination. Like Shaftesbury, Leibniz envisions that internal resources and characteristics of the mind will become a partner with nature and then interpret that union. Knowledge depends, to use Fichte's later terms, on both the ego and the non-ego; it is sensuous, demonstrative, and intuitive. Locke had suggested this himself in the fourth book of the *Essay Concerning Human Understanding.* Above all, knowledge affects what we believe in, our faith, and how we act. This imaginative process places new emphasis on the individual.

Leibniz highlights at least three themes that volley back and forth and gain pace throughout the Enlightenment. Figures as dissimilar as Kant and Keats take them up. Leibniz's first theme is that, while the imagination turns outward and inward uniting the self with the external, it can also differentiate between them. We become conscious of the self in a profound way. We develop apperception (*s'appercevoir*). "*J'aimerois mieux distinguer entre perception et entre s'appercevoir.*" The concept of self-consciousness is present in Cartesianism, too. *Cogito, ergo sum* can be taken as a sign that self-consciousness had attained increasing importance in philosophy. Spinoza and Malebranche also express concepts of self-consciousness. According to Leibniz, self-consciousness, in the broad and positive sense, is an imaginative act. The impact of this concept for Romanticism—and for the modern world, especially romantic and modern literature—cannot be underestimated. It is at once the very stuff of Byron's irony, Wordsworth's sincerity, and Keats's questionings.

Leibniz's second theme is that consciousness of self leads directly to the active production of an image of the self, an identity. This identity comes from connecting time past with time future, from experience that not merely is receptive but also allows the self-aware individual to act and suffer and become.[16] Our identity is a creature of the imagination. Hobbes, Hazlitt, Coleridge, and Keats explore this theme. Schelling sees his age as one of self-consciousness and personal identity. The Romantics come to believe, as Leibniz did, that personal identity is self-evolving, that it does not depend solely on reason or the senses, on fact or spirit, but on these united and given a distinct character by "*la puissance active*" working in nature and the mind.

Leibniz's third theme emphasizes that the apperceptive and self-evolving individual turns to a nature that also is changing and evolving. Between the individual and nature there is, as Keats says, "a greeting of the spirit." The self comes to participate; it realizes and knows more. Leibniz puts it another way. A person with a lively imagination, an enthusiast in the good sense of the word, "*aura l'avantage d'avoir des idées plus vives et en plus grand nombre; ainsi il auroit aussi plus de connoissance.*" Good memory, passion, and strong imagination—which a poet ideally has—permit us to conceive of things and feelings with electrifying strength. This enthusiasm or fire—similar to the ancients' belief in the divine fire and inspiration of the poet—signifies the divinity in us, "*Est Deus in nobis.*" This is the daemonic, and Leibniz cities Socrates and his daemon. Leibniz believes that the greatest power for knowledge, wisdom, and understanding comes from an imaginative vision. We greet nature, and even as we do so, we are creating it, as well as our own identities.[17]

The influence of Leibniz reflects his uncanny reconciliation of new and old. The pervading thought in 1700 was not so eclectic. Hobbes and Locke, Newton and Descartes, acquired self-appointed disciples, who were less open and catholic than their masters. An army of popularizers and salon intellectuals, eager for certainty, narrowed the sights and jettisoned the speculations of their heros. Even Christian Wolff later diminished the spirit of Leibniz. In this atmosphere, often partisan and mechanistic, Leibniz managed to integrate the classical trust in reason, a sense of wonder, theology, psychology, and scientific inquiry. The importance and concept of the imagination, especially on the Continent, would grow largely from the range of thought found in Leibniz.

It is hard to appreciate Leibniz's achievement simply because the romantic period assimilated so much of his viewpoint. Familiarity with Wordsworth, Blake, Shelley, Rousseau, Goethe, Keats, and Coleridge can make Leibniz seem second-hand. But the reverse is truer. Born in 1646, Leibniz came a century before. He cut leaves in the cosmic and holy books, and his thought inspired the confidence and outlook necessary to what these later writers would express in poetry.

# 4

# THE CREATIVE IMPULSE:
# ADDISON THROUGH AKENSIDE AND
# THE 1740s

*I*n the last year of Shaftesbury's life, 1712, when at forty-one he was battling consumption at Naples, Joseph Addison wrote his *Spectator* series on "the pleasures of the imagination." These papers elevate "imagination" and rescue it from a morass of critical terms. Addison places the word in a solution of attitudes that crystallize around it and begin to form a comprehensive idea bearing directly on poetry and the arts.

The membrane separating English philosophy and psychology from poetry and literature had, since Hobbes, been highly permeable, as could also be said of Germany after about 1770. By an osmosis of ideas each area of endeavor now flowed to the other. Often a single man turns philosophic or speculative thought to the uses of poetry or criticism. Hobbes, Hume, and Coleridge are good examples. Addison's series on the imagination provides English poetry and criticism with a quasi-philosophic and aesthetic underpinning, something only Sidney, Bacon, and Hobbes had attempted before.[1] In a sense, the idea of imagination becomes the first artery joining philosophy and psychology with the arts and criticism. And the idea of the imagination has continued to be the strongest link between speculative thought and the theory of literature.

Addison was probably not conscious of the lift he gave to the relationship between literature and philosophic thought. What he was doing seemed, in a way, only natural. Familiar with Locke and Shaftesbury's work, he tried to apply the vigor of new thought and psychology to the appreciation of nature, literature, and art. "Imagination" became an attractive vehicle. "The pleasures of judgment" would have sounded ridiculous. Besides, the need for judgment had been so persistently urged that the concept had become threadbare and routine. Not much better would have been "the pleasures of wit." Already that term had acquired widely disparate meanings. To employ it would have led to a series of commonplaces, or else to a futile struggle against them. "The pleasures of invention" might have worked, but Addison speaks not only about the creative act but about the appreciation of art, the intrinsic comparison between nature and a finished poem or painting.

After Addison's series, interest in the imagination as a critical concept gathers force quickly. By the 1720s and 1730s many critics and poets consider it the highest gift and value of art. In 1744 Akenside's *Pleasures of Imagination* fortifies this new attitude and expresses the growing unity of imagination as a literary value and as an idea with philosophic and religious importance.

In late seventeenth-century criticism and the commentary of poets themselves, we find that "imagination" enjoys a frequent but dissipated usage. No critic or poet develops a theory of imagination or seems consistent in what is often alternative praise and censure of that power. For one thing, the word "imagination," or "fancy," had not, by 1700, become connotative in a broad sense. It meant a fairly limited power connected, in the main, with the simple formation of images. This is even true to some degree in Addison. Though Hobbes uses fancy and imagination in a variety of ways, some of them with the broadest implications, he was unusual; in addition, his main interest is in psychology rather than poetry. Shakespeare, Puttenham, and Cowley had spoken about imagination or fancy as a far-ranging power. Yet on the whole, "imagination" in the late seventeenth century was hemmed in by a snarl of critical terms. It was in part a question of vocabulary and semantics. "Wit," "judgment," "enthusiasm," "invention," poetic "fire" or "ardor"—all these are mixed and compared with "imagination." In some instances these values and attributes are taken to be part of the imagination. In other cases imagination is identified as a constituent part of these qualities. Most frequently the imagination is opposed to judgment. The word also felt the influence of French criticism during the last forty years of the seventeenth century. Among its numerous effects, French criticism tended both to swamp imagination with terms and distinctions that were often abstract and rigid in theory, and to impose rules on English criticism simply because many French observations were parroted by minor English figures who thought themselves "critical" in the way a person believes he can improve his thinking by wearing someone else's wig.

For these reasons, the early neoclassical period is commonly said to have "distrusted" the imagination. At least that is what we say from hindsight, when the prevailing attitude then is compared with the exploratory mood in the middle and even the first decades of the eighteenth century. In fact, early neoclassical criticism suspected "imagination" and choked its potential no more than previous periods of literature. Viewing imagination askance and with some reservation had been a common practice for centuries. The early neoclassical stance was no more adverse in its strictures than critics and writers had been before.

Dryden exemplifies the vacillating attitude of the Restoration. In the *Epistle Dedicatory* to *The Rival Ladies* (1664), he warns that "imagination in a poet is a faculty so wild and lawless, that like a high-ranging spaniel, it must have clogs tied to it, lest it outrun judgment." But Dryden was not writing a critical treatise; seven years later, the year before Addison's birth in 1672, while not denying the importance of judgment, he radically changes his emphasis and tone. The production of a dramatic work by a poet is "the largest field of fancy, which is the principal thing required in him . . . Judgement, indeed is necessary in him; but 'tis fancy that gives the *life-touches*, and the *secret graces* to it."[2] Imagination imitates nature but also injects the wonderful and surprising. There was certainly interest and curiosity about the imagination. One reason that before Addison it suffered under almost universal qualification was that critics, especially those following rules, apprehended how powerful a faculty it could be.

John Dennis checks the imagination with reins of judgment, but he wants Pegasus to be full of "passion" and "warmth." The "great Parts" of a poet are first "a lively, and a warm, and a strong imagination," then "a solid and piercing judgment." The way to teach reason is not through a reflective, self-enclosed mood but by transport and inspiration: "Passion is the chief thing in poetry."[3] Similarly, Addison praises Pindar's "noble sallies of imagination" and, though himself later labeled "coldly correct" by Joseph Warton, refers to the race of natural genius as those who have "most heat and life in their imaginations."[4] A variation on the classical premise of instruction and pleasure, this view offers nothing essentially new, and Dennis, in his claims for "enthusiasm," relies on Longinus, with a Christian slant.[5] But once reason embodies passion, then the line between reason and the inflamed imagination—which, according to Dennis, convinces us of the reality of things not present or not experienced—becomes wavy and even breaks. One enters the realm of what Bacon had once called "imaginative or insinuative reason," perhaps the source for Matthew Arnold's later "imaginative reason."[6] As Edward Young relates in *Night Thoughts*, passion elevates reason. This mixing and mutual reliance of reason, vivid images, and passion expressed by Dennis was to become important for the associationists and for critics in general who, like Hume, Archibald Alison, and Hazlitt, stress the mind's inner excitement of response and creation.

### ADDISON'S INFLUENTIAL TREATMENT

In the *Spectator* series on "the pleasures of the imagination" (Nos. 409, 411–421), Addison does more than popularize the notions of Locke or provide the title and materials for Akenside's poem. Expanding Locke, Addison adds many new ideas. Although he does not pursue any one of these approaches to the imagination at length, they all became important and were more forcefully expressed and explored during the latter half of the century. Addison's fashionable series of 1712 was familiar to every man of letters. These dozen papers influenced—to name a few—Pope, Akenside, Francis Hutcheson, Hume, the Wartons, Johnson, and on the Continent, the "Swiss Critics" Bodmer and Breitinger.

At first it seems that Addison simply distinguishes two "pleasures of imagination" and bases them on Locke's division of simple and complex ideas. Addison calls the pleasures of imagination either "primary" or "secondary," terms Coleridge used a century later, intending to clarify levels of imaginative power. Addison's primary and secondary "pleasures" are not, of course, quite the same thing as primary and secondary powers of imagination, but, on the other hand, they go beyond passive responses. Both kinds of pleasure correspond to and arise from the mind actively at work, and so the "primary" and "secondary" pleasures are roughly equivalent to "primary" and "secondary" activities of the imagination itself.

For Addison, the primary imagination reproduces or copies mentally what we receive directly from experience, especially visual images. But "we have the power of retaining, altering, and compounding those images . . . into all the varieties of picture and vision." This is the "secondary" imagination, which involves an internal and distinctly psychological process. Throughout the essays Addison works more fully toward this less visual, less sensuous, and more psychological description of the imaginative act. He becomes intrigued with the way the mind reworks and transposes what it has sensed and, with this altering power, produces new combinations and ideas. Addison frees himself from the concept of imagination as something based on vision and the literal sense of "image." The imagination "has something in it like creation; it bestows a kind of existence, and draws up to the reader's view several objects which are not to be found in being. It makes additions to nature." Shakespeare's Caliban is a creature of imagination, while Hotspur or Caesar "might have been formed upon tradition, history, and observation."[7]

Thus Addison speaks of imagination as indispensable not only to taste and appreciation but also to the imitative or creative power of art. The secondary imagination gives rise to art as an imitation (not a copy) and supplement to nature. Mimesis, the classical foundation of art, becomes an imaginative act. We create by imagination and also appreciate through it, for the pleasure of art derives from that comparison with nature which the art work forces us to make. Art throws the mind into activity and comparison; this activity can arouse many responses—intellectual, emotional, and sensuous. It also elicits a delight in the artist's skill, a curiosity why he can be suggestive and catalyze such pleasurable comparisons. As Johnson was to say in *Rasselas*, "When the eye or the imagination is struck with any uncommon work the next transition of an active mind is to the means by which it was performed."

Addison believes that language and poetry capture and hold the imitative process best because words are the most versatile medium. They allow the mind freedom to present and to interpret, in a new and unified form, varied elements of experience and spots of time. The whole basis of fiction, the making of poetry from which poetry derives it name, is most appropriately called imagination rather than wit, skill, or feigning.[8]

In contrast to the traditional ideal of beauty as the regular and rational harmony of parts, Addison voices a *je ne sais quoi* attitude about beauty that implies an intuitive grasp of the beautiful through the power of imagination. "We are struck we know not how," he says, "and immediately assent to the beauty of an object, without inquiring into the particular causes and occasions of it." Influenced by Shaftesbury, Addison anticipates and helps to form the later Enlightenment's quest for beauty as an intuitive and aesthetic grasp of the world, a feeling which receives its finest poetic statement from romantic genius. Furthermore, Addison, like Locke, sees the associative and imaginative process as varying from person to person. He takes a step in the direction of the personal and the subjective as the basis, at least in part, of creating and judging art. The focus is more on the individual than it had previously been.[9]

In addition, Addison emphasizes two positive and exceptionally important values in criticism, values which become extremely important during the remainder of the century and which preoccupy, at one time or another, every critic of worth. These values are novelty—or originality as it was later known—and the sublime. Here, in a crucial link, Addison ascribes the power of these qualities to their effect on the imagination. After discussing decorum and the unities in dramatic poetry, he adds that "there is still something more essential to the art, something that elevates and astonishes the fancy, and gives a greatness of mind to the reader, which few of the critics besides Longinus have considered." This is the sublime, and Addison makes this "greatness" indispensable to the best art. Similarly, he places stress on "everything that is new or uncommon." This novelty or originality "raises a pleasure in the imagination, because it fills the soul with an agreeable surprise, gratifies its curiosity, and gives it an idea of which it was not before possest." In adding novelty and the sublime as criteria for art, Addison pays more attention to the effect of art on the mind's internal response. The reasons for judging and appreciating become more psychologically based, a tendency that by the late Enlightenment dominates critical thinking and establishes new criteria for intuitive beauty, novelty, and the sublime.[10]

Although Addison does not nuance or ramify many of his ideas about the imagination, he throws off a great many which, like sparks, do not have much mass themselves but are bright and hot enough to ignite larger fires. He attempts to clear the confusion between fancy and imagination by making them synonymous. His attempts fail, but he recognizes the problem. He also perceives the immense sway of imagination in life as well as in art and remarks "how great a measure of happiness or misery we are capable of receiving from the imagination only." This point was to become one of Johnson's central themes in his moral writings and the basis for *The Vanity of Human Wishes*. Addison hints at another of Johnson's themes when he says, in phrasing similar to Johnson's, that "our imagination loves to be filled with an object, or to grasp at anything that is too big for its capacity." It is a restless power, never entirely under rational control. Like Johnson, Addison sees this as a potentially treacherous "defect."[11]

The same paper (No. 412) that discusses the insatiable character of the imagination also turns to a different topic, the blending of the senses—not real synaesthesia, where one sense is used to characterize another, but a coordination and multiple interpenetration of senses through a common center in the mind, an idea that would fascinate Hazlitt three generations later. Addison explains that, "if there arises a fragrancy of smells or perfumes, they heighten the pleasures of the imagination, and make even the colours and verdure of the landscape appear more agreeable; for the ideas of both senses recommend each other, and are pleasanter together than when they enter the mind separately."[12]

The word "recommend" is the crux here. Addison seems to use it in a fairly literal way; each different sense leads into the others until they seem to repeat and add to each other, forming a total impression where the whole is greater than the sum of parts.

By the last essay (No. 421) the imagination has so broadened in scope for Addison that he speaks openly of its application to literature, morality, and criticism. He expresses a sophisticated philosophical concept, the mind's interface between the material and intellectual worlds and its ability to break down dualism by transferring one world to the other, a theme later important to Coleridge, Schelling, and to German thought on the imagination in general. Addison may have been thinking of Shakespeare's lines that imagination gives to airy nothing a local habitation and a name and bodies forth the shape of things unknown. Most of all, this last paper shows how, even in the two weeks his series occupies, he has begun to sound out the psychological intricacies of the imagination.

On the mind's ability not only to receive impressions and compose them into ideas but also to transpose ideas back into material impressions, Addison is specific in assigning the source of this power to "the pleasures of the imagination." These pleasures

> are not wholly confined to such particular authors as are conversant in material objects, but are often to be met with among the polite masters of morality, criticism, and other speculations abstracted from matter, who, though they do not directly treat of the visible parts of nature, often draw from them their similitudes, metaphors, and allegories . . . A truth in the understanding is . . . reflected by the imagination; we are able to see something like colour and shape in a notion, and to discover a scheme of thoughts traced out upon matter. And here the mind . . . has two of its faculties gratified at the same time, while the fancy is busy in copying after the understanding, and transcribing ideas out of the intellectual world into the material.

In this respect, Addison suggests that the exercise or pleasure of the imagination depends on a full and directed interplay and integration of as many faculties and operations of the mind as possible. His shortcoming is that when he makes an observation, he often fails to make a strong case for it. He settles for a polished veneer and does not vigorously pursue his numerous and incisive suggestions. He is not concrete or extended enough for his assertions. As Johnson says, he often thinks rightly but faintly. The slight enervation and generality, however, cannot tarnish the fact that he brought many ideas into the light and air where others could see, examine, and develop them. What he lacks in penetration he makes up for with activity. No one else in the first half of the English Enlightenment sprinkled as many seeds for a later understanding and development of the imagination as Addison.

## A GROUNDSWELL OF INTEREST

The *Spectator* papers step outside bounds of the ordinary. For example, Pope's *Essay on Criticism*, published the year before, in 1711, and written in 1709 when Pope was twenty-one, is an encyclopedia of neoclassical rules and premises. Typically, it contains only one reference to the imagination (l.58) and a few minor uses of "wit" for what we now think of as imagination. But in two later prefaces, both written after Addison's series, Pope changes his stance considerably. He is older and relying less on Horace and Boileau. The *Preface* to his translation of the *Iliad* (1715) abounds with praise for Homer's inventive and imaginative work:

> It is to the Strength of this amazing invention we are to attribute that unequal'd Fire and Rapture, which is so forcible in Homer, that no Man of true Poetical Spirit is Master of himself while he reads him. What he writes is of the most animated nature imaginable; everything moves, everything lives, and is put in action ... The Reader is hurry'd out of himself by the Force of the Poet's Imagination, and turns in one place to a Hearer, in another to a Spectator.

As the *Iliad* progresses, Homer's imagination "grows ... and becomes on Fire like a Chariot-Wheel, by its own Rapidity." Imagination is the inventive power, and Pope turns more to this "strength," "fire," "rapture," and "force of the poet's imagination" than to the clichés he gracefully versified six years earlier. He even told Joseph Spence that he had planned to write a Persian fable "in which I should have given a full loose to description and imagination. It would have been a very wild thing."[13] Pope's *Preface* to his edition of Shakespeare (1725) again champions original genius. Milton and especially Shakespeare, both growing in popularity, perhaps did as much to promote the esteem of imagination as any work of criticism or philosophy.

Addison's basic approach not only stands at the threshold of sharper critical interest in the imagination, like that shown by Pope, but also paves the way for psychological and aesthetic evaluation at large, which would soon be put to critical use. Francis Hutcheson's *Inquiry into the Original of Our Ideas of Beauty and Virtue* (1725) combines Shaftesbury with a few elements of Locke and adds an Addisonian flavor. Hutcheson, who later became professor of moral philosophy at the University of Glasgow, states we have an "internal sense" (similar to Leibniz's *"sens interne"*) that perceives beauty. It is an internal "sense of beauty" and yields to no rational explanation. Similarly, we possess a moral sense, also internal and intuitive. The capacity of these internal senses is actually much like Addison's concept of the imagination, especially the "secondary" pleasures. Hutcheson is not writing literary criticism, but when he and others begin to talk about beauty in nature as dependent on man's internal sense, they encourage criticism, insofar as criticism professes aesthetic values, to base itself on something in man's inner makeup that is imaginative rather than rational. Burke and the associationists soon extend this tendency and take the small additional step of calling Hutcheson's "internal sense" the imagination. Hutcheson's brief definition of beauty as "Uniformity Amidst Variety" is also not far from Coleridge's "multëity in unity."

By the 1720s and 1730s the imagination begins to acquire a distinctly positive character. It becomes the power not only to invent images but also to animate and excite, providing what Dryden called the "lifetouches" and "secret graces" of art. Imagination, in effect, means something naturally pleasant and enjoyable. And poetry, which can imitate nature so well that it touches all the senses, including the internal senses, relies chiefly on imagination. Leonard Welsted, in an anticipation of Wordsworth's "Reason in her most exalted mood," implies in *Concerning the Perfection of the English Language* (1724) that poetry—the imagination—blends and unifies ideas and acts like an extended reason: "Poetry depends much more on imagination than other arts, but is not on that account less reasonable than they; for imagination is as much a part of reason as is memory or judgment, or rather a more bright emanation from it, as to paint and throw light on ideas is a finer act of understanding than simply to separate or compare them."

Following Addison, several poets praise and try to explain the imagination in didactic or reflective verse. *The Excursion*, a poem by David Mallet in 1728, suggests that the imagination, by going beyond the senses and external reality, can transcend nature. It was this transcendent or escapist idea of poetry that Keats exploited so well but also came to question. As an internal and psychological power, it transports the reader to "extended space" and "superior worlds":

> Companion of the muse, creative power,
> Imagination! at whose great command
> Arise unnumber'd images of things,
> Thy hourly offspring: thou, who canst at will
> People with air-born shapes the silent wood,
> And solitary vale, thy own domain,
> Where contemplation haunts; oh, come, invok'd,
> To waft me on thy many-tinctur'd wing,
> O'er earth's extended space: and thence, on high,
> Spread to superior worlds thy bolder flight,
> Excursive, unconfin'd.

Mallet was, like Hutcheson, of Scottish family having changed his name from Malloch in 1724, and he became friends with both James Thomson and Pope.

During the middle years of the century, a number of poems express belief in the universal order of beauty and harmony by appealing not to a mechanistic operation of physical laws but to an intuitive and moral sensibility. These poems include John Gilbert Cooper's *The Power of Harmony* (1745), Henry Brooke's *Universal Beauty* (1728–1736), and James Harris' *Concord* (1751). Later, the creative power behind beauty and virtue was to be celebrated by John Ogilvie in *Providence* (1769) and by the American poet Philip Freneau in *The Power of Fancy* (1770). But none of these poets support and extend the ideas of Addison and Shaftesbury as much as Akenside does in one of the most successful poems of the 1740s.

### AKENSIDE: A COSMIC VISION

Mark Akenside's *The Pleasures of Imagination* serves as a poetic appendix to Addison's *Spectator* series and, through Addison, to Locke. But as Addison expanded on Locke and brought art and aesthetics to bear on Locke's nugatory ideas of psychology, so Akenside adds to Addison.[14] *The Pleasures of Imagination* appeared in 1744, thirty-two years after Addison's papers. During that time the idea of imagination was fanning out to include more and more; Akenside sees the imagination not only as the power that compares nature with the artist's imitation but specifically as the one creative and inventive force itself. He anticipates Alexander Gerard, Tetens, and Coleridge when he describes the blending of ideas by the imagination as it forms works of art. He also views the power of imagination as the hinge connecting experience and perception with moral judgment. Lastly, imagination serves religion, to the extent that if imagination is disordered, it becomes the primary source of evil. But when guided properly, it gives a sense of the cosmos as created by God and existing in harmony with man.

Akenside grafts large artistic, philosophic, and religious concepts, which in themselves were not new, onto the imagination in such a way that they depend completely upon the imagination for their activity and conviction. He brings within one framework elements of artistic, moral, and religious thought that had developed over the previous eighty years. The influence of Milton—his cosmology as well as his style—and of the new Platonists and Shaftesbury merge with the concept of the Great Chain of Being. Akenside's poem also reflects the sense of nature and universe—in vivid detail as well as in infinite distances and time—that appeared in Thomson's *Seasons* (1726–1730), and it reflects earlier eighteenth-century moral and aesthetic thinkers, such as Hutcheson, who were combining the intuitive, Platonic strain of Shaftesbury with the empirical one of Hobbes and Locke.

With this moral and aesthetic outlook Akenside introduces the poem, saying that the imagination mediates between "bodily sense and the faculties of moral perception."[15] In order words, he does not put imagination forward as a moral power itself but maintains that it alone permits the exercise of moral judgment. Without imagination, morality would remain latent, too general and abstract for human effectiveness. As the imagination connects the moral sense to the sensuous world, it encourages an aesthetic appreciation of experience that combines with moral power, until what fits a pattern of moral judgment and can be verified through the senses also becomes beautiful and pleasing. So Akenside speaks of the "trinity" of the beautiful, good, and true, which actually is one, echoing Shaftesbury. Beauty is the seal and promise, holding the letter of the good within the envelope of truth:

> Thus was Beauty sent from heaven,
> The lovely ministress of Truth and Good
> In this dark world; for Truth and Good are one,
> And Beauty dwells in them and they in her,
> With like participation.[16]

The weakest spot in this lovely and ideal construction is that Akenside never explains the origin of our "faculties of moral perception," whether this power is derived from education, upbringing, and tradition, is innate, or is both. Yet Shaftesbury had already dealt with this problem. He remarks on Locke's *Essay*, "Innate is a word Mr. Locke poorly plays upon." The point is not when ideas enter the mind, but "whether the constitution of man be such that, being adult and grown up, the ideas of order and administration of a God will not infallibly and necessarily spring up in him."

Akenside follows Addison's notion that imagination provides delight by comparing imitations (art) with nature itself, but Akenside turns more to the ability of imagination to produce these imitations in the first place. In both God and man he refers to the "creating" and "the plastic powers" that "labor for action" and give form to intangible ideas.[17] Imagination assumes a more active role, which recalls Locke's "power" to form complex ideas from simple ones. But Akenside puts it on a grander scale. He means that imagination, "the plastic powers," are responsible for creation itself and for all that man creates as art. In art, the form that most fulfills this creative urge is poetry, "an unlimited representative" in service of the imagination.[18]

In the image of the abyss, borrowed from Milton and later used by Wordsworth and perhaps punningly by Coleridge in his "Abyssinian maid," Akenside finds the source of all that fascinates "The Child of Fancy"; like Addison and Hobbes, he uses "fancy" interchangeably with "imagination":

> with loveliest frenzy caught,
> From earth to heaven he rolls his daring eye,
> From heaven to earth. Anon ten thousand shapes
> Like spectres trooping to the wizard's call,
> Flit swift before him. From the womb of earth
> . . . they come . . .
> . . . and the dark abyss
> Pours out her births unknown.[19]

Akenside, in borrowing from a speech of Shakespeare that was quoted repeatedly throughout the century, recognizes the importance of "frenzy" or passionate and emotional transport in the creative process. He sees in the imaginative process an instinctive drive toward the unity and inner harmony of the completed work of art, the blending and fusing of ideas until they form a whole. And this whole process is, by implication and analogy, similar to God's "creating power," which works continually in the universe.[20] The poet or artist turns to the cosmic abyss, "and mortal man aspires/To tempt creative praise":

> He marks the rising phantoms; now compares
> Their different forms; now blends them, now divides,
> Enlarges and extenuates by turns;
> Opposes, ranges in fantastic bands,
> And infinitely varies . . .
> . . . . . . . . . . . . . . . . . . . .
> . . . At length his plan
> Begins to open. Lucid order dawns;
> And, as from Chaos old the jarring seeds
> Of Nature, at the voice divine, repaired
> Each to its place . . .
> . . . . . . . . . . . . . . . . .
> . . . by swift degrees
> Thus disentangled, his entire design
> Emerges. Colors mingle, features join,
> And lines converge: the fainter parts retire;
> The fairer, eminent in light, advance;
> And every image on its neighbor smiles.[21]

The final shaping of this design into something with color, shape, and sound Akenside calls "Promethean art," a motif that runs back through Shaftesbury to the Renaissance and is mentioned later by Reynolds in his seventh *Discourse* and revived by Carlyle in *Sartor Resartus*. Akenside elaborates the Renaissance concept of man as a second maker and attributes this power specifically to the imagination.[22]

Some verbs that Akenside uses to describe the shaping power of imagination are the same or similar to those used later by Gerard, Tetens, and Coleridge when they list the activities of imagination. Gerard, author of *An Essay on Genius* (1774), read Akenside; Tetens borrowed from Gerard and cites him; Coleridge eagerly read Tetens, Akenside, and probably Gerard. We shall see one thread running through these writers, a connection ranging over seventy years. But for now we should note the particular verbs Akenside employs, for they reappear. The imagination "blends" and "divides"; the images and ideas, caught up and controlled by its power, "mingle," "join," and "converge." The imagination "enlarges," "extenuates," and "varies" its materials until a single new and unified image or work of art is produced.

Akenside predates by twenty to thirty years the descriptions of Gerard and Tetens concerning the imaginative process of combining ideas into a new and harmonized whole. The conclusion is inevitable that the beginning and the core of this way of outlining imaginative powers, culminating in Coleridge, starts with Akenside, who casts an eye back on Addison, Hobbes, and Locke for his own raw materials. Much of what Akenside says about the creative process, relatively briefly and in verse, will become expanded in prose criticism and psychology of the next three decades.

*The Pleasures of Imagination* was so popular, so widely read by critics and educated people interested in letters, ideas, and philosophy, that it challenged Thomson's *Seasons* as the *de rigueur* poem for learned circles, as well as being one of the foremost works discussed by more strictly "polite" groups, local book clubs, and philosophical societies. It is an indication of keen interest in the subject of imagination that such a long and didactic poem, one without plot, characters, or historical and national interest, and one completely lacking in the "romantic" or exotic appeal of a work like *Ossian*, should have been so widely read, quoted, and discussed. That Akenside's notoriety waned after the 1770s is largely because he had effectively spread his message and interest: it had become thoroughly assimilated into thought and criticism, and his own work no longer retained its novel and singular quality.

Aside from describing the moral nature of imagination and the shaping activity of "creating" and "plastic powers" (phrases that enter the century's critical vocabulary), Akenside turns directly to the relationship between the artist, the second maker, and the original and on-going creation of the universe.

The creative artist participates in the divine shaping of the cosmos, a joining of the world of spirit with the world of matter. This same hope that the poet's imagination mediates between ethereal spirit and earthly

life appears in Keats, though in a somewhat different context. Akenside
suggests what Shaftesbury implied and what Leibniz stated categorically—a pre-established harmony of mind and nature, spirit and matter.
By use of, if not belief in, this harmony, the poet makes nature and man
into one and binds them together through what Coleridge would call
"humanizing nature." Akenside phrases this sense of nature "humanized" by the imagination:

> Some heavenly genius, whose unclouded thoughts
> Attain that secret harmony which blends
> The ethereal spirit with its mould of clay;
> Oh! teach me to reveal the grateful charm
> That searchless Nature o'er the sense of man
> Diffuses, to behold in lifeless things,
> The inexpressive semblance of himself,
> Of thought and passion.[23]

The opening paragraph of Coleridge's "On Poesy or Art" expresses
the same concept in similar language. "Art," says Coleridge, is "the
power of humanizing nature, of infusing the thoughts and passions of
man into every thing which is the object of his contemplation." The
"power," as Coleridge designates it, and the "grateful charm . . . to be-
hold," as Akenside calls it, are the same in their ability to weave man
and nature into one fabric and establish or reveal "that secret harmony"
of spirit and matter. To call imagination a "power" or "charm" that secures a "secret harmony" is a way of referring to it with almost holy
fervor and reverence, somewhat like the ending of Coleridge's *Kubla
Khan*. Akenside's insistence on an inevitable bond between morality
and the imagination was additionally attractive to Coleridge.

In a modest way, then, and with a poetically conventional diction,
Akenside presents the idea that imagination establishes and uncovers a
harmony of being between man and nature as well as within the various
parts of man's own nature. The mind, by an imaginative and "harmonious action of her powers,/Becomes herself harmonious." In "outward
things" the mind desires "to mediate" and bring closer "the sacred
order" to its own "kindred order." In a similar way, Coleridge calls art
the mediatress between man and nature. Nature, for Akenside as for the
Romantics, is a symbolic veil. Appealed to and seen imaginatively, it
leads to the godhead itself, and through nature "we feel within ourselves
His energy divine."[24]

In all this optimism, Akenside touches on an aspect of the imagination
that would lie dormant for sixty years, until Coleridge and especially
Schelling, pushing imagination to the limit as an explanation for the
basic facts of the cosmos, take it up again. Johnson touches on it, but in a
directly moral and more concrete fashion. According to this theme, the

unbalanced and disordered imagination is the source of moral evil. "The origin of Vice," explains Akenside, is "from false representations of the fancy, producing false opinions concerning good and evil."[25]

There is a distinct lack of specificity to Akenside's outline of the actual mechanism of evil springing from the imagination, but he points to two causes. Instead of working with reason, imagination completely dominates the powers of belief. We soon believe whatever we imagine. The result is illusion and pretense. Second, given the natural make-up of man, a powerful and illusory imagination feeds and encourges the passions of self-interest: "ambition," "Revenge," "Lust," and "wishful Envy." In Johnson's moral essays, this false stoking of the passions by imagination becomes a central theme, as in Keats does the illusory quality of imagination, especially in art.

In fact, some lines from Akenside, although they lack Johnson's taut energy and concrete examples or allusions, sound like *The Rambler:* "Hence the fevered heart/Pants with delirious hope for tinsel charms"; and Akenside, telling how fancy "sheds a baleful tincture o'er the eye/Of Reason, till no longer he discerns,/And only guides to err," anticipates the line in *The Vanity of Human Wishes*, "How rarely reason guides the stubborn choice."

Akenside does not vie with Soame Jenyns in explaining a scheme of natural or cosmic evil. The evil of the imagination is human. It remains for thinkers like Schelling to attribute to God an imaginative and creative power that can become distorted in a way analogous to man's false imagination. Imagination's bad tendencies, according to Akenside, are known and can be controlled, but its scope, creative power, and direct contact with the "secret harmony" of the universe are only beginning to be explored. This is the final impression left by Akenside and the one that propelled itself into popular thought, psychology, and criticism.

## THE HIGHEST IDEAL OF POETRY

From 1710 to the 1750s, the imagination had risen in stature considerably. It acquired a moral, aesthetic, and even religious value that was almost exclusively positive. To many it became the single most desirable quality in poetry. Pope died in 1744 and Swift a year later. As satire and didactic verse loosed their stranglehold, the ode and lyric regained much of the place they had enjoyed in the previous century. Even though emulation of the Pindaric ode was often poor, that form's wild flights and sudden swellings of passion and "fire" soon made it a favorite. Not long after Akenside's *Pleasures of Imagination*, William Collins and Joseph Warton proclaim imagination as the central poetic attribute.

In 1746 Warton prefaces his *Odes on Several Subjects* with a short manifesto. He "is convinced that the fashion of moralizing in verse has been carried too far, and as he looks upon invention and imagination to be the chief faculties of a poet, so he will be happy if the following odes may be looked upon as an attempt to bring poetry into its right channel."

In the first ode in Warton's book, "To Fancy," fancy appears in the allegorical guise of a "Nymph, with loosely-flowing hair,/With buskin'd leg, and bosom bare." Although the poem is transparent in its technique and even sounds artificial, it is a clear and open plea for a new approach to poetry based on the imagination. (Warton does not distinguish fancy from imagination.) The creative power, he says, is the most important and mysterious gift of a true poet. Fancy waves "An all-commanding magic wand" and carries us, as does imagination in the chorus to *Henry V*, on "rapid wings" over the barriers of time and space. Fancy begets enthusiasm, "vital aid," "energy divine," and "unexhausted fire." Poets following her go "Beyond cold critic's studied laws" and overwhelm our souls with feelings and sentiments. Invoking Spenser and calling Fancy to "come/From thy lamented Shakespear's tomb," Warton tries to create a new kind of poetry by restating and redefining the ideal power of poetic invention and emotion, which he believes was disregarded by poets immediately preceding him. Not surprising for the author of *The Enthusiast: or, The Lover of Nature* (1744), he beckons the hopeful spirit of poetic imagination to venture closer to nature, "Where never human art appear'd . . . Where Nature seems to sit alone." Imagination casts a primitive aura, and the maid of Fancy sports "brows with Indian feathers crown'd."

Warton is perhaps a less gifted poet than Addison, whose "artful" and "coldly correct" work he rejects in *The Enthusiast* in order to recapture Shakespeare's "Warblings wild." But the significance of "To Fancy" is not in style, diction, imagery, or form. Warton's poem is important not for its poetry but for its message. He announced that England needed a new poetry and that this poetry should be inspired by and based upon a faith and confidence in the creative imagination.

William Blake, whose imagination combined the cosmic, political, religious, personal, and poetic—and who championed the name and power of imagination—was one of the poets to answer Warton's invocation. Born in 1757, Blake was writing verses in the early 1770s. But the vanguard of rising movement is often its extreme element, and Blake, in many ways the most brilliantly singular of the new poets of the imagination in the latter half of the century, remained in comparative obscurity. Blake's vision is unique and highly personal, but even in the 1740s and 1750s it was not wholly unpredictable. He read extensively in philosophy and poetry. The Bible, Milton, and Bunyan were among his favorites, but he also picked up the call to a new poetry from critics and poets like Warton, Collins, Thomas Warton, Sr., Isaac Watts, and Edward Young. And although Blake disliked Locke, seeing only one side of him, he was also a product, like the American and French Revolutions he supported, of the very toleration and spirit of free and individual inquiry that Locke had eloquently preached.

In the same year as Joseph Warton's *Odes*, Collins' *Ode on the Poetical Character* appeared, later admired by Coleridge. In this poem, difficult to interpret, "Fancy" is the highest poetic power and is regarded as an analog to the divine creation. The idea is like Akenside's, but Collins writes in more vibrant and urgent language:

> Young Fancy thus, to me divinest name,
>   To whom, prepar'd and bath'd in heav'n,
>   The cest of amplest pow'r is giv'n,
>   To few the godlike gift assigns,
>   To gird their blest prophetic loins,
> And gaze her visions wild, and feel unmix'd her flame.

The verses are not really visionary and prophetic, but that is the quality Collins desires. Recalling Milton, he laments the poor prospects for imaginative poetry in his own and the coming generation. Yet Collins, like Warton, is helping to establish the tenor and taste that will encourage a new kind of poetry.[26]

Ten years later, in 1756, Joseph Warton dedicates his *Essay on Pope* to Edward Young and makes his second important plea for the imagination: "It is a creative and glowing imagination, and that alone that makes the poet." Although Pope, and neoclassical verse as a whole, was rich in genius, Warton implies that the whole ambiance of Pope's poetical world was less than ideal. However admirable, it fell short of Shakespeare and Milton. "The 'man of rhymes' may be easily found," explains Warton, "but the genuine poet, of a lively plastic imagination, the true maker or creator is . . . a prodigy." Here, as in Akenside's "plastic powers," the word "plastic" is associated with the imagination. William Duff will use it often again to refer to imagination, but its most famous context is in "esemplastic," where Coleridge uses it to approximate the German *Einbildungskraft*.

The mid Enlightenment bestows new literary premium on the imagination. Critics and poets are rapidly becoming confident that it alone permits the greatest poetry, of a kind found by skipping the high neoclassic mode and returning to Milton and the Elizabethans, to Chaucer, and to Homer. The ability to imitate and, more important, the gift of invention are incorporated into the new and rangy view of imagination.

It becomes more of a trusted power and, harkening back to Renaissance and classical inferences, a human reflex of God's creative energy. The classical idea of the poet as a maker or feigner remains, but critics and poets increasingly insist upon imagination as the essence of poetry and the key to its magic and greatness. This is done, at times, almost to the exclusion of any other powers. Lord Monboddo in his *Origin and Progress of Language* (1773) sums up the opinion that was widespread when Coleridge was an infant:

> The imagination has ... a *creative* power ... is conversant with the future as well as the past and paints ... scenes that never did exist, and it is likely never will; for it may be said to create even the materials of those scenes ... formed upon the model of objects that have been presented by the sense[s] and are, as it were, imitations of them ... This is that great work of imagination, which is the foundation of all the *fine arts*, and stamps men truly *poets*, or *makers.*[27]

# 5

# THE INNER STRUCTURE OF LIFE:

# HUME AND JOHNSON

*A*lmost exact contemporaries, David Hume and Samuel Johnson are two of the most powerful and informed minds of the eighteenth century. In argument and reasoning their intellects move undaunted; opponents, like Soame Jenyns and James Macpherson, discover themselves often crushed by a force of thought as swift and unrelenting as the muscles of a python. The minds of both men are in close touch with concrete human experience. What is more, they are as agile in thought as they are trenchant. They touch the bedrock of human activity and behavior.

For both Hume and Johnson, however diverse and even antipathetic they are in other ways, imagination becomes the central fact of experience and life. They are empiricists in a broad sense—that is, they rely on external nature, on observation, and on the analysis of what is actually felt and seen. Johnson dismissed Berkeley, whose empiricism had been carried so far that it had become subjective idealism and recognized only the existence of mind, by kicking a stone and claiming, "I refute him thus!" And Hume, although a self-proclaimed skeptic, admitted that he could support skepticism only so far, and that he would dodge a carriage in the street if it were bearing down on him. Yet Johnson and Hume see something even more important than their fundamental recognition of the external world, the way in which the mind reacts and orders experience according to its own desires, uncertainties, and fears. The drama of the mind and of its passions, as it confronts other people and the world, is directed, overwhelmingly, by the imagination.

For both men, the existence and active working of the imagination is perhaps the most important empirical fact and certainly an inescapable one. The imagination is not matter, and it is not "received" by any of the senses, but it alone explains how we face change, connect the past, present, and future, and direct our actions. Without imagination the psyche could not swim and make its way in the sea of events surrounding it. It would only float, like a chip of wood, at the mercy of each passing wave and tide. The imagination is so imbedded in our natures that it, more than anything else, controls our lives. This recognition largely gives Hume his psychological acuity and Johnson his profound wisdom as a moralist.

To each of them imagination is a capricious power, fundamentally getting man into more trouble and superstition than good. As Swift said, man is not rational, only an animal that can be described as *capax rationis*, capable of reason. Hume and Johnson realize that the imagination is the one power that we can use to understand circumstances around us, and also the principal or only means we can use to respond, however misguidedly, to the world as it jars against and cracks the vessel of our feelings and hopes.

Their comments on the imagination fall into two categories that are intrinsically connected: psychology and morality. But they never formulate a psychological system or invoke a rote series of moral rules. In a way, this is because the awesome role that the imagination plays in human life will not let them. In their recognition of this fact, and in their application of it to specific situations, lie a great deal of the power and truth of their thought.


HUME AND THE ACTIVE UNDERCURRENT OF THE MIND

Relying utterly on an empirical approach, Hume discounts the possibility of transcendental knowledge, but he also shies away from mechanical explanations of the mind. To him, the metaphysical and the mechanical indicate respectively too little observation and too much hunger for certainty. While he rejects the ideal and transcendental, he is equally suspicious of empirical systems.

In Hume's view, the mind is a whole unit with few internal barriers or bridges. Emotions mingle with ideas and change their intensity or force. A tide of passions, sometimes "calm" and sometimes "violent," pounds the shore of reason. This tide both erodes and builds; it sculpts the entire coastline. Sense impressions, like constant winds, set up more motion in the area. The breakwater of the understanding partly calms and orders, but not completely. Real activity of the mind occurs at exactly that spot where the waves break and all elements converge, a slurry where reason mixes so thoroughly with passion that it is no longer possible to distinguish the two. Now this slurry forms an under-current which mixes together all the effects of sense impressions, reason, understanding, and passion. This undercurrent flows incessantly and gives one common direction to all these combined activities of the mind. It is responsible for "the vivacity of our ideas" and diminishes or augments their hold on the mind. It can either propel thought shoreward or create an undertow. This shifting, mixing force in the psyche is imagination. It is the active undercurrent of the mind.[1]

Hume calls "impressions" those stimuli we receive directly from the outside world through our senses. "Ideas" are the mind's later reproduction of these impressions. These ideas may be identical to their original impression or they may not. If they are, then such ideas come simply and directly from memory. But in reproducing impressions as ideas, the imagination may transpose, wrench them out of sequence, divide, or even fuse them. The association of ideas obviously lends a hand in this process, but Hume discovers a richer and more complicated arrangement. The imagination interfuses and combines passions with ideas. Every thought has an emotional charge varying from slight to great. This is one of the central points in Hume's "Dissertation on the Passions" (1757). The imagination orchestrates the crescendo and harmony of feeling and thought. It gives ideas direction, "uniting them in one action."[2] We feel or think of something strongly or faintly, according to the force of imagination. In his *Treatise of Human Nature* Hume says simply that, "The memory, senses, and understanding are therefore all of them founded on the imagination, or the vivacity of our ideas."[3]

But once passion is roused, it grips and controls the mind. Passions are "slower" to stir than the imagination, but when they are moved, their force is overpowering. Hence a "contradiction" seems to arise between passion and imagination: passions lurk everywhere, and when awakened, they usurp all force. The vivacity of our ideas is then no longer governed by the imagination but by the greater momentum of passion. The key to resolving this "contradiction," however, ultimately depends on imagination itself. Since passion is actuated by imagination in the first place, imagination can initially direct the passion. Thus, argues Hume, we may feel great affection for a man, but little for his servants or children. This is because passion cannot move easily from a large object to "lesser" ones. But if our imagination first connects, by "nearness" or "contiguity," the servants and children with the man himself, then the sluice gate of our affection immediately opens in their direction, too.[4]

Hume's notions seem occasionally mechanical. He relies somewhat on Locke and cites the "rules" of association: contiguity, resemblance, and cause and effect. But Hume always insists on the complexity of the mind; we separate our faculties and call them different names, but they all interconnect. For example, with regard to the passions, the mind is not like a clay tablet or

> like a wind instrument, which, in running over all the notes, immediately loses the sound when the breath ceases; but rather resembles a string-instrument, where, after each stroke, the vibrations still retain some sound . . . Each stroke will not produce a clear and distinct note of passion, but the one passion will always be mixed . . . with the other.

Imagination itself wavers back and forth between the strong passions of hope and fear. The psyche moves in perpetual motion and mingling. When contrasting passions mix, they do not cancel out each other. They alternate, and such alternation may heighten the impact of each passion. Following this reasoning in his *Preface* to Shakespeare, Johnson argues that tragic and comic scenes often reach their intense points when juxtaposed. Throughout the late eighteenth century, in both England and Germany, the "mingled" or "tragicomic" drama became increasingly popular, in part because it was seen to reflect more accurately the real state of human psychology.[5]

Under an internal pressure ready to erupt any time, the passions and imagination rise to the surface when heated by uncertainty. The imagination is a *completing* power. It makes us open to suggestion, a value on which literary critics later in the century placed increasing emphasis:

> Nothing more powerfully excites any affection than to conceal some part of its object . . . which at the same time that it shows enough to prepossess us in favour of the object, leaves still some work for the imagination . . . the effort, which the fancy makes to complete the idea, rouses the spirits, and gives an additional force to the passion.

Lack of uniformity in the object—or even its total absence—can suggest and inflame passion. Hume believes absence magnifies strong passions and kills weak ones in the way that wind fans fire but blows out a match. The passion suggested may bring hope or fear, pleasure or grief. And, the "completing" inference does not have to be true.[6] When Joseph's brothers show the bloody coat of many colors to their father, Jacob imagines that his favorite son has been torn apart by a beast.

This last example introduces one of Hume's central themes: the imagination is very easily deceptive. He is not just raking up the well-worn "dangers" of the imagination. His point is that the imagination can be grossly misleading because it is so pervasive and ever-present.[7] The mind cannot escape its sway. The imagination has an inertia of its own, which busily seeks out new objects or conjures up groundless fears. It is always ready to seize power and establish an inner tyranny over reason. But we cannot disregard the imagination; all faculties, including reason, are crippled without it.

Hume concludes that the imagination is "a principle so inconstant and fallacious" that if we follow it we doom ourselves to false reason as often as not, but to ignore it sentences us to no reason at all. As W. C. Gore explains, imagination was "the only element left to Hume which could carry anything, it was the only element possessing the quality of continuity and capable of transcending the present moment. Hence it was loaded down with the great objective categories of causation and substance; and . . . it broke down under the strain."[8]

Hume keeps the faculty of judgment outside the sphere of imagination. Imagination may produce fictions or beliefs, but even beliefs are of a lower surety than "ideas of the judgment." Yet in the end, because Hume gives for the dangers of the imagination the reason that it is all-pervading, the net effect is to stir more interest, not suspicion, in the power.[9]

The imagination acts so vividly, with such uninterrupted force, that in filling ideas with passion and feeling, it may actually reconvert those ideas back into immediate and lively impressions. The grip of these impressions on the mind can be as keen as sense impressions. This kind of activity is the source of psychosomatic disease, as Coleridge analyzed it. But such an activity can also create sympathies with other people or situations. It fosters what Adam Smith was soon to call "fellow-feeling," the basis of morality. Hume does not dwell on this aspect, but his notice of it was one starting point for the fascination with sympathy that later swept the century. "Sympathy," he explains, is "the conversion of an idea into an impression by the force of imagination." Hume briefly but clearly makes imagination the power behind sympathy.[10]

In "On Tragedy" (1757), Hume contends that "imitation is always of itself agreeable." The action of a tragedy "makes the time pass easier . . . and is some relief to that oppression under which men commonly labor when left entirely to their own thoughts and meditations." The imagination must be filled in some way. Imitation forces it to compare and to complete at least three things: the object imitated, the imitation or work of art itself, and the mind's own reactions or self-reflection concerning the interplay of the first two. Without such an engagement the imagination is liable to become a cannibal and turn on itself. Johnson himself remarked that when he was in low spirits in the early 1760s, he would go to the theater "more than in former seasons," not out of admiration for the plays, but "to escape from myself"—that is, to engage his restless imagination, to fix it, in expectation, on something external before it bruised the mind within. It was escapism, a safety valve. But the theater, like art in general, automatically encourages the imagination to compare the action of a play with the state of human nature as each of us knows it individually. The potential of the imagination is released rather than left to fester, and art becomes a purgative for the human spirit.[11]

Finally, as the active undercurrent of the mind, imagination for Hume unifies the intention or design of any creative project, as in Hobbes, Akenside, Gerard, Duff, Tetens, Schelling, Kant, and Coleridge. This is especially apparent in genius. The events a writer relates, claims Hume, "must be connected together by some bond or tie: They must be related to each other in the imagination, and form a kind of *unity*, which may bring them under one plan or view." This idea, found in Akenside and others, receives deeper practical and psychological treatment from Hume. The mind of genius is purged from all spurious and tentative wanderings of creative power. It collects and sorts images and ideas until they slip together like interlocking pieces of a puzzle and form one picture. Where this picture has the force of truth and is also most complete, the imagination is most enlivened. History and biography may be accurate in their facts and inferences, but poetry excites the mind more. The poet not only has the opportunity to order facts and events, but also invents them.[12] He thus achieves a stronger and more continuous bond between the expectation he stirs up in the reader and the objects he creates to fulfill that expectation. This psychological approach to the genius and effects of poetry was seized on by many who followed Hume, whether they agreed with his thought as a whole or not. Fellow Scots, such as Duff, Gerard, Kames, Smith, Stewart, and Alison, pursued and investigated Hume's claim that imagination is at the core of both sympathy and the creative power of genius; while for Hazlitt and Coleridge, sympathy is an essential part of genius.

Hume jolted the scene. He challenges the concept of thought as distinct from emotion not merely because he reveals that thought calls on emotion and passion, but also because he shows the extent to which thought and feeling—under the sway of the imagination—are intrinsically connected. Thought takes on the force not of something that happens to the thinking part of the mind but of something that happens in the whole mind. The activity is internal and complex. This opened up a keener psychological approach. In 1751 Hume wrote Gilbert Elliot that even his own researches were "a perpetual struggle of a restless Imagination against Inclination, perhaps against Reason." British empiricism was becoming broader and less systematized. Hume had repercussive effects, too. Men like Alexander Gerard, who learned much from Hume, were read avidly by the German psychologist Tetens, who was to have a strong impact on Kant and Coleridge. For the imagination, as for so much else, Hume is a pivotal figure.

## JOHNSON'S MORAL STANCE

Johnson's special importance for the subject is only beginning to be realized. He does not approach the imagination as a theoretical psychologist nor as one seeking to unlock the secrets of artistic creativity or of a grand cosmology. His focus is directly on life, on how and why hope, fear, and desire tend to occupy so much of our time and energy in the pursuit or contemplation of imagined rewards, calamities, and happiness. Johnson is not dealing, at least not theoretically, with the creative side of imagination but with something just as vital: how the imagination constructs so much of the shape and content of daily life and thought, which in themselves become the subject of art and literature.

In Johnson's literary criticism, when we find specific discussion and not what is implied or taken for granted, the imagination has a relatively minor role, largely because of the two genres in which his major criticism is written. The *Preface to Shakespeare* (1765) is in the traditional form of a general apologia, followed, as is fitting for the preface to an edition, by a discussion of editorial principles and practice. And the *Lives of the Poets* (1779–1781), commissioned by a group of publishers, were intended as short biographical introductions to fifty-two poets, though Johnson could not refrain from supplementing what was expected with critical analysis. In neither of these forms of criticism would explicit discussion of the imagination have seemed relevant to him. But he thought well of the new psychological criticism beginning to explore the subject. He praised Burke's *Philosophical Inquiry into the Origins of the Sublime and Beautiful*, and also Lord Kames's *Elements of Criticism*, both of which base criticism and aesthetics on a broad psychological foundation.

Touching the subject *en passant* in his critical writing, Johnson tends to use the word "imagination" in a somewhat conventional way, as would be expected from the writer of the *Dictionary* concerned to stabilize the meaning of words in the norm in which they had been used from about 1600 to 1750. Imagination is essentially, as he says in the *Dictionary*, "the power of forming ideal pictures; the power of representing things absent." By the word "imagination" the high Romantics meant a combination of abilities and functions of mind working at their highest pitch and turning creatively to the production of something new. For this idea Johnson prefers the term "genius"—"a mind of large general powers, accidentally determined to some particular direction," "a mind active, ambitious, and adventurous, always investigating, always aspiring," and of which the "highest praise" is "original invention." Genius would be impossible without imagination, "the power of representing things absent." But this power becomes effective as genius when its vividness is supplemented by knowlege and judgment. "Imagination," claims Johnson in his *Life of Butler,* "is nothing without knowledge." Yet he is not thinking of separate faculties and reacts against routine tendencies to compartmentalize the mind. "It is ridiculous to oppose judgment to imagination; for it does not appear that men have necessarily less of one as they have more of the other."[13] During the trip to the Hebrides, when William Robertson repeated the "cant" notion that "one man had more judgment, another more imagination," Johnson replied, "It is only, one man has more *mind* than another."[14]

If we go beyond the literary criticism, we discover that no major author before the Romantics is more concerned with the imagination or devotes to the subject a larger share of his work than Johnson in his writing on human nature. He especially probes the human imagination in the ten years from *The Vanity of Human Wishes* (1749) through the essays in the *Rambler, Adventurer,* and *Idler* to *Rasselas* (1759). In this writing the major premise and ultimate lesson is the extent to which people, individually and collectively, are in almost every way "of imagination all compact." The question is what to do with this restless, hungry, creative, and unpredictable capacity of mind that is so radically built into human nature. Given Johnson's moral stance, he dwells on the darker potentialities of imagination and on how we can try to avoid the illusion and self-deception that these potentialities involve. He recognizes the seductive power of the imagination and the extent to which "helpless man" is caught in its grip.

Johnson's treatment of the imagination has a panoramic scope because he saw clairvoyantly the interconnection of the imagination at every point with what might now be called the libido. Everything we mean by desire, wish, hope, or fear and despair is primarily the product of the imagination, except for elementary biological needs and instincts; and even these are constantly being permeated, magnified, or altered in their direction by the imagination. The imagination—as Coleridge said later, though in another context—is a *"completing* power." It is forever leaping ahead—or particularly as one grows older, backward—to some end, image, or pattern, and in the process it fills out and extends the incomplete experience and stray memories of passing moments. "The truth is that no mind," reports the philosopher Imlac to Rasselas, "is much employed upon the present: recollection and anticipation fill up almost all our moments."* The thin line of the present is in constant motion, and

* Throughout this and the following three paragraphs I am indebted to W.J. Bate, *The Achievement of Samuel Johnson* (1955), ch. 2 ("The Hunger of Imagination").

the greater part of our ideas, or for that matter our feelings, arise from what is "before or behind us"— in short, from the imagination as it fills the "vacuity" and "insufficiency" of the fleeting moment. Imlac, the philosopher who has taken his pupils to see the Great Pyramid, implicitly contrasts two uses of this recourse "to the past and future for supplemental satisfaction." He defends the study of history as a sane, valuable way of satisfying the imaginative appetite, but he also points to the Great Pyramid as an example of this appetite when used in another way:

> It seems to have been erected only in compliance with that hunger of imagination which preys incessantly upon life ... Those who have already all that they can enjoy, must enlarge their desires. He that has built for use, till use is supplied, must begin to build for vanity ... I consider this mighty structure as a monument of the insufficiency of human enjoyments.[15]

At the same time, the imagination always extrapolates from context, sifts out and disregards elements from the confusing welter of experience that would otherwise distract effort and blur focus, leaving us paralyzed in neutrality. As a result, we create for ourselves a simpler, more concentrated conception than reality can ever fulfill. Yet this concentrated vision, in one respect, forms the basis of all dramatic art, which is a distillation of life. This thickening of events and passions is suggested by the German *dichten*, to make more dense, or to compose, especially poetry.

But Johnson is particularly fond of exploring this aspect of imagination as it applies to daily life. Often we dwell only on the expected delights of travel, recreation, or change of job, find the results disappointing, but then proceed to do the same thing all over again. "The married praise the ease and freedom of a single state, and the single fly to marriage from the weariness of solitude." The aspiring author dreams of happiness once his book is published, then finds that there are complications he had not foreseen and that his happiness has increased far less than expected. So with ambitions of every kind, including the pursuit of riches, fame, and position. The actual experience when it arrives— mixed, complicated, embarrassed with qualifications and contrarieties— seldom matches the condensed simplicity of the extrapolative character of the imagination. "Yet, when the same state is again at a distance, imagination paints it as desirable."[16]

This projective and extrapolative character of the imagination would be innocent except that it also leads to most of the evil in human life, evil inflicted by human beings on each other—as distinct from "natural evil," such as sickness, accident, or natural catastrophe. The way to an imagined good or desire, such as money, power, or fame, is often dictated by the deliberate or even ruthless practice of envy, the desire to "pull others down" and to relieve the sense "of our disparity by lessening others, though we gain nothing to ourselves." On a grand scale, wars for land and prestige—a word that, like "prestidigitation," originally meant illusion or something purely imagined—or conflicts of creed and opinion are the result of imagined outcomes or imagined ideals, very few of which satisfy in the end.

The chapter in *Rasselas* entitled "The Dangerous Prevalence of Imagination," is perhaps Johnson's most thorough and harsh exposure of the trap hidden in imagination:

> No man will be found in whose mind airy notions do not sometimes tyrannise, and force him to hope or fear beyond the limits of sober probability. All power of fancy over reason is a degree of insanity . . . it is not pronounced madness but when it comes ungovernable, and apparently influences speech or action.
>
> By degrees the reign of fancy is confirmed; she grows first imperious, and in time despotic. Then fictions begin to operate as realities, false opinions fasten upon the mind, and life passes in dreams of rapture or of anguish.

It is true that what Johnson says here is superficially matched by almost every previous writer who has anything to say about the imagination.[17] Johnson would have read, for example, the remark of Marcus Aurelius in his *Meditations:* "The thoughts and imaginations upon which you frequently dwell will fix the character of your intellect; for the soul takes its tint from the imagination" (Bk. V). But most earlier writers describe the working of the imagination merely in conceptual terms. Imagination, they say, projects one forward or backward, or into another's condition or feelings, and completes a pattern from suggestion and isolated details; it sifts, selects, and recombines. By contrast, Johnson puts imagination dramatically, with concrete vividness, practicality, and range. He writes from experience. Himself a man of strong, at times overwhelmingly turbulent imagination, he confronts it so constantly that he cannot minimize its effects. This gives his thinking about the subject a direct authenticity, a resonance and body lacking in more detached or theoretical writers.

Johnson brings to its highest pitch the rationalist suspicion of the imagination, the feeling of many writers in the earlier part of the Enlightenment that there were "dangers of imagination" in contrast to its pleasures. After Johnson, this distrust of imagination slackens, although it reappears in Goethe and Keats. Perhaps one reason is that no one could state this distrust more powerfully and more convincingly than Johnson had already. Things yet to be said and topics of the imagination yet to be explored would have to assert the positive side of that power or else run the risk of repeating rather than creating.

Johnson probes the unconscious mind, too, with a brilliant, stubborn persistence unrivaled before Freud. He is aware that the door is always open between imagination and every impulse, instinct, and emotion, at every level from the rudimentary to the sophisticated. This leads to a less compartmentalized, more dynamic conception of the mind than is common among contemporaries writing in the 1750s. It also leads him to conceive of the simplifying, extrapolative activity of the imagination in a way consistent with what is now thought of as its archetypal character, something so rooted in the human psyche that it can be viewed as partially responsible for certain forms, structures, and kinds of characters that recur in all literatures.

Dealing with another aspect of the unconscious and imagination, Johnson comes closer than any writer before Freud to understanding the psychology of repression.[18] For Johnson, this means a blocking of the imagination's search for fulfillment, forcing it to skulk away and then tunnel back through various forms of regression, transference, fixation, hypochondria, and hostility. He had "studied medicine diligently in all its branches," wrote Hester Thrale, "but had given particular attention to the diseases of the imagination."[19] Moreover, the form of therapy to which he turns as the most effective treatment of the "diseases of the imagination" is essentially a "dynamic" one, in keeping with the dynamic character of the imagination itself; his therapy is not a futile attempt to suppress imagination but is an effort to redirect it through activity, or at times counteractivity, such as exercise, habit, focus, or even distraction. This he discovered during his own mental breakdown between the ages of twenty and twenty-five, and the lesson was reinforced by reading and attempting to apply George Cheyne's study of melancholy, *The English Malady* (1733), in which the same form of therapy is advocated, though in general terms. Finally, though Johnson conceives the omnipresence and power of the imagination as vividly as the high Romantics forty years later, he differs from them in being much less able to trust the imagination. He does not see it, by itself, as "constructive" in a healthful and optimistic sense. True, it is indispensable in every good or creative act—intellectual, moral, or both. Idealism itself is the extrapolation of a desired pattern or form. Charity or compassion would not be possible without imagination: "All joy or sorrow for the happiness or calamities of others is produced by an act of the imagination . . . placing us, for a time, in the condition of him whose fortune we contemplate."[20] This sympathy is taken for granted, but it will not happen automatically. The theme of Johnson's poem *The Vanity of Human Wishes* and of most of his moral essays is the necessary and constant cleansing and rectifying of the "hunger of imagination" through reason, religion, and the stability of fact. Imagination needs the *katharsis* of

Greek drama, a moment to recognize and to accept things that cannot be changed, no matter what personal consequences they may have.

Johnson's view may seem too dark and not a healthful corrective for romantic optimism. But at least it supplements the high romantic view and highlights one side of the imagination on which they did not dwell. Even Coleridge, long before he expressed an immense confidence in the imagination, which he held until his late forties, wrote a poem in which he briefly admits much of what Johnson said. In the seventh stanza of his *Dejection: An Ode* (1802), despair and horror result when the imagination turns in revenge on the self and plucks apart rather than constructs the hope of inner harmony. Being capable of creating that harmony, the imagination brings more devastation than any other faculty when it turns on the self and, instead of connecting everything with trust and confidence, tears the mind apart with doubt, apprehension, remorse, and paralysis. Allowing for obvious differences in style, that crucial stanza, expressing what Coleridge was fighting so hard in himself, could have been written by Johnson.

# PART TWO

# A Broader Stage

# 6

# NEW AESTHETICS AND CRITICISM: THE ASSOCIATIONISTS AND THE SCOTS

*T*he associationists form a broad school of thought whose psychological discoveries were to affect profoundly aesthetics, criticism, and the interest in genius and creativity from Hobbes through J. S. Mill and the mid nineteenth century. Our interest in them falls roughly from 1750 to 1820. The "association of ideas" basically means that the mind groups together habitually, almost instantaneously, ideas or images according to certain patterns or, as they became known, "laws of association." These laws include the possibility that two or more ideas may be experienced coincidentally in one place or at one time in the past, and so they recur together ("contiguity"); or one idea may be the "cause or effect" of another, such as dawn and the lark's song it awakens (*Romeo and Juliet*, III, v). Finally, images may "resemble" each other, in the way that a winding road appears from a hilltop to be a carelessly tossed ribbon.

Soon the process of association becomes very complex. Not only does each mind store a unique and huge volume of images, but it also connects its own passions, feelings, and habits with these images. There are so many ideas, images, and feelings that they cross and fuse in innumerable ways. Carried to its logical conclusion, the association of ideas represents a lively, essential, and unresting proclivity of mind.

Aristotle briefly mentions that the mind connects memories in certain patterns, and others reiterated and embellished his observations during the Middle Ages and the Renaissance.[1] But British empirical psychology makes the association of ideas central to an understanding of experience. By pursuing theories of perception, the coalescence of ideas, passion, memory, sense experience, and the internal or transforming power of mind, associationist thinkers provide an indispensable development to the concept of imagination. They apply association to the whole self and attempt to explain all facets of the psyche.[2]

Hobbes, using the words "succession," "coherence," "sequence," "consequence," and "series," discusses the formation of a train of imaginations or thoughts as a notable characteristic of the intellect. The actual phrase "association of ideas" does not appear until the fourth edition of Locke's *Essay Concerning Human Understanding* in 1700. He assumes that ideas either are simple and fuse or compound themselves into complex ones, or, once complex, decompose into smaller units. Less sensationalistic and physically oriented in his explanations than Hobbes, Locke uses the "association of ideas" to account only for accidental differences of mind between individuals. It is not intended as a basic principle of psychology, nor does it explain—as reason does—the natural connection of ideas.

An instance of Locke's association of ideas occurs early in *Tristram Shandy* (I, Ch. 4), where Tristram's father, whenever he wound the clock in the hallway before retiring (always "on the first Sunday-night of every month throughout the whole year"), would connect this activity with "some other little family concernments," one of which produced Tristram. Thus, says Tristram, "from an unhappy association of ideas, which have no connection in nature . . . my poor mother could never hear the said clock wound up,—but the thoughts of some other things unavoidably popped into her head—and *vice versâ:*—which strange combination of ideas, the sagacious Locke . . . affirms to have produced more wry actions than all . . . prejudice whatsoever."[3]

Berkeley divides mental activity into "sense ideas" and ideas formed by the imagination, which are weaker. All ideas are interconnected by the power of "suggestion." With Berkeley association becomes a fundamental element in empirical psychology. In the 1730s and 1740s John Gay, cousin of the poet, emphasizes the way in which ideas coalesce or mix in groups and applies his theory to a utilitarian ethic.* Returning in part to Hobbes, Hume carefully redefines the principles of association. Ideas are connected by either resemblance, contiguity in time and space,

---

* See John Gay's "Dissertation on the Fundamental Principle of virtue," an introductory essay to Edmund Law's translation of Archbishop William King's *Origin of Evil;* a 1747 work, "An Enquiry into the Origins of the Human Appetites and Affections, Showing How Each Arises from Association," if not by Gay himself, shows his influence. See Howard C. Warren, *A History of the Association Psychology* (1921).

or cause and effect. Hume distinguishes "impressions" from "ideas." Impressions imply an admixture of feeling, sensation, passion, and emotion, and may exert greater impact or "intensity" than ideas. Association is, from then on, thrown open to emotions and feelings as well as to images and ideas.

David Hartley's *Observations on Man* (1749) expresses the first thoroughgoing theory of association. His system, a combination of psychology and physiology (neurology), makes association the power or agent of absolutely all human activity. There is not one involuntary or voluntary idea, motive, or personal feeling ("idea of sensation") that does not stem either from direct sense experience exciting the nerves and our "white medullary substance," or from a coalescence and mixture of nervous vibrations caused by numerous other ideas. Complete and unified, his synthesis would appeal over forty years later to Coleridge when he was studying at Cambridge. Hartley combines the intellectual and emotional aspects of psychology with "scientific" reasoning, ethical principles, and religious belief. Not one vibrating chord of human experience escapes his explanation. But he was dogmatic. Harmony and comprehensiveness of outlook are achieved only because he tunes every string to the same key of association.

Before we explore the major associationist contributions to the idea of imagination, we might briskly survey the remaining important men involved, concluding with Thomas Brown who died in 1820. Almost as important in the history of associationism as Hartley, partly because his fame in other areas helped to popularize his work, is Joseph Priestley. Best remembered for his discovery of oxygen, Priestley was a Unitarian minister, a moralist, and a critic of considerable talent, as he reveals in his *Lectures on Oratory and Criticism* (1777). He was a committed liberal in politics and championed the American cause. Later, in 1794, he emigrated to the United States, following his three sons who had gone the year before. He settled in Northumberland, Pennsylvania, and died in 1804. Having mastered Hartley's doctrine of association, Priestley sensibly concluded that Hartley's *Observations on Man* had not won the popular attention it deserved because it was too long and included the needless *impedimenta* of Hartley's physiological conjectures. Priestley abridged the work into a manageable and coherent volume, *Hartley's Theory of the Mind* (1775), in which he plays down Hartley's neurological speculations and follows Hume in emphasizing the emotional side of associationism.

Alexander Gerard and William Duff both use association to explain the powers of genius in the arts and sciences. These two writers combine elements of association with the more intuitional approach favored by the Scottish School. Thomas Reid, who held positions at Aberdeen and later succeeded Adam Smith in the chair of moral philosophy at Glasgow, had become interested in philosophy after reading Hume. He opposes Hume's skepticism and position that we do not perceive any real and necessary connection between distinct experiences, and instead he emphasizes the spontaneous and habitual power of the mind to make immediate judgments. Dugald Stewart expands Hume's principles of association to include "contrariety."

Abraham Tucker, influenced by Locke and Hartley, carries Hartley's concept of the coalescence of ideas to the point where constituent ideas in a "compound" are not obscured by the presence of others but are actually transformed into new ideas when they fuse together. *The Light of Nature Pursued* (1768–1778), though primarily an ethical work, ventures into an organic and fluid associationism. In the 1790s Archibald Alison would expand Tucker's observation that qualities in art and nature such as beauty and sublimity are really states of mind produced almost entirely by association. In *Zoönomia* (1794–1796) Erasmus Darwin, grandfather of Charles, attributes sympathy, creativity, and the fusion of sense impressions (synaesthesia) to ideas in a "state of combination." Related ideas are connected so that each one triggers the others. This fabric of ideas he relates to muscular motion and physiological development.

Thomas Brown, the brilliant student and colleague of Dugald Stewart at the University of Edinburgh, wrote a critique of *Zoönomia* in 1798, when he was only twenty years old. His later *Lectures on the Philosophy of the Human Mind* bridges the gap between Scottish intuitionalism and English associationism. Like Berkeley, Brown uses "suggestion" to describe a train of ideas. The *Lectures,* published several months posthumously in 1820, propose a "spontaneous chemistry of mind" responsible for all mental activity, a concept later developed by J.S. Mill. Brown explains "voluntary reminiscence" and the "constructive imagination" in terms of association. Also a poet, he brought to his work a practical and sensitive understanding of the arts.

Associationism in the eighteenth century thus expands from a limited and mechanistic aspect of the intellect to an organic, encompassing psychological principle informing aesthetics, criticism, and ethics. The progress of associationism can be seen as the drama of empiricists seeking to widen their horizons, to include more of the complexities of experience, yet always to explain these complexities and nuances by as simple and empirical a principle as possible.

## A NEW CRITICISM

The associationists, with their pervasive influence on the developing concept of the imagination, also reflect the appreciation and criticism of the arts from a psychological point of view, as in James Beattie's *Essays on Poetry and Music, as They Affect the Mind*, written in 1762 but published sixteen years later. These aestheticians and critics for the first time discuss literature and artistic values as they relate directly to intricate psychological processes in both the artist and the audience. They follow Addison's lead but go considerably beyond him. One major tool in their critical examination is the association of ideas, and the deeper the psychological criticisms and studies proceed as a whole, the more the imagination evolves as their central point of focus.

A number of Shaftesbury's followers, most of them Scots, like Francis Hutcheson, had combined an intuitional strain with the empiricism represented generally by Locke. They emphasized two issues, the sense of beauty and the moral sense. We see this reflected in a discussion appearing in Robert Dodsley's *The Preceptor* (1748), which links "moral images" and "natural beauty" through the connecting power of imagination.[4] Dodsley—publisher for Akenside, Young, Gray, Burke, and Johnson—designed *The Preceptor* as a popular course in self-education. The points concerning morality and aesthetics as derived from the imagination show how familiar and essential this topic was now considered. By the middle of the century many thinkers were exploring how the mind joins ideas and seems to intuit from its "coalition of imagery" both moral and aesthetic values. These writers, who may generally be classed as the "Scottish Common Sense School," were trying to elaborate not only Shaftesbury but also the nature of that "power" Locke held responsible for the formation of complex ideas. They saw an extension of this power and asked how complex ideas themselves are associated into even larger conceptions and values. Imagination, and with it the association of ideas, became their immediate interest.

George Turnbull's *Principles of Moral Philosophy*, appearing in 1740, four years before Akenside's long poem and almost a decade in advance of Hartley's major work, discusses three essential points. First, Turnbull credits the law of association with our familiarity and ease of movement in nature. We find directions to our homes, learn to like certain foods, allude to books, wear specific colors and shapes of clothing, and even read language all by associating ideas with each other in a multiple way that amasses and integrates habits and various methods of action:

It is plainly in consequence of this law [association], that we so quickly learn the connexion established by nature between the ideas of different senses, those of the sight and touch, for instance; so that we are very soon able, even in our infant state, to judge of such . . . connexions with great facility, ease, and quickness . . . Those connexions and appearances, by which we judge immediately of magnitudes, distances, forms, and other qualities, may be called the language of nature . . . And it is by means of the law of association, that appearances, found by repeated experience to be connected with effects, do recall those effects . . . so soon as they recur, or are re-perceived. It is, indeed, in consequence of the law of association, that we learn any of the connexions of nature.[5]

Second, Turnbull argues that although by association and reasoning "truths may be rendered evident and certain to the understanding . . . yet they cannot reach our heart, or bestir our passionate part, but by means of the imagination." In other words, the imagination draws feelings into our acquaintance with "the connexions of nature." The result is that, as Gloucester said, we see nature feelingly.

Finally, Turnbull leaps to an important consideration of literature and genius. He describes the act of invention strictly in terms of the association of ideas and their imaginative ordering. He anticipates Duff and Gerard in outlining the creative process and suggests that this very process, and not reason, is the most truthful way to view nature and its relation to the self:

Invention is nothing else but the habit acquired by practices of assembling ideas or truths, with facility and readiness, in various positions and arrangements, in order to have new views of them. For no truths can be placed in any position or order with respect to one another, but some . . . relation or quality of these ideas, must appear to the mind. And discovery of a new or unknown relation can be nothing else but the result of placing truths, objects, or ideas, in some new or unobserved position . . . Every different juxtaposition of ideas will give us a new view of them, that is, discover some unknown truth.[6]

Edmund Burke's earliest important work, published in 1757 and written largely while he was a student at Trinity College, Dublin, is the famous *Philosophical Enquiry into the Origin of Our Ideas of the Sublime and Beautiful.*[7] Although not oriented strictly to the association of ideas, the *Enquiry* is perhaps the most fertile and suggestive of all psychologically based criticism and aesthetics in the mid Enlightenment. Its popularity sent it through over half a dozen editions in the first sixteen years. Lessing translated Burke into German, and the *Enquiry* stimulated the interest of Moses Mendelssohn and of German aesthetics generally in the second half of the century. While the content of the book is not concentrated and fails to express any comprehensive stance, understandable for such a youthful work, Burke ventures with brilliance. Two years before Adam Smith's *Theory of Moral Sentiments* (1759), Burke investigates the nature and importance of sympathy. He also develops ideas of suggestiveness and "obscurity," which become important to literature and the arts as the century progresses.

Starting with the assumption that nature merely reaches us through the senses, Burke bases the fuller, dynamic relationship between mind and nature on the imagination. Passages can be used to put his position in a simplistic and purely empirical light; he explains that "the imagination is only the representation of the senses"; elsewhere he says that qualities in nature are "acting mechanically upon the human mind by the intervention of the senses." But Burke works away from these notions. The imagination connects our inner passions and our capacity for feeling and action with what we experience directly. It has a power to reorder experience and to cast nature in a new mould:

> The mind of man possesses a sort of creative power of its own; either in representing at pleasure the images of things in the order and manner in which they are received by the senses, or in combining those images in a new manner, and according to a different order. This power is called Imagination; and to this belongs whatever is called wit, fancy, invention, and the like.[8]

As Burke became famous in politics, his reputation gave a boost to the *Enquiry*. Its general premise about imagination is even repeated in discussion groups like the Literary and Philosophical Society of Manchester. On February 12, 1783, Thomas Barnes read a paper to that society entitled "On the INFLUENCE *of the* IMAGINATION, *and the* PASSIONS, *upon the* UNDERSTANDING." Barnes reiterates the general attitude popularized by Burke: "All the pleasures of *Taste* depend absolutely upon a vigorous and cultivated imagination. Even in the *actual contemplation* of the *scenes of nature, imagination* is as necessary to refined pleasure, as the eye. Perhaps we might . . . call it, the *eye of the mind.*"[9]

Concerning the passions, which we feel internally as distinct from what we receive from the senses, Burke says that "the imagination . . . principally raises them" and then mixes them with the impressions of nature. Burke even remarks that there is "a chain in all our sensations; they are all but different sorts of feelings." The imagination mediates between and joins the inner self with the external world. It is the basis for forming our conceptions of what is beautiful and sublime—of whatever in nature is identified with an aesthetic quality. It is the basis of taste. Furthermore, aesthetic judgment reflects not only the "natural properties of things" as we experience them directly, but also our associations: "It must be allowed that many things affect us after a certain manner, not by any natural powers . . . but by association."[10]

It is a tribute to the intellectual vivacity of Edinburgh in the 1750s and 1760s that Lord Kames's *Elements of Criticism* (1762) remains as fresh as it is. Already sixty-six when the book appeared, Kames could have slipped into a mechanical, rule-studded handbook, a stable approach reminiscent of the century's early years. But the same circle of thought and the same atmosphere that, after Hume, went on to produce Gerard, Duff, and Smith also informs Kames's work.

His *Elements* typifies the psychological approach to criticism pioneered by the Scots. (Hume's essay "On Tragedy" is another example.) Kames intends his work "to draw the rules of criticism from human nature, their true source."[11] This principle or bias means that critical and aesthetic values like beauty, sublimity, and novelty are defined more along lines of the mind's reaction and assimilation of external objects and works of art than in terms of intrinsic qualities in the objects themselves. His chapter titles indicate this procedure, such as "Perceptions and Ideas in a Train," "Emotions and Passions," and on a "Standard of Taste," which he bases in part on some traits of human nature that are universal.

In his first chapter Kames defines the work of art "that is conformable to the moral course of our ideas" by likening it to "an organic system, its parts . . . mutually connected." This "organic system," a forerunner of the general Romantic ideal of organic unity found in Hazlitt, Coleridge, and so much German thought, is attained, Kames believes, by "culture and discipline" operating on "a bold and fertile imagination." Practice and effort encourage the artist to judge the relative importance and order of the associations he experiences between ideas and to create from them art with a new sense of unity.

Kames extends the method of Burke's *Sublime and Beautiful*, investigating more keenly the interplay of emotion, thought, and imagination—the mind's internal processes—and their bearing on or actual determination of values in perception and taste. Although Kames's concept of the imagination is fairly common for that time, he helps to establish the difference between internal and external, subjective and objective. Other thinkers and critics soon develop the idea that the imagination, and with it art, mediates between and unifies these "opposites," even as it mediates between faculties within the mind itself.

Kames tries hard to be exact and stimulating in his approach, yet the work as a whole is diffuse. Perhaps sitting on the bench as a judge for a number of years squelched the growth of literary flair. His most suggestive remark on imagination itself is that it exerts "ideal presence."[12] This presence may be vivid or weak. The important point is that it does not rely on the actual presence of objects but reproduces images in the mind. These images arouse emotions and thoughts usually excited by a "real presence" in the senses. But Kames, unlike Hume, never explores this process. He lacks an active or productive sense of the mind and its emotions. Every psychological characteristic is predominantly passive, as if it were always reacting but not generating or originating. Kames hardly mentions genius or any power capable of forming images from the associated ones that the mind stores and recalls. These more creative aspects of imagination attracted Duff, Gerard, Priestley, and later Stewart. But Kames is on the same stairway that they ascend. He has not turned back or followed a dead end, but provides a capacious landing place. Like Burke and many of the associationists, Kames had influence in Germany, especially on Mendelssohn, Herder, Lessing, and, through Lessing, on Kant and Schiller.

## EXTENSIONS AND REFINEMENTS

Hartley's all-encompassing system attracted Joseph Priestley. In introductory essays to his own abridgment of Hartley's *Observations on Man*, entitled *Hartley's Theory of the Human Mind* (1775), and in his *Lectures on Oratory and Criticism*, written in 1762 but published in 1777, Priestley catches specific points of associationism and ramifies them. He does not use the analytical format of propositions and scholia favored by Hartley, who was imitating Newton, but what he drops in apparatus, he gains in clarity and reasonableness.[13] Where Hartley viewed imagination as a particular *kind* of association, Priestley comes close to implying that it has the *power* of association. Imagination assumes a broader and more active role in "the internal agitation" of the mind. "*Joint impressions*" and complex sensations or ideas, giving either pleasure or pain, all become involved with the imagination. Any activity of imagination is "more or less compounded of almost all the other intellectual pleasures and pains too."[14]

Following Hartley and Hume, Priestley remarks on the "fluction of mind" caused by passions, which participate in the association of ideas and are mixed or magnified by that process. He presents a concept of mind in which the ebb, flow, and coalescence of interacting passions and ideas form a complex whole, an "abridgment" of experience, which may appear in the imagination.[15] In *Oratory and Criticism* this concept informs particular insights about literature and psychology. A vivid or strong passion, whether or not it is "*present* and *real*," affects the imagination. Art and literature may affect us as strongly as our own actual experience. The "particular terms" and concrete language of literature give passions and characters greater impact. An obscure hint or a suggestive use of words "sets imagination strongly and effectually at work."[16] Implying the existence of a passion, or using a single word to represent it, often inflames feeling more than a direct description or statement. Properly guided, the reader quickly imagines a whole design and senses its total impact.[17] All effects "crowd upon his mind in one *complex sensation,* and affect him with all their powers united." Abstractions and general terms, such as are found in advanced societies, often inhibit the concrete and suggestive power of words that flourished in earlier ages. The power of metaphor, common in early or folk writers, encourages the associative power to achieve a "unity of the whole" in artistic expression. Taking a theme later discussed by Coleridge, Priestley contends that poetry can give more pleasure than prose. Verse combines more elements of composition which, when related well to each other, exemplify his observation that "the greater the design, and the more difficult we imagine the execution of it to be, the greater pleasure we receive." Throughout his criticism Priestley implies an aesthetic principle in the imagination by using the familiar phrase, "pleasures of the imagination." He does not elaborate a theory of beauty or investigate the relationship of aesthetics to judgment, but he allies imagination closely with a sense of the agreeable.[18]

In fiction or fantasy, "only one single effort of the imagination" is needed to give "assent" to a whole series of improbable characters and events.[19] "Assent," the equivalent of Coleridge's "willing suspension of disbelief," was also used by Hartley and Addison. That single imaginative effort, according to Priestley, affords the pleasure found in reading "the history of such beings and powers as far exceed every thing human." Furthermore, what we find enjoyable to believe, we are more inclined to believe in reality. Genies, fairies, heathen gods and goddesses, knights-errant and necromancers easily stir the young mind, while in older persons, imagination is more regulated. Priestley here fuses several concepts. Imagination usually matures with the individual, but a single instance of its exertion may at any time arouse enjoyment from a whole train of associations, no matter how improbable, provided they are consistent with each other. He does not mention the force of imagination in fiction or fantasy as a "danger" or "folly," a label that leaped to the minds of many in the previous generation.[20] Johnson noted time and again the too powerful influence that romances and fantastic stories had over his own imagination, and his experience reveals another, more troubling interpretation of imaginative "assent."

The natural conformation of our feelings to those of another with whom we identify, also excites imaginative pleasure. Priestley stresses how quick this reaction is. Vivid associations immediately excite the mind. Many "feelings are instantaneous and constant, and to appearance *simple,* yet they are . . . the offspring of association . . . by a thousand sensations and ideas, which it is impossible to separate and analyze."[21] In witnessing comparatively large and grand objects, or in feeling rare and strong *"sentiments and passions,"* the imagination exercises considerable effort. We become conscious of "the strength and extent of our own powers." This effect, a mixture of the intellectual and emotional, is the sublime. Priestley fixes the strength of the sublime in art or experience in direct proportion to its accompanying degree of imagination, a subject later treated by Archibald Alison.[22]

## ASSOCIATIONISM AND THE CREATIVE PROCESS

Psychologists and thinkers were now, by the 1770s, recognizing the association of ideas as an extensive activity involved in the creative process. Like Kames and Priestley, they turned this discovery to critical use and attempted to show how an author's understanding of the association of ideas in others, or how his own associations, appear in his work. Gerard in his *An Essay on Genius* (1774) elaborates on a passage from *The Tempest* (II, i). Alonso, King of Naples, voyages with his son to celebrate his daughter's marriage at Tunis. On returning, their ship is wrecked in a storm, and the son is believed drowned. The king's company try to assuage his grief by recalling his daughter's marriage, but he explodes:

> You cram these words into mine ears against
> The stomach of my sense. Would I had never
> Married my daughter there! for coming thence
> My son is lost, and, in my rate, she too,
> Who is so far from Italy remov'd,
> I ne'er again shall see her: O thou mine heir
> Of Naples and Milan, what strange fish
> Hath made his meal on thee?

Gerard explains these lines by the principle of association. The marriage suggests the voyage; Alonso associates the voyage with his son's death; in turn, this compels him to realize the distance he is removed from his daughter, a distance so great as to be a second kind of death. Entangled in sorrow, Alonso can then only revert to its original cause, his son's death, "to view it in every light, to conceive many circumstances relating to him, his being his heir, his being entitled to large dominions."[23]

Gerard also points out how a strong passion like grief channels association and selects only those images and thoughts that are amenable to or reinforce the passion. Strong feeling has the creative force of a design. In this and many other ways, the critical use of associationism was becoming widespread. As late as the 1790s it is a common explanation of poetry, especially of dramatic speeches that bare the inner thoughts of a character. Richard and Maria Edgeworth in *Practical Education* (1798) remark:

Homer, in the speech of Achilles to Agamemnon's mediating ambassa-
dors, has drawn a strong and natural picture of the progress of anger . . .
Whenever association suggests to the mind of Achilles the injury he has
received, he loses his reason, and the orator works himself up from argument to declamation, and from declamation to desperate resolution,
through a close linked connexion of ideas and sensations.[24]

The theory of association was pushed to an interesting critical extreme. Again, as in numerous instances of psychological interest in an
author's suggestive particulars, Shakespeare is the subject. Walter
Whiter's *A Specimen of a Commentary on Shakespeare Derived from
Mr. Locke's Doctrine of the Association of Ideas* (1794) examines passages in Shakespeare that exhibit an accidental but repetitive association
of images—not, this time, on the part of one character, but in Shakespeare's own mind. Following Locke in assuming that association does
not rest upon reason but is highly individualistic, Whiter shows in his
best example how the images of false friends, dogs (usually a spaniel),
fawning, licking, candy, and melting are all connected. When Shakespeare mentions one of these, the others seem to ride along like burrs.
Antony's lines (IV, xii) provide an example:

> The hearts
> That *spaniel'd* me at heels, to whom I gave
> Their wishes, do *discandy, melt* their *sweets*
> On blossoming Caesar.

The same or similar images recur in *Timon of Athens, Henry IV Part I,
Richard II,* and *Hamlet.* Lines from *Hamlet* (III, ii) show the drift of
the pattern:

> No, let the *candied tongue lick* absurd pomp
> And crook the pregnant hinges of the knee
> Where thrift may follow *fawning.*

Whiter hopes that, by recognizing this kind of association, textual problems, such as what word Shakespeare actually wrote, might be solved.
Furthermore, his title, beginning *A Specimen of a Commentary,* suggests that the book offers only a small sampling of clusters and that more
study could ensue. In 1935 Caroline Spurgeon's *Shakespeare's Imagery
and What It Tells Us* followed this lead and incidentally made use of the
same grouping of images instanced in Whiter.[25]

Although Whiter based his study on Locke's idea of idiosyncratic associations, there is a certain logic to the connections between fawning,
spaniels, traitorous friends, licking, and candy. There is even a proverbial ring about the group. Most of Shakespeare's images in fact have
some obvious or natural connection with those that repeatedly occur
near them. But still, Whiter's point holds: Shakespeare, over a period of

months and years, habitually associates certain images with others, and this is concrete evidence of how, in at least one way, the process of creative composition works within the poet's mind. Three decades before Whiter, in the middle of the century, the study of associationism, brought into contact with Homer, Milton, and Shakespeare, had already catalyzed a rapidly expanding inquiry into the imagination of genius.

# 7

# INVESTIGATORS OF GENIUS:
# GERARD AND DUFF

*T*he Enlightenment liked to speak of itself as an age of criticism. It hoped to infuse art, science, and politics with a "spirit" of exploration and planned curiosity. It sought what Leibniz, Coleridge, and Gerard call a "method." Something quite different from Descartes' method, this was to be a total approach to life, learning, and even creativity, based on an awareness of natural laws and of the natural constitution of human mind and heart. Philosophy and psychology unite with literary and aesthetic criticism, as Ernst Cassirer says, "in all the eminent minds of the century."[1] After 1750, this union turns increasingly to an interest in and a brilliant exploration of the human imagination, a faculty that, even more than reason, is seen to reveal the place and truth of man's experience and to unlock that mysterious reflex and counterpart of the cosmos, as vast and as wonderful, the individual psyche.

One effect of this interest in the imagination was to create in large degree what we ordinarily call "Romanticism." Goethe summed it up bluntly by saying that this age of great literary talent—what we think of as Romanticism—sprang from the cradle of philosophy: *"Epoche der forcierten Talente entsprang aus der Philosophischen."*[2] Philosophers treated their work not simply as a metaphysical puzzle but primarily as a servant to understanding human nature. They provided an ambiance of ideas that encouraged literary and aesthetic expression. The Enlightenment, remarks Cassirer, "joined, to a degree scarcely ever achieved before, the critical with the productive function and converted the one directly into the other."[3] The hope that another such critical age might pave the way for a creative one was later voiced by Matthew Arnold in his essay "On the Function of Criticism at the Present Time" (1864).

But the Enlightenment's view of the imagination had one immense advantage that the later nineteenth century failed to recapture: it focused on the source of creative power, on what permits the unified operation of all faculties, and at its highest pitch, on what constitutes genius and creativity in art. Simple as it may sound, the imagination became so vital and released so much potential brilliance because it is an idea about the way ideas and expressions are formed. It is protean. It deals with the very source of genius and creation and touches the nerve center of human achievement. It brings with it self-confidence and self-reliance. A premium on the imagination encourages the genius and the poet in their faith that what they say is more than decorative, that their creations can awaken the soul and reach truth.

Because the study of genius examines the highest talent and relates many ideas and human powers in the context of individual lives and details, it brings together nearly all aspects of the imagination. The study of genius also places the idea of imagination in a rarefied atmosphere—as Coleridge knew, who often "apologizes" that genius is too uncommon to be commonly understood and that the imagination of genius alone should not be trusted as a guide to life or as a form of salvation. But Coleridge also knew that it is exactly in the rare atmosphere of genius, in asking what genius is and what promotes it, that we discover the richest and most meaningful concept of imagination, a discovery made first by the Enlightenment and ultimately shaping and animating the romantic burst of poetry and achievement. Two of the earliest and most insightful investigators of genius are Alexander Gerard (1728–1795) and William Duff (1732–1815).

### "IT IS IMAGINATION THAT PRODUCES GENIUS"

Gerard broke the mold of run-of-the-mill British associationists. His *Essay on Taste* (1759) and, even more important, *An Essay on Genius* (1774) move associationism and the theory of imagination onto a higher and richer plane.[4] So important to Gerard is the role of imagination, and with it the association of ideas, that imagination begins to assume the power previously ascribed to judgment. As judgment is assimilated into imagination, it becomes more immediate and intuitive. It loses the distinction of a conscious and superior power. The barriers developed by faculty psychology continue to disintegrate as Gerard pushes for a more unified and enlarged concept of imagination.

In scientific discoveries and in works of art, the imagination not only accumulates piecemeal associations but simultaneously conceives a "design" or plan informing the whole effort. This plan suggests an organic unity that instinctively selects those ideas which will fit the finished creative work and automatically rejects others:

> As the magnet selects from a quantity of matter the ferruginous particles, which happen to be scattered through it, without making an impression on other substances; so imagination, by a similar sympathy, equally inexplicable, draws out from the whole compass of nature such ideas as we have occasion for, without attending to any others.[5]

Each individual carries out this process according to the unique bent of his own genius. An internal stimulus, unaccountable for by any impression received from sense experience, motivates his imagination to complete and fill in the design.

Gerard also stresses that "passion" shares in the associative process, especially in poetry, either by suggesting an idea or by drawing into unity and giving one cast to images and thoughts otherwise unconnected. Passion can in this way help to form a large design or structure of ideas. The mind charged with feeling more easily identifies in an imaginative way with its subject, or with another person whose feelings are similar. When passion fixes on a particular object or person that is related to or associated with other ideas, the person or object begins to acquire the nature of a symbol. Gerard and his colleagues in the Aberdeen Philosophical Society, among them Thomas Reid, Dugald Stewart, and James Beattie, avidly read and discussed Hume, whose analysis of the passions intrigued them all.[6]

By bringing both "passion" and "judgment" within the scope of imagination, especially as it works in the fine arts, Gerard gives a more organic, responsive, and immediate picture of the mind. His *Essay on Genius,* translated into German in 1776, two years after its publication in England, is primarily a study of imagination (much of the *Essay* Gerard delivered in lecture and discussion form from 1758 to 1769 at the Aberdeen Philosophical Society). Genius, he says, depends on invention, the ability to make "new discoveries in science" or to produce "original works of art." Invention in turn derives solely from the faculty of imagination. In simple and bold terms, "It is imagination that produces genius." A passionate or habitual frame of mind and other faculties, such as memory or judgment, affect the imagination, but none of them provides the necessary and immediate sources of genius. A man of genius forms relations between previously unconnected perceptions and thoughts ("ideas") because his imagination associates them with a "peculiar vigour."[7]

Several characteristics of the imagination combine to produce this enlarged power of association, and Gerard's discussion of them blazes a trail through the whole *Essay.* The more ideas a mind possesses, the greater are its chances of forming new combinations. "Comprehensiveness" or "fertility" of imagination necessitates a large and varied store-house of perceptions presented by memory. The "activity" of the imagination moves like an underground stream, seen only occasionally but always flowing. In the friction and jostle of ideas, speed and agility act in the same way that heat precipitates chemical reactions. "Activity" implies that the imagination is not only quick but restless and even obsessive. The mind becomes inspired and gains internal momentum. It fixes on a train of thought, becomes "enraptured with the subject," and begins to identify with it. This "enthusiasm," reminiscent of Dennis, propels more associations. It is not a "passion," because its object is only continued activity. It does not color or affect the ideas actually associated but speeds the process. This rapidity is crucial. It is the "fire of genius," the "divine impulse," and without this "elevation and warmth of imagination" genius never fulfills its potential.[8]

Gerard assumes the conventional associationist view about the role of the senses, habit, and memory in creating and connecting ideas. For example, repeated associations become petrified and stagnant. Starting with one idea, a person may be in the habit of forming a particular series, but this process is often just "circumstantial." To others his train of thought may appear forced or illogical. An otherwise clear writer can be tricked by habit into unnatural transitions and imagery. He has become so familiar with his own ideas that in the effort to communicate, he leaves unexpressed links in his thought that others are not able to take for granted.

Gerard takes a significant leap when he analyzes the way passion excites and channels imagination. Passion, which is an emotion turned to some particular object or experience, either catalyzes ideas together or unites with them itself. More of the complex feelings with which the mind digests and reacts to experience are thrown into the mixing bowl of association. The imagination blends thoughts and passions until they suggest each other. Feelings are not only *"conjoined,* but also *mixed* and blended so perfectly together, that none of them shall be distinctly perceivable in the compound which arises from their union." The passionate mind rushes forward, which "often occasions an abruptness of thought." A poet moves from image to image quickly, relating them through one strong passion. In this sense, feeling provides a framework or design for many ideas, which all receive "a tincture from that passion."[9]

An image, when intimately and habitually associated with many connected thoughts and feelings, begins to take on the force of a symbol. So not only does passion aid in forming a whole design, it may also create a particular image or symbol that represents a larger context of values, ideas, and emotions. As English poetry changed in the later eighteenth

century, this new sense of symbolism replaced more flaccid and pas-
sionless images copied from classical figures and stock poetic diction.[10]

Passion—really the whole emotional side of the psyche or "sensibility
of heart"—also permits a poet to identify more closely with the subject.
"Entering into the sentiments" of another person and assuming those to
be his own, he can then imagine and consequently imitate, not merely
describe, the real nature and character of his subjects' feelings. "This is
indeed so difficult, that the best poets cannot always perfectly attain it."
Gerard believes that Shakespeare is the most successful. Through his
chapter on "The Influence of the Passions on Association," Gerard establishes a fundamental principle of sympathetic identification. To the
1780 edition of his *Essay on Taste*, first published twenty-one years earlier and translated into German and French in 1766, Gerard added a
lengthy section on the associative power of imagination, concluding it
with remarks on "the force of sympathy, which enlivens our *ideas* of the
passions infused by it to such a pitch, as in a manner converts them into
the passions themselves," an idea already stressed by Hume.[11]

Although Gerard echoes the traditional concept of judgment as a faculty that checks absurd or random associations, he draws it closer to the
imaginative process and nearly incorporates it into the function of the
imagination itself. Judgment is not, as it is in Dryden, Dennis, and Addison, a power to control and subordinate imagination. Instead it is a
complementary aid to perfect and to assure the justness of the "design"
already sketched out by imagination. When a genius judges his own
work, he is simply developing a "regularity of imagination," which is by
no means the same thing as subjecting a completed imaginative work to
some higher power. When a genius changes his work, he exercises "the
posterior essays of imagination, affected by new associations in repeated
views of the subject."

Judgment, in other words, becomes a "methodising power" actually
belonging to imagination itself, a notion Coleridge later pursued in his
*Essay on Method*. By making judgment share in the associative process,
the mind of genius gains a "correct" imagination and can follow out the
design of its work with an "instinctive infallibility." Ceasing to follow a
strict faculty psychology, Gerard observes mental traits that do not
seem to fit the mechanistic theories of association. He removes the tyranny of the concept that experience is the touchstone of the mind and
presents ways in which the mind itself becomes the touchstone of experience.

The imaginative mind does not connect ideas one at a time like chain
links. It conceives a whole design almost at once, which it then fills out
and gives body to by particular associations. Each scientific discovery or

artistic work has a governing form or plan. The mind thinks simultaneously of specific parts and of their one organizing principle. Speaking of a genius like Homer or Newton, Gerard states, "No sooner is a design formed, or the hint of a subject started, than all the ideas which are requisite for completing it, rush into his view as if they were conjured up by the force of magic." In science the desire to reach a solution, in art the force of passion, create a unifying tendency. One idea immediately suggests a whole form. In a similar way, each aspect of the imagination leads directly to the total cooperation of all aspects. "In every individual, genius is like an organized body, the form of which arises from the manner in which the several members are combined, and is altered by every [even] the smallest change in the size or portion of any one of them." This statement expresses the essential germ of an organic philosophy. As Schelling, Coleridge, and others were later to explain, the artist should imitate the inworking, creative, and organizing spirit of nature, the *natura naturans*, rather than copy or imitate nature's outward form and appearance, the *natura naturata*.* Working toward a unified group of associations, the mind, concludes Gerard, readily develops a self-correcting and self-regulating capacity. The conception of a design "breaks in of its own accord, and, like an antagonist muscle," counteracts any idea improper to the larger scheme.[12]

Of course no two minds will associate ideas in the same way, if for no other reason than that they have not encountered the same experiences or felt the same passions. In fact, one individual may easily vary and modify his own imaginative effort. Many different plans for discovery or writing may enter into his consideration. But the diversity of imagination among different people cannot be fully explained by their acquaintance with dissimilar ideas. It must, "in a great measure, be resolved into original differences in the constitution of the mind" or "in the turn of men's imaginations." When each individual alters the method of his own association, he reveals a "flexibility" of imagination that gives his own mind "numberless combinations that are wholly new," as well as differentiating him from other individuals. Complex passions and circumstances wholly his own enter the associative process and enhance the singular nature of his genius. In all these operations, an internal stimulus or inner and active self-identity drives imagination forward.[13]

The importance of individualism in Gerard dawns into an insight far removed from the cruder empiricists' view of the mind as a *tabula rasa*. Intelligence is more self-aware and possesses the inherent potential for its own development. We become, says Gerard, aware of all the operations and passions of our own minds. This convinces us of the existence

* See below, pp. 313–319, 333, 358.

of our own consciousness, which "is even a prerequisite to . . . perception" of any external ideas. In this way, each individual is able, "without any information from experience, by a natural and inexplicable principle, to infer the existence of himself as the percipient and agent." This point—that the self or the intelligence exists and is aware of its own existence before it turns to the external world—becomes a central feature of thought in much German transcendentalism and in Coleridge as well.[14]

In the *Essay on Genius* Gerard presents a volatile combination of the individuality of imagination and the mind's ability to become self-aware and consciously reflect on its own existence, thought, and feeling. Together, these elements contribute to the growing importance placed on the character and life of the artist. They are soon used as avenues to attain some of the finest artistic expression of the past two centuries (and some would twist them to justify the most self-indulgent and ridiculous excesses). Gerard attains great insights. He promotes a movement in the arts and in thought with consequences that perhaps went beyond his own deepest analysis. But his acumen searches out what is important for the success of potential genius. He asks thinking questions and is one of the leading figures to establish a new critical climate of ideas. Soon this climate produced what became the ideal of romantic genius and of those individuals who grew up to exemplify it.

### DUFF'S PLASTIC POWER

In his *Essay on Original Genius* (1767) William Duff, although at times contradicting himself, attains a view of the imagination as a broad and natural power whose scope in poetry is "absolute and unconfined."[15] By differentiating "original" genius from genius, he proposes a degree of imagination less dependent on the faculty of judgment, more vigorous in conceiving the design of a creative work, and superior to "artificial rules" of criticism. A talented poet would be most likely to express his imagination in a society that paid more attention to elemental human passions and the world of nature than to luxuries and literary analysis.[16]

Duff begins his book by warning that imagination alone is not sufficient for genius. Yet especially when he talks about poetry, he enlarges on the imagination until it begins either to absorb or to rely less on other faculties. It permits the mind to reflect on its own operations. Ideas and sense impressions are gathered together and shuttled in and out of the "repository of memory" by the imagination. Its "compass," "depth," "fertility," and "ardor" account for the whole associative process. Taste, which is the aesthetic judgment vital to produce works of art, shares such a mutual influence with imagination that the two can be seen as one operation of the mind, combining both response and active creation.[17]

Duff, like Akenside before and Coleridge after, often refers to imagination as a "plastic" power. The word suggests shaping and molding, also continuity, range of movement, and a plan or design. Although at one point he denies that the imagination offers the plan or outline of a creative work, elsewhere he emphasizes that it forms and unifies the ideas and "materials" it has collected. "The Imagination must guide the hand in the design and execution of the whole." The most gifted or original genius has such a powerful imagination that he "combines at once every homogeneous and corresponding idea" and "sketches out a creation" of his own.[18] The mind gains an immediate and intuitive sense of what is proper. Judgment, in effect, is pushed into the background.

Even while incorporating more faculties into the imagination, Duff in one instance implies a difference between fancy and imagination. The fanciful mind has wit and humor which, by an uncommon description or by a quick, even "superficial" connection of ideas, produce pleasant or agreeable sensations. An imaginative individual, who may possess this ability to please, really organizes his ideas into a more "extensive combination," a whole work completely shaped by the power of invention.[19]

The *Essay on Original Genius* contains in embryo several points that later typify romantic criticism. Duff remarks that poetic imagination reveals itself early in life by a certain "grandeur" and "luxuriance" of expression that ripens into mature genius.[20] Coleridge pursues the same theme in Chapter 15 of the *Biographia*. In other words, imagination contains an inward potential, an inner *Geist* or reservoir of power, that grows and perfects itself. To recognize and pursue this development, Duff devotes about one-third of his book to an illumination of works of genius by reference to characteristics of the imagination. In many instances he is interpreting literature through the use of psychological principles. The imagination, for him, becomes closely related to imitation or *mimesis*. One of the by-products of this approach is an awareness how imagination creates myths and symbols. These act as a code and give the psyche a quick and powerful way to represent complex beliefs, associations, archetypes, and feelings. For Duff, Greek mythology exerted great impact as "a system of ingenious Fiction." It attracted him in the way it also attracted Keats: both saw in it a strong and concrete expression of the inner life of the mind. Also, in a manner similar to Coleridge's and Blake's fascination with the Bible, Duff felt entranced by the imaginative and "remarkable boldness of sentiment and expression, by the most poetical figures of speech," found in the sacred texts of Eastern and Egyptian mythologies.[21]

Scattered throughout Duff's *Essay* are indications that his concept of genius and imagination is working toward a totality of response. The mind integrates all of its intellectual and emotional capacities and relates them directly to the natural world. However, no two individuals are alike, because each has an intrinsic "bias" peculiar to himself, that is, a particular way in which his own imagination unifies his faculties and expresses his reaction to external scenes and to experience.

> The outward organ, by which these sensations are conveyed, is supposed to be equally perfect in both [individuals]; but the internal feeling is extremely different. This difference must certainly proceed from the transforming power of Imagination, whose rays illuminate the objects we contemplate.[22]

At the same time that the individual imagination creates a subjective self, it lends that self a unified and coherent outlook by collecting and transforming all experience. Nothing escapes the imaginative power. Duff does not speculate on the truth or accuracy of imagination in the subjective self. His mechanical discussion of judgment is hardly a corrective force, because he does not always consider judgment a superior power. It merges with and is often subordinated to imagination.

Considering that imagination transforms all experience and relates it to the function of the whole mind, Duff concludes that a fairly primitive or early stage of civilization fosters the most imaginative genius. Such relatively simple societies present fundamental experiences that have tremendous impact on the faculties of the mind.[23] The passions and ideas excited are basic, which incites the imagination to combine them into more complex and refined forms of expression. Highly developed societies have, in effect, already assumed and carried out imaginative combinations. The individual imagination feels distracted by what many others have done before. Duff summarizes the last section of his *Essay on Original Genius* with the long title:

> That original Poetic Genius will in general be displayed in its utmost vigour in the early and uncultivated periods of Society, which are peculiarly favorable to it; and that it will seldom appear in a very high degree in cultivated life.

In this sense, the man of genius in an advanced society is literally prevented in the exercise of his transforming power of imagination.[24] He is presented with little more than the transformations of others. He loses contact not only with the natural world but also with his own fundamental nature. The harmony of his being cracks under the strain.

There is another important aspect concerning the totality of imaginative response discussed by Duff's *Essay*. As the mind perceives and transforms its experience of the natural world, it not only combines and connects ideas and objects but searches out their origin and cause of creation. This enthusiastic curiosity is especially common to the philosophic imagination. By presenting speculations about causes and the original creation, it leads the mind to consider the existence and nature of divinity. Duff cites Plato, whose imagination led him to contemplate "the existence and unity of the supreme Being."[25] The philosophic genius, adding to his imagination greater reason and judgment than are necessary in the poet, unlocks the secrets of things. Through reason *and* imagination, the philosopher approaches the religious aspect of nature and the ultimate unity of God. This idea, greatly elaborated, Coleridge later made central to his thinking.

Both Gerard and Duff drive a wedge between genius in the fine arts, especially poetry, and genius in philosophy or science. In science more judgment or "regularity" of imagination is necessary.[26] Gerard does not see the cleavage of imaginative content in the arts and in science as complete; however, a genius rarely has enough flexibility of imagination to erase all differences separating artistic efforts from scientific invention or analysis.[27] Keeping a conventional emphasis on the role of "reason" or judgment in philosophy and empirical science, Gerard and Duff begin to apply "taste" as a name for aesthetic judgment that will aid and "instigate" the artistic imagination. In both writers, taste carries a subjective flavor. It is not completely bound to facts and phenomena. It has an emotional and personal character. Duff calls taste an "internal sense," which does not direct the imagination but intertwines with it.[28]

Gerard pursues taste in the arts with a wide range of implication that includes ideas of beauty, pleasure, delight, suggestiveness, enthusiasm, and agreeable sensations.[29] Furthermore, taste for Gerard draws on the passions and is easily affected by them. By beginning to substitute taste for judgment in the arts, both Gerard and Duff further relaxed the reins of reason and encouraged creative works with greater aesthetic and emotional content.

Scottish and English associationists, and the new interest in genius dependent on them, gained considerable and almost immediate attention in Germany. Johann G.E. Maass devotes the last third of his revised *Versuch über die Einbildungskraft* to a history of associationism from Socrates to 1797, the date his second edition appears, and titles it *"Beiträge zur Geschichte der Lehre von der Vergesellschaftung der Vorstellungen."* He summarizes the work of Hartley, Priestley, Kames, and

Gerard, interweaving them with numerous German works on associationism in the last thirty years of the century. Empiricism and the association of ideas enjoyed a legacy extending back to the early eighteenth century in Germany. As Maass points out, Hobbes, Locke, and Hume, among the British, were influential. Leibniz, too, speaks of the association of ideas in the *Nouveaux essais,* published in 1765, which Maass quotes (Liv. II, xxxiii): "man as well as the beasts is liable to connect by memory and by his imagination whatever he has observed together in his perceptions and his experiences."[30] Maass recognizes that the full blending and association of ideas is necessary for Leibniz's "Pre-established Harmony." Maass also reveals that German critics and psychologists were drawing on the same classical authors as were the British. Duff, Gerard, and Priestley make extensive use of Plato, Aristotle, Longinus, Cicero, and Quintilian. By the 1770s these were well-known sources.

In 1777 at Göttingen the first history of associationism appeared, Michael Hissmann's *Geschichte der Lehre von der Association der Ideen.* This book reflects the rising interest in the subject. The year before Christian Garve had translated Gerard's *Essay on Genius* into German, and in the same year Tetens, warmly acknowledging the ideas of Gerard, produced his *Philosophische Versuche über die Menschliche Natur und ihre Entwicklung.* And Tetens' *Versuche* was profoundly to affect and even to create the whole interest in the imagination in Kant, who himself praises Gerard on several occasions. Although Schelling did not agree completely with the British associationists and their criticism of the arts, he states in his *Philosophie der Kunst* (1802) that in "the period immediately preceeding Kant . . . the well-known theories of the fine arts established [in Germany] were those whose principles were the psychological axioms of the English and French."[31]

# PART THREE

# The German Foundation

# 8

# SHADOWS A CENTURY LONG

$\mathcal{B}$y the beginning of the nineteenth century, German thought had developed a concept of the imagination that was more complete and far-reaching in philosophical terms than anything envisioned in England. The German development had grown from a set of circumstances that were considerably different.[1] Until the 1770s, intellectual contact between the two nations had been sporadic and frequently indirect. Even into the 1800s the sharing of ideas was fairly limited, with Germany far more receptive to England than England to Germany. This is partially because, in sheer bulk and quality of literature, England had more to offer. Few Englishmen—with the exceptions of Coleridge, Crabb Robinson, and later Carlyle—paid such careful and knowledgeable attention to the startling rise of German thought and literature after 1750 as German professors, poets, and writers did to the whole canon of English literature and particularly to Engglish speculative thought since Hobbes.

The German spirit investigating the idea of the imagination was more systematic. Tiedemann, Sulzer, Brucker, Platner, Maass, the Schlegels, Fichte, Schelling, Kant, Novalis, Tieck, Schiller, Goethe—all participated in relatively close-knit literary and philosophical movements. They knew and often lived near one another. They shared writings and ideas in a way quite foreign to the more individualistic, less organized, and often eccentric British. German universities provided a gravitational center for lectures, debate, sharing ideas, the communal spirit of intellectual discovery, and disagreement, which could lead to new points of view. Small courts and circles, like those at Jena and Weimar, served the same purposes. (In Great Britain, it was the Scottish universities and philosophical societies that offered similar opportunities for the adventure and mixing of ideas.) Books, treatises, and poems were written quickly in Germany and read immediately after publication. From before the beginnings of the *Sturm und Drang,* a flurry of activity and frequent personal contacts saturated intellectual life and guided the evolution of every major idea and literary form. Eager to throw off the French yoke as the century progressed, the Germans banded together. There was an astonishingly deep interplay between philosophy and the creative arts. In England, Gerard, Duff, Kames, and then Blake, Coleridge, Keats, Wordsworth, and Shelley tried to unify the philosophic and the poetic imaginations. But Tetens, Sulzer, Platner, Kant, and then in the next generation the Schlegels, Schiller, Fichte, and Schelling analyzed and constructed more comprehensive and more fully articulated ideas of the imagination in its exquisite relation to both art and philosophy. The systematic spirit of the Germans, as well as their enthusiasm and distrust of mechanism and rules, attracted and deeply impressed Coleridge.

German writers and thinkers were receptive and eager to explore English literature, criticism, and moral philosophy. The formulation of the idea of the imagination in Germany depended significantly on English influence. Yet the Enlightenment and Romantic development of the idea in Germany flowed not only from England but from a great many internal causes and contributions. Whereas the eighteenth-century history of the idea in England can be compared to the kindling of a small fire, first of twigs, then of successively larger pieces of wood, the rise of the idea in Germany is closer to a spontaneous combustion bursting from many different materials.

Before we examine the details of the various and related elements that converge to form the German idea of the imagination, we might make a compact survey, not stopping to explain here, but simply to list: the immense range and influence of Leibniz in metaphysics, logic, cosmology, and psychology, as a commentator on empiricism, an investigator of *a priori* conditions in nature and the mind, and the founder of the system of Pre-established Harmony, which insisted on the reality of *active force* in both nature and the human psyche. There was a lively interest in Continental philosophy as a whole, including Descartes, Malebranche, and Spinoza. The impact of British aesthetic and moral philosophy was significant, especially through Shaftesbury, who provided in the later eighteenth century a way to interpret Spinoza that fostered Romantic Spinozism and opened Spinoza's pantheism to the imagination, saving his system from its congenital dualism. The interest in empirical psychology and associationism led to a psychologically based criticism drawing heavily on both the association of ideas and the new studies on originality and genius, especially by Locke, Hume, Kames, Priestley, Hartley, and Gerard. A persisting influence of the older, "scholastic" philosophy of the Middle Ages and the Renaissance, which England had virtually forgotten, offered not only key terms but essential ideas to construct a new concept of the imagination. Another factor was the "critical philosophy" of Kant, his followers, and some of his opponents, all of whom studied the transcendental, without ignoring the sensuous, as thoroughly as the British had examined the empirical and empirical psychology. German mysticism, represented largely by Jakob Boehme, was also influential.

The new "science" of aesthetics, first formulated by Alexander Baumgarten in his *Aesthetica* (1739) and *Metaphysica* (1739), which drew not only from the Greek past but from Shaftesbury and, through the "Swiss Critics" Bodmer and Breitinger, from Addison.[2] Hellenism brought not only the model of the Greek fine arts but also Plato, Longinus, and Plotinus to bear on German thought. The growing popularity of and interest in the primitive, in *Volkspoesie* and *Urgeschichte*, in the "pure" and original, was spurred by the rage for Homer and *Ossian* and promulgated by Johann Georg Hamann and Herder. After 1750, adulation of Shakespeare was marked, as was the hope for a corresponding natural and powerful German or "northern" poetry . A violent reaction developed to French criticism and culture as artificial, unimaginative, overly rational, and class-oriented. Finally, a tendency toward polarities or opposites in thought developed, contradictions that needed to be reconciled or caught up in some larger synthesis, as in Kant, Hegel, and Schelling. The polar or thesis-and-antithesis tendency was to lead to the dialectical and synthetic nature of German Romanticism.


### FIRST PRINCIPLES

Leibniz lies at the heart of German Enlightenment thought. Like a pulsating star, he radiates a strong field of influence in all directions. His idea of an active force in both the mind and nature gives the universe and the human psyche a common, dynamic power through which harmony between the two is attained. Not only in metaphysics and in the natural sciences, but in psychology as well, this transforming force binds together the natural world, the individual, and all the internal processes of each. There is no such thing as a separate entity; the flux and force of mind and cosmos acting in both things and ideas unify elements in each "separate" identity, each thing, person, or idea. Leibniz is like the person who stakes a claim by riding around a vast tract of land from sun-up to sunset. The work of coming generations then falls largely within the perimeter he marks off, and thinkers who follow cultivate what he has already surveyed. The scope of Leibniz saved German thought from becoming boxed into the corner of pure empiricism.

Shaftesbury had helped the British extricate themselves from rigid empiricism, and his emphasis on the becoming and striving of the individual moral life, his search for ultimate principles and for the nature of both divine and human creation, was equally attractive to the German Enlightenment. Shaftesbury had a continuing influence on German thought during the century. He merged the horizons of philosophy, artistic theory, moral sensibility, and feeling. Anyone who took up these topics separately soon found that in Shaftesbury's thought they flowed into each other, not by any *a priori* rules but by an imaginative exercise of perception and by the individual's active ordering of experience. The unity of Shaftesbury's work—its combined grasp of the individual life and passionate love of nature—helped to set the groundwork for the imagination as a power of enthusiasm that joins and interprets the characteristics of man with the ideal potential of the universe that is manifested through the natural world.

Both Leibniz and Shaftesbury (at least the general aesthetic represented by Shaftesbury) fell into the hands of pupils with more specialized interests. But though Christian Wolff and Alexander Baumgarten narrowed the original intention of the two larger-minded men, they cultivated particular points so intensely that, temporarily contracting the range of Leibniz and Shaftesbury, they eventually arrrived at a greater number of articulated positions. After all, the highest flights of Shaftesbury and the most profound remarks of Leibniz were, by their very nature, suggestive and even vague. They could be interpreted in many ways, and to have any continued influence, they had to be narrowed and anatomized, if only to save them from static generality or passive acceptance. The positions of the important philosophers are in this respect like works of the better poets; they invite a multiplicity of views and interpretations, which must be traced out and voiced.

### THE NEXT GENERATION

Christian Wolff (1679–1754) selectively systematized Leibniz's thought. He was more formalistic than Leibniz and supported rationalism in a more confining sense of the term. Yet it was mostly through Wolff that Leibniz filtered into the German universities. Wolff gives specific and defined instances of what, in Leibniz, had been more impressionistic and speculative. This attempt to ferret out exact principles trivialized them at times, but also kept them alive and open to discussion. For example, in his *Psychologia Empirica* (1732), and to a lesser extent in his *Psychologia Rationalis* (1734), Wolff distinguishes between *imaginatio, phantasma, phantasmata,* and the *Facultas fingendi.** Wolff's work is remarkably fertile, for he can be interpreted as distinguishing the reproductive from the productive imagination. *Imaginatio,* he says, reproduces what the senses have perceived yet is now absent from them. But the *Facultas fingendi,* to which Wolff devotes a thirty-page chapter in the *Psychologia Empirica,* is defined thus: "*Facultas phantasmatum divisione ac compositione producendi phantasma rei sensu nunquam perceptae dicitur* Facultas fingendi."[3] That is, the *Facultas fingendi* is the shaping, joining, and plastic power of the mind that fashions and produces ideas and images in a new and transformed totality that has never been presented to the senses before. This faculty is productive, as opposed to the reproductive operation of *imaginatio.* The productive power of the *Facultas fingendi* roughly corresponds to the "power" that Locke said the mind uses in forming complex ideas; in this sense Locke, too, had differentiated between a reproductive and a productive faculty. But Wolff dwells on this distinction and tries to characterize it. Although he is not here speaking about poetry or art, he does make clear that the mind has a productive capacity, one that may generally be called "imagination" but is on a different and higher level from the reproduction of what the senses register.

Wolff has been generally ignored as too mechanical and compartmentalized. But here, in the early 1730s, he is putting succinctly a major development in the eighteenth-century history of the imagination, one we have discussed in Hobbes, Locke, Akenside, and Gerard, and one that will reappear in Tetens, Kant, Schelling, and Coleridge. The application of Wolff's views to the theory and criticism of poetry and the arts helped to inject vigor into the last thirty years of the century and the first thirty of the next. His *imaginatio* and *Facultas fingendi* point to all later divisions in German criticism, psychology, and philosophy between the power of reproduction and the different, higher power that shapes new ideas and images, a power variously called *Dichtkraft, Dichtungskraft,* or *Dichtungsvermögen,* a power that alone produces the artistically and aesthetically creative acts of the mind. Wolff investigates, too, the dangers and satisfactions of the *Facultas fingendi* and discusses the influence of will, desire, and judgment on his version of both the reproductive and the productive imaginations.

Wolff combined empiricism with implications of Leibniz's organic and dynamic relationship between mind and nature and the dynamic quality of nature itself. Wolff even speaks of the *Facultas fingendi* in its power to produce "hieroglyphics" and "symbols," concepts that be-

* The *Philosophia Prima Sive Ontologia* (1730) should also be examined in conjunction with these two works. Wolff's own cross references to it are numerous. For Wolff on "fancy" vs. "imagination," see below, pp. 176–177.

come vitally important throughout the century in their relationship not only to art theory but also to studies of ancient poetry and imaginative myths. In essence, Wolff pursues and tries to define the premise, found in more broad-minded empiricists like Hobbes and Locke, that "there is a power" which joins and combines ideas to produce new ones. But Wolff carries the analysis of this power to a new stage and gives it special significance and clarity. It now has a larger, more clearly defined potential and directly serves those who use psychology to explain how the mind and the inner sensibility create art and what characterizes the genius of a poet. The idea of creative imagination is closely related to Wolff's *Facultas fingendi*.[4] Coleridge, for example, read the *Psychologia Rationalis* and probably encountered Wolff's discussions of the imaginative power and its levels.

The work of Wolff received full body and dimension from his pupil Alexander Baumgarten (1714–1762). To the dry and rational analyses of his teacher, Baumgarten added the consideration of what he calls "aesthetics," the first modern use of the word. In 1739 his book *Aesthetica* expanded the logical and reasonable investigations of Wolff to include "the lower or sensitive" parts of the soul. Drawing from the same tradition that produced Shaftesbury's, Addison's, and Hutcheson's concern with what is now generally called aesthetics, Baumgarten added another side to the imaginative power, a moral and artistic bent which was to combine with Wolff's rational and deductive approach.

The "Swiss Critics" J. K. Bodmer and J. J. Breitinger already reflected such a confluence of ideas. Bodmer, who published a prose translation of *Paradise Lost* in 1732, and Breitinger ardently tried to introduce English literature to the Germanic world. In their "modern" views they opposed and finally helped refute the school of Gottsched at Leipzig. Acquainted with Locke, Shaftesbury, Addison, Italian critics, and Leibniz, they turn directly to questions concerning the psychology of art. *Die Discourse der Mahlern,* written by both men and modeled after the *Spectator,* and Bodmer's "Dichtkunst, Malerei, und Bildbauerei," as well as his *Von dem Einfluss und Gebrauche der Einbildungskraft zur Ausbesserung des Geschmacks* (*Influence and Use of the Imagination in the Improvement of Taste,* 1727), all exhibit a repugnance to French authority and rules and a tendency to favor free association and passion because they stimulate the poet to rivet his attention on an object in order to portray its total essence and character. The act of comparing nature with an imaginative reconstruction of it is, as Addison had said, at once the impetus and pleasure of art.

Then, in a spurt of activity, Bodmer and Breitinger wrote three important critical works that champion the autonomy of the poetic and imaginative world. Breitinger's *Kritische Dichtkunst* (1740), which opposes Gottsched's treatise of the same title, was soon joined by his friend Bodmer's *Von dem Wunderbaren in der Poesie* (1740) and *Kritische Betrachtungen über die poetischen Gemälde* (1741). Bodmer stresses the freedom of the imagination and, following the conviction of Leibniz that there are many possible creations always ready to be materialized, he calls on the poet to "imitate the *powers* of nature in transferring the possible into the condition of reality."[5] Here we get a foretaste of the later and heavy emphasis on the ability of art not only to recreate sensuous nature but also to share with and use the moving powers, forces, and ideals in the cosmos to depict a new and transformed material world.

In this critical position, new to the Germanic world, Bodmer was following Italian critics and also Addison's praise of what he called the "fairy way of writing." By "fairy," Addison indicated something imaginative, not childish or ridiculous. The *Faerie Queene* or *A Midsummer Night's Dream* are examples. Happily for Bodmer and Breitinger, Klopstock's *Der Messias* (1748) vindicated their views.* Klopstock's work was a thrust into the enemy camp, for he published it in Leipzig, the stronghold of Gottsched and his followers. It was Klopstock, too, whom Coleridge visited when he studied in Germany, for the great poet of the middle of the eighteenth century in Germany, and the practitioner of the theories of Bodmer and Breitinger, did not die until 1803.

### STIRRINGS OF A GRAND SYNTHESIS

Added to this rich and varied field, which was permitting the idea of the imagination to spread out simultaneously in many directions, was an undercurrent that strove to unify these directions into one harmonious or at least comprehensive view. Kant himself emerges from this spirit of mediation, this drive to blend Wolff's formalism with British empiricism, scientific experimentation and mathematics, and also to confront the overall questions of religion, aesthetics, morality, and art. The new and comprehensive view, broadly called the "critical philosophy," had some of its first roots in the work of C. A. Crusius, Leonhard Euler, and J. H. Lambert. Yet these men could not attain the psychological accuracy or approach the transcendental synthesis of Kant who, borrowing from the psychologist Tetens, developed the role of the imagination in the critical philosophy. The opportunity came for the critical philosophy as both empirical psychology and the more intuitive or aesthetic approaches broadened and spilled into each other.

* In 1751 Bodmer himself published two weak imitations of Klopstock, *Die Sündfluth* and *Noah*.

Something very curious had happened. Hard-rock and uncompromising empiricism had inevitably led to empirical psychology, the study of the way in which the mind works. Yet how the mind works, its limits and characteristics, is one of the major components of all transcendental philosophy. The whole question of knowledge and values had moved from outside the self to inside the self. Experience became the study of philosophy, says Santayana, and psychology, "for the philosophers, became the only science . . . The irony of logic actually made English empiricism, understood in this psychological way, the starting-point for transcendentalism and for German philosophy."[6] It happened just as Leibniz had noted: each philosophical system carries within itself the seeds of almost all other systems, including that of its own "opposite." Coleridge, too, makes nearly the same analysis in the *Biographia:* as soon as materialism "becomes intelligible, it ceases to be materialism. In order to explain *thinking,* as a material phenomenon, it is necessary to refine matter into a mere modification of intelligence."[7] The philosophy of matter had become, of its own accord, the philosophy of intelligence.

Writing in the 1790s, Maass takes an historical perspective on the subject. He finds this development from the empirical to the psychological in Greek philosophy, where first the "object of consideration was the external sensory world. Greek philosophy proceeded from this, as must the philosophy of all peoples . . . It is more difficult to reflect on internal development, and particularly on that of the psyche." The very change from the purely empirical to the psychological led to and encouraged the study of the imagination. In his *Versuch über die Einbildungskraft,* which Coleridge read and used in the *Biographia,* Maass concludes that the shift from the empirical to the psychological results in a new and vastly important place for the idea of the imagination: "So it was first after the time of Socrates that psychology could begin to sprout from its seed. But as soon as one began to construct this science, the imagination was especially bound to attract the attention of the investigator."[8] As Maass explains it, this was exactly what was happening in the eighteenth century, too.

The shift from empirical to transcendental, and to an enlarged view of philosophy that embraces both the sensory and the ideal by realizing that they are not separate, continued from 1750 through the 1790s and later, especially in England. The rigid and mechanistic interpretations, the naive notion of a simple *tabula rasa,* had already foundered. They could not survive the rich and diverse philosophical climate of Germany. In 1765, Leibniz's *Nouveaux essais* gave straightforward empiricism, viewed as a complete answer, the *coup de grâce.* Wolff and, in the 1770s, Tetens brought empirical psychology to a higher level of sophistication. The works of Gay, Hume, Smith, Priestley, Tucker, and

Kames, also known by the 1770s, eclipsed the physiological empiricism of Hartley, Bonnet, and Condillac as exemplified by Albrecht von Haller's *Elementa Physiologiae Corporis Humani* (1757–1758). Yet Haller, like so many of these thinkers an individual of diverse intelligence, corresponded with Bodmer and was open to the drive for a new and imaginative national literature.

### THE QUICK RESPONSE TO ASSOCIATIONISM

As a sign of the speed and success with which the association of ideas and associationist criticism (a product of empirical psychology) was developing in Germany, we can turn to a small but remarkable volume, Michael Hissmann's *Geschichte der Lehre von der Association der Ideen*, published at Göttingen in 1777. Hissmann traces figures in associationism from Plato to Ernst Platner, including Aristotle, Quintilian, Hobbes, Locke, Leibniz, Wolff, Hume, Condillac, Kames, Reid, Beattie, Priestley, and Gerard. He notes that much of the impetus for modern associationism came from John Gay and that Wolff should be given credit for the popularization and spread of associationism in Germany.[9]

The last section of Hissmann's book holds special interest. Drawing on Tucker's *Light of Nature Pursued** (Hissmann calls Tucker by his *nom de plume*, Edward Search), Hissmann devotes his concluding pages to a new topic, the difference between associated and compound ideas and on the nature of trains of ideas. Hissmann distinguishes ideas that are simply associated from those that, according to Tucker, form a train and then an organic and compact whole, such that one idea conjures up a whole mass (*"die ganze Menge"*). Hissmann, led by Tucker, goes beyond the association of ideas to a blending, joining, and unifying of them. In ideas that are bonded together (*"zusammengesetzten"*), boundaries between them disappear. The ideas become, as Hissmann says, "so precisely linked together, that a single whole results." In fact, this new operation is the act of a creative imagination, the willful unifying of ideas into one whole, similar to what Coleridge means by the secondary imagination. Hissmann explains, "The characteristic of compound ideas rests in the unity of the associations in one single whole."[10]

Furthermore, as Gerard had done and as Tetens was doing that very year (1776–1777) in following Gerard, Hissmann finds this process of uniting ideas in creative work and in poetry. Like the English critics, he quotes Shakespeare to exemplify the principles of association that can connect everything into one whole, rejecting—by a sort of intuitive

* See below, pp. 162–165.

judgment—what is not useful. By the end of his history, Hissmann turns fully in the direction of art and criticism, and concludes that "The genius runs through a mass of associations without losing his thread."[11]

Johann G. E. Maass's *Versuch über die Einbildungskraft* (1792 and 1797) is a more thorough and prolonged treatment of the imagination than is Hissmann's work. Yet Maass is not a startling thinker and adds little to Hissmann's observations about the development of associationism into an organic outlook where the mind sees and creates things in their totality —a kind of outlook that Hazlitt would best exemplify and apply to the arts. Maass does show, however, that the empirical and associationist traditions remain vigorous in Germany through the 1790s. This empirical strain is maintained in the orderly studies of Ferdinand Ueberwasser, G. E. Schulze, J. F. Ströhlin, J. L. Gosch, and A. J. Dorsch, especially in Ströhlin's *Philosophische Rede über die Associationsgesetze unserer Begriffe* (1788) and Dorsch's *Über Ideenverbindung und die darauf gegründeten Seelenzustände* (1788).

### THE PSYCHOLOGY OF THE IMAGINATION
### ENTERS ARTISTIC THEORY: PLATNER

Both Hissmann and Maass are primarily empiricsts and historians of the work of others. More particular and original studies threw the idea of the imagination into new perspectives. For example, four years before Tetens' *Philosophische Versuche über die Menschliche Natur und Ihre Entwicklung* appeared in 1776–1777, and four years before Gerard's *Essay on Genius* became so popular in Germany, Ernst Platner in 1772 published his *Anthropologie für Aerzte und Weltweise* (*Anthropology for Doctors and Philosophers*). Platner, like Wolff, was already thinking with acuity how to define the difference between *Phantasie* and *Einbildungskraft*. More important, Platner's *Anthropologie* starts from the standpoint of a physiologist and an empirical psychologist but then unifies empirical psychology with a belief in the immateriality of the soul, the *Geist* or psyche. The result is an idea of the imagination that draws on both the concrete and the abstract, the real and the ideal. (Eighteen years later, in 1790, Platner came out with an enlarged version of the *Anthropologie*, whose title indicates what a far-ranging net could be cast combining principles of empiricism and inherent qualities of the psyche: *Neue Anthropologie für Aerzte und Weltweise Mit besonderer Rücksicht auf Physiologie, Pathologie, Moralphilosophie und Aesthetik*.)

Turning to what he calls "*Genie in der Einbildungskraft*," Platner assumes that there are different types of genius in the larger sense of the word, such as genius for observation ("*Genie in der Beobachtung*") or a genius for invention ("*in der Erfindung*"). The striking thing here is that he identifies *Genie in der Einbildungskraft* with art and with artistic creativity. Imagination is the power to present in concrete, particular forms and expressions what before had been only general and abstract knowledge, hazy feeling, or impression. The poet's imagination provides a local habitation and a name. By "abstract," Platner does not mean incapable of concrete presentation but previously lacking in concrete form, up to the time it becomes the object of an imaginative act. As he explains, "The genius of the orator, the poet, the artist, and the actor originates from this liveliness of the imagination in the presentation of abstract ideas and shows itself in all manner of sensory presentations of a general nature, in personifications, metaphors, and similes."[12]

Poetic invention, maintains Platner, requires three attributes: fancy ("a lively and extensive mechanical fancy") to supply a large initial mass of ideas; a lively imagination ("*eine Lebhafte Einbildungskraft*") to connect them, create new wholes, and give these new ideas and images sensory form; and an organizing power, or special faculty of the soul ("*eine besondere Fähigkeit der Seele*"), to give the whole production feeling, beauty, and the aesthetic sense that reconciles opposites and contrarieties.[13] Although Platner restricts "*Einbildungskraft*" to the second stage of this threefold scheme of poetic invention, he is touching on the same kind of poetic process that would be defined further by Tetens, Schelling, and Coleridge, and for which "imagination" or "*Einbildungskraft*" eventually became the one most commonly accepted word. In Tetens and many others, *Dichtkraft* or *Dichtungsvermögen* is used to characterize the highest act of artistic creation, which Coleridge was to call the "secondary imagination," but for Schelling and for the great figures of Romanticism, especially after 1790, "*Einbildungskraft*" becomes the more positive and encompassing word. "Imagination" is, as Coleridge found out, the only natural translation into English of *Einbildungskraft, Dichtkraft,* and its cognates.

Imagination was becoming the central theme in the consideration of genius and creativity in the arts by the 1770s. By the next decade it held unquestionable supremacy, and it no longer was possible to sift out German criticism and psychology based on empiricism from that based on intuitional-*cum*-aesthetic principles. In so many writers the two mix thoroughly. Empiricism, idealism, aesthetics, art, poetry, philosophy, genius, and creativity are all being tightly drawn together by their common thread, the concept of imagination.

# 9

# THE NEW FOCUS
# OF LITERATURE AND MYTH

*I*n the 1770s the crescendo of German studies on imagination, the creative power, enthusiasm, and genius became pronounced. These culminate in the 1790s with works intended to be comprehensive, such as Maass's *Versuch über die Einbildungskraft*. These books exhibit an agglomeration of empirical psychology, intuitionalism, poetic theory drawn from Homer to the present with emphasis on the nature of enthusiasm, and a belief in the ideal spirit or *Geist* of the imaginative act leading to philosophical and religious considerations. On the whole, these studies place the imagination at the center of the fine arts, especially poetry, and are well informed about both the history of and contemporary critical commentary about the idea of imagination in England, France, and Germany.

A telling example of the myriad discussions is the work of Leonhard Meister (1741–1811), professor at Zurich, where Bodmer and Breitinger had published. Although Meister proceeds in a cautious way and does not make unbounded claims for the imagination, he approaches what he calls *"der Zauberglas der Einbildungskraft"* ("the magic glass of the imagination") with enormous respect for its power and importance in human nature. Meister's four books overlap in content, as their titles indicate: *Ueber die Schwermerei* (2 vols., 1775–1777) was followed by *Versuch ueber die Einbildungskraft* (1778), and in 1795 both *Über Aberglauben, Einbildungskraft, und Schwärmerey* and his most suggestive work, *Über die Einbildungskraft in ihren Einfluss auf Geist und Herz*.

In each of these books, Meister speaks eloquently of the persuasive grip of the imagination over the mind—over all beliefs, actions, and acts of creativity. The imagination provides the driving force not only behind superstition but also behind religion, orthodox as well as fanatical and pantheistic. Imagination excites and is excited by passion; it is the strongest attribute of visionaries and enthusiasts. Imagination serves as the nexus and control of every human response and action that deals with more than the most simple and purely demonstrable, material side of experience. The roots of Meister's theme run back through notions of poetical frenzy and religious mysticism, through Spinoza and Boehme, both of whom Meister cites, and into the religio-philosophical mysteries of the neo-Platonic, cabalistic, and Egyptian schools, all of which had been uncovered since the middle of the eighteenth century in Germany by systematic studies in the history of philosophy and the fine arts. But Meister assigns the radical and inevitable cause of all human beliefs and darkly brilliant intuitions to the imagination and the intense feelings it generates.[1]

Meister perceives a potential danger in this overwhelming strength of the imagination, a threat of self-deception, of tragic excesses and obscurity (*"Ausschweifungen der Einbildungskraft"*), which German thinkers in the late eighteenth and early nineteenth centuries never minimized as much as their English counterparts did. Meister's answer to this potential danger is to ally the imagination, with all its creative and mystic powers, to philosophy. This union, he believes, forms a true alloy of the mind's otherwise disjointed capabilities. It brings the whole man together—heart, soul, body, brain, and feelings—and it establishes the individual's place in society.[2] In short, all human uncertainties, beliefs, intuitions, and feelings of truth are governed by imagination, and these, if joined to a love of wisdom, knowledge, and moral values, fulfill man's estate in the highest degree. The imagination should permeate life. An interesting contrast to Meister's hope for the imagination is John Trenchard's skeptical rationalism in *The Natural History of Superstition* (1709). By a different route, Meister aims at a goal similar to that which attracted Keats, a rich imagination, yet one which will save the artist from being simply a dreamer caught in superstition and escapist fantasy. In fact, it had always been the great humanists, and often the religious poets like Dante and Milton, who held out the gift and promise of the poetic imagination as a high road to philosophy.

### SULZER'S ESSENTIAL ANALYSIS

Meister's thoughts carry him into the uncertain air, and trying to follow him can cause an attack of *Schwärmerei* in the sense of confused vertigo. But during the years that Meister was writing about the farthest reaches and hence most powerful and poorly defined stretches of the imagination, others approached the idea from new directions. Thinkers interested in the theory, appreciation, and criticism of the fine arts, especially poetry, were now focusing on an analysis of the imagination.

Johann George Sulzer's *Allgemeine Theorie der Schönen Künste (General Theory of the Fine Arts*, 4 vols., 1771–1774, 2nd edition 1792–1799) sums up the generally accepted place of the imagination in the arts throughout the latter half of the eighteenth century in Germany. Sulzer's striking and condensed articles on *Einbildungskraft* and *Dichtungskraft* show how well-formed and directly the "romantic" concept of the imagination comes from the Enlightenment. The *Allgemeine Theorie* is an extensive encyclopedia of terms used in the fine arts, which frequently resembles Jean Baptiste Du Bos' *Critical Reflections*. Sulzer devotes little attention to psychological or metaphysical background, so what he assumes is telling. The power of the imagination in its elementary perception, its contribution to memory, and its reproduction of both ideas and inner feelings or intuitions is completely taken for granted. Sulzer, who knew Bodmer, focuses directly on imagination in the arts, and he assumes imagination to be a massively important power of the mind in general, and everyone, he implies, is now taking this for granted. His purpose is therefore to examine imagination "only in so far as the superior gift of the artist and as its effect on works of taste can be admired." Specifically, the imagination "is really the mother of all the fine arts, and through it especially the artist differentiates himself from other men." Only in the soul of the artist does imagination work with a pre-eminent liveliness and elastic power. The imagination of the artist converts a mass of ideas, feelings, and impressions into the sensuous and identifiable work of art, which distills, unifies, and symbolizes experience. In order to accomplish this, the imagination must be profuse and vivid, but also regular, directed to one end, and sharing in some kind of organized judgment. "*Leichtigkeit*" (an ease that makes no mistakes), "*Lebhaftigkeit*" (vivacity or liveliness), and "*Ausdehnung*" (range) are qualities of the artistic imagination, recalling Gerard's "activity," "fertility and regularity," and "methodizing power" of the imagination of genius.[3]

Imagination is capable in itself of absorbing and assuming all these "separate" qualities. It is the surest foundation of taste and aesthetic value. Furthermore, the artist's imagination usually fixes on an object with intensity and enthusiasm. This gusto and concentration on the particular, seeing deep into the nature of a thing, becomes an important tenet of romantic art, poetry, and criticism. In England it is best expressed by Hazlitt and Keats.

The imagination, says Sulzer, also works most powerfully when it brings forth the specific and the particular to act as a symbol of a larger network of associated ideas and experiences. The concrete particular is important because the imagination sees in it the suggestion of something much larger. Handled by a genius, the most common word comes alive and resonates with meaning. As an example, Sulzer gives the poignant phrase in the sixth book of the *Aeneid,* *"Tu Marcellus eris,"* where Aeneas, peering as a visionary into Rome's future, foresees simultaneously both the brilliant promise and the tragic death of Augustus' nephew and son-in-law, nineteen-year-old Marcellus, who promised to be a second great Marcellus. The verb *eris* invokes a profound sense of Rome's history and predicament shortly after the civil wars. Virgil was writing soon after the death of Marcellus, in 23 B.C., about the forebearer of Rome, Aeneas, who is pictured as looking ahead from far in the past to both the auspicious hope and the terrible death of the noble young man. The meaning of *eris*, besides "you will be," seems just as clearly to be "you would have been" or "you will have been." The future promise, the tragic sense of human events, the gates of horn, the gates of ivory, are all embodied in this one word, at which Octavia, hearing Virgil read it aloud, is said to have fainted. Sulzer thus stresses what becomes a major critical preoccupation for the Romantics, how the imagination creates highly specific touches (similar to Dryden's "life-touches"), symbols, and words to present something in life that is so full of feeling, meaning, and the richness of experience that it seems ineffable. It cannot be described, only suggestively evoked.

By implication, the imagination fuses the particular with more universal feelings and ideas. As Sulzer states, imaginative art also activates the imagination of the audience, an idea that goes back at least as far as Addison. This is how "suggestivity" works, by engaging the completing power of the audience's own imagination. "Then the imagination of those who hear or see the artist's work comes to his aid. If through any of the latent qualities in the work this imagination takes on a vivid effect, it will thereupon complete what remains by itself."[4]

We should remember that this is a short article, not at all militant or earth-shaking in tone, and one that has roots directly in the heart of the Enlightenment. This fact sinks in all the more when we discover that Sulzer makes two crucial distinctions routinely assumed to come largely from later romantic theory. Sulzer's own distinction between "fancy" and "imagination" is reserved for the complete chapter on that topic. The other is his distinction between *Einbildungskraft* and *Dichtungskraft*, which parallels Tetens' and Gerard's distinction discussed in the next chapter. It also prefigures Schelling's and Coleridge's division of the imagination into primary and secondary levels.

From 1770 on, the tendency to separate *Phantasie, Einbildungskraft,* and *Dichtungskraft,* or their equivalents, is a common practice in German thought. Sulzer's major points concerning *Einbildungskraft* and its higher, more lively and creative counterpart, *Dichtungskraft*, though not so rich in philosophical implications as either Schelling's or Coleridge's positions, are lucid and viable. Moreover, Sulzer intentionally restricts himself to the fine arts. "The poetic power," he says, "is a special attribute of the imagination, and is the more extended and vivid." This special power, *Dichtungskraft*, combines more and invents the forms to present its unified combinations in a better organized, directed, and inspired way than "imagination" taken in the broader sense. *Dichtungskraft* presents an altered and transformed experience and shapes images or things that have never before been directly apprehended through the senses: it is "the power to create images (concepts, perceptions) from objects of the senses, and of the internal sense, that have never been immediately perceived before." In order to accomplish this creative act, *Dichtungskraft* must pull apart, rearrange, or "melt" the disjointed and dissolved elements of experience and then, with this raw material (*"abgezogene und schwere Begriffe"*), fashion new images, characters, and ideas. *Dichtungskraft* creates, finally, a wholly new and total impression. It idealizes in the sense that it tries to fulfill an ideal, and hence truthful, form through the creation of new being, new individuals, and new images. *Dichtungskraft* generates an organic work of art in its idealized or perfected totality (*Vollkommenheit*). Sulzer describes this complex, with an echo of Theseus' speech: "Through the poetic power, abstract and difficult notions take on a bodily form by which they are vividly and easily grasped; through this power characters, morals, actions, and incidents acquire the highest level of convincing probability in which each particular is set in its own proper light and the truth of the whole becomes more visible."[5]

The general and "lower" power of imagination itself (*Einbildungskraft*) presents us with the world—it continually images the world *into* us, similar to Coleridge's eternal act of creation of "the infinite I AM" repeated in the "finite mind." Thus Sulzer says of *Einbildungskraft*, "Through it, the world—as far as we have seen and experienced it—rests in us." But when linked to the poetic power, as *Dichtungskraft*, it becomes "the creatrix of a new world." The special reach of *Dichtungskraft* permits the imagination to shape a new universe of experience, the "golden world" of Sidney's *Apology*, a world in which Shelley's embers of divinity in man catch fire. In Coleridge's phrase, the person who creates and enters this world has "drunk the milk of Paradise." By the power of *Dichtungskraft*, argues Sulzer, "We place ourselves in the midst of a paradisical scene of overflowing riches and charming agreeableness."[6] This concept is found in Shaftesbury, Addison, and Hamann as well; it goes back at least as far as the neo-Platonic strain in Renaissance Italian criticism. Many critics of the eighteenth century and even Hobbes, seemingly rigid in his empiricism, hint at this higher world of imaginative truth. The important thing is that Sulzer splits the imagination into two levels and defines them carefully. As a result, there is an increased stress on art and on the individual artist, as well as a deeper analysis of the imagination and a new reverence for it.

Sulzer makes a special claim for poetry. The other arts, he asserts, address themselves to the senses. We hear music, dance and painting we see, but the words of poetry are actually directed to the reader's imagination and not to his senses. The poet, therefore, expresses the highest potential of *Dichtungskraft:* "Among artists the poet requires this power in the highest degree, because he seeks to cultivate the widest range of presentation, and also especially on this account, that he never writes for the senses, but for the imagination."[7]

This double-barreled quality of poetry, which capitalizes on the range of *Dichtungskraft* in the artist and the corresponding range of imagination (*Einbildungskraft*) in the audience, places it first among the fine arts. For much the same reason Schelling was to call poetry the most "ideal" of all the arts. As examples of great artists, Sulzer picks Phidias, Shakespeare, and Samuel Richardson.*

### IN THE CRITICAL WHIRLWIND

Sulzer's references include Tetens, Platner, Duff, Gerard, and Muratori. But to get a better idea of the profound and widespread sharing of interest in the imagination from 1750 through 1790 in Germany, one must turn to a unique book. This is the *Litterarische Zusätze* [*Literary Supplements*] *zu Johann George Sulzers allgemeiner Theorie der schönen Künste* (1796) by Friedrich Blankenburg, which draws on the surprising number of books on the imagination that were known in Germany in those crucial decades. Under *"Einbildungskraft"* Blankenburg cites Tetens, Gerard, Duff, Meister, Maass, and Platner (Gerard is given the largest summary). He includes James Beattie's *Dissertations Moral*

* Sulzer may have included Phidias the sculptor because of passages in Plotinus (*Enneads* V. viii, i), Cicero (*Ad M. Brutum Orator*, ii, 8-10), and Seneca (*Epistle* LXV) that were well known in the eighteenth century and which stress that Phidias did not copy nature but imitated the ideal and formative beauty that nature had engendered in his own mind. Coleridge's distinction between copy and imitation, as well as his idea of art imitating primarily the beautiful in nature, draw support from these passages, too. Sidney in his *Apology for Poetry* had made the same claim as Sulzer for the ideal superiority of poetry: "whereas other Arts retain themselves within their subject, and receive . . . their being from it, the poet only bringeth his own stuff, and doth not learn a conceit out of a matter, but maketh matter for a conceit."

*and Critical* (1783) and D. Tiedemann's *Untersuchungen über den Menschen* (1778). Works by Christian Garve, Gerard's translator, and by E. L. Wieland are cited, as is G. H. Richerz's 1785 German translation of Muratori's *Della forza della fantasia umana.* The list even includes Pico della Mirandola's *De Imaginatione sive Phantasia* (in the 1533 and later editions) and an esoteric work by the Marquis de Feuquières, *Phantasiologie, ou Lettres philosophiques... sur la faculté imaginative* (1760).

The thirty-five entries under the article on *"Genie"* contain many references to the imagination as the essential characteristic of genius. Spanish, French, English, and German works are represented, among them the studies or remarks on genius by Du Bos, Addison, Duff, Gerard, Reynolds, and Beattie, and even the minor contributions of Thomas Belsham and J. W. Parsons (*Hints on Producing Genius,* 1790). The German list is rich, too, with early studies such as S. F. Trescho's *Betracht über das Genie* (1755) and C. F. Flögel's essays appearing in *Vermischten Beytrage zur Philosophie und den schönen Wissenschaften* (1762) and his own *Geschichte des menschlichen Verstandes* (1765).

Of particular importance in Blankenburg's research is a little-known discussion by P. Gäng entitled *Vom aesthetischen Genie und seinen Eigenschaften* (1785). Gäng differentiates the genius or imagination of the artist (*"Dichtkraft"*) from the imaginative power of other individuals, and thus he joins the marked tendency to divide imagination into at least two levels. Genius "is a markedly higher, more distinguished degree of the mind's faculties, which make the person in whom it appears skillful in the creation of work of pre-eminent quality; and the constituents of which are a sprightly, expansive, and lively fancy (*Phantasie*), and a ready, strong, and extensive imagination (*Dichtkraft*)."[8] Here is another distinction between fancy and the artist's imagination.

Although Blankenburg indicates how thoroughly and acutely the idea of the imagination was developing, there are other works on the subject than those he names, and considerations wider than his bibliographical approach suggests. For example, Sulzer's *Theorie der Dichtkunst* (1788) reinforces the importance of the imagination. It is not only sensory observation, says Sulzer, that garners and supplies the elementary materials for images, but imagination itself, which is a life-giving power. It reaches the realm of spiritual powers and ideas, and with this power it unifies dissipated and abstracted ideas and notions, transforming lifeless things into living forms (*"die Dichtungskraft, die abgezogenen Begriffen einen Korper giebt, die leblose Dinge in lebendige Wesen verwandelt"*). The images that result are different from those found in nature (*"Die Lebhaftigkeit der Einbildungskraft ist die einzige Quelle dieser*

*Bilder"*). Furthermore, Sulzer views the imagination as a power that, to produce good art, must be charged with passion, feeling, enthusiasm, and intensity of purpose.[9] Such qualities reflect an aesthetic outlook, which is a throwback to ideas of Longinus, John Dennis, and Shaftesbury, as well as to the feeling, benevolent sides of the imagination. Another work of Sulzer's, *Unterredungen über die Schönheit der Natur* (1774, but written in the 1760s), posits an aesthetic and moral sensibility responsible for the human warmth and dimension of the imagination.

### THE REGROUNDING OF PHILOSOPHY

In the strengthening conviction of Sulzer and others that poetry creates a new and different world, a world where sensible things may be the direct embodiment of forces and ideals, the theory of imaginative creation interpenetrates with the critical philosophy. The imagination, in effect, works through poetry to present a sensuous imitation of the transcendental and spiritual worlds in general. This produces a "higher" aesthetic that goes beyond visible nature and comes face to face with the forces and essences of nature, whether permanent or themselves in evolution and flux. The role of the imagination widens as it participates in this new imitation, one that is *geistig*, even *geistlich*, receiving support from the critical philosophy, from the rampant interest in neo-Platonism, and from those, like Blake, Hamann, Lessing, and Coleridge, who revered the Bible as a holy poem "imitating" the Word and spirit of God.

In the study of the Bible, as well as of early Egyptian and Greek religious poetry, there was fresh interest not only in the origins of language but also in the early sacred texts and why they seem to be beautifully poetic in their profound mixture of the sensual and the spiritual. Looking back to the Bible, to Egyptian, and to Indic myths, both scholars and poets started to create what we might call the anthropology of the imagination. Robert Lowth's *De sacra Poesi Hebraeorum praelectiones* (1753) was annotated by J. D. Michaelis in its first German edition in 1758, and in 1787 it appeared in its first, familiar English translation, *Lectures on the Sacred Poetry of the Hebrews*. Lowth's popular work influenced Hamann and one of Hamann's early admirers, Herder.

These men also drew from the work of others, including Michaelis himself. Hamann envisioned language as divinely inspired, a form of heavenly music turned to words. Herder's *The Spirit of Hebrew Poetry*—translated by the American James Marsh and published in Burlington, Vermont, in 1833—is an example of what the new interest in biblical poetry was accomplishing.[10] Here, in a nexus, converge the beliefs that man carries within himself an inspired gift of expression and that he possesses a natural poetry springing from his inner being and reaching up through the natural world, using nature as its source of images, until it attains an awareness of the divine expressed through nature yet "above" the material universe. Here, too, the imaginative process is seen in the context of what the natural man, unspoiled by a highly developed and artificial civilization, can create and how—in this condition—natural genius transforms things in the natural world into myths and symbols of the divine.[11] Blake is at the heart of this long and complex tradition. The study of ancient sacred poetry led many to believe that religious verse is the most powerful utterance and proof of the inherent relationship between God's creation and the creativity of man. Writers and critics encouraged new attempts at religious poetry, hoping to free the imagination to express that relationship between God and man which had already established many patterns and archetypes from the author of Genesis to John Milton.

An expanded sense of imitation and a confidence in the ability of man's imagination to body forth ideal forms and spirits naturally releases the deepest potentialities of myth and symbol, for these are intended to imitate not sensuous nature itself but that which is of itself creating, generative, and formative. The aesthetic that in writers like Burke had held relatively close to the empirical and sensuous was preserved but now lifted into another realm.

In 1787 Christoph Meiners (1747–1810), professor of philosophy at Göttingen, published his *Grundriss der Theorie und Geschichte der schönen Wissenschaften*. This work exemplifies the striking transition taking place from an aesthetic that is largely empirical and sense-oriented to one that retains the empirical but also seeks to attain the spiritual and active force of the ideal which shapes the material world in the first place. This aesthetic depends on the imagination to penetrate into the ideal world and, as Coleridge would say, to "elaborate essence into existence." The background Meiners has in mind reflects both the empirical or real and the spiritual or ideal. He mentions both Burke and Hogarth (the *Analysis of Beauty*), as well as Hutcheson, Kames, Gerard, Beattie, and Hugh Blair. But Meiners turns equally to Winckelmann, Anton Raphael Mengs, Moses Mendelssohn, and Sulzer—all of whom tend to be less empirically bound than the British, but who recognize the absolute necessity of the empirical and the concrete, without which art could not exist. As a result, Meiners sees the imagination as it presents not simply the real and the natural but also the spiritual, that which we call "unreal" in the sense that it has not hitherto appeared in the physical world. The products of an imagination that directly imi-

tates these ideals and forms are symbolic and carry within themselves a
greater diversity of meaning and representation of beauty and truth.
This greater diversity is brought to bear through the unified medium of
the symbol, which itself must be concrete and sensuous.

In his chapter *"Ueber das Imaginativ-Schöne, oder über die schönen
Werke der Einbildungskraft,"* Meiners states his fundamental premise
that the imagination presents

> not only real circumstances as they appear in nature, but it also embel-
> lishes the beautiful, and even the indifferent and the ugly, transforms the
> real, creates things that never were, and places both real and imaginary
> things in orders and combinations different from those in which they are
> ever found in the real world. It is not surprising, therefore, if its beautiful
> productions are, according to the variety of symbols it employs, of such a
> great diversity.[12]

Sulzer himself had said of *Dichtungskraft*, the highest level of imagination, *"durch sie wird das geistliche Wesen der Dinge uns sichtbar"*—
through it the spiritual essence of things is made manifest to us. The
concept of the imagination, then, as applied to a wider aesthetic realm
and extended to the spiritual, ideal, and transcendental, helps explain
the repeated use of *Geist* to characterize the power of artistic genius. But
many factors promoted the union of poetry, imagination, philosophy,
and ultimately religion. Much of the impetus came from antiquarian research and from philosophy, in the latter case not only from Kant and
the critical philosophy but from a systematic revival of interest in the
history of philosophy that reinterpreted neo-Platonism, myths, mysteries, and Spinoza.

Meiners shared this renewed vision of philosophy, now fortified with
a belief and confidence in the imagination. He wrote on ancient Egyptian religion and on the anthropology and thought of early Russia. He
produced a history of religion, works on ancient Greece, and an intellectual history of the first centuries A.D., titled *Beytrag zur geschichte
der denkart der ersten Jahrhunderte nach Christi geburt, in einigen
betrachtungen über die neu-platonische philosophie* (1782). Meiners
was carrying on an established practice in writing these studies. Jakob
Brucker (1696–1770) was one of the more remarkable people engaged in
this work. Rector of the *Stadtlateinschule* in Kaufbeuren, Bavaria,
Brucker wrote two monumental works, *Historia critica philosophiae*
and *Kurtze Fragen aus der philosophische Geschichte*. The table of
contents of *Kurtze Fragen* could provide topical notes for Coleridge's
*Philosophical Lectures*, themselves in the vein of Brucker and Meiners,
among others.

As the neo-Platonists, Pythagoreans, and Spinoza were resurrected,
they were reinterpreted not only through a deepened historical under-

standing but also through the newly ground lens of imagination. In turn, reinterpreting philosophy in this way enriched and expanded the idea of the imagination. Just as the "Eastern Tale" from the late seventeenth century, Pope, Andrew Ramsay's *Travels of Cyrus* (1728), and Coleridge's *Kubla Khan* helped release the imagination, so the study of Plotinus, Proclus, Synesius, the Bible viewed as mystical philosophy, and the relatively recent pantheism of Spinoza seemed equally likely to attribute almost holy powers of knowledge and intuition to the imagination. Just as philosophy and religion were seen as processes evolving in time, so the imagination, including the collective imagination of mankind, was seen to hold the promise of recognizing and achieving a transformation and development of what is real and empirical through the formative and active power of the ideal and the spiritual.

### ESCAPING REASON AND ALLUSION

Research turned not only to the history of philosophical thought, including aesthetics, but to the history of myth as well, and the result was freer play in what was considered acceptable, and greater range in what was considered desirable, for products of the imagination. This new research and curiosity held wide implications for the idea of the imagination.*

Giambattista Vico, whose important third edition of *The New Science* (1725) appeared in the last year of his life, 1744, hoped to establish a rational study of myth and of the early development of man.[13] The more Vico pursued his work, the more he realized that the first cause of myth is not really external; it is not found simply by studying the revolutions of the moon or the cycle of crops. The cause is internal, seated in man's complete nature, in his emotional and archetypal character, only part of which is rational. Vico concluded, according to Burton Feldman, that "Not reason but imagination must ... be the key to myth." And myth involves religion, too. Vico's greatest impact was not felt until after 1800, but he was read somewhat in the eighteenth century, especially in Germany, by Herder among others, and his work indicates that a rational study of history and ancient fragments was actually enlarging upon the generation and evolution of the mind's imaginative power.

Throughout the middle of the eighteenth century, German studies

---

* Readers familiar with studies of myth in the eighteenth century will recognize my use of *The Rise of Modern Mythology*, *1680–1860* by Burton Feldman and Robert D. Richardson (Bloomington, 1972); also Frank Manuel, *The Eighteenth Century Confronts the Gods* (Cambridge, Mass., 1959).

turned to Greece and the Hellenistic world. At Göttingen, also renowned for the study of modern literatures, J. M. Gesner and his successor Christian Heyne attempted to understand the origins and meaning of Greek art more completely than anyone ever had before. Although largely philological in orientation, Heyne's work discusses myth and aesthetics at length. Relatively ignored is the insightful work by Karl Philipp Moritz, especially his *Götterlehre oder mythologische Dichtungen der Alten*, published in Vienna the year before Moritz died in 1793 in his late thirties. Goethe may have collaborated on the *Götterlehre*. The beginning of this book summarizes many ties that the later Enlightenment had found linking myth, religion, and the imagination. Moritz, who spent time in England and remarks in his *Travels* about the popular appeal of *Paradise Lost*, distills several decades of the mingled interest in the ancient world, religion, and man's creative impulse:

> Mythological poems must be considered as a language of imagination: as such, they make a world for themselves . . . The essence of imagination is to form and shape . . . It flees the concept of a being which has no beginning; in imagination, all is origin, procreation and birth, as in the most ancient stories of the gods. None of the higher essences or beings which imagination represents is eternal; none derive from unbounded power.

The imagination, then, is eternally creative, like Coleridge's "primary" and presumably "secondary" imagination. It catches the flux and mutability of the world in sensuous shapes and deifies the "higher essences" of the world, in which the "primary principle . . . is power, to which all else is secondary."

Moritz takes a major step when he identifies the basic impulse of myth with the imaginative transformation of the transcendental and the ideal powers and essences of nature into the concrete and actual. Yet, he states, "none of the higher essences or beings . . . is eternal." As the imagination catches the spiritual and the material in their mixing evolution and apprehends this poetry of the cosmos, it also "seeks to make its forms as individualized as possible: so imagination transfers the concept of these higher and prevailing powers . . . to beings now represented as actual, and to these are attributed the birth, names, genealogy, and form of men."[14] Schelling and Coleridge would reiterate that imagination is the principle of individuation and consequently of personal identity. Moritz's formulation shows the probable influence of Leibniz and Shaftesbury, and the certain influence of the neo-Platonists, the new theories of the fine arts, and the researches into the past that attempted a history of consciousness.

Moritz indicates that myths, symbols, and art in general were being considered as the bodily and immanent manifestations of the mind's transcendental ideals of nature and even of the mind itself. In the first instance, Poseidon and all the myths and poetry about the sea were, to the Greeks, the best definition of the *Ding-an-Sich*, or, we might say, the *Kraft-an-Sich* of the sea. In the second instance, Narcissus and Eros were part of the expression of archetypal human nature. In this way, art could answer the "scientific" and psychological inquiry that Vico, Tetens, Kames, and many others had put: what is the nature of man, and what does it tell us about art? By the work of his imagination everything in him is expressed and given outward form. To understand what his poetry means is to understand the inner man, the material world, and those higher ideals that work through both the material world and the inner psyche. Poetry and psychology, like poetry and philosophy, are able to interpret each other through the translating medium of the imagination. Keats was magnetically attracted to Greek myth for some of these reasons, as was Shelley, though Shelley's interest is more exclusively Platonic, more concerned with unchanging, permanent truths and ideas. In myth we also give tangible form to the interaction between the actual and the "unreal." Women give birth to a god's child, or mortals challenge the mythic forces of nature; this mixture of the truth of poetry with the truth of external reality, this compounded experience, which Moritz calls a "twilight horizon," is possible only through the imagination.

Winckelmann and Lessing turned the rising Hellenism to a direct consideration of aesthetics and art theory, hoping to affect the practice of contemporary artists. This development strengthened through the 1750s and 1760s. Germany was having a love affair with Greece, and the concept of the imagination matured in the southern warmth of this amity. The German admiration of the Hellenic was not merely romanticized, at least not in the shallow sense, but reflected real knowledge and thought. Scholarship was trying to answer questions about Greek art that would indicate something about the Greek spirit and imagination, questions that would help the modern artist. The ideal, as Edward Young had said in his *Conjectures on Original Composition* (1759, translated the next year into German), was not to imitate the *Iliad* but to emulate the spirit and the values that had caused and supported the flowering of ancient Greece. There had been since the early years of the century a corresponding interest in the older expressions of the Nordic and German imaginations. In England Thomas Gray, William Stukeley, Hugh Blair, and Thomas Percy tried to piece together the elements of the Nordic, the Welsh, the Druidical, and other early phases of man's "northern" imaginative experience and creations. These, as much as Greek myth, stirred interest and stimulated artists. *Ossian* and even *Faust* can be seen as outgrowths of this general attitude, highlighted by the feeling that southern myths look "outward," while northern ones peer "inward" to the psyche and ultimately to the psyche's contemplation of itself.

Herder, who markedly influenced the young Goethe, approaches most of these avenues of the imagination, including myths from different cultures, ancient poetry, religion, origins of language, anthropology, art history, the history of philosophy, and symbolism, and his octopal reach interconnects and vitalizes the bonds between these various avenues, each one of which was revealing—even as it was being revealed by—the increasingly complex and wonderful idea of the imagination.

From the early 1770s, half a dozen years before Tetens' *Philosophische Versuche* and almost ten years before Kant's first *Critique*, Herder stirred the currents of new ideas. Working on a religious and quasi-mystical foundation, gained in part from Hamann—a foundation that acts as a substratum for much of his work—Herder began to import and to theorize about English criticism of Shakespeare and also of "primitive" works, including *Ossian*.[15] Through Herder, the influence passed into German criticism of such works as Thomas Blackwell's *An Enquiry into the Life and Writings of Homer* (1735) and his *Letters Concerning Mythology* (1748), and Robert Wood's *Essay on the Original Genius of Homer* (1769, first published under another title in 1767).

Since the 1730s and 1740s in England there had been an interest—more amateur than the German interest bursting on the scene ten to twenty years later—concerning the imaginative qualities of primitive poetry and of myth. Akenside's *Pleasures of Imagination* had appeared in 1744, the year Herder was born, but Akenside also wrote another long and startling poem, *Hymn to the Naiads*, which Douglas Bush has described as "the most notable mythological poem of the century." To the *Hymn* Akenside appended learned notes on the nature of myth, which imply that the possibilities of myth remain open to modern writers. In composing myths, the poet is free to turn his imagination to "representing the mutual agreement or opposition of the corporeal and moral powers of the world: which hath been accounted the very highest office of poetry."[16]

Herder follows, elaborates, and connects some of the suggestive but scattered work of the early and middle part of the century. He crystallizes it into large and inspired concepts having to do with the philosophy of history, types of myth in various lands and cultures, the origin of language, great indivdual poets, and the anthropological and historical causes of poetry—all of which have, as a *locus communis*, the human imagination. Herder also encouraged writers of the 1770s and 1780s, like Goethe, not to imitate Greek myths but to turn to stories belonging to the Germanic and Nordic past.

### THE RENOVATION OF SPINOZA

The ferment of critical and historical ideas underwent a further heated change when it assimilated the rising influence of Shaftesbury and Spinoza. In Shaftesbury the Germans saw not only an emphasis on feeling and on moral sentiment but also a Platonism, or neo-Platonism, that was *geistlich* and operated in and through the natural world. Shaftesbury's work encouraged the belief that nature is a work of art through which the artist's spirit is creatively moving. As the long-standing interest in Shaftesbury intensified, it helped to initiate a fascination with Spinoza, who had remained in the relative background during the early and middle years of the century. Approached in the spirit of Shaftesbury and interpreted through the idea of the imagination, Spinoza could fit in with a dynamic, organic view of the universe in which there is no dualism. In fact, the idea of the imagination solved the potential problem of dualism in Spinoza and permitted him to challenge Leibniz as the modern philosopher with the greatest openness for development and for applications to aesthetics, morality, and religion.[17]

Spinoza uses *imaginatio* in two senses. However different, they are not contradictory, and both senses, already traditional in his own time, persist to the present day. *Imaginatio* is first a term for sensation, a neutral and passive receptivity that contains neither truth nor error.[18] Without denying this rudimentary psychological definition, Spinoza also identifies imagination as the prophetic and visionary power, the gift to receive divine truth and to transform it into particular symbols and myths. This is the imagination later proclaimed by Blake, Shelley, and in some moods by Wordsworth, the kind of imagination that Coleridge found expressed in the writings of Jakob Boehme and Eziekiel. In his *Tractatus Theologico-Politicus* (1670) Spinoza says: "As the prophets perceived the revelations of God by the aid of imagination, they could indisputably perceive much that is beyond the boundary of the intellect ... The prophets perceived nearly everything in parables and allegories ... for such is the usual method of imagination."[19]

Yet these two rather conventional treatments of the imagination do not represent Spinoza's most striking contribution to the idea as a whole. He provided an opportunity, for it was his pantheism (or at least what was often interpreted as his pantheism) that offered a philosophy to which another concept of the imagination could be engrafted. The result was a new and remarkable scheme of thought. The idea of a transforming and active imagination in man, God, and nature affords the thought of Spinoza a dynamic quality it otherwise lacks. Romantic Spinozism is largely a result of his system as interpreted by and tailored to a concept of the imagination as force. This imagination lends a power of creativity, of interchanging what is material and what is spiritual, of seeing the infinite in the finite, which rescues his philosophy and prevents it from collapsing into what many thought to be an entropy governed by bare logic. Although Spinoza continued to have bitter opponents, Schelling's comment in *Ideen zu einer Philosophie der Natur* (1797, 2nd edition 1803) is typical of the reverential attitude toward him—a comment that was almost surely influenced by Jacobi's *Ueber die Lehre des Spinoza* (1785, enlarged 1789): "The first who with full consciousness looked upon spirit and matter as one, thought and extension simply as modifications of the same principle, was Spinoza. His system was the first bold design of a creative imagination that in the idea of the infinite, pure as such [that is, remaining as purely One in itself], immediately conceived the finite, and recognized the latter only through the former."[20]

Without the newly expanding idea of the creative imagination, Spinoza's system encountered a barrier insurmountable from both sides. Either the infinite was chopped into a finite number of pieces, or a finite number of pieces were put together to constitute the infinite, and hence the divine; the spiritual and material, as also the One and the many, seemed isolated from each other. If only the infinite One could create and yet also be *in* what it created as "separate" and finite! The imagination was now seen as an active force, a creating God, and thus as a creating drive in nature that continually affirmed and extended itself through the particular yet flowed from the original idea of the infinite, and this creative imagination was, to many, becoming the holy fountainhead. In addition, the study of ancient myths of creation, such as those of the Greek gods Pan and Demiurgos or of the Hebrew Eloiah and the tetragrammaton, added a rich and diversified fabric of speculation and poetizing that was interlaced through the original framework of Spinoza.

# 10

# THE GREAT METAMORPHOSIS:
# TETENS AND KANT

*T*he works of Kant form an isthmus across which ideas passed and were transformed as they migrated from the Enlightenment to Romanticism. Kant added much, especially in his transcendental deduction, aesthetics, and the notion of synthesis. Yet he received the idea of imagination primarily from Tetens, the amazing psychologist who was familiar not only with British works on criticism and philosophy but with several other traditions, from strict empiricism to the schools of Leibniz and Shaftesbury. Tetens himself drew extensively on mid-century associationism and commentators on genius, notably Alexander Gerard.

Kant and Tetens stand like two colossi in their concepts of the imagination. Although Kant's stature may seem more imposing, it is only because of his greater fame and influence deriving from the other subjects he treated. For on the nature of the imagination, Kant stands largely on the shoulders of Tetens, who in turn is well informed about nearly all eighteenth-century views of the imagination as they had been formulated by 1775. In both these thinkers the concept of the imagination is the crucial element in their work, the idea on which more advances, questions, uncertainties, and assertions center than on any other single idea. To understand the idea of the imagination in Enlightenment and Romantic Germany, it is necessary to understand both what Tetens says about the imagination and how Kant carries the idea, once placed in his hands, into a new realm and destiny.

## TETENS' CENTRAL IMPORTANCE AND
## INDEBTEDNESS TO GERARD

Johann Nicolaus Tetens (1736–1807) links together British associationists and investigators of genius, especially Gerard, with German transcendental thinkers, Kant in particular. He directly influenced Coleridge. Tetens' whole approach is psychometaphysical, and his major work, the *Philosophische Versuche über die menschliche Natur und ihre Entwicklung* (*Philosophical Essays on Human Nature and Its Development*), probes how the psyche, through complex and interconnected faculties, relates itself to the outside world. The two volumes of the *Versuche* appeared in 1776–1777 and fall between Leibniz's *Nouveaux essais* and Kant's major works. Kant carefully studied the *Versuche*. In 1804 on Malta Coleridge was reading Tetens, and on Christmas Day he wrote in his notebook, "In the Preface of my Metaphys. Works I should say—Once & all read Tetens, Kant, Fichte, &c—& there you will trace or if you are on the hunt, track me."[1] In his marginalia on the *Versuche* (I, xii), Coleridge speaks of "so sound a thinker as Tetens." Tetens, born twelve years before Hartley published *Obervations on Man*, was still alive when Coleridge read the *Versuche*. Tetens' life spans all major developments from mechanical associationism to a high-blown, transcendental idea of imagination. In the *Versuche* are seen, either directly or in solution, the distinction between "fancy" and "imagination" and also the various levels or degrees of imagination itself that were soon to be explored by Kant, Schelling, and Coleridge. So Tetens is, in the true sense, a seminal figure.

Tetens gave the imagination a huge scope, his treatment of it covering the first one hundred fifty pages of the fifteen-hundred-page work. He seems to have placed it first in the book because of his awareness that he was introducing relatively new and important complexities to psychology. He divides imagination into three levels, an arrangement that gives flexibility to the empirical approach and lightens the starch in the scheme of faculties. Accordingly, imagination is responsible for direct perception, for all of the mind's subsequent manipulations of what it first perceives, and for the highest or "creative" power of forming new images and ideas. Breaking new ground, Tetens lumps together these three levels to form *Vorstellungskraft*, "the power of presentation" or of "presenting images internally," which is imagination in the broadest and most encompassing sense of the word.[2]

He carefully establishes names for each of the three levels. The first is *Perceptionsvermögen* or *Fassungskraft*, the ability to coordinate and sort sense impressions into meaningful images. One step up from this level is *Wiedervorstellungskraft*, the power of representation. This is not the same as memory. Although it includes the copying function of memory, it can represent images in an altered state. It can join or separate them, reorder them, play with and juxtapose them, in a way they could never appear to the immediate power of perception. This *Wiedervorstellungskraft* Tetens calls, more specifically, *Phantasie* or *Einbildungskraft*. These last two terms are for him synonymous, though he prefers *Phantasie*. But whichever he uses, he categorically does not mean by these terms the ability to create wholly new and unified images. That power, the highest level of the imagination and the sole province of genius, he calls *Dichtungsvermögen* or *Dichtkraft, ein "bildende, schaffende Kraft,"* a forming and creating power.

The concept of the first and most simple level, *Perceptionsvermögen*, is straightforward.[3] In psychology and philosophy, the meaning of perception was fairly well established. We order and collect immediate sense impressions into objects and ideas that we understand, which have meaning beyond mere physical stimuli. We form in our minds a picture of reality that is capable of repeating the complex relationships actually existing in the world. This power of perception is essentially what Coleridge means by the "primary imagination," the "repetition in the finite mind of the eternal act of creation in the infinite *I am*." Coleridge here was drawing on Tetens and, among others, Schelling, who very likely studied Tetens, too.[4] This perceptive power is also what Kant sometimes refers to simply as imagination (*Einbildungskraft*) and what Tetens and later Schelling say is the "common" meaning of the word. Tetens identifies his *Perceptionsvermögen* as the *"facultas percipiendi."*[5] Coleridge's "primary imagination" is the "prime agent of all human Perception."

*Phantasie* or *Einbildungskraft*, for Tetens the second level of imagination, reorganizes perceptions and uses them like building blocks. Here Tetens uses the routine example of Pegasus, but with a new intent. He shows that such a figure is the product not of the highest level of imagination but of *Phantasie*, the middle level. The creature is a combination of two ideas, a horse and wings. The result is "new"; that is, a flying horse does not exist in nature. But it is produced by a static compounding of ideas. Neither idea changes or interacts with the other. They are, literally, just stuck together. This inventive but mechanical *Phantasie* corresponds to Coleridge's definition of "fancy." *Phantasie* operates *"nach der Regel der Association"* ("according to the rule of association"). In its power of representation "consists the law of the Association of Ideas." Coleridge's "fancy" plays with "fixities and definites" and "must receive all its materials ready made from the law of association."[6]

When Tetens comes to the highest stage, *Dichtungsvermögen*, his energy and excitement burst out. *Dichtungsvermögen* builds on but goes beyond the middle level. It not only rearranges, it creates: "The psyche cannot only place and order its representations as does the curator with a gallery of pictures, but is itself a painter and invents and composes new paintings."[7] New images are formed. These appear to us to be simple and uncompounded; that is, they do not have the joints or seams that characterize the products of *Phantasie*, such as Pegasus. These new images are the result of a special process, which thoroughly mixes, blends, and fuses a series of images into one, which itself has a unified and final appearance, as if it occurred naturally and was not contrived in a routine way. Referring to this product, Tetens says, "It possesses something unique in itself that is not present in the individual listing of its components, and is thus far a new representation; but also a *simple* one for us, because we differentiate far less of the multiplicity in it than we do in the constituent parts out of which it is formed."[8] The whole is greater than the sum of its parts, and in the completed whole none of the parts are discerned because they so fully mesh and transform together.

Tetens' highest level of imagination is analogous to Coleridge's "secondary imagination." The verbs that each man uses to describe this poetic and genial power have a remarkable similarity. Tetens explains *Dichtungsvermögen* by its activities: "*Sie kann . . . trennen, auflösen, verbinden, vermischen . . . die mit innerer Heftigkeit die Einbildungen bearbeitet, auflöset und vermischet, trennet und zusammenziehet, und neue Gestalten und Erscheinungen schaffet*" ("It can . . . separate, dissolve, unite, blend . . . with inner intensity it arranges, dissolves and blends images, separates and draws them together, and creates new forms and appearances"). He implies that the power of genius alone includes "*Entwickeln, Auflösen und Wiedervereinigen . . . Ineinandertreiben und Vermischen*" ("generating, dissolving, reunifying . . . interfusing and blending").[9] These strings of words closely parallel Coleridge's definition of "secondary imagination," which "dissolves, diffuses, dissipates in order to recreate." Where this imagination cannot succeed completely in its attempt, it tries at least "to idealize and to unify." Coleridge speaks in the *Biographia* (ch. 14) of the poetic imagination as one that "blends, and (as it were) *fuses.*"

In their operation, then, secondary imagination and Tetens' *Dichtkraft* are nearly identical. Moreover, both powers form a single image from the mingling and interaction of many. Coleridge summarizes this concept in the word "esemplastic," to shape into one. The "first law" of *Dichtkraft*, according to Tetens, is that "Through an activity of the representational power, various simple representations become unified in one."[10] As an example of this unifying and inventive power, Tetens cites Swift's Brobdingnagians and Lilliputians. This instance is like Johnson's representation of the fantastic creatures in Pope's *Rape of the Lock* as a product of original and imaginative genius.

But Tetens is not the one source, or even the principal source, for Coleridge's distinctions. Schelling made such distinctions in his *System des transzendentalen Idealismus,* and in writing chapters 12 and 13 of the *Biographia,* Coleridge at times followed this major work of Schelling and even lifted passages from it. The parallels between Coleridge and Schelling are significant. For example, Coleridge's "esemplastic" is close to the *"In-Eins-Bildung"* of Schelling.* A natural inference is that Schelling, like Coleridge, studied Tetens. Coleridge would thus have received Tetens directly and also through the genial intermediary Schelling, who had ideas of his own about the imagination and how it fits into an overall philosophic and religious scheme. This last characteristic of Schelling's concept of imagination appealed to Coleridge. And finally, Tetens himself has an earlier source to whom he is deeply indebted, Alexander Gerard.

Tetens' approach is more psychological than philosophic or aesthetic, but he binds *Dichtkraft* closely to the idea of genius. He often leans in the direction of an artistic outlook. He certainly did not get this sense that artistic genius and imagination are intimate, that the highest form of imagination goes beyond mere association of ideas and is a necessary facet of genius, from the Swiss naturalist and psychologist Charles Bonnet, nor from the wildly general theories of the naturalist George Buffon, both of whom he occasionally cites. Although Locke, Wolff, and Leibniz discussed the unification of several ideas to form a new idea, they never broached or really suggested the treatment of genius.

However, Tetens read and was captivated by Alexander Gerard's *Essay on Genius* (1774). Gerard insists that the power of genius in poetry and in all the arts is more than a simple association of ideas; it is the association carried to such a degree that ideas and images meld and transform into something new and original. When Tetens explains that *Dichtungsvermögen* enlarges the usual sphere assigned to imaginative power, he identifies this extension with Gerard's idea of imaginative genius. Explicitly, *Dichtungsvermögen* is *"die, selbsthätige Phantasie; das Genie nach des Hrn. Girards [sic] Erklärung, und ohne Zweifel ein wesentliches Ingredienz des Genies"* ("the self-activated [or self-willed] imagination, genius according to Gerard's explanation, and undoubtedly an essential ingredient of genius"). The power is not limited to poets. Tetens acknowledges that his *Dichtkraft* is precisely what Gerard has described as the imaginative power of genius; he is simply extending the analysis of his Scottish predecessor and enthusiastically

* See below, pp. 302–305, 317, 322.

notes the source: "Gerard, the insightful observer of genius—and this is for him the power that is here called the creative imagination [*bildende Dichtkraft*]—perhaps has given most fully the particular rules for which new associations of ideas are formed by the imagination [*Dichtkraft*]."[11] Gerard to Tetens, then Tetens to Coleridge—with the added interpolations of Schelling—is one line of direct contact.

Gerard's *Essay on Genius* had been immediately and warmly received in Germany. Favorable reviews appeared throughout 1775 and 1776, at least a year before Christian Garve's translation. The *Neue Bibliothek der schönen Wissenschaften* praised Gerard's work and in 1776, the year after, the *Göttingische Anzeigen von Gelehrten Sachen* and the *Neuer Gelehrter Mercurius* continued the enthusiastic comments. Indicative of the importance seen in Gerard is a comment from the *Allgemeine deutsche Bibliothek*: "A splendid book! The gist is this: genius expresses itself most conspicuously in invention, which is caused by the imagination, and this in turn depends on the association of ideas . . . this work is a major achievement. Most of the examples are cited from Shakespeare."[12] This summary grasps the order of essential points in the *Essay on Genius*. Gerard's use of literary authorities was well accepted, but it was examples from Shakespeare that proved irresistible.

### IMAGINATION AND WILL

When choosing labels for the highest level of the imagination, *Dichtkraft*, Tetens had in mind Gerard's idea of genius. *Dichtungsvermögen* or *Dichtkraft* is the plastic, shaping power of genius, or the power to write poetry. *Dichten* means either "to caulk, to make tight (as with a seam)" or "to write or compose, especially poetry." Both meanings are germane. The plastic, forming power of the highest level of imagination fuses together ideas and images in order to form new ones. These are more than merely old ideas reorganized and connected: images and feelings, like reacting chemicals, produce a single result that is dense and compact in associations. In fact, *dichten* can mean "to make tight" in the sense of making more dense. Perhaps the closest thing in English to this sense is Theseus' statement that the lunatic and lover "are of imagination all compact." Of course, he says that the poet is, too, and this is precisely the second meaning of *dichten*. The poet or genius bonds and fuses images and feelings into a new and meaningful whole.

What in the psyche accounts for the "extended" yes "separate" powers of the highest level of imagination? The answer Tetens offers is not categorical, but suggestive. First, he says that as we analyze any function or faculty of the mind, we discover that the complex and creative levels subsume and build on the lower ones. *Dichtungsvermögen* is, in this sense, an extension, an expansion in degree, a swelling of the *Phantasie*.[13] "Let fancy be made into a degree proportionately more extensive, refined, vivid, and stronger," and it produces the *creative* imagination.[14] Coleridge describes secondary imagination as an "echo" of the primary imagination, the same in kind but varying in mode and higher in the degree and range of its operation. He does not, however, like Tetens, say that it echoes "fancy." Coleridge, too, says that fancy plays with what is fixed and dead; imagination is by contrast "living" or "*vital*," Tetens' "*lebhaft*."

Yet it does not seem plausible that one level becomes a different and "higher" one merely by intensifying its activity. There would be no qualitative change. Tetens explains that *Dichtungsvermögen* is also a "separate" power as well as one that extends the lower levels of the imaginative process. It has an element peculiar to itself: "*Sie ist die selbsthätige Phantasie; das Genie nach Hrn. Girards* [sic] *Erklärung.*" "*Selbsthätige*" here does not mean "spontaneous" fancy in the sense that when we open our eyes, vision is spontaneous. Tetens has already described *Phantasie* itself as often spontaneous in this way, as in dreams, so "*selbsthätige*" indicates an added quality. Here it means something like "self-activating" or "self-generating."[15] The power excites and exerts itself; *Dichtkraft* controls and designs its own activity even as it is carried away by it. It is spontaneous in the sense that once it excites the mind, *Dichtkraft* becomes, as Gerard says of the imagination of genius, like a willful instinct that operates with no second thought. It is the ancient idea of divine inspiration or enthusiasm and has a "methodizing power." It acts like "an internal stimulus" that pushes the creative act to its own completion.[16] The force of imaginative genius really has the force of passion, of strong desire for a certain end, which may be characterized as "will." Its power implies greater self-consciousness—not the self-consciousness of a stuttering actor but of the mind directing its own thoughts and creations with the aid of the strong feelings that those thoughts and creations produce. "*Selbsthätige*" could even mean "self-willed."

Coleridge was aware of this kind of interpretation. He had his copy of Maass's *Versuch über die Einbildungskraft* bound with Friedrich Jacobi's *Ueber die Lehre des Spinoza*, and in Coleridge's marginalia on Jacobi's book we find comments on this very question of "*Selbsthätigkeit.*" Jacobi says (XXXVIII), "*Wille ist reine Selbsthätigkeit, erhoben zu dem Grade des Bewusstseyns, welchen wir Vernunft nennen*" ("Will is pure self-activation, elevated to the level of consciousness that we call reason"). Coleridge, meeting this usage of *Selbsthätigkeit*, wonders if "spontaneity = Selbsthatigkeit" or if there is a larger possible meaning.

It is clear to both Jacobi and Coleridge that the idea of *"selbsthätige"* implies something more than a simple or instinctual spontaneity. It means a kind of willful and direct insight, part of an activity of mind that is urgently self-willed or self-activating. For certainly genius, which alone possesses Tetens' *Dichtkraft* or *"selbsthätige Phantasie,"* combines deliberate planning and effort with spontaneous and free force. It is more than "mere receptivity"; it is also active. For Schelling, the highest level of imagination, which he, too, identifies with genius, unifies the *"absolute Willensakt"* with *"Willkür, oder die mit Bewusstsein freie Tätigkeit,"* the absolute act of will with choice, or the consciously free faculty.[17] And for Coleridge, the secondary imagination—the imagination of poetic creativity and genius—is distinguished in one way from the primary imagination by "co-existing with the conscious will." In Coleridge, as in Schelling, Tetens, and Gerard, the unification of the conscious with the unconscious, and of the spontaneous with the willful, helps to differentiate works of inspired genius from the inventive but comparatively cramped efforts of minds that either dream aimlessly or else create mechanically. The spontaneous and the consciously willed may also bear a relation to Schiller's emphasis on the instincts for "free play" and "form." On December 27, 1804, two days after remarking that those who want to "trace, or if you are on the hunt, track me," should read Tetens, Coleridge—reading Tetens at that time—makes a long entry about the nature of the will and the relation of the will to feeling, thought, and the imagination. This entry is speculative only but shows that Coleridge was already, probably in direct connection with reading Tetens, considering the will and its relationship to imagination.[18]

To the imagination, especially to *Dichtkraft*, Tetens ascribes additional qualities that were to speed the eighteenth-century birth of Romanticism. Speaking of the third and highest level, *Dichtkraft*, Tetens says simply, *"Von ihr kommt alles Originelle."*[19] In the next generation, Schelling would proclaim that the unique feature of the literature of his day was this very stress on originality: *"Erstens . . . ist das Grundgesetz der modernen Poesie Originalität (in der alten Kunst war dieses keineswegs in dem Sinn der Fall)."*[20] Tetens is one of the first to state explicitly that imagination, or genius, is the *only* source of everything original; in England, Gerard, Duff, and Young are candidates. This idea, during the century's last quarter, permeated the critical atmosphere.

Tetens' *Dichtkraft* is, like Hume's "imagination," a completing power. It follows the lead of suggestion, involves passion, and extends creatively what the outside world only implies. Imagination gives mental inferences concrete form and shape. It is strongest when it unifies what is real and concrete, what has been experienced, with the "fiction" or more fantastic bent of the mind. Milton's picture of Hell or, to use

Tetens' own example, Swift's description of the Lilliputians and their empire is each an instance of a mixing of the familiar and common with the novel and impossible. Here the imagination is both convincing and delightful.[21]

In a broad psychological context, imagination connects the outer sense with the inner process and workings of the mind. It does so to such an extent that imagined sensations, hopes, and fears become real to us, and we experience physical sensations of what may only be in our minds.[22] We grow cold and sweat, supposing, as Theseus says, "each bush a bear." Tetens revamps, probably unknowingly, Hume's remarks about the reciprocity of inner and outer sense when the imagination operates between them. Psychology and physiology pass into one another.

Perhaps following the lead of Leibniz in the *Nouveaux essais*, Tetens claims that in its productive function as *Dichtkraft*, the imagination creates images (*das Bildliche*) for ideals that would otherwise remain disembodied in the mind's internal conception of them. Leibniz used the example of a regular polygon; our imagination represents its ideal form through the invention of a formula and thus the ideal "shows through" an image that we can see. Tetens makes essentially the same point using the circle. The image of this ideal form, of all ideals, is created by the imagination, by *Dichtkraft*.[23] Kant a few years later stresses that the imagination operates in this capacity according to a method or procedure, a "schema," one instance of which might be Leibniz's formula for the construction of regular polygons. Schelling and Coleridge, both conversant with Leibniz, Tetens, and Kant—and Coleridge with Schelling himself—finally contend that the imagination has the power of intellectual intuition. It intuits, and then creates in sensory form, the ideal. This may be one reason Coleridge says that the "secondary imagination" struggles "to idealize and to unify." The imagination has an idealizing tendency. Moreover, it—not reason—is our window on the intellectual world, a world in which reason is imprisoned until freed by the imagination. Imagination becomes the organ, the organon, for perceiving ideas of reason and communicating them to the understanding.

Tetens is not quite so enthusiastic as Schelling and Coleridge later become. He shares Bacon's reservations, and soon Kant's, concerning the intuitive power of creative imagination alone. But the imagination, as Gerard and Duff said, is the mark of philosophical and scientific, as well as of literary and artistic genius. As Einstein remarks in his paper "On the Method of Theoretical Physics," "To him who is a discoverer in the field of theoretical physics, the products of his imagination appear so necessary and natural that he regards them not as creations of thought but as given realities." This view would have been congenial to Leibniz, Gerard, Tetens, Kant, Schelling, and Coleridge. The "method" of the imagination in its intuitive and creative role was important to them all. Einstein's own "Method of Theoretical Physics" simply became one manifestation of it.

The figure of Newton, as Wordsworth describes him "Voyaging through strange seas of Thought, alone," had become for many eighteenth-century thinkers a symbol not so much of reason but of the imagination. Newtonian physics, the law of gravitation itself, was an ideal presence in nature discovered and expressed by the imagination. The more philosophically inclined of the Romantics, such as Coleridge, Goethe, Schelling, Wordsworth, and Shelley, could always see a union of the scientific and the literary through the mediation and method of imagination. What was perhaps most intriguing about this view of the imagination as the organon of scientific and philosophical truth, of knowledge about the laws of nature, was that it need not be at all incompatible with the view of imagination as the receptor of divine truths, as the vatic or prophetic voice. They were two sides of the same effort; give a flip to one and the other resulted. In both instances the imagination was uncovering and expressing ideals, something outside the realm of ordinary sensory experience, whether it was the law of gravitation or the law of the prophets. Nature, as well as the Bible, was God's poetry. In both cases the imagination expressed its findings through something concrete, a formula or a metaphor. In this vein, too, Coleridge calls Burke a seer or prophet because he could "see" the principles or ideals of human action and government and then put them to use in the context of a real and imperfect society.[24] This legislator was an unacknowledged poet of the world.

Relying on Gerard, Tetens uses the association of ideas but also goes beyond that principle because it is too limited in itself to account for real creativity. Tetens accepts the association of ideas as necessary but not sufficient for the *Dichtkraft* of genius. It is employed in the creation of new ideas and forms, but it alone cannot make them. The association of ideas enlarges the stock of images in the mind, which provide the poetic power with more material for shaping and fashioning. The association of ideas essentially offers multiple images or ideas, hooked together like cars in a train. *Dichtkraft* streamlines these images into unified wholes.[25]

By 1775 English and German thinkers shared several basic and crucial assumptions about genius and imagination. This is one reason Coleridge later found Schelling and Kant so congenial. It is not that these men were caught up in the gusts of an anonymous *Zeitgeist;* they were the moving spirit of the age themselves. In fact, Tetens touches on philosophic issues or polarities that Coleridge and Schelling were to relate more directly to the imagination. These issues have as their common focus a split (*Kluft*) between the human psyche and nature, a split which encouraged the "return to nature" and became one of the fundamental reasons for the very existence of Romanticism: Romanticism was to heal this gash. Tetens expresses the split in four ways: the mind and the world (nature), internal and external, the transcendent and the sensory, subjective and objective.[26] These polarities later become pairs of those very "contradictions" and "opposites" that, for Schelling and Coleridge, only the imagination, or art, can unify and thus join the soul of man to nature.[27]

Tetens enters the movement of thought like a subtle melody, one that swells, becomes rich, is repeated, and finally dominates other themes. He is at a crucial balancing point. Behind him stretches the legacy of seventeenth- and eighteenth-century rationalism, mechanistic science, and psychology. Ahead of him opens the vista of imagination: transcendentalism, organic sensibility, and a romantic, philosophic quest for the unity of soul and cosmos.

### KANT AND A NEW SYNTHESIS

Kant emerges from two prominent strains in mid-Enlightenment German thought, and his views on the imagination reflect an attempt to mediate between them. One strain descended from Leibniz, Wolff, and Baumgarten, the pupil of Wolff. It emphasized the inherently organic, dynamic sensibility of the mind and its harmonious understanding of the world. It had a moral dimension and explored the effects of ideas on belief and action. It included strong religious overtones. Shaftesbury, who appeared in German translations beginning in 1738, added further impetus to this general philosophical attitude, as did the increasing popularity of Spinoza. Later in the century, Friedrich Jacobi was a radical proponent of this web of ideas, which had a strong Platonic flavor and introduced Plotinus in earnest to German thought.

The second strain, to which Kant pays equal attention—at times stressing one more than the other, then reversing and urging on its "opposite," but always trying to fuse the two—is the empirical and associationist psychology and, on a slightly different plane, the science and mathematics of the late seventeenth and early eighteenth centuries. The principles of this more concrete and "scientific" school were set down in large part by Hobbes, Locke, Newton, Hume, and British empiricism in general. Certainty is derived from direct observation, or as in geometry and physics, the realities of time and space are cornerstones of knowledge. Although Tetens is an excellent example of the psychological and empirical infusion into German thought, he, like Kant, also expressed the belief that ideas, principles, values, and truths are built into the psyche and are not the exclusive product of experience.

Kant tried to combine the two general tides of thought more completely and fully than had Tetens or any other thinker of that period. Kant swam in a confluence of ideas that would have drowned most other men. At one time or another he tried to incorporate them all, and his attempts to leave nothing out show up in his varying interpretations of the imagination: empirical, psychological, *a priori*, rationally deductive, innate and intuitive, logical, geometrical, transcendental, synthetic, Newtonian, aesthetic, and idealistic.

Kant stands as the great repository for almost all eighteenth-century ideas of the imagination. This is the source of his seeming confusion and struggle with that topic throughout the entire body of his work. As his twentieth-century commentator H. J. de Vleeschauwer concludes, the problem of the imagination in Kant is "singularly complicated." It is an unstable part of his thought. Like a rare radioisotope, it sheds an eerie glow and seems to change its form into different elements. Kant's first reference to imagination is in the *Reflexionen*, published the same year as Johnson's *Dictionary* (1755), and he was still writing about the imagination when Schelling's *Transzendentalen Idealismus* appeared in 1800. During this forty-five year span Enlightenment ideas, owing in significant part to Kant, flowed together, jostled, and produced the volatile and powerful romantic trust in imagination.

In trying to reconcile the two streams of thought we have mentioned, Kant realized that he could not simply alternate his vantage point. He had to create a third concept of imagination that would synthesize the present views into a unified whole. There is an adage, started by Kant himself, that he could not help thinking "in threes." Indeed his formulation of the imaginative power falls into three stages, corresponding to the two major systems of thought with which he was grappling and a third system that strives to incorporate and harmonize the two. Also, he imposed a reconciliation within each of the two views of the imagination, for no one system or psychology is so monolithic that it does not have its own internal divisions that need to be connected.

Not only can we but we must talk about different concepts of imagination in Kant.* It is a versatile but baffling power, and he even resorts to it when he needs a solution that may contradict, or at least not coincide with, what he says about it elsewhere. Although his definition of the imagination cannot be neatly paraphrased, it is extraordinarily complete because, like a full dictionary entry, it is really a series of defini-

---

* For a deatiled but rather strangely organized study of the whole question of the imagination in Kant, see Hermann Mörchen, *Die Einbildungskraft bei Kant,* 2nd ed. (Tübingen, 1970).

tions and usages, some overlapping, others quite distinct, which together convey the meaning of the idea and echo the intellectual and philosophical milieu of the time.

In the first place, Kant recognizes an imaginative power based on direct sensory contact with reality. The basis of this power is empirical, and it depends on the association of ideas. It reproduces and connects sense experiences, building a comprehensive understanding of reality. Unfortunately, Kant does not clearly distinguish it from memory, but as a larger and more comprehensive power, it seems to include memory. This *reproductive* imagination works from particulars and phenomena in nature, "from the bottom up," until it organizes and relates all faculties of the mind by referring them directly to sensory experience. For Kant, this imaginative power is grounded in a subjective perception of the phenomenal world. Behind it lies the eighteenth-century tradition of empirical psychology, presented in Germany most completely by Tetens.[28] This view of imagination holds a prominent place in the first edition (1781) of the *Critique of Pure Reason*.

Almost immediately, however, Kant began to consider what he had sacrificed by relying heavily on the empirical approach. The idea of innate powers of understanding, or the *"sens interne"* of Leibniz, would have to be modified, if not wholly abandoned. And any case for objectivity based solely on empirical evidence was hard to make, as Hume had shown. Moreover, the seemingly indisputable truths of Newtonian mechanics and Euclidean geometry seemed ignored. Fragment B12 of the *Lose Blätter* (January 20, 1780) shows that there was an inner struggle in Kant's mind about the exact nature and place of both the "empirical" and the "transcendental" imaginations. By the second edition of the *Critique of Pure Reason*, published in 1787, Kant shifts ground on the imagination.* Although he does not delete all references to it as empirical and reproductive, he now stresses its transcendental or "pure" function. In other words, the imagination no longer takes as its yardstick the observed phenomena of nature as they are gathered piecemeal and fitted together. It takes instead certain logical principles, the *a priori* rules of time and space, as its first condition and from these produces an order which it imposes on experience itself. The transcendental imagination, as Kant had suggested in the first edition, produces an "objective affinity," which is "a necessary consequence of a synthesis in imagination, grounded *a priori* on rules."[29] The psychological bias of the "reproductive" imagination thus succumbs to a more "rigorous" and supposedly

---

* For discussion of the dual nature of the imagination in the *Kritik der reinen Vernunft*, see Norman Kemp Smith, *A Commentary to Kant's "Critique of Pure Reason,"* 2nd ed. (1923 [1918]), pp. 260–268, 337–338.

more objective approach. Kant gives the faculty of "judgment" new prominence. It helps to determine the order and value of experience. The categories provide an outline for the imposition of this order. The imaginative power of "pure" synthesis is thus a transcendental principle operating upon a phenomenal world.

This position continues to some degree in the *Critique of Judgment* where, in the introduction, Kant refers to imagination "as the faculty of intuitions *a priori.*" Relying on the power of "judgment," imagination works "from the top down" and mediates between established or postulated categories of understanding and actual sense experiences. This "productive imagination"—productive because it molds experience to its own power and preconceptions based on laws of geometry, logic, theoretical science, and reason—does not preclude the existence of a "reproductive" faculty, but it dominates that power. The productive imagination may, like the reproductive, use images to give a pattern to experience, but it also creates schema that do not exist in nature. In Kant's example of the experience of a quantity of five of anything, the reproductive imagination may picture these five things exactly as they appear separately, or it may represent them with an image thus: . . . . . But the productive imagination imposes an imaginative schema on the experience and develops a kind of shorthand for the things it perceives. It creates a numeral, such as "5," which bears no empirical resemblance to its meaning but which is clearly understood. Language and, even more, the printed word are a complicated interweaving of schema. The educated mind becomes habituated to these schema, uses and responds to them without thinking:

> The schema is in itself always a product of imagination. Since, however, the synthesis of imagination aims at no one intuition, but only at unity in the determination of sensibility, the schema has to be distinguished from the image (*Bild*). If I place five points one after another . . . I have an image of the number five. But if I think only of a number in general, whether it be five or a hundred, this thought is more the idea of a method whereby a multiplicity (for instance, a thousand) may be represented in an image in conformity with a certain concept than it is the image itself. For with a number such as a thousand the image can hardly be seen at once and compared with the concept. This idea of a universal procedure of imagination in providing an image for a concept, I call the schema of this concept.[30]

Actually, Leibniz had said much the same thing in the *Nouveaux essais*, where he distinguishes between idea and image rather than between image and schema, but his point is essentially the same and the example he uses seems to have stuck in Kant's mind. Leibniz had noted that we have an idea of a thousand-sided polygon but can form no accurate image of it in our heads. We need a formula (Kant's schema) to represent the angles and sides of this, or any, polygon, and it is from this formula that we can construct an image of the polygon and understand it.

Kant, however, proceeds to a more general statement about the productive imagination. In its transcendental activity, he says, "We ourselves . . . introduce into appearances that order and regularity which we name nature." The productive imagination serves as a partner to "formal intuition," the mind's ability to apprehend ideas or patterns that explain experience, transfer it to a code, like mathematics or language, and give it order. Imagination creates schema that permit formal intuition to affect and become connected with the infinite particulars of the sensory world. The Pythagorean School would be an example of prizing a kind of "formal intuition."

The productive imagination links the universality of formal intuition to the concrete actuality of what is experienced. Without its language and its ability to communicate, the mind's power for analysis and ordering, called "reason," would remain latent, abstract, and out of contact with the material world.

But if the second edition of the first *Critique* swerves away from an empirical bias, Kant recognizes that, in order to satisfy the inescapable facts of empiricism, the imagination cannot impose *all* order on experience, like a cookie mold cutting a sheet of dough. Thus, Kant works toward a concept of imagination that will synthesize the two strains of thought, empirical and transcendental—strains that Schelling would say are nothing less than the "real" and the "ideal" worlds. Kant's imaginative power will not be a harmony or combination of other powers but something *sui generis,* an independent power, a *"tertium medium,"** making possible a synthesis of the dialectic he was facing.

This desire for a grand synthesis by the imagination, enlarging and fusing its powers to incorporate the real and the ideal, the empirical and the transcendental, moves forward tentatively and suggestively. Sometimes it results in contradictions, as when Kant speaks of the "empirical faculty of the productive imagination" or refers to the transcendental imagination as both productive and reproductive. Whether it starts from *a priori* transcendental principles or from empirical observations, the imagination is always heading in the other direction, always trying to bridge the gap between the two. But however Kant uses it, it is everywhere an instrument for unity within the powers of the mind and also for unity of the mind with external reality.

One central problem for Kant was to show that the two strains of the

---

* Coleridge's *"tertium aliquid"* in the *Biographia Literaria* (ch. 13) presents a similar idea, following the premises of Kant, Fichte, and Schelling.

imagination actually do converge. It is on this postulate, or even this hope, that the overall unity of Kant's work depends. The search is essentially for a pre-established harmony, where objective truth and subjective perceptions become one. This is the hope that Fichte and Schelling took up, Fichte from the subjective side of the "ego," and Schelling (after having first followed Fichte) from the ideal or transcendental side. Their extension of Kant's implications about an overall unity of the imagination led Coleridge to say that these two men were, especially on the subject of imagination, "completing" Kant and carrying his work to its conclusion.

For Kant, the unity that Leibniz had assumed to be true was extremely hard to prove. We can compare it to the building of a long tunnel through a granite mountain. From the side of the categories and the postulated *Ding-an-Sich*, the side of formal intuition, the transcendental and *a priori* rules of time and space, the productive imagination starts to head into the mountain, destined to reach the other side of phenomena and experience. Meanwhile, from the empirical side, the reproductive imagination sets out in the opposite direction, struggling to cut through to the goal of understanding. The question is whether or not the two tunnels will meet precisely and form one perfect tunnel, which guarantees an objective understanding of reality. Or will the two miss in the middle, run askew, or hit each other at an angle?

At times Kant suggests that the imagination, in its most comprehensive sense, can actually coordinate the efforts of these two attempts. Not only is it a part of each one in its subsidiary roles of "productive" and "reproductive," but it also hovers over the whole and directs the two to become one. It is the key and pivotal power to understanding the mind, nature, and the mind's understanding of nature. But it is nearly impossible to demonstrate such a thorough and unified activity of the imagination, a proof which empiricism demands but which Kant could not show so easily as the conditions of time and space. Thus Kant wavers, saying in one place that the synthesis of the imagination depends on the conditions of experience in time and space, but elsewhere clinging to the idea that even the conditions of experience in time and space, and hence the categories, are themselves founded on an overall synthesis of mind and nature that is performed by the imagination.

### UNANSWERED QUESTIONS

With Kant, the stage was set in Germany for the entrance of the romantic faith in the imagination, for he suggests that this "blind power, hidden in the depths of the soul," affords the most satisfactory answer to the puzzle of man's relationship to nature and his ability to experience and react to nature as one unified being. The development of Kant's concepts of the imagination has been commented on extensively, and we should highlight this metamorphosis here. It is a drama of effort and uncertainty, in which Kant wrestled with ideas that seemed too contradictory to reconcile and too important to deny.[31] His first reference to the imagination involves an early connection of the categories to faculty psychology in *Reflexionen* (1755). Imagination is paired with "possibility." The 1770 *Dissertatio* essentially makes nothing of the imagination, and neither does the 1775 *Duisburg'sche Nachlass*. After reading Tetens (on May 17, 1779, Hamann wrote to Herder that Kant had Tetens always before his eyes, and Kant himself mentioned the use of Tetens), Kant gives the imagination a distinctly empirical and psychological flavor in the first edition of the *Critique of Pure Reason*, which was altered in the second edition, although retaining a residue of the statements of 1781.

The alterations Kant was making in his concepts of the imagination are complicated (or enriched, depending on one's view) by the number of terms he employs for ideas which might all be translated with the single word "imagination." *Einbildungskraft, Phantasie, Grundvermögen der Seele*, and *Perceptionsvermögen* indicate the debate not only about the nature of the imagination but about what term should be established in order to gain a common acceptance and agreement about "the imagination." As Coleridge would note in the marginalia in his copy of Maass's *Versuch über die Einbildungskraft:* "The word Vorstellung has been as often mischievous as useful in German Philosophy."

In his struggle to chart an accurate map of this bewildering territory, Kant takes up the broad question of the psychological mechanism that directs the imagination. What initiates and guides its power? Is it the will—and, if so, what exactly is the will? Imagination might be a conscious power or a "blind power hidden in the depths of the soul, of whose operation we are hardly ever aware."[32] Is it something spontaneous, and to what degree does it mix passive response with active creation?

Kant does not answer these questions with definite conviction. An aura of mystery surrounds his attempts at either psychological or logical precision. Yet dealing with the imagination, Kant realizes that he faces a complex power. Just as the nervous system involves an intermingling of chemistry, electricity, conscious control, and involuntary reaction, so the imagination itself seems to be the organic union of separate parts whose intimacy in working together makes them almost impossible to distinguish.

This uncertainty and complexity about the triggering, force, direction, and processes of the imagination had great repercussions for romantic notions about the ways in which art is produced and the artist creates. For as imagination became more identified with artistic power, genius, and originality, understanding its operation meant getting at the core of the creative process and the psychology of genius. In asking how the imagination functions, Kant was really inquiring about what permits art, even great art, and what kind of mind produces all that we consider creative and original.

Kant, like Tetens, was attracted to Gerard. There had been a great deal of confusion and debate, Kant indicates, about the nature of genius, but one source offered clear and solid observations that had not been surpassed: "Gerard, an Englishman, has written about genius and his views on it are the best, even though the subject is treated by other writers as well."[33] In a very important way, Kant's reading of Gerard catalyzed his own thoughts about imagination and genius and about the nature of the productive and reproductive imaginations, including the role of the will in imagination. A passage that deals with all these complex and interrelated topics appears in Kant's *Menschenkunde oder philosophische Anthropologie*. Kant ascribes to Gerard the observation that genius is built primarily on "productive imagination." Kant maintains that genius therefore relies on this productive power, which is its particular hallmark, but must also have a fruitful imagination in general to supply its productive power with the materials from which it selects:

> Gerard ... says the most significant characteristic of genius is the productive imagination; for genius is most of all to be differentiated from the spirit of slavish imitation, so that one believes this spirit to be the most unfit to approach the condition of genius. Genius thus grounds itself not on the reproductive imagination but on the productive, and an imagination fruitful in providing images and representations gives to genius a great deal of material from which to choose.

The productive imagination of the genius, for Kant as for Gerard, creates something new and self-sufficient rather than copying or making a mechanical imitation of something that already exists.

Kant then divides the productive imagination into two stages. One of these, he says, is a willfully productive capacity, which is raised to the level of design and exists in accordance with some discretionary consideration or desired end. The other stage of the productive power is *"Phantasie,"* which is not connected to a willed purpose. Many writers, he adds, confuse *Phantasie* with the more willed and discretionary imagination. All these points he puts briefly:

> This productive power is divided into the willed and the unwilled imagination. The willed imagination consists in the fact that one can exercise

the activity of imagination with discretion, let images well up and disappear, and shape them according to one's desire. The unwilled imagination is called fancy (*Phantasie*), and although many writers have indeed confused the two, common usage already gives occasion to differentiate them.[34]

Kant—like Wolff, Gerard, Sulzer, and Tetens before him, and like Schelling and Coleridge after him—is employing his own vocabulary and defining words as he goes in order to clarify as many aspects of the imagination as possible. In this case, he is dealing with the creative imagination, its productive capacity, and the role of both the will and an unwilled "fancy." By *"willkührlich,"* Kant clearly means discretionary, aimed at some end, and not arbitrary or random. The term carries much the same weight as Coleridge's phrase "co-existing with the conscious will," used in the definition of the secondary imagination. But Kant, like Coleridge, understandably confuses his case. He uses the word *"Imagination"* (not uncommon in German of that time—Schelling also uses it), with the result that fancy (*"Phantasie"*) in this passage becomes a part of the productive imagination. Kant does not even employ the rather common terms found in Tetens and Sulzer, *Dichtungskraft* and *Dichtkraft*.

Thus Gerard, Tetens, Sulzer, Kant, Schelling, and Coleridge were talking about the same or similar concepts, and each man was trying to establish a common vocabulary and accepted definitions, or connotations, for these concepts. Some, like Kant and Coleridge, saw more facets and questions than others. Therefore, their analyses and discussions are harder to follow and run more risk of being self-contradictory. Sometimes these thinkers are writing exclusively about the fine arts, sometimes about philosophic thought, and sometimes about psychology. And the remarks of each individual are often spread over many years. It is not that the concept of the imagination taken in all its possible meanings breaks down under this strain; rather, the one poor word "imagination" cannot always imply the intended meaning each time it is used.

In the end, too, we must realize our tendency to look at remarks on the imagination for a clarifying and simplifying statement. We find dead-ends, labyrinths, and mazes. The vocabulary becomes unsteady, the definitions weak and unstable. But there is also a bright side to this situation. If nothing else, the confusion and the struggles of the best thinkers and writers of the Enlightenment and the Romantic period indicate what a powerful, complex, and subtle force the imagination is. It would be disastrous to conclude that Tetens or Coleridge is the real authority on the imagination, or that any writer received his thoughts about the imagination ready-made from the law of association and his own memory. And although the remarks of all these individuals on the subject of the imagination are frequently complicated and various, and amassed from many different sources and readings, so are modern ones. Like different ships on the ocean, these writers traversed the same waters, but when each one read his own position, it was rarely on the exact spot that anyone had passed before or would do so again, including himself. Yet only in this manner could the whole potential of the imagination be explored and put to use.

While neither the *Critique of Practical Reason* (1788) nor the *Prolegomena* (1781–1785) adds significantly to the groundwork and investigations contained in the two editions of the *Critique of Pure Reason*, both the *Critique of Judgment* (1790) and the *Opus posthumum* unfold more facets of the imagination, and these are closely allied with art and aesthetics. The imagination remains fundamentally productive but now operates more with reference to aesthetic sensibility. In rough terms, the premise is becoming one more of taste and feeling than of logic. However, Kant shows no deep interest in the emotive or passionate side of imagination. It is something cool and collected. Harmonized with reason and judgment, imagination determines or at least recognizes aesthetic values such as beauty. Kant does not, though, place moral values strictly within the purview of imagination. The deduction of the categories and "formal intuition" drop out of the picture. The intellectual side of the imagination is still foremost—indeed in Kant it is never wholly absent, even in the empirically reproductive imagination—but now this intellectual side seeks aesthetic appreciation of the phenomenal world. Schema of understanding give way to the taste and values we associate with art.

Kant in no way camouflages the fact that with the *Critique of Judgment* he is turning the imagination to a new consideration, one that is aesthetic and subjective. The imagination, having put on new robes, assumes an importance equal to its place in the first *Critique*. Kant is specific about the centrality and unique characteristics of the imagination when it is involved in aesthetic judgments. He makes his position clear at the outset of the *Critique of Judgment*:

> If we wish to discern whether anything is beautiful or not, we do not refer the representation of it to the Object by means of understanding with a view to cognition, but by means of the imagination (acting perhaps in conjunction with understanding) we refer the representation to the Subject and its feeling of pleasure or displeasure. The judgement of taste, therefore, is not a cognitive judgement, and so not logical, but is aesthetic—which means that it is one whose determining ground *cannot be other than subjective.*[35]

Kant discusses the "free play" of the imagination in aesthetics and in poetry, an idea that Schiller was to expand into a short theory of the arts, where the instinct for form and the instinct for free play work together. The imagination, explains Kant, enjoys "free play" in poetry, and nature sustains this free play in its own activities, as in the changing shapes of a fire or the ripplings of a brook. These things attract our attention because they are really engaging our imagination. On a broader front, Kant's remarks about imaginative free play in the *Critique of Judgment* have profound implications. Whatever in nature is in process, in the act of moving, changing, evolving to another state, transforming and metamorphosing, whatever undergoes any kind of sea-change, draws the eye of the imaginative power to it. And then the imagination, as it produces poetry or art, not only imitates the object it sees but imitates the actual process of change, the force behind the change and the full context of it. Imagination captures the life and the activity of the world, not just its seemingly static forms or its sensory and material shell. So the cataract at Lodore will always be something less than Alph the sacred river.

The *Opus posthumum* suggests that Kant's desires and intentions, like those of many other seventeenth-century and Enlightenment thinkers, are ultimately involved with the attributes of God and with the art or mystery of creation. The work indicates one strong current of German philosophy for at least the next generation, a current into which both Fichte and Schelling plunged. In its suggestivity it marks the transition between the philosophy of the Enlightenment and that of high Romanticism. In the *Opus,* Kant makes the human imagination the condition of the constitution of space. God, the original creator and hence the original condition of all things, becomes *"eine Dichtung,"* a prototype of art. Kant also speaks of *"dichtende Vernunft,"* a "composing (or poetizing) reason," that is, an active and transforming reason, a power that essentially creates through and is brought to life by a productive power, *Dichtkraft*—the imagination.

The idea of God as an artistic creator complements the notions of genius, art, and imagination already presented in the *Critique of Judgment.* There, drawing on the increasing fascination with genius and original creation, Kant had added another hue to the spectrum of imagination. Imagination is the one original and creative faculty. The reproductive capacity of the imagination is not discarded but is now made to serve this productive power. The artist's productive power turns aesthetic ideas into sensible objects. Art is the expression of aesthetic ideas, and the artistic genius possesses these ideas along with an extraordinary imagination to transform them into matter, color, sound, shape, and texture. The artist has a third attribute, *Geist,* which in a cryptic but intriguing sentence Kant closely allies with the imagination: "Spirit is the principle of animation, of upward movement—of talent, of the soul's powers—through ideas; and therefore it is the principle of a purposeful, animated imagination."[36] This spirit, which recalls Leibniz's *"esprit,"* links the idea with the real and the objective with the subjective. Art fulfills the requirements for the meeting of the empirical and transcendental, the productive and reproductive. Kant verges on proclaiming for the fine arts, the arts of genius, a supreme philosophical value.

It was becoming necessary for art and the imagination to be viewed not as the reflex of philosophical truth and reason but as their source and purest means of expression. Carrying these ideas further and stressing their idealistic bias, Schelling developed his *Philosophie der Kunst*, one of the great high-Romantic theories concerning art, philosophy, and their mutual reliance on the imagination. In Germany, after Kant, there could be no more significant thinkers of the Enlightenment. The tide of Romanticism was rushing inevitably forward.

## PART FOUR

# Faith in the Imagination

# 11

# THE PSYCHE REACHES OUT:
# SYMPATHY

*O*ne of the major themes of mid and late eighteenth-century thought, both moral and aesthetic, is the power of sympathy. It becomes especially important for English Romanticism. Coleridge, Wordsworth, Hazlitt, and Keats all share this legacy. Sympathy forms the cornerstone of Hazlitt's writing on both moral thought and the arts in general. The idea of sympathy—how the individual feels for other people and approaches the world at large, how he identifies with others or even with inanimate nature—had become intimately connected with the idea of the imagination.[1] Adam Smith put the case succinctly in his *Theory of Moral Sentiments* (1759) when he said that sympathy, which for Smith constitutes the whole of man's moral sense, relies completely on the imagination. As we approach Hazlitt and the Romantics, we are confronting the culmination of a century of thought. Hazlitt returns time and again to the wellsprings of Hobbes, Butler, Locke, Shaftesbury, and the associationists, particularly Tucker and Priestley. For the fundamental premise of Hazlitt, which struck him as a young man, is that the imagination governs both our relationships with other people and our understanding of the natural world. In Hazlitt we see the grand combination of sympathy and imagination in morality, in associationism, and in a ready aesthetic sensibility that has both empirical and intuitional sides.

The idea of sympathy began to attain importance early in the century. Shaftesbury had said, "All things sympathize." On a high philosophical plane, sympathy could be considered the cohesive force behind an organic view of the universe. Yet on a more manageable scale, sympathy also becomes that special power of the imagination which permits the self to escape its own confines, to identify with other people, to per-

143

ceive things in a new way, and to develop an aesthetic appreciation of the world that coalesces both the subjective self and the objective other. Yet as Hazlitt would point out, abstraction, though necessary, is dangerous by itself. We turn to the specific, for it is the particular and the individual that engage the imagination, embodying its creative power, and which eventually lead the whole mind to an understanding of things as they relate to each other. "We can conceive nothing clearly in the abstract," maintains Hugh Blair in his *Lectures on Rhetoric and Belles Lettres* (1783); "all distinct ideas are formed upon particulars."[2] Earlier in 1776, George Campbell's *Philosophy of Rhetoric* compared the remark in Luke (12.27), "Consider the lilies how they grow," with a revised version in which all particular words are generalized: "Consider the flowers, how they gradually increase in their size."[3]

### SYMPATHY IN ITS FUNDAMENTAL FORM: HUTCHESON AND ARBUCKLE, COOPER AND CAMPBELL

The interest in sympathy, which by the middle of the century was becoming strongly linked to the concept of the imagination, emerged as a by-product of the Enlightenment debate about the moral nature of man. The contention of Hobbes that man is basically selfish seemed so convincing, given his premises, that no one could forget it. One writer after another, starting with Richard Cumberland in his *De Legibus Naturae* (1672), tried to answer Hobbes. Religious apologists could waive Hobbes's assumptions, but that would not satisfy those impressed by the new science and the new psychology.

For many, Shaftesbury offered a viable alternative in his argument on behalf of the "inner sense" or the "moral sense." He developed the major point of Cumberland: men's social affections are just as "natural" as those impulses and appetites that Hobbes calls "selfish." We have a capacity, as open to cultivation as any other, to recognize moral virtue and to prefer it for its own sake. More subtle was the argument of Bishop Joseph Butler in his *Sermons* (1726). He sides with Shaftesbury in asserting that social affections are as natural as self-preservation, but he also resurrects the Stoic argument that "pleasure" is not necessarily the first aim of our desires or appetites. Our desires have an object, and "pleasure" comes only as a result of attaining that object. We get pleasure because we want a thing for its own sake, not because an inner hedonistic drive tells us that we shall feel "pleasure" by securing it. The distinction is crucial and was to be incorporated as an essential premise in Hazlitt's manifesto on behalf of the sympathetic imagination, his *Essay on the Principles of Human Action* (1805).

By the 1720s and 1730s the argument against Hobbes was taken further onto Hobbes's own ground. Shaftesbury and his followers, the "benevolists," were joined by psychologists and associationists who showed how an empirical outlook could reveal a powerful, sympathetic, and tender side of human nature. Francis Hutcheson and James Arbuckle dwelt on man's innately sympathetic moral nature, yet they also emphasized how this sympathetic nature could be deduced from experience, from an empirical awareness of human behavior and society. Arbuckle connected the idea of sympathy directly to the imagination. Hutcheson, in his *Inquiry into the Original of Our Ideas of Beauty and Virtue* (1725), separates what Shaftesbury had called the "moral sense" from the "sense of beauty" and argues that man has a natural tendency toward the good. Hutcheson's book is better known than the work of Arbuckle, yet Arbuckle first combined the general notion of aesthetics with two other elements, Addison's "pleasures of the imagination" and Arbuckle's astonishingly original thought that the imagination is responsible not only for artistic and aesthetic pleasure but also for the ability to put oneself in the place of others. Arbuckle made this observation at least thirty years in advance of Adam Smith's and Burke's comments about sympathy and imagination.

In his *Collection of Letters and Essays* (1728, first published as *Hibernicus's Letters* in 1722), Arbuckle speaks of the imagination as "divinely implanted" to act as a moral faculty. Social affection, benevolence, the Golden Rule—all would be impossible if we were unable to sympathize with others and feel as they do. "Hence," says Arbuckle, "we may see the Wisdom of our Creator in giving us this Imaginging Faculty." It is possible that Burke, growing up in Dublin where *Hibernicus's Letters* had been published, read them as a student. At any rate, tucked away in Arbuckle's essays is a strong and direct connection between imagination and the power of sympathy.

Imagination, for Arbuckle, has a free play that can turn anywhere and permits us to feel for others. Yet this free play is also that very quality of the imagination responsible for some of its most delightful artistic compositions. Arbuckle calls this free play of the imagination "Castle-building." It is another way that the imagination makes it possible for a person to escape from the husk of a subjective ego. Thomas Reid later suggested that Addison was the first to call this play of the imagination *"castle building,"* although Sidney says in his *Apology:* "wholly imaginative, as we are wont to say by them that build castles in the air." In this act the imagination, continues Reid (writing late in the century), combines not only creative power but "judgment, taste, moral sentiment, as well as the passions and affections."[4]

Archibald Campbell and John Gilbert Cooper either picked up the idea of sympathy and imagination from Arbuckle or developed it on their own. The connection between the imagination and sympathy was, before 1750, already established, but it was not common. Campbell, in his *Enquiry into the Original of Moral Virtue* (1734), proposes that sympathy is a kind of imaginative substitution or identification. And Cooper, whom Edmond Malone called the "last of the *benevolists*," speaks of the "sympathizing Warmth of . . . Imagination."[5]

The title of the book in which Cooper makes this remark, *Letters Concerning Taste* (3rd. ed., 1757), rightly suggests that the moral and sympathetic nature of the imagination was rarely separated from aesthetic concerns. In fact, the power to sympathize and to identify with someone or with something was already viewed as a highly valuable part of the poet's free play of imagination. Shaftesbury had praised the poet as one who grasps "the inward form and structure of his fellow creature" and is himself "no certain man, nor has any certain or genuine character." The poet is "annihilated" by throwing himself into the object or the person he imitates, and thus the poet's own subjective nature is absorbed into the objective world, creating a poem or work of art that captures the fullest possible human perception of nature and of other individuals. As Pope had praised Homer for his imaginative invention and for the fire of his enthusiasm, Shaftesbury praises Homer as "the great mimographer": "He describes no qualities or virtues; censures no manners; makes no encomiums . . . 'Tis the characters who show themselves. 'Tis they who speak in such a manner as distinguishes them in all things from all others, and makes them ever like themselves . . . The poet . . . makes hardly any figure at all, and is scarce discoverable in his poem." This sympathetic power of the poet also gives him the ability to suggest characters or qualities of things with great economy and accuracy. Sympathy makes us more open to suggestions, and more able to make them. For the poet, remarks Shaftesbury, "A few words let fall on any slight occasion, from any of the parties he introduces, are sufficient to denote their manners and distinct character. From a finger or toe he can represent . . . the frame and fashion of a whole body."[6]

These maxims of Shaftesbury are similar to those of Keats more than a century later. Keats even uses Shaftesbury's word "annihilated" to express the submergence of the poet's own character in his material. The connection with Keats is natural, since Keats was relying to a great extent on Hazlitt, who inherited the eighteenth-century tradition of sympathy in both its moral and its critical aspects. Keats also uses the image of a chameleon to describe the ideal poetical character, a usage probably suggested by Hazlitt himself. Perhaps Hazlitt, or less likely Keats, had read Zachary Mayne's *Two Dissertations Concerning Sense and the Imagination* (1728), which makes a general case for the imagination in its capacity to sympathize with or to become like what surrounds it. Mayne couches this general observation in a specific image: the imagination is "like the Cameleon, of which Creature it is reported that it changes its Hue according to the Colour of the Place where it happens to be."[7]

## HUME AND BURKE

Unwilling to assign our propensity for sympathy to a simple cause, Hume shrewdly analyzes the various psychological reasons for the sympathetic impulse. At the root of all these reasons is the imagination, but for Hume, the imagination is a faculty too pervasive and general to rely upon for a detailed explanation. He turns instead to specific examples, which reveal complex motives. In the *Treatise on Human Nature* (1739), he remarks that "We naturally sympathize with others in the sentiments they entertain of us." Our self-esteem is at stake, so our interest is heightened. With a wry twist Hume ventures the case of a man with stinking breath who is always concerned with or "sympathizing" with what others think of him and with the way he is offending their senses. Also, says Hume, it is of course other people that most resemble our own selves in their desires and passions and so they have "an advantage above any other object, in operating on the imagination."[8] But our natural interest in others, our gregariousness, is not always sympathetic. When examined closely, sympathy is likely to turn out to be nothing more than a contagion or infection of feeling. This kind of experience—indeed all sympathy—only repeats our own original feelings and whips them into a state of excitement. As both Hume and Johnson noted repeatedly, strong feelings, of whatever kind, are more likely to engage the mind and to give pleasure than weak feelings. A great deal of what passes for "sympathy" is merely intensity of feeling.

Hume's sharp and ambivalent attitude toward sympathy comes out, too, in the way he criticizes the notion of sympathetic identification. For one thing, the force of envy and the tendency to revert to our own concerns permit only a short lease of time to any real identification: "No force of imagination can convert us into another person, and make us fancy that we, being that person, reap benefit from those valuable qualities which belong to him." We have difficulty in identifying, in a sympathetic way, with the better side of someone else, especially if it is a side better than our own best. And if we do make such a sympathetic identification, it soon vanishes. Hume concludes that "no celerity of imagination could immediately transport us back into ourselves and make us love and esteem the person."[9] We cannot be two people at once, nor another person for long.

Yet in the midst of this brilliant and tart psychological penetration, Hume never denies the power and the natural inclination of sympathy. He simply wants to examine certain motives and show the complexities involved. If one "faculty" had to be chosen as responsible for the ability to sympathize, it would, for Hume, be the imagination. He, like many others, Burke among them, also stresses that within our sympathetic power the same principle operates in considerations of aesthetics as in judgments of morality.

On both the aesthetic and moral planes, however, Burke is more ready than Hume to speak of an unqualified "force of natural sympathy." Writing in the *Enquiry* (1756), Burke devotes a whole section to "Sympathy, Imitation, Ambition." He says that in observing others, "we are moved as they are moved," and our "sympathy must be considered as a sort of substitution." Burke offers two curious examples. Jacob Spon's *Recherches d'antiquités* (1683) mentions the bizzare case of the philosopher Tomasso Campanella (1568–1639), who got inside people by imitating their every gesture in face and body "and then carefully observed what turn of mind he seemed to acquire by this change." Thus sympathy often relies heavily on the relationship between mind and body, a lesson later allegorized to an extreme in *Dr. Jekyll and Mr. Hyde*. Burke's second example is of Blacklock, the blind poet who, like Helen Keller, used a kind of sympathy to grasp the essence of things and could "describe visual objects with more spirit and justness" than many endowed with perfect sight.[10]

Burke in general follows the lead of Addison that it is the imagination, with its ability to arouse passions and feelings and with its openness to the suggestions of words, that naturally forms the basis of all imitations. But then Burke calls attention to the "affecting arts," those that engage us completely in their subject. This form of imitation relies on sympathy, which thus appears as a certain kind of imagination—imagination capturing the full nature of a thing or person in all its emotional and associational involvements. Poetry, which does not describe to the senses but engages the imagination of the hearer, has as its business "to affect rather by sympathy than imitation; to display rather the effect of things on the mind of the speaker, or of others, than to present a clear idea of things themselves." So often, says Burke, "We yield to sympathy, what we refuse to description."[11] If, as Keats was to say, the poet has a "design" upon us or is too well-schooled in verisimilitude, our interest is not immediately caught.

Burke's analysis is somewhat confused, understandable in the larger context of the *Enquiry* and forgivable at the age he wrote the book. Yet he stands, next to Hume and Smith, as one of those figures who generated intense speculation and interest about sympathy and its connection with the imagination. The popularity of the *Enquiry* alone assured a large audience for Burke's hazy but suggestive remarks about imaginative sympathy. Burke, Smith, and Hume each admired the work of the others on sympathy. They kept an open mind on the subject because they realized its complexity, and in the approach of the others each could see an important new consideration.

In the years immediately preceding the appearance of Smith's *Theory of Moral Sentiments* (1759), a landmark in mid-century writings on sympathy and the imagination, there was an increasing interest in the subject. Several books discussed sympathy. These do not necessarily mention the imagination, and most deal with morality rather than poetic theory, but they all indicate the interest in what was thought to be an essential but little-understood part of human nature. In 1753 James Balfour's *A Delineation of the Nature and Obligation of Morality* appeared, followed the next year by two works that also illustrate the rise of sympathy, David Fordyce's *Elements of Moral Philosophy* and James Burgh's *The Dignity of Human Nature*. Thirty years after his first influential book, Hutcheson published *A System of Moral Philosophy* (1755), which mentions sympathy as a permanent quality in man's nature.[12] Thomas Nettleton's *Treatise on Virtue and Happiness* was, by 1754, entering its fifth edition. In two chapters titled "Of Sympathy and Social Affection" and "Of the Moral Sense," Nettleton contends that our moral sense is directed primarily to an abstract idea of beauty and good, whereas it is sympathy that aids in the actual practice and application of the moral sense to everyday situations.

The idea of imaginative sympathy struck home even to Johnson, usually wary of the imagination as a guide. In *Rambler* 60 (October 13, 1750), he makes a sweeping assertion: "All joy or sorrow for the happiness or calamities of others is produced by an act of the imagination, that realizes the event . . . by placing us, for a time, in the condition of him whose fortune we contemplate; so that we feel . . . whatever emotions would be excited by the same good or evil happening to ourselves."

### SMITH'S FORMULA

Adam Smith's *Theory of Moral Sentiments* (1759) opened the floodgate to a rising tide of interest in the sympathetic imagination. His book became hugely influential. Many authors, among them Hazlitt,

Thomas Brown, and Shelley, built their arguments with an eye to his. The educated world discussed him in everyday conversation. He had written an encompassing book, and the first few pages clearly stated its premise: sympathy is the basis of all moral thought and action, and the sole agency by which this sympathetic feeling operates is the imagination.

In addition to Smith's psychological acumen, his premise had a broad foundation. It implied so much. The mind has an innate power of sympathy. Interest in others often overrides our selfish impulses and, what is more, gives pleasure to ourselves. As it prompts actions that alleviate the sorrows of others, it also increases our own joy. But we do not do good in order to feel good; we do so because it falls within our *instinctive* power:

> Though our brother is upon he rack . . . it is by the imagination only that we can form any conception of what are his sensations. Neither can that faculty help us to this any other way, than by representing to us what would be our own, if we were in his case. It is the impressions of our own sense only, not those of his, which our imaginations copy. By the imagination we place ourselves in his situation . . . we enter as it were into his body, and become in some measure the same person with him.[13]

The imagination heightens and vivifies our awareness of another's feelings until those feelings dawn into reality for us and we feel them just as intensely as he does—perhaps more so.

Consider, says Smith, the case of a madman who unwittingly strolls near a cliff. Our alarm exceeds his fear. Or the subject of our apprehension may be beyond help, or not even want our help, yet we still feel what he feels and react with sympathy. "The mob, when they are gazing at a dancer on the slack rope, naturally writhe and twist and balance their own bodies . . . as they feel that they themselves must do if in his situation."[14] The more accurately and completely our imagination reproduces the circumstances of another in our mind, the more readily the feeling of sympathy is excited. Imagination, therefore, encourages us to know a situation, to ascertain events surrounding a person, and even to learn the character and passions of the person who is the object of sympathy.

The art of biography depends on a sympathetic imagination. It is no coincidence that the remark of Johnson quoted above is in the *Rambler* issue that centers on problems and advantages of biography. We escape the monotony and confinement of our own lives. The same kind of escape also occurs, says Smith, when we discover that another person has sympathized with us. That awareness binds us to him in a process of reciprocation and pleasure. We are more than flattered; we are moved—

and being moved incites us to follow our own imaginative power to a reciprocal sympathy.

In Smith, sympathy and imagination are not synonymous. The imaginative act of recreating, in our own mind and emotions, what another person feels must precede the actual exercise of sympathy. The moral and social result of fellow-feeling is predicated upon an initial working of the imagination. The imagination changes how we feel and what we sense. This transformation generates, or taps, that sense of concern and interest leading us to act for the sake of others. Smith's simple and forceful premise darted down like a shaft of sunlight in a century that, since Hobbes, had been darkened with moral systems based on self-interest. The imagination, already accepted as a vital and innate faculty, now became absolutely indispensable to the exercise of man's basic social and moral instinct, his "fellow-feeling" or sympathy.

### SYMPATHY IN *MIMESIS*

After 1760, Smith and Hume provided a nucleus around which moral philosophers, especially other Scots like Reid, Stewart, Hutton, and Brown, clustered in their discussions of imagination and sympathy. The effects of Smith and Hume percolated down through the early nineteenth century. For instance, in 1790 Archibald Alison regarded Smith's *Moral Sentiments* as "the most eloquent work on the subject . . . that Modern Europe has produced."[15] Literary critics, the associationists in particular, also shifted to the idea of sympathy and included it in their analyses of genius and the poetical character. Burke and Shaftesbury had earlier urged sympathy as a trait in developing the greatest mimetic power. The poet does not speak for himself but gives each character or scene an articulate tongue of its own to break the sable chain and dumb enchantment. Now, starting in the 1760s and 1770s, the poet's sympathetic power began to be seen as an adjunct of his imagination, and critical thinking increasingly explored this relationship. Saturating this approach was the example of Shakespeare. Immensely popular, Shakespeare seeemed to fit perfectly the ideal of a writer blessed with sympathetic imagination and the ability to identify completely with his own creations. When critics wanted to exemplify how a poet's sympathy could reveal a character or capture the essence of an object, they turned repeatedly to Shakespeare. This tendency became one of the more pronounced interests of romantic criticism.

James Beattie crisply summed up the attitude of many writers when in 1778 he said that "the philosophy of Sympathy ought always to form a part of the science of Criticism."[16] Critics began to connect imaginative sympathy with the process of imitation. Dugald Stewart, in lectures delivered during the 1790s, ventured the opinion that sympathetic imagination facilitates a kind of imitation desirable above all others. The artist does not trace the superficial and obvious but moves within his characters and scenes so that they seem to be illuminated from the inside out, glowing in their entirety, in the way that designs on a jack-o-lantern leap out into a kind of three-dimensionality when a candle is placed in the hollow center. In his *Essay on the Dramatic Character of Sir John Falstaff* (1777), Maurice Morgann echoes Shaftesbury when he says, "Every man . . . has two characters; that is, every man may be seen externally, and from without;—or a section may be made of him, and he may be illuminated from *within*."[17] Sympathetic imagination permits the artist to present the whole world as it is transformed and viewed from the standpoint of the one character or object he is imitating. The poet gives witness to the world as it is experienced through the medium of another person or point of view.

Gerard points out that the ability to sympathize with a person or with a situation depends on the extent to which the imagination captures and traces the flow of associations that occur in the person's mind and feelings, and how well the imagination follows the chain of effects that one passion produces as it amalgamates and directs the particular thoughts and associations of that other individual. In his *Essay on Taste* (1759), Gerard remarks that the imagination possesses a force of sympathy that "enlivens our *ideas* of the passions infused by it to such a pitch, as in a manner converts them to the passions themselves." Suddenly we are not thinking about what a character thinks, but feeling as he feels. We are enmeshed in his associations and passions with their particular objects, which are highly individualistic. Yet the associations and feelings of another that the imagination recreates are not random, excepting the madman—though even he, like Shakespeare's clowns and fools, may have a method and message. Some feeling or desire, some idea or bent of mind marshals these particulars into a full-bodied personality. Instead of describing only a "ruling passion" or repeating a type, the artist can create an individual by presenting personal associations, habits, and words as they are aligned and linked by an overarching desire, such as the ambition of Richard III. Macbeth is ambitious, too, but a completely different character; sympathetic imagination works from individual particulars and wipes away the fuzzy diffractions of general description.*

* See e.g. Thomas Whately's *Remarks on Some of the Characters of Shakespeare* (1785), which lay at least fifteen years in manuscript. Whately compares Macbeth and Richard III and perhaps would have done more in the field of criticism had he not suspended literary work to complete his *magnum opus, Observations on Modern Gardening* (1770).

When the sympathetic power is engaged, says Gerard, "the most distant hint is sufficient to direct the imagination to an object which is congruous to the present disposition of mind."[18] For example, following the stripping off of Lear's rank and dignity, his self-respect, and finally his barest comforts, exclamations of his that might otherwise sound vague become poignant and rich with meaning. "Didst thou give all to thy daughters, and art thou come to this?" he says. And underneath we hear the more passionate and terse cry, "What! have his daughters brought him to this pass?" The line conjures up the whole of the tragedy.

Sympathy becomes what Gerard calls a "happy structure of imagination," an infallible principle of organization that seems automatically to select what the poet should and should not imitate in order to present a convincing and complete portrait. Sympathy prevents the poet's imagination "from turning aside to wander in improper roads."[19] Sympathy, as it were, conditions or sensitizes the imagination to concentrate its creative power along certain lines that will result in the most unified and insightful imitations.

One result of this sympathetic guiding of the imagination is the ability to capture what is "natural," not what is concocted by an artificial scheme or mechanical rite of composition. Critics now begin to stress a speech and diction that Hugh Blair identifies as the *"natural* language of passion."* In this movement we can already see the basic romantic emphasis on the language of feeling, on what Wordsworth calls the language of "a man speaking to men." Blair, in his *Lectures on Rhetoric* (1783), explains that, "There is no possibility of speaking properly the language of any passion without feeling it."[20] In rough terms, "poetic" or "artificial" diction blocks the full exercise of sympathy. Stock words and phrases tend to hobble the imagination, preventing it from creating or perceiving those particular ways in which a person speaks or reacts with feeling to a situation. A stilted and frozen vocabulary, especially one of abstract description, cannot possibly express what Dryden had called the "life-touches" of art.

### THE EXAMPLE OF SHAKESPEARE

To Gerard, Kames, Blair, and Beattie, the *"natural* language of passion" did not emerge as a text or precept standing by itself. They believed in it and promoted it, to a large degree, as a commentary on the text of Shakespeare. At no other time from Dryden to the present has the figure of Shakespeare been more in the critical limelight, and at no other time have the ideas of sympathy and imagination been more openly confronted and explored than from 1760 to about 1825. This was the period of "bardolatry." Shakespeare was worth a legion of critics, and his language became a model for new poetic speech based on the sympathetic imagination. "Pray you, undo this button," and "Out, damned spot!" were lines carrying greater force than any lengthy, abstract argument about the effect of emotional and natural language.

The secret of Shakespeare's power lay in his ability to identify with his own creations. As early as 1664, Margaret Cavendish had noted that he seemed to "metamorphose" himself into his characters.[21] Shaftesbury considered the whole of *Hamlet* to be a kind of long soliloquy in which Shakespeare had effectively become the young prince. At least three critics of the 1760s and 1770s valued and dwelt on this sympathetic nature of Shakespeare's imagination. In her *Essay on the Writings and Genius of Shakespeare* (1769), Elizabeth Montagu praises the dialogue and expressions in Shakespeare's plays because they unfold "the internal state of the persons interested, and never fail to command our sympathy. Shakespeare seems to have had the art of the Dervise, in the Arabian tales, to throw his soul into the body of another man, and be at once possessed of his sentiments, adopt his passions, and rise to all the functions and feelings of his situation."[22]

Five years later in 1774, William Richardson, in his *A Philosophical Analysis and Illustration of Some of Shakespeare's Remarkable Characters*, puts Shakespeare's range and gift of sympathetic identification in an image that would later be used by both Hazlitt and Coleridge: "He is the Proteus of the drama" and "changes himself into every character." For Richardson, not only is the power of forming characters essential to dramatic invention, but the writer must imitate them "in their natural expressions, the passions and affections of which they are composed."[23] In Richardson's opinion, Shakespeare unites these capabilities: he creates characters, then lets them speak for themselves, only endowed with a Shakespeare's tongue.

As one critic put it, Shakespeare's imagination creates such truthful and individual characters that it is tempting to speculate about their off-stage existences and wonder what they are saying and doing after their exit. Morgann, in his landmark *Essay on the Dramatic Character of Sir John Falstaff* (1777), remarks that, with all of Shakespeare's characters, it is fit to consider them "rather as Historic than Dramatic beings," an attitude that extends down at least to the famous reaction, "How many children had Lady Macbeth?" Each character is really a complex image, and Shakespeare possesses "a wonderful facility of compressing, as it were, his own spirit into these images." Each line, phrase, and remark thickens with associations and is "in fact relative, and inferring all the rest."[24] The poetic composition in which associations imply and modify one another and in which the poet has a "wonderful facility of compressing" his spirit into images closely approximates both the literal and literary meanings of the German *dichten* and *Dichtungskraft.*

With the example of Shakespeare living through and "metamorphosed" into all his characters, the critical plea for a "*natural* language of passion" sounded far more solid and convincing than it would otherwise have been. Shakespeare, as Kames remarked in his *Elements of Criticism,* "is superior to all other writers in delineating passion." And by passion, Kames and others did not mean only turbulent or fierce emotions. They had in mind something like the list of qualities Shaftesbury had considered to be passions: "anger, ambition, desires, loves, eager and tumultuous joys, wishes, hopes, transporting fancies, extravagant mirth, airiness, humour, fantasticalness, buffoonery, drollery." Shakespeare seemed to capture all these not by "a laboured *description,*" as Gerard said in reflecting a common distinction, but by "a natural *representation* of the passion."

### SENSIBILITY

The sympathetic imagination that represents passion by getting inside of it, feeling and expressing it, produces strong and vivid results. The poet, filled with his subject in a powerful way, gets "carried away." Plato had said, "Who would be a poet cannot be master of himself." Shakespeare could transport himself into his creations, and this was one way to interpret that "poetic transport" or "divine inspiration" which classical authors had commended. The classical phrases, however, were becoming clichés. The late Enlightenment replaced them in part with the word "sensibility," and as a meaningful way to describe a poet's attributes, it remained a valuable and common watchword for at least two generations. Today "sensibility" is apt to be used in a general or ill-defined way and, in the plural, often as a mildly satiric jab, implying an affected or overdelicate taste. For the late Enlightenment, the Romantics, and much of the earlier nineteenth century generally, "sensibility" really stood for the susceptibility or ability of the poet to identify with his creations in a feeling way and to express that feeling in passionate and natural language. Ultimately, the whole concept rests on the imagination. As Stewart said in his *Elements of the Philosophy of the Human Mind* (1792), "What we commonly call sensibility depends, in a great measure, on the power of the imagination."[25] John Ogilvie, writing almost twenty years earlier in 1774, had said that the "facility of entering deeply into the feelings of the heart" is a distinguishing feature of "those writers who will always stand in the highest rank."[26]

Not only the poet but the critic, claimed Gerard, ought to possess "a sensibility of heart, as fits a man for being easily moved, and for readily catching . . . any passion that a work is fitted to excite."[27] Beattie also identified "sensibility" and "enthusiasm" with the poet's power of sympathizing with and feeling for "every part of his subject."[28] Priestley, in his 1777 *Lectures on Oratory and Criticism*, published the year before Beattie's observations, had remarked, "The more vivid are a man's ideas, and the greater is his *sensibility*, the more intirely, and with the greater facility, doth he adapt himself to the situations he is viewing."[29] "Sensibility," which has in the twentieth century seemed a rather vague critical word, is rooted directly in the idea of the sympathetic imagination, which explains why it became so popular, though it later fell from overuse. Imagination implies a certain openness, even a vulnerability to the world and to the feeling of others. George Campbell put it well when he said that "Sympathy is not a passion, but that quality of the soul which renders it susceptible of almost any passion."[30]

The ancient "poetic transport," "frenzy," "enthusiasm," and "inspiration" were thus seen as part of that sympathetic power of the imagination to get out of itself and feel its way strongly and vividly into other people and even into the forms of nature. As long as there was no immediate danger of becoming hurt, the poet and his audience might also pleasurably identify with distressing or potentially dangerous situations. This was, in a way, the beginning of the "romantic" stress, which could easily be cheapened, on the suffering hero or heroine. In the late eighteenth century, it was a relatively new phenomenon in serious literature. Thomas Barnes' paper entitled "On the Pleasure which the Mind in Many Cases Receives from Contemplating Scenes of Distress" appears in the *Memoirs of the Literary and Philosophical Society of Manchester* (Vol. I), and indicates the critical and psychological interest in this area.

The idea of sympathetic imagination applied not only to the poet but to his audience and, in the case of a playwright, to the actors who would perform his plays. Aaron Hill, in his *Essay on the Art of Acting in which the Dramatic Passions are Properly Defined and Described* (1779), warned that if an actor is to be successful, his "Imagination must conceive a strong idea of the passion " to be represented, and he "never must attempt its imitation, till his fancy has conceived so strong an image, or idea, of it, as . . . when it is undesigned and natural."[31] The idea of the sympathetic imagination began, in the 1760s and 1770s, to change acting styles and to affect the audience's reaction, especially to scenes of pathos and passion.

EMPATHY

"Empathy " is a word never used in the English Enlightenment or the Romantic period. A translation of the German *Einfühlung*, it means "in-feeling" or "feeling into" something. In the late nineteenth and early twentieth century, Rudolph Hermann Lotze and Wilhelm Wundt developed *Einfühlung* to an aesthetic doctrine, which was explained more fully by Theodor Lipps in his *Ästhetik* (1903–1906). E. G. Titchener, a pupil of Wundt, coined the English translation "empathy," and Vernon Lee popularized it. However, empathy was not at all a new concept. Herder had used *Einfühlen* ("empathy") to describe the cast of mind of an artist endowed, as Isaiah Berlin interprets it, "with historical insight and imagination" and able to "feel himself into" (*sich einfühlen*) the individuality and variety of human experience.[32] Coleridge had spoken of an imaginative union of the *percipi* and the *percipere*, the "perceived" and the "perceiver." In short, what we now call "empathy" was very much alive in the late Enlightenment, although the English word did not exist. "Sympathy," to our present confusion, was often used instead.

One difference between empathy and sympathy can be put in basic terms (though there are qualifications). Sympathy we might properly reserve for an imaginative feeling or identification with another human being. After all, as Hume said, human beings most resemble each other, and so they sympathize with each other more readily than with anything else. This sounds like a tautology, but is not always so. Smith put his finger on the point when he said that when we sympathize with someone, we are actually working up our own feelings into duplicating his; we can do this because one person has fundamentally the same emotional and intellectual make-up as all others, at least when compared to other animals. The question remains as to whether a person can truly sympathize with something that is not human, or is just projecting human values, emotions, and reactions onto an animal, or even onto an inanimate object, and then sympathizing with those projections. Perhaps we can feel as the creature feels, yet perhaps we are also "humanizing" it, especially if the animal already has some degree of similarity with human nature. Shakespeare's passage on "poor Wat" the hare, in *Venus and Adonis*, of which Coleridge was so fond, provides a good example of empathy that is almost sympathy—the frightened hare is described in nearly human terms.* But how are we to sympathize with a tree or, as Keats said he did, with a billiard ball? Plants and things have no senses as we know them. Yet there is nothing "wrong" with projecting human attributes or senses onto them. Coleridge thought Shakespeare unsurpassed in his power to render nature "humanized." Thus, Shakespeare gives an empathic description of a natural process which, in turn, is applied to the feelings and passions of a character: "My way of life/Is fall'n into the sear, the yellow leaf." There is another twist. However much we sympathize with another, we can never be sure that our imagination is accurately reproducing what he feels. We may misconstrue his experience. This may then not be sympathy but a form of empathy, projecting how we imagine a person feels and then identifying with that (false) projection?

Arguing about the two words is fruitful, for there are—or can be—helpful differences. But a specific case of either sympathy or empathy is worth many general definitions. The late Enlightenment in England got along rather well with "sympathy" alone, and critics extended its range to an imaginative feeling for, or even an identification with, animals and objects. Much of the result of a sympathy for particulars in nature was an aesthetic sensibility, a concord of nature with the mind as associations were aroused in the mind by those scenes before it, or even by imagined ones, like Satan's flight through chaos. In the late eighteenth century, much of this aesthetic doctrine fell into two categories, the beautiful and the sublime. They, like so many aesthetic values, seemed to depend entirely on the power of imagination and its accompanying associations.

An object with which we have personal associations may act like a symbol and prompt our imaginations to recreate certain experiences. Beattie says, for example, that we may "see in ruins a house in which we have long lived," and proceed to reconstruct from it many memories.[33] But the imagination also responds to enduring aesthetic forms in nature, which act similarly on everyone. Burke says that we sympathize with the *power* of certain things, such as storms, and not with the things themselves. In this way one value, like the sublime or the beautiful, may show through many different natural scenes because our imaginations associate all these scenes with one *kind* of feeling.

In his *Elements of Criticism*, Kames asserts that our "sense of order" is attuned to "the order of nature." So "thinking upon a body in motion, we follow its natural course. The mind falls with a heavy body, de-

---

* A marvelous passage in Cowper's *Task* (IV 336–356), in which he describes a man, his cart and horses in a snowstorm, exemplifies how "We may ... sympathize with others" and gives concrete form to the "feeling into" a subject that so many poets and critics were beginning to value highly.

scends with a river, and ascends with flame and smoke." Sluggish motion in another person or object creates or suggests to us a feeling of languor. Water plunging through rocks gives a tumultuous sensation.[34] It is not hard to see how this immediate and emotional bond between the self and nature reveals an imaginative state of mind closely related, for example, to passages in the *Prelude*.

Archibald Alison, in the *Principles of Taste* (1790), remarks that in observing the "forms" of objects, we may feel a sympathy or a feeling *with* the shape itself, and this produces an aesthetic emotion within us. A fine and winding line, such as Hogarth's serpentine "line of beauty," is beautiful "not of itself, and originally," but because we identify with it. Its shape and sense of motion coincide with our feelings of "ease and volition" as we follow the line with our eyes.[35] Similarly, when a ball we have hit or thrown is beyond our influence, we still yell or apply body english to change its flight. Priestley had used this example first, almost twenty years earlier. "What is more common," he said, "than to see persons in playing at bowls, lean their own bodies, and writhe them into every possible attitude, according to the course they would have their bowl to take?"[36]

As early as 1769 Daniel Webb had noticed that empathy with natural objects often depends on the ability of the imagination to follow, anticipate, and complete some *movement* in those objects or sounds. In his *Observations on the Correspondence between Poetry and Music* he relates the motion of music and the progress of human passions to the completing and anticipating power of the imagination. His work is just one indication of how *ut pictura poesis* was becoming *ut musica poesis*.[37] "If music owes its being to motion," states Webb, "and, if passion cannot well be conceived to exist without it, we have a right to conclude, that the agreement of music with passion can have no other origin than a coincidence of movements." In a general way, the imagination follows a movement or a developing form of nature and often impresses the direction or feeling of this movement, in an empathic way, onto its own creations: "The imagination may be raised by movements of expansion; hence its agreement with pride, wonder, and emulation. But as these passions and their movements tend naturally towards increase, it follows, that the images here employed may be enlarged and dilated."[38]

Both sympathy and empathy dissolve the boundary between the objective, outside world, and the subjective self. The imagination can, by a process of identification, extend the self out into the world and into other people. The result is neither strictly subjective nor objective, but a fusing of the two. Shakespeare accrued so many sympathies with his diverse creations and he compounded so many individual subjective natures that, perhaps of all the poets, he may be called "objective," for the objective world can be seen as the total interworking of all of its individual beings and identities. In the 1770s and then through the Romantic period as a whole, the imagination was looked upon more and more as a power that not only worked in the mind but could really connect and even unite the self with the outside world. Empirical psychology, especially in the hands of the associationists, was now—with the idea of the imagination well established—turning to the external world and trying to resolve the polarities of self and nature, subject and object, internal and external, perceiver and perceived.

# 12

## THE PSYCHE REACHES OUT: COALESCENCE AND THE CHEMISTRY OF THE MIND

*A*side from a direct discussion of sympathy and the sympathetic character of the imagination, the associationists and the Scottish thinkers explored how the imagination forms its comprehensive recreation of the world and how, in a way, the self then becomes or assimilates that recreation. The self and the world meet most completely not through the senses but through an imaginative process. This (though for the British it is defined more loosely) is the same question that German philosophy was then facing under the heading of the *"Ich bin"* and *"Es gibt"* systems.

The associationists now lifted the concept of the imagination to a new and more sophisticated plane, one in which organicism and active process, rather than simple mechanism, govern the associative activity. Abraham Tucker, Archibald Alison, and others speak of association as a modifying, combining, and coalescing process. They analyze how the imagination conceives of and arranges the external world, how imagination recreates within each mind the surrounding reality and places aesthetic value upon it. The work of these associationists, from 1770 on, has much to do with imagination as a perceptive and connecting activity rather than as a strictly creative power turning to the arts. But for the most part, the simple faculty psychology is discarded or at least used with an awareness than it is a simplifying schema of things. These associationists are speaking about what the Germans, often developing points from the British, were already considering as the most fundamental level of the imagination,* and what Coleridge would call "pri-

* See above, pp. 119–120.

mary imagination." The associationists now viewed the imagination as the true connecting link between the individual, subjective self and the universe at large.

## TUCKER'S "TRAINS" AND "COMPOUNDS"

Abraham Tucker's *The Light of Nature Pursued* (1768–1778) rambles through seven volumes of ethics, metaphysics, and loosely-spun but often striking philosophy.[1] Hazlitt's second book was an abridgment of it. He appreciated Tucker's breadth of interest, keen observations on the mind, and use of examples drawn from daily life. (In Germany, Tucker was known by his *nom de plume*, Edward Search.) He is an empiricist's empiricist who relies more on his own particular observations than on a system abstracted from many observations, inevitably distorting the experience upon which it is supposed to be based. To the imagination he assigns all "sense appetite and instinct," all sensation, and—most importantly—all forms of human perception and knowledge that we "fall upon by experience, or grow into by habit and custom." All of these as "the produce of the imagination" have one thing in common: they arise from or represent *all* spontaneous or involuntary activity in the mind. Imagination is the "perceptive" power, and it furnishes the only way we have of representing, collecting, and associating what the external world impresses on us. Without imagination, the mind would perpetually remain what it is at birth, "a meer blank."[2]

Tucker discriminates between two basic kinds of imaginative "combinations." Association forms "trains" of ideas, and "composition" fuses simple ideas into compound or complex ones. Associative "trains" may "grow so bulky that we cannot take them in at one glance, but are forced to turn about them . . . in order to view them a side at a time." However, in this case, each idea in the train almost always excites "some part of the assemblage." This "quality of cohering in our ideas" means not only that each idea connects with the ones immediately before and after it, but that its effect spreads throughout the whole. Impressions leave "a spice and tincture" by which they operate on and select all subsequent ideas. The mind tends to synthesize as much as possible. "Imagination is not so scanty but that it can exhibit several objects to our notice at once." As trains of thought become more familiar and habitual, they may unite into compounds, which we sense as one idea. If the trains are too long for this conflation, then their "middle links frequently drop out or pass so swiftly as not to touch the notice."[3]

In compounds, all links coalesce or fuse into one amalgam, which "may have properties resulting from the composition which do not belong to the parts singly whereof it consists." Tucker here carries association to a new level, "composition," where ideas melt into and transform one another, producing a whole that can be entirely different from its component parts. In composition ideas "so mix and as I may say melt together as to form one single complex idea." The mind continually overlays or groups together separate but related impressions until they crystallize into a unified whole handled as one single impression:

> Thus the taste of sugar . . . joins with the colour we saw . . . and the hardness we felt . . . and the ideas of a certain colour consistency and sweetness make the complex of sugar. By degrees we add more ingredients to the compound, further experience informing us of other qualities constantly attending what we have already comprehended under the idea of sugar whenever they have an opportunity of showing themselves, and hence we learn that sugar is brittle, dissolvable, clammy, and astringent.[4]

Drawing on memory, experience, and habit, the mind adds "fresh ingredients to the compounds formed . . . in our imagination" and extends its range. Trains and compounds soon act as single ideas and group together to form even larger compounds and trains: "The idea of the Iliad in the vulgar contains no more than an old story of a siege wrote in Greek verse: but . . . there arises in the mind of the poet or critic ideas of the fable, the characters, the sentiments, the figures, the diction, any of which being altered they would not acknowledge it to be Homer." The imagination becomes a completing power that threads together many compounds. This "makes the imagination like a wilderness cut into a multitude of short alleys communicating together by gentle and almost imperceptible windings."[5]

Our perceptions no longer depend on what is immediately present to our senses. We develop an "internal fund," which is made possible because "sensations after their disappearance leave ideas of themselves behind in the reflection . . . We talk of seeing cubes and globes, but in reality our sense exhibits no such objects to the mind: we can at most see only three sides of the former and one hemisphere of the latter, but imagination supplies what is wanting to compleat their figures." Likewise in a picture, where objects lie level, "the roundness and protuberance we discern in them cannot come from the sense but must be drawn from our internal fund."[6]

Although Tucker obscures this internal activity by connecting it with a change in the disposition and "mechanical play of our organs," his final point is clear and important. The imagination fosters a ready and intuitive power of judgment that draws on accumulated perceptions and reflections. This judgment occurs "to the thought instantly and involuntarily without deduction of reason or chain of consequences."[7]

We look at the moon and judge instantaneously that it is far away. But if our imagination had not already provided us with other perceptions

and a cumulative sense of experience, we could not make such a judgment. Tucker gives a charming illustration. A boy, born blind, gains
sight at age fourteen: "One evening he was lost, and upon searching they
found him upon the leads of the house. It seems he had been in the street
and upon seeing the Moon peep a little over the roof he was going to
climb up the tiles in order to catch her."[8]

When our perceptive and intuitive power of imagination is turned to
some purpose by volition, "careful instruction," or "care and diligence,"
it becomes, for Tucker, the second and only other major faculty of the
mind. The "understanding" unites the reflective and judgmental powers
of imagination with the power of will. Imagination is therefore "active"
or consciously and deliberately controlled. Imagination and understanding enjoy a curious relationship. On the one hand, imagination always supplies the materials and perceptions on which understanding
operates. Understanding is therefore derivative of imagination. "But on
the other hand understanding . . . makes over a part of her purchases to
imagination." That is, "by making us so compleatly masters" of certain
deductions or acts, the understanding provides these "ready at hand
without requiring any time or trouble to rummage for them."[9] A voluntary act, like balancing or making sense out of what seems a confused
mass of letters, becomes involuntary or automatic. We walk and read
without the original will needed to learn such activities. They become
part of our more automatic or imaginative nature.

In these various aspects, "understanding often begins and terminates
in imagination." All our proceedings are a mixture of voluntary and
spontaneous processes, but imagination must come first.[10] It is the bedrock of all else, the only prerequisite of development and growth in the
mind. By stressing the fusion, melting, and coalescence of ideas, Tucker
altered the usual mechanical metaphors of associationism into ones that
suggest organic flow and continuity.

Since the imagination encompasses all complex ideas and compounds,
qualities or ideals like sublimity, taste, beauty, and sympathy emerge as
nothing more than particular aspects of the perceptive power at large.
These concepts are simply related trains and compounds that exert various specific effects on our feelings or adhere to certain other groups of
ideas. Qualities like the sublime or "fine humour" in writing cannot
"convey a great deal more than they express," because "this More must
be something the mind has already in store and they only draw it up to
view." Similarly, we cannot know what to desire in order to satisfy a
craving, until we have experienced and perceived what actually does alleviate our appetite: "Little children, when uneasy through hunger or
sleepiness, do not know what is the matter with them, and are so far
from being moved by appetite towards the gratification of it that they

fight against their victuals and other methods of relief when applied to them." Like desire, sympathy is also gained by the "inadvertent notice of repeated trials," then re-enforced by "design and industry."[11]

Some perceptions arise in the imagination more easily than others. We readily conceive of a square, but a ten-sided polygon, half of whose sides are half as long as the remaining five sides, is more difficult. The tendency or disposition of our habituated minds produces the "cast" or "mold" of imagination. Our store of perceptions may lead us to view objects or ideas with great ease or, as in the case of optical illusions, with error. Imaginative perception is, however, the only basis of judgment. Tucker denies first principles of reason and innate ideas. Man can attain moral certainty, but "knowledge, that is, absolute certainty was not made for man."[12] The imagination provides so much, yet it cannot pretend "to penetrate quite to the fountain head" of truth and Godly reason. However, Tucker's pseudonym Edward Search, the revelations of his amazing chapter "The Vision," which is a speculation on the mystery of "Psyche" in the cosmos, and the Lucretian motto of his first volume, *"Juvat integros accedere fontes"* (it is a pleasure to approach the pure fountains), all suggest that the human imagination strives to repeat and know the wonder of God as revealed through the creations of the infinite "I am."[13]

## ALISON AND AESTHETIC VALUES

Archibald Alison, in his 1790 *Essays on the Nature and Principles of Taste*, attributes the "emotions" of beauty and sublimity solely to the power of association.[14] Aesthetic qualities, which he terms "ideas of Emotion," are not, as Burke suggested, intrinsic to things themselves but exist in the psychological or internal realm as "the signs or expressions of such qualities [in natural phenomena] as are fitted by the constitution of our nature, to produce emotion." Sensations and objects from the "material world" produce their effects "by leading our imaginations" to associate them with earlier experiences.[15] The mind, for example, is so engaged by a particular scene or poetic image that it quickly attaches a series of its own images and memories to what is appearing before it at the moment. In other words, "the imagination is employed in the prosecution of a regular train of ideas and emotion."[16]

The interplay of mind and the external world catalyzes in the mind its latent associations and feelings, which have been collected over a long period of time. Set off by something external, our whole mind becomes involved, and it is the mind's expression alone that is truly beautiful or sublime. In this way, single experiences or objects have the power to produce "analogies with the life of man, and bring before us all those images . . . which, according to our peculiar situations, have the dominion of our hearts!"[17] The process is spontaneous and immediate, no power of will is needed. Alison combines Scottish intuitionalism with a spontaneous associationism similar to Tucker's. Editions of *Principles of Taste* appeared for over fifty years. Francis Jeffrey, by an enthusiastic review of the 1811 edition, which he condensed five years later for his article on "Beauty" in the *Britannica*, strengthened and extended Alison's influence in criticism and aesthetics.

Much of the second half of the *Principles of Taste* examines objects, forms, colors, sounds, or motions in nature that produce the associations called beautiful or sublime. "The howling of a Storm,—the murmuring of an Earthquake . . . the Explosion of Thunder," all are associated with danger and consequently are sublime. The idea of power or might we connect with "the fall of a cataract" or "the dashing of the Waves," and this idea also suggests sublimity. Alison shows acumen in implying that when images are associated, the power of suggestion is what makes them sublime or beautiful. The "low and feeble Sound" which precedes great thunder is "more sublime in reality than all the uproar of the storm itself." It is "the forerunner of the storm and the sign of all the imagery we connect with it." The suggested associations form the essence of the emotion or response we feel. When the associations are dissolved, "the sounds themselves cease to be Sublime."[18]

Alison's theory and examples result in a crucial point. All sense of taste would at first appear to be personal and subjective, the product only of circumstance, accident, and idiosyncracies. "Peculiar habits," national differences, the effect of our employments and education, all create diversity in taste. The yellow color currently found distasteful in dress, remarks Alison, is the rage of China. A farmer finds that hay fields arouse only thoughts of sweat and worry, while to a party in a coach they give a beautiful prospect. Early societies possessed their own "instinctive associations," such as the regularity of meter in verse, which alter with the progress of art and change the criteria of taste. However, not all associations are completely relative. For Alison, the imagination has general characteristics similar enough in all people to establish a range of acceptable taste, within which there is personal diversity. After all, the images we link to feelings are themselves derived from the external world, and people inevitably share similar experiences. Some associations, like those of fitness or utility in architecture, are "permanent" or commonly agreed upon because of the nature of the materials and space at hand. In poetry, images cannot be scattered at random. They must have "some general principle of connection which pervades the whole" and which all readers recognize.[19] In other words, taste, and with it the imagination, combines subjective and objective values. Personal experience itself is largely determined by the limits and natural constitution of the mind, as well as by the common fund of elements in the external world that supplies each individual with a distinctive catalogue of images.[20]

### KNIGHT, BROWN AND THE "CHEMISTRY OF MIND"

Associationist psychology and aesthetics did not simply flare up in the last half of the eighteenth century and then rapidly subside to make way for a "more romantic" mood. Rather, the movement continued throughout the Romantic period and was instrumental in creating the critical mind, and to some extent the taste, of that period. And as associationism remained popular, it increasingly magnified the idea of the imagination, now by far its single most important topic for critical discussion. For example, Richard Payne Knight (1750–1824), scholar of mythology and ancient art, wrote a widely-read, succinct work on associationist aesthetic theory, *An Analytical Inquiry into the Principles of Taste* (1805), which treats in detail the relationship of association with every aspect of the imagination, from madness to military architecture, and from sculpture to manners and etiquette.[21] Crucial to art, and to all uses of the imagination, are "mental sympathies" aroused in us. Our strongest sympathies, evoked by what we most admire, reach their height when triggered by suggestion, as in the small but significant detail, rather than by exact copy. Similarly, when we know people too well, even if it is the knowing of love, our desire weakens. Knight then works toward an ideal of genius as the "normal" person whose insight represents "the norm of human experience."

Fifteen years later, in his 1820 Lectures on the *Philosophy of the Human Mind*, Thomas Brown joined British associationism with Scottish intuitional psychology and developed an encompassing, organic theory of imagination. It could be called frankly "romantic," yet it emerged directly from thinkers like Hume, Knight, and Alison. Brown prefers the work "suggestion" to association, because it indicates that the mind moves in a series of steps to relate ideas, images, and emotions that perhaps never before have been joined through direct sense perceptions or through any of the established principles of association, such as resemblance or contiguity in time and space.[22]

The imagination works by an accretive process. Like a developing organism, it ingests material from the outside world, differentiates its own structure, and grows more complex, yet never loses its integrity and sense of being one life. The process, almost a form of mental digestion, is always working. All reminiscence and imagination depend at first not on our will but on various conceptions, which break the surface of consciousness in related patterns. We cannot "will the existence of any particular idea; since this would be to suppose us either to will without knowing what we willed, which is absurd—or to know *already* what we *willed to know*, which is not less absurd . . . . If we select images, with the view of *forming a particular compound* [of images], we must already have formed this *compound.*" Once a single image or conception takes hold of the mind, the power of suggestion presents "image after image . . . in the perceived fitness or unfitness of certain images for a particular design." The mind may be charged or biased by a "general *desire*" or by "other more particular and subordinate desires," which act like a filter and permit only selected images.[23]

In other words, imagination is wrongly called "a peculiar intellectual power." It is a complex series of stages in the construction of a final product whose completed form is, as it were, an anticipated shadow coming from out of the future, the prescience of a finished whole, that during the imaginative process is always casting back a formative outline to guide the filling in and fitting together of component parts. Imagination

> is not the exercise of a *single power*, but the development of various *susceptibilities*,—of *desire*,—of *simple suggestion*, by which conceptions rise after conceptions,—of judgment or *relative suggestion*, by which a feeling of relative fitness or unfitness arises, on the contemplation of the conceptions that have thus spontaneously presented themselves . . . We may term this complex state, or series of states, imagination, or fancy,— and the term may be convenient for its *brevity*.[24]

This fluid, dynamic sense of imagination as a succession of interconnected states Brown calls the "spontaneous chemistry of mind."[25] It mingles "the mere forms of matter" as well as "the affections of the soul . . . in its spiritual creations." Both external and internal worlds become one in the mind. Himself a poet, Brown tried to discover what sets apart creative imagination from the more "humble" sort. The imagination of a writer, he believes, is impassioned, full of strong desire, and fixes its attention so as to choose and order images, to focus on one end to which all activity is subordinate.[26] A poet's desire for the unity and meaning of his work is especially emotional. His ability to create analogies between the external world and human life, and to express these analogies, is "a very natural result of that susceptibility of vivid emotion, which . . . is usually conceived to be characteristic of the poetic temperament."[27] The poet uses images in a way not suggested by direct sense experience. Lucan compares a decaying oak to the decay of a human mind. This analogy he created; his invention did not depend on the two images having previously appeared successively, in point of time, in his own mind. The speed with which genius creates such analogies justifies many so-called "faults" of poets, such as Hamlet's mixed metaphor about taking arms against a sea of troubles.[28]

In its emotional state, the poetic imagination exerts "a greater elevation" that suggests more related images and thoughts than could be grasped otherwise. The imagination then will "diffuse itself over them all, as if they were living and sympathizing parts of itself." The images are *"coalescing,* as they rise." We invest nature with our own feelings and sympathize with it as a part of ourselves. An object in nature, "the *symbol* . . . becomes representative of the enjoyment itself." We fix and embody our feelings in a real object, which gives us something more comprehensive, "one general impression of reality." In a similar way, people become the object of each other's response. Brown follows in the line of sympathetic imagination represented to him chiefly by Smith, Alison, and Hazlitt.[29]  ,

Brown argues, too, that while the imaginative process is complex and sympathetic, it is not hopelessly subjective. "The irregularities of individual association are more and more counteracted by the foresight of the diversities of general sentiment," until finally whatever we think and feel is to a large degree that "which we foreknow that others are to feel." Although personal taste and imagination vary somewhat, "there is still one universal harmony that seems to animate the whole." Brown goes so far as to say that because of sympathetic imagination, "Every individual has thus the aid of all the powers of every other individual." In its final measure, imagination becomes sympathetic not only in a symbolic but also in a moral way.[30]

Although often loosely organized in his explanations, Brown sees imagination as an immense power, one cast over many activities like a huge net of fine and weightless mesh, drawing them into one organic whole. This sense of totality suggests "the Omniscience of the Sovereign Intellect." God's power is revealed to us as we scan His creation. This is possible because "in the complex process of imagination . . . there are truly no limits,—not in external things . . . —not in the affections of the soul . . . —not even in infinity itself."[31] Brown belongs to the long line of empiricists who found religious, even mystical experience by working from facts of observation in what they considered an upward progression.[32] The imagination is everywhere; it is "a species of virtual omnipresence." This embracing idea is similar to Coleridge's thought of "the primary imagination" as a repetition in the individual mind of the acts of creation performed by God, the infinite "I am." As Brown notes, the universe thus may "be said to be comprized in a *single retrospective thought of man"* that rapidly retraces all human knowl-

edge and sympathies.[33] For Coleridge, the universe in its great multiplicity is, when taken as one thought, the "choral Echo" of "the great
I AM."[34] With a phrasing that recalls Coleridge's remark on the imagination as forming a "harmonized chaos," Brown argues that the imaginative power of suggestion gives "its own *unity* to the innumerable objects
which it comprehends, and like the *mighty Spirit* which once hovered
over the confusion of unformed nature," is able to "*convert into a universe* what was only *chaos* before."[35]


### BELSHAM, DARWIN, AND SCOTT

As Hazlitt, born in 1778, passed from his late teens to his early twenties, he could look about him and see an array of new works on "intellectual philosophy" that combined associationism—now with its more
organic view of the coalescence of ideas—and sympathy. These works
fall in the generation between Alison's *Principles of Taste* and Brown's
*Lectures*. Priestley had tutored Hazlitt at Hackney College and naturally influenced him, but Hazlitt could also turn to another of his tutors
there, Thomas Belsham, whose *Elements of the Philosophy of the Mind*
appeared in 1801. Belsham relies at times on Hartley, and when he does,
his view of the imagination slogs along in a deterministic and mechanical way. But Hazlitt, speaking of Hartley's rigid associationism as the
nerves' game of "battledore and shuttlecock," rejected it—as would
Coleridge—for something more like Belsham's own idea of coalescence.
Although Hartley still had impact, Tucker, Priestley, and Belsham were
turning associationism in another direction, one more organic and complex.

Erasmus Darwin in his *Zoonomia* (1794–1796) and his *Botanic
Garden* (1789–1791) stressed both the natural presence of sympathy
and a coalescing of ideas that remakes or creates new impressions. As biology gained a stronger foothold in the sciences, metaphors of plant and
animal life were increasingly used to characterize the nature of genius
and the imagination.[36] Johnson, Young, Gerard, and Morgann had employed the organic growth of plant life to describe the mental process of
genius, and Morgann had used it to describe Shakespeare's own understanding how the human mind operates: "Bodies of all kinds . . . possess
certain first principles of *being*, and . . . have an existence independent of
the accidents, which form their magnitude or growth . . . each plant and
each animal imbibes those things only which are proper to its own distinct nature, and which have besides such a secret relation to each other
as to be capable of forming a perfect union and *coalescence* . . . Shake-

speare appears to have considered the being and growth of the human mind as analogous to this system."

Published in 1805, the same year as Hazlitt's *Essay on the Principles of Human Action* and Knight's *Analytical Inquiry*, Robert Scott's *Elements of Intellectual Philosophy* sets out a few important points in its otherwise routine approach. Scott, a pupil of Stewart, says that the imagination associates and modifies its materials and operates in both "passive" and "active" modes. Imagination and sympathy yoke together and work as one reflex or faculty. These points resurface in Coleridge's *Biographia*.

Belsham, Darwin, and Scott contributed in a minor way to the idea of the imagination around the turn of the nineteenth century. They capture notice because they influenced Hazlitt, Brown, and perhaps Coleridge, and also because they exemplify how British associationism, in the fifty years since Hartley, metamorphosed itself and broadened to include an organic vision of how the imagination encounters, makes sense of, and recreates the external world. Sympathy, coalescence, and an awareness of the complex, reciprocal workings of rational planning, unconscious habit, desire, and both moral and aesthetic values converged to give the idea of imagination dimensionality and depth. It had become a power attuned to human experience in all its variety. The imagination had become not simply the power to perceive, or to escape the self and identify with others, or to create, connect, modify, and relate, or to grow and augment its own flexible strength, but all these powers, and each seemed like one of several vital organs within the body of the larger idea.

# DISTINCTIONS BETWEEN FANCY
# AND IMAGINATION

$\mathcal{C}$oleridge's famous distinction be-
tween "fancy" and "imagination" used to be thought either to have originated with him or to have had an obscure German source. But actually
a growing distinction between the terms took place in English usage
throughout the eighteenth century, and in much the same direction in
which Coleridge developed or ramified it.[1] The first surviving statement
by Coleridge of his own distinction occurs in a letter of 1802. Eight
years before this, however, Mrs. Piozzi, in her *British Synonymy*
(1794), noted that a "well-instructed foreigner" will discover a difference in the way the words are used "in a conversational circle." Milton's
*Paradise Lost*, for example, will be said to show "a boundless IMAGINA-
TION," whereas Pope's *Rape of the Lock* will be spoken of as "a work of
exquisite FANCY."[2] Moving back a few years, we find a confirmation of
this in James Beattie (1783): "According to the common use of words,
Imagination and Fancy are not perfectly synonymous. They are, indeed, names for the same faculty; but the former seems to be applied to
the more solemn, and the latter to the more trivial, exertions of it. A
witty author is a man of lively Fancy; but a sublime poet is said to possess a vast imagination."[3] A few years earlier still, in 1772, Sir Joshua
Reynolds in his Fifth Discourse remarks that "Raffaele had more taste
and *fancy*, Michel Angelo more genius and *imagination*." This is a
fairly casual statement, and it is different in kind from what Beattie and
Mrs. Piozzi are saying. But in all of these instances, "imagination" is the
more commendatory term and it, more than "fancy," is associated with
creative vigor and range. For instance, in John Moir's *Gleanings or Fu-
gitive Pieces* (1785) fancy is an "embellishing," "connecting," and "dis-
posing" power that provides "new combinations" of images, but it is
imagination that "creates or fabricates."

## THE EARLY REVERSAL OF TERMS

As this distinction developed, it involved a reversal of the traditional distinction between the two terms. Coming from the Greek, *phantasia* carried with it the suggestion of creativity and play of mind, with the possible implication of license and illusion as a by-product of that freedom. The Latin *imaginatio*, on the contrary, had a blocklike, Roman solidity derived from the primary word "image," which referred to a mental concept as much as a visual "image." It was akin to the word "imitation" and carried with it a sense of fidelity and accuracy. But precisely because *phantasia* suggested a greater freedom of mind, whether for creative insight, for perception, or for illusion, the word "fancy" began to bear the brunt of suspicion or distrust thrown by seventeenth-century rationalism and, above all, by the fashionable colloquial speech that echoed it. Hobbes is perhaps the last major writer to favor the use of "fancy" for the greatest creative and inventive freedom of the mind. Locke's comparison between "real" and "fantastical" ideas in the *Essay Concerning Human Understanding* tends to disparage the term "fancy" itself as something unconnected with reality. Leibniz, although he places less stigma on the fantastical, makes a similar comparison between *"les idées réelles"* and *"les idées phantastiques ou chimériques"* in the *Nouveaux essais*. In Chapter 30 of Book II, he implies that the imagination is involved not only in a synthetic perception of the real world but also in the creation of wholly new images and unities that, although they do not actually exist, seem natural and possible and are therefore "real" in that sense. Leibniz is giving the imaginative power two levels.

In the search for a new or different word to express what seventeenth-century rationalism seemed to leave out, the more solid word "imagination," with its implication of being firmly rooted in the concrete, was at hand. It seemed freer from error and illusion.[4] By the 1660s, Dryden is already using the word "imagination" in a larger and richer sense. A poet's "imagination" includes three qualities—"invention"; "fancy," which is the "variation," enriching, and shaping of the particular thought; and "elocution," or the gift of language.[5] Addison (1712) wanted to "fix and determine" these two terms, which were becoming more important and should therefore be used in a less "loose and uncircumscribed sense." His attempt to stabilize them involved trying to make them synonymous.[6] But the growing division between them was too far advanced for Addison to have much effect. Walter Harte, too, in his poem *An Essay on Reason* (1735), equates the powers of fancy and imagination, although perhaps giving fancy more importance: "Imagination thence her flow'rs translates;/And Fancy, emulous of God, creates." And Andrew Baxter, a follower of Addison, also defines imagination and fancy as being alike in his *Enquiry into the Human Soul* (3rd ed., 1745). But on the whole, the two terms were splitting apart.

## MID-CENTURY DISTINCTIONS

Significantly, Addison himself uses "imagination" far more than "fancy," the reverse having been true in Hobbes, and Akenside solidified this tendency by entitling his poem *The Pleasures of Imagination*. In Shaftesbury's *Characteristics* (1711), "imagination" is the stronger word. Fancy suggests "mental abandon," which Shaftesbury exemplifies by the same passage from Otway's play, *Venice Preserved*, that Coleridge a century later was to quote as a favorite illustration of "fancy" ("seas of milk, and ships of amber").[7] Another favorite illustration of fancy for Coleridge was the poetry of Spenser which, he claimed, was blessed with "imaginative fancy." Burke had remarked in his *Enquiry*, which Coleridge read, that descriptions like Spenser's are not as affecting as imitations guided by the imagination; Spenser's descriptions are instead "formed by fancy." In a similar vein, Joseph Warton notes that Pope had imagination but "indulged it not." This failing checked the full development of his power, and Warton chides him for forming "himself upon the Grecian and Italian sons of *Fancy*." The key to what was happening is seen in Johnson's *Dictionary* (1755). Although his primary definition for each word virtually equates it with the other, his important second definition of "imagination" attributes to it a meaning and a dignity that he does not give to "fancy"—he says of imagination that it is a "conception, image of the mind, idea."

Except for Johnson's definition, the implied distinctions cited so far are not, in the rigorous sense, critical or philosophical. The first of these distinctions is provided in William Duff's seminal *Essay on Original Genius* (1767). The similarity with Coleridge's later distinction is striking. The imagination can both discover "truths that were formerly unknown" and "present a creation of its own"; it is at once "inventive and plastic"; it is the essence of "genius." "Fancy," on the contrary, is a form of association and memory; its "proper" function is simply "to collect the materials of composition," which in Coleridge's phrase would be its "aggregative and associative power." Fancy, according to Duff, can be "extravagant and lawless"; and in its ability to yoke together distantly related ideas in an unexpected way, it is the parent of "wit and humour."[8]

Abraham Tucker generally takes a favorable view of the imagination in his *Light of Nature Pursued*, but he speaks of "that noted liar

Fancy," whose operation is unregulated and undirected.[9] Finally Thomas Reid, in 1785 looks back in retrospect on the whole century of thought.

> From the constitution of the mind itself there is a constant ebullition of thought, a constant intestine motion; not only of thoughts barely specula-tive, but of sentiments, passions and affections, which attend them.
> This continued succession of thought has, by modern philosophers, been called the *imagination*. I think it was formerly called the *fancy*, or the *phantasy*. If the old name be laid aside, it were to be wished that it had got a name less ambiguous than that of imagination, a name which had two or three meanings besides.[10]

Reid has hit not only on the slow yet discernible reversal of "fancy" and "imagination" from the late seventeenth to the late eighteenth century, but also on the new confusion arising from the fact that imagination must now stand for "two or three meanings."

### A NORM

Finally something of a norm is reached in Dugald Stewart's *Elements of the Philosophy of the Human Mind* (1792), which approaches the subject in an analytic and systematic way. In brief, "imagination" is a far more comprehensive term than "fancy." It is the coalesced activity of four different functions or faculties of mind, one of which is "fancy." First, "imagination" includes the power of "conception" itself, or "sim-ple apprehension, which enables us to form a notion." Uniting with this are the power of "Abstraction," meaning the ability to pluck out or ex-trapolate particular elements or characteristics for the purpose of re-combining them in a new context, and "Judgment or Taste," meaning informed or inspired tact in selecting the elements to be abstracted and reconceived in another form. The fourth element is the "association" of ideas or images "according to relations of resemblance or analogy" in order to "collect materials for the Imagination." When this gift of associ-ation is characterized by "liveliness" or quickness and by "luxuriance" in the range or variety of what it can pull together, it can conveniently be called "Fancy." It differs from "wit" only in one significant way. "Wit" applies to the general gift for making new combinations of what-ever kind, including abstract ideas; and the pleasure it gives is produced by surprise at an unexpected result. "Fancy," however, is always leap-ing from the "intellectual and moral to the concrete world," to the images and "appearances with which our senses are conversant"; and the pleasure it gives is produced not only by surprise at the unexpected but in part by the images themselves.[11]

Coleridge thought highly of Stewart and without doubt had read these passages from his principal work. We may note also two followers of Stewart, though both of them are now forgotten. Robert E. Scott in his *Elements of Intellectual Philosophy* (Edinburgh, 1805) associates "fancy" with a form of "wit," which he interestingly illustrates with the same passage from Butler's *Hudibras* that Coleridge later uses to illustrate "fancy" ("And like a lobster boil'd, the morn/From black to red began to turn").[12] Two years later, Thomas Cogan in his *Ethical Treatise on the Passions* (Bath, 1807) defines "fancy" as simply a lively, ingenious play of mind. "Imagination," in contrast, "forms the embryo of everything which originates from human intellect." It is the open avenue, the active agent and transmitter to the mind, of "every portion of knowledge" that is not, at that very moment, being directly brought by sensation.[13]

In 1820, three years after the *Biographia* appeared, Thomas Brown makes a conscious and careful effort to distinguish beween fancy and imagination. But he apparently had not read the *Biographia*, for he does not repeat Coleridge's own distinction. Brown's work shows, however, that thinkers were still trying to sift out the meanings of the words. "Fancy," explains Brown, is only "a general term." It means that many unrelated images float into or suggest themselves to the mind. But a writer or artist, in his desire for a unified whole, exerts or establishes "a predetermining selection" of images. "Such is the frame of the mind, *in composition of every species, in prose or verse* . . . It is a continued *exercise of imagination.*"[14]

### GERMAN DISTINCTIONS: WOLFF, SULZER, TETENS

In Germany almost every discussion of the imagination during the last third of the century contains either a direct or an implied distinction between "fancy" and "imagination." Although there is no clear-cut correspondence in all these distinctions, at least one generalization can be made. Most of them assume fancy (*Phantasie*) to be mainly an associative power that supplies the mind or the inner eye with numerous images, usually connected by some associative principle. But the imagination fuses, combines, transforms, and orders images so that they produce an artistic or aesthetic unity.

In addition, the German critical and philosophic writers, from Wolff through Schelling, realized that what is called the imagination or the imaginative process actually consists of several complex operations, some of which vary in degree or in kind. Thus, writers like Tetens and Sulzer, who on the surface equate *Phantasie* with *Einbildungskraft,* also employ other terms like *Dichtungskraft* or *Dichtungsvermögen*. More than the English, the Germans were prone to give specific names and definitions to the various operations of the imaginative process and thus to avoid the "two or three meanings besides" that Reid complained about concerning the word "imagination" in English.

Writing in Latin in the early 1730s, Wolff painstakingly defines the difference between imagination and fancy in his *Psychologia Empirica* and his *Psychologia Rationalis*. He dismisses *phantasia* as the name of a faculty and prefers to use *imaginatio* for our ability to reproduce images. *"Phantasia vero pro facultate imaginandi sumitur."* In this, Wolff believes he is following Aristotle. Rather mechanically, *imaginatio* supplies images culled directly from experience, called *phantasmata*. (*"Ideam ab imaginatione productam Phantasma dicimus."*) The creative mind, however, takes these *phantasmata* as raw materials and renovates and transforms them into new wholes. The faculty that performs this creative act Wolff calls the *Facultas fingendi*. If Wolff's Latin were to be directly translated into English, the distinction would become one between "imagination" and "the faculty of joining or unifying." But Wolff is really driving at something like the distinction Coleridge was later to make between fancy and imagination. Although Wolff does not assign perception to a primary imagination in the way that Tetens, Maass, and Coleridge later do, he differentiates between a reproductive power that responds to the association of ideas (*imaginatio*) and an active, creating faculty (*Facultas fingendi*). Wolff's distinction thus follows the same lines as Coleridge's distinction between fancy and imagination.

We face a similar situation in the work of J. G. Sulzer. In brief, as we have already noted in passing, Sulzer distinguishes not between *Phantasie* and *Einbildungskraft*, but between *Einbildungskraft* and *Dichtungskraft*. (This is natural, for Sulzer read Tetens and cites him.) Yet his discrimination between these two terms carries somewhat the same weight as Coleridge's definitions in the *Biographia*. In his *Allgemeine Theorie der schönen Künste* (1771–1774, rev. 1792–1799) and his *Allgemeine Theorie der Dichtkunst* (1788), Sulzer indicates that *Einbildungskraft* associates images, but *Dichtungskraft* unifies and molds them into a poetic or idealized, finished product. Sulzer's distinction enters a middle ground, carrying with it something of Coleridge's later division between primary and secondary imagination. Sulzer tends to drop *Phantasie* as a separate and full faculty, in the same way Wolff did, because it does not appear as a separate entry in his *Allgemeine Theorie der schönen Künste*. But both *Einbildungskraft* and *Dichtungskraft* do. *Einbildungskraft* is for Sulzer a combination of Coleridge's primary imagination *and* fancy. His *Dichtungskraft* is then closely equivalent to Coleridge's secondary or poetically creative imagination. Whereas Coleridge's distinction is three-fold (fancy and primary and secondary imaginations), the distinctions of both Wolff and Sulzer are essentially two-fold.

Sulzer does, however mention the *Vorstellungskraft* as the most basic level of imaginative power. This roughly corresponds to the perceptive power or *Fassungskraft* in Tetens and to the primary imagination in Coleridge. Tetens in fact affected Sulzer's revision of the entries on *Einbildungskraft* and *Dichtungskraft*. *Phantasie* for Sulzer then becomes the poet's repository for images and ideas, the "weapons" that help him win over the hearts and minds of men ("*Phantasie ist das Zeughaus, woraus er die Waffen nimmt, die ihm die Siege über die Gemüther der Menschen erwerben helfen*").[15]

With Tetens and his *Philosophische Versuche* (1776–1777), we have a German distinction that is clearly tripartite. Tetens' apparent equation of *Phantasie* with *Einbildungskraft* is only superficial, relating to his nominal labels and not to his concepts. For Tetens employs *Dichtkraft* and *Dichtungsvermögen* to express the highest, creative, joining and modifying reach of the mind. *Phantasie* is really a power of association. He likens it to a curator who can rearrange pictures in a gallery but cannot himself paint new ones. At a more fundamental level is *Fassungskraft*, the power of perception, and at a more advanced level is *Dichtungsvermögen* or "*die* selbsthätige Phantasie," the self-activating or self-willed power to produce new, unified images and works of art. We should keep in mind, too, that Tetens—and through him both Sulzer and Kant—are indebted to Gerard.

All these wonderful terms—beginning with *Dicht*,—lasted for only a generation or two in Germany, and by the time of Schelling in the late 1790s, *Einbildungskraft* had come to bear the weight of two or three possible meanings, one of which Sulzer and Tetens had once indicated by their use of *Dichtungskraft*. As these resonant terms beginning with *Dicht* began to pass out of a common critical parlance, both *Phantasie* and *Einbildungskraft*, taking up the slack, assumed a greater load and acquired more implications. Starting in the 1770s, therefore, but especially by the 1790s, *Phantasie* and *Einbildungskraft* were less often equated, for there was frequently no *Dichtungskraft* against which to lump them together. Critics and thinkers like Platner, Maass, Kant, and Schelling began to concentrate on differentiating between the words *Phantasie* and *Einbildungskraft*, because they were not, in general, employing the *Dicht*-terms. Such distinctions between "fancy" and "imagination" are not the first ones, however, in Germany. These thinkers are shifting semantic, not conceptual ground. Often poetry or art is only one part of the subject, so they are tempted to drop the *Dicht*-terms as being too narrowly associated with the fine arts. Kant, Platner, Schelling, and Maass typify this trend, and their discriminations between *Phantasie* and *Einbildungskraft* reveal an intellectual content similar to the distinctions between *Einbildungskraft* (or *Phantasie*) and the *Dicht-*terms.*

## PLATNER'S 1772 DISTINCTION

In his 1793 *Philosophische Aphorismen*, Ernst Platner specifically distinguishes between fancy and imagination: "When fancy (*Phantasie*), in respect to the clarity and liveliness of its images, attains a superior level of perfection, then it is called imagination (*Einbildungskraft*). All men have fancy; only unusually good minds possess imagination. The difference is like that between judgment and shrewd sagacity."[16] Imagination is a higher and a more perfected or complete power with greater liveliness, meaning, judgment, and purpose. Platner also expresses the increasingly common assumption that fancy is subsumed by the imagination, which alone accounts for the gift of genius. *Einbildungskraft* is, for Platner, a more synthetic act, where associations are not strung together but shaped more actively.

Twenty-one years earlier, in his 1772 *Anthropologie für Aerzte und Weltweise*, Platner had noted four aspects to the difference between *Phantasie* and *Einbildungskraft*. First, Platner views *Phantasie* as the mere presentation of images, mechanically associated in a way that acts through the nervous system. This association can be spontaneous or willed, ordered or random, yet it is "mechanical" because the images associated are not transformed; they reappear in the bits and pieces in which they were first experienced. Second, fancy is, in its association of images, a primary source of the comic, as Coleridge would later stress. Comic writers, states Platner, have a lively fancy. This statement is unique in the German distinctions between fancy and imagination, for although Maass makes a connection between wit (*Witz*) and fancy in his *Versuch*, he does not single out comedy as a result of fancy. The observation later becomes one of the more intriguing elements in the English distinctions, for it rescues fancy from being completely overshadowed by imagination. Third, Platner argues that fancy need not be governed by any principle of reality. It is free-flowing and relatively untouched by fact: "The presentation of ideas [or images] without ref-

---

* Cf. P. Gäng, *Aesthetik* (1785), quoted in Blankenberg, *Litterarische Zusätze:* genius has *"eine leichte, ausgebreitete lebhafte Phantasie, und eine fertige, starke, ausgedehnte Dichtkraft."*

erence to reality and without the test of possibility, verisimilitude and proportion, is fancy."[17]

And last, Platner categorically separates fancy from imagination: "*Ich unterscheide die Einbildungskraft aus guten Gründen von der Phantasie.*" For one thing, the power of invention stems directly from imagination and not from fancy. When associated ideas and images thicken in the mind, this is fancy; but when they pack and cluster together so tightly that greater unity can be discerned, this is an act of imagination. In association, our ideas, images, and their objects start to link together, mechanically, and then in some cases the objects become "very closely compounded through a gradual mixing or cohesiveness of ideas. This last operation of the imagination requires more genius than the first, when individually remembered ideas are presented." In imagination there is a greater power of coherence and unity. When Platner enumerates the qualities of "*Das erfinderische Genie,*" he includes as two separate qualities "a lively and extensive mechanical fancy, which brings forth a large quantity of particular ideas," and "a lively imagination through which these ideas are presented to the psyche in a vivid and concrete manner not only as particulars, but together in a complex."[18] Platner's distinction, carried through a good part of his 1772 *Anthropologie*, came two years before Gerard's *Essay on Genius* and four years before Tetens' *Philosophische Versuche*. Though not appearing in a specifically artistic or literary context, his distinction becomes important to literary discussions and criticism. Significantly, Coleridge read Platner's 1772 *Anthropologie*.[19]

## MAASS, KANT, AND SCHELLING

Although Platner refers to different levels of liveliness in the fancy ("*Von den Graden der Lebhaftigkeit der Phantasie*"), the highest of which is presumably *Einbildungskraft*, his distinction is essentially a two-fold one, between fancy and imagination. The three-fold distinction in Tetens between a fundamental imagination as the power of perception, fancy as an associative power, and a higher imagination (*Dichtungskraft*) as the creative and unifying force, crops up again in J. G. E. Maass's *Versuch über die Einbildungskraft* (1797), which, like Tetens' *Versuche*, Coleridge read and used heavily in the *Biographia*.

Aware of the confusion and proliferation of terms, Maass tries to explain *Einbildungskraft* in two ways. First, it means "*im engsten Sinne,*" the simple power of perceiving and reproducing images in their unchanged state. Here, imagination is involved in the act of perception, *"und das ist ihre ursprüngliche Thatigkeit."* But *Einbildungskraft* can also be used *"im weitesten Sinne des Worts,"* or *"in der weitesten Bedeutung,"* and in this sense it is a creative and poetic act that separates, alters, and reforms images. Maass likens its activity in this higher stage to a chemical reaction. When two images are acted upon by this higher state of the imagination, it is "like a chemical mixing of them, when they are so combined that we can no longer differentiate them one from another, and from them proceeds a third simple image itself."[20] This "chemical" simile would be echoed in Friedrich Schlegel's *"chemischer Witz,"* Thomas Brown's "chemistry of mind," and in J. S. Mill's "mental chemistry." In his concept of the higher nature of *Einbildungskraft,* Maass relies on the work of Tetens and, through Tetens, of Gerard.

Between the two levels of *Einbildungskraft* Maass places *Phantasie.* At times it is hard to distinguish *Phantasie* from the higher and more active level of *Einbildungskraft,* but there is at least one point of difference. Although *Phantasie,* says Maass, can indeed change images, it cannot unite or join them into new, simple images with the complete action of the higher level of *Einbildungskraft.* In other words, while *Phantasie* does not deal simply with "fixities and definites" in that it can alter images, it cannot recombine them into one simple image or symbol. That last unifying task in the creative process is reserved for the higher level of *Einbildungskraft,* which is a deeper perception of the world, or a poetic perception of a greater world.

In a spirit of dissection, Maass then slices up his three levels, the two of *Einbildungskraft* and the one of *Phantasie.* Although his terminology grows cumbersome, he discriminates two significant categories: spontaneous or unwilled associations as compared to associations where the will operates to join together images.[21] This distinction between unwilled and willed associations has a rough analogy in both Kant and Coleridge. One of the ways Coleridge distinguishes secondary imagination from primary is that the secondary imagination is "co-existing with the conscious will."

Kant's distinction between *Phantasie* and *Einbildungskraft* is based on the will itself, at least in the important quotation from the *Menschenkunde,* the same passage in which Kant attributes to Gerard the observation that *"die productive Einbildungskraft"* is the most important characteristic of genius. *Phantasie,* for Kant, is that part of the productive imagination which is unwilled or spontaneous. He makes a further, albeit confusing, distinction between *Phantasie* and *Einbildungskraft* in his *Anthropologie in Pragmatischer Hinsicht* (1800), a book Coleridge owned. Fancy is not under our conscious control. It "plays ... with us" and is a kind of spontaneous, freewheeling imagination. But then by identifying fancy with "creative imagination" (*schöpferische Einbildungskraft*), Kant raises the unanswered question of its relationship to the "productive imagination."[22]

Schelling discerns at least three or four levels of the imaginative or productive power. His specific distinction between *Phantasie* and *Einbildungskraft*, which runs throughout his works, is presented most clearly in his *Darstellung meines Systems der Philosophie* (1801) and his *Philosophie der Kunst* (1802), where he devotes sections of several pages to the general problem of distinction between them.

Schelling consistently uses *Phantasie* to represent the juxtaposition and rearrangement of what is already created in nature or in art. *Phantasie* deals with external appearances, does not change them but moves them, like chess pieces, to create new situations and relationships. The imagination is more a *productive* power. It creates new images and ideas. It is not limited to the rearrangement of what is real but invents symbols and shapes the world of ideas into physical being:[23]

> In relation to fancy (*Phantasie*) I mean by imagination (*Einbildungskraft*) that in which the productions of art are conceived and developed, fancy as that which views them externally, as art projects them in their outward form, and insofar as art also represents them. It is the same relation between reason and intellectual intuition. In the reason and similarly from the materials of reason, ideas are created, and intellectual intuition is the mental ("inner") representative [of them]. Fancy thus is the intellectual intuition in art [as imagination is its reason].[24]

In addition to this distinction, imagination enjoys a special relationship with reason. Whereas reason stands as the ideal potential or the conceived possibility of the existence of something, the imagination "potentizes" reason and transforms the intellection of reason into sensuous reality. Fancy, on the contrary, can deal only with those things that already have been created through the force of imagination. "*Denn Einbildungskraft bezieht sich auf die Vernunft, wie Phantasie auf den Verstand. Jene produktive, diese reproduktive.*"[25] Tetens himself had connected *Phantasie* with the understanding (*Verstand*), and he claimed that the law of the association of ideas "is only a law of fancy in the reproduction of ideas."[26]

Among the many German distinctions between fancy and imagination, ranging over seventy years from Wolff through Schelling, several facts stand out. First, the distinctions are not all the same, but they are similar. Second, as the Enlightenment progresses, there is a marked tendency to rely more and more on *Phantasie* and *Einbildungskraft* and to drop other perfectly good terms, such as those beginning with *Dicht-*. Third, the German distinction between fancy and imagination is caught up in other distinctions, for many German thinkers, like Coleridge, divide the imagination itself into levels. Fourth, the German thinkers are oriented to a psychological and philosophical direction. They are less apt than the English to speak of specific literary works or writers as fanciful in contrast to those that are imaginative. Finally, while the German distinctions have the same general thrust, in no case is a single previously made distinction the one source of a later one. By the last thirty years of the century a number of distinctions were available, each influenced by one or more previous writers, both German and English. Duff, Gerard, Beattie, and Reynolds were all read in Germany.

Each generation must struggle with the words it uses to act as symbols for its most important ideas. To some extent we are able from hindsight to look back on the period from 1660 to 1820 and to trace the growth and involutions of the distinctions between fancy and imagination and their related terms.* But thinkers then, as we do now, found it hard to measure the climate of ideas; words responded like drops of mercury, slippery and inconstant, yet the only things capable of registering change precisely because of their fluid and responsive nature.

* For further distinctions in Hazlitt, Wordsworth, Fichte, Schiller, and Goethe, see below, chs. 15–16, 18–19, and my Introduction to the *Biographia* in the *Collected Coleridge*.

# 14

# A PLATEAU IN BRITAIN AND
# DEVELOPMENTS IN AMERICA

*B*oth Sir Joshua Reynolds and Dugald Stewart represent the culmination of a long development in Enlightenment England and Scotland.[1] Like Kant in Germany, they stand on a plateau from which rises directly the Romantic movement. Kant is a great synthetic thinker, and Reynolds and Stewart are more purely summarizing figures. But in the breadth and generality of their statements about the imagination, they reflect how dominant the idea had grown in art and speculative thought.

## ENGLAND: REYNOLDS

Writers and artists tend to be associated with specific dates, often the year of a famous work or a year in the middle of their productive careers. But most individuals, unless they die young, cut across a swath of time that extends three or four decades. Sir Joshua Reynolds was twenty-one when Akenside's *The Pleasures of Imagination* appeared (1744). In 1786, two years after Johnson died, Reynolds delivered his thirteenth *Discourse* at the Royal Academy, where he was its first president. In that year, within walking distance of the Academy, fourteen-year-old Coleridge was enrolled at Christ's Hospital School, reading Plotinus, reciting poetry, and discoursing on metaphysics in the courtyards and archways.

Reynolds' *Discourses* span twenty-one years (1769–1790). They form a coda, the quick and final repetition of themes developed over several decades. The first five are concerned with "classical" concepts, such as imitation, decorum, and "general nature." The sixth and seventh

(1774, 1776) reflect the growing distrust both of reason as narrowly and abstractly interpreted and of the neoclassic over-reliance on system, method, and rules. The thirteenth *Discourse* reveals the increasing centrality of the idea of the imagination. Essentially, Reynolds uses it to replace the function of reason in the arts. Like the concept of the sublime, it offered a great deal to the new psychological criticism without necessarily either threatening the classical ideal of moral purpose or sweeping away all assumptions of the classical approach based on the imitation of nature.

Caught up in the groundswell of interest in the imagination, Reynolds subtitles his thirteenth *Discourse:* "Art Not Merely Imitation, But under the Direction of the Imagination." The development of the *Discourses* and the change in Reynolds' stance symbolize the progress and force of the imagination as an idea after 1750. During the 1770s and 1780s it was giving theoretical backing and a philosophical or quasi-philosophical foundation to the interests of psychology and the concrete. It unified these interests and began to supersede "reason." Reynolds' *Discourses* reflect the play of pieces that was passing on the larger critical board. The pair "genius and imagination" become, as the *Discourses* progress, inseparable. Reynolds adds another critical voice to those already proclaiming that human passion responds most fully to the imagination; feeling saturates art. Reason, he maintains, "is required to inform us when that very reason is to give way to feeling."[2]

He pries further apart the widening meanings of fancy and imagination. Fancy is for him slightly derogatory. It harbors delusions, and he uses "fantastical" in a disparaging sense.[3] By the thirteenth *Discourse*, he finds "imagination" wholly desirable and drops "fancy" as having any real meaning in discussions about genius.

The son of a clergyman, Reynolds extends the tendency of Akenside and Tucker. He asserts that imagination lifts man's consciousness to an awareness of the divine, "to the desires of the mind, to that spark of divinity which we have within, impatient of being circumscribed and pent up by the world which is about us."[4] If the wording were changed slightly, this might be mistaken for Wordsworth or for a sentence from Shelley's *Defence of Poetry*. Here again, the path of imagination wends its way to the top of a promontory, where at the edge it stops abruptly, looking out onto the spaces of theology and metaphysics.

In art, the value of suggestiveness is not as an imitation of nature but as an imitation of or incitement to an activity of mind, which then anchors itself in nature as it turns to particular situations. The artist does not present a *camera obscura* view. Rather he imitates "what it is *natural for the imagination* to be delighted with" and what finds an analogy in the mind. The whole "object and intention" of art is "to gratify the mind by realising and embodying what never existed but in the imagination." In these general premises, Reynolds anticipates Hazlitt's critical stance and Coleridge's belief that the arts serve as a mediator between man and nature.

Reynolds downgrades reason as a deductive and truthful measure of the arts. Reason had too long been made to stand for "partial, confined, argumentative theories," which Reynolds characterizes as "principles falsely called rational." He harkens back to Greek humanism where man is the measure of all things, not man's systems or formal contrivances. With finality and assurance, he defines the imagination as the response of the whole individual turning to particular ideas and actions. The imagination connects the particular to the universal; it unites the specificity we always find in individual situations with "the accumulated experience of our whole life."[5]

From its commerce with the world, the mind develops an "habitual reason" or a sense of taste—"a sagacity which is far from being contradictory to right reason, and is superior to any occasional exercise of that faculty." This sagacity, when turning actively to the production of art, is really the imagination. It "does not wait for the slow progress of deduction, but goes at once, by what appears a kind of intuition, to the conclusion."[6]

Reynolds is describing an *organic* function of the mind or psyche. The imagination shuffles and integrates its material so rapidly and unreflectively that minute acts and decisions seem to merge instantaneously into larger plans and important choices. "A man endowed with this faculty feels and acknowledges the truth, though it is not always in his power . . . to give a reason for it . . . many and very intricate considerations may unite to form the principle." The imagination shapes the ungainly, complex thing we call experience. It simplifies experience, yet it can do this without denying any detail of fact or feeling.

Reynolds concludes that "the imagination is the residence of truth. If the imagination be affected, the conclusion is fairly drawn."[7] He is the first Enlightenment thinker to formulate bluntly and without qualification a belief becoming widespread: truth is attained through the imagination and, more specifically, through imaginative art. From this point, it was a short step for the high Romantics to conclude that truth in art can be the truth of life, nature, and the cosmos, that imagination is the highest organ of philosophy, and that art is the only way to climax philosophical inquiry. Reynolds' assertion that "imagination is the residence of truth" is the prototype of later avowedly romantic ones. A. W. Schlegel's *Lectures on Dramatic Art and Literature* (1809–1811) left his friend and companion Madame de Staël with the impression "that imagination, far from being an enemy to truth, brings it forward more than any other faculty of the mind."[8]

The importance of Dugald Stewart (1753–1828) lies not in the novelty of what he said but in the fact that he was so widely read. Though he began his career as professor of mathematics at the University of Edinburgh when he was twenty-two, he was at heart a moralist. Within three years he supplemented his work by a course of lectures on ethics, and by the time he was thirty-two he had become professor of moral philosophy, succeeding Adam Ferguson. His eloquence attracted students that included Walter Scott, Francis Jeffrey, Thomas Brown, James Mill, and Archibald Alison.

Stewart's *Elements of the Philosophy of the Human Mind* (1792), later followed by two supplementary volumes (1814, 1827), are a popular exposition of the "Common Sense" approach of his mentor Thomas Reid, updated by insights from associationist psychology. In his synthesis of Scottish intuitionalism and the association of ideas, the imagination occupies a central place. Stewart maintains that imagination is not a single "faculty" of the mind. It is a coalescing of four distinct faculties or functions of mind and is genuinely present only when all of these combine and interfuse.

In Stewart's analysis of this "complex power," imagination is not the simple addition of these four faculties of conception, abstraction, fancy, and judgment or taste. It is the reacting and compounding of them to form a whole greater than the sum of its parts. The imagination becomes not just another static faculty but a real force or originating power, similar to the German sense of *Kraft* or of *Produktionsvermögen*. This "complex power" or animating spirit becomes so important for Stewart's scheme of thought that the chapter on imagination climaxes his book and acts as the unifying element that caps the other concepts and holds them together like a keystone.

For Stewart, the imagination has both moral and creative attributes. It can be a sympathetic power so important that, as Stewart remarks, "I have often been inclined to think that the . . . coldness and selfishness of mankind may be traced . . . to a want of attention and a want of imagination." Stewart's concept of the imagination as a power that needs to be engaged in order to attain the highest moral and social good anticipates the reasoning of Hazlitt a decade later. Stewart sees the imagination as "the great spring of human activity, and the principal source of human improvement."[9]

As Hazlitt himself would do, Stewart moves from the moral force of the imagination to its indispensable place in the fine arts, genius, and poetry. When imagination is possessed "in an uncommon degree," says Stewart, it forms the groundwork of all poetical genius and creativity. In the fine arts as a whole, genius springs from "a cultivated taste, combined with a creative Imagination."[10] With Stewart, as with Reynolds, the imagination has become the hub of all important values, the axis around which everything turns.

## DEVELOPMENTS IN AMERICA

Just as American philosophy from the late 1700s to the middle 1800s was, especially in schools and colleges, largely imported from the Scottish Common Sense thinkers, so American critical and aesthetic theory in the same period took as its model the works of Kames, Hugh Blair, George Campbell, Alison, and Jeffrey. Also helping to shape the idea of the imagination as it appeared on the western horizon was a belletristic awareness of and admiration for the poetry of Akenside, Gray, the Wartons, Cowper, Chatterton, and even Coleridge and Wordsworth. America produced numerous odes to genius and poems praising fancy. Although most are conventional, one is definitely not, and we shall examine Philip Freneau's "The Power of Fancy" (1770), which is remarkable for its adaptation of themes expressed by Gray, Collins, and Joseph Warton, while adding a fresh vision of a New World shimmering with fancy. Finally, a moral sense that was derived in part from the Scottish School but owed much to Addison and Johnson kept American thinkers and poets mindful that imagination goes deeper than fiction and aesthetics to exert, as one essayist puts it simply, "influence on life." As Goethe and Keats were so acutely aware, imagination *intensifies;* it intensifies both happiness and sorrow.

Until the 1820s and 1830s, when Coleridge entered the philosophical consciousness of America largely through James Marsh's edition of the *Aids to Reflection* (1829) and subsequent reviews such as that by Frederic Henry Hedge in *The Christian Examiner* (1833); and until German studies began to attract serious academic attention, the attitude toward German transcendentalism and ideas of the imagination was negative. Although not fully representative, an 1801 letter in the Philadelphia *Port-Folio* indicates the initial resistance to German philosophy, often born not so much of a contrary view as of a simple lack of acquaintance: "In every department of science and literature, what loads of trash burden the stalls of Leipzig . . . but none, perhaps, so much as in that of metaphysics, and moral philosophy . . . A disciple of Kant, one

Fichte . . . has written a book, ridiculing the ideas of a future life . . . and of a supreme Being . . . [Fichte] now wanders about Germany, scribbling, and holding himself forth, as the victim of persecution."[11]

These circumstances in the young republic help us realize how instrumental Coleridge and Carlyle were in bringing German thought into the ken of English-speaking people. Emerson saw the Germans first through the eyes of these two men. We shall not undertake the huge task of tracing the course the idea of the imagination took in America after about 1820. But we should note that before the 1820s America, too, like England and Scotland from the late 1770s to the early 1790s, was on a plateau. Only after the interjections of Coleridge and Carlyle, and after the simultaneous arrival of German thought from other sources, did Emerson, Hawthorne, and Poe turn to a deeper American scrutiny and exercise of the imagination.

America in the late eighteenth century was not directly concerned with the imagination as an idea because, as a group of colonies and later as a nation, it had not yet obtained a weight of intellectual and literary tradition or a sense of its own civilization being over-refined. To develop a critical, let alone an analytic or philosophical, idea of the imagination demands a considerable degree of self-consciousness. And perhaps the degree of self-consciousness necessary for such an idea did not develop until Emerson began *Nature*, in 1836, with the remark: "Our age is retrospective . . . It writes biographies, histories, and criticism." Years later, in 1880 at the Concord Lyceum, Emerson summed up the tenor of the age during his youth: "The key to the period appeared to be that the mind had become aware of itself. Men grew reflective and intellectual. There was a new consciousness." In these *Historic Notes of Life and Letters in New England*, Emerson also recalled of himself and his circle that "Germany had created criticism in vain for us until 1820, when Edward Everett returned from his five years in Europe" to exert as a teacher at Harvard an influence "almost comparable to that of Pericles in Athens." But before 1820 no Everett had returned, nor was the mind yet sufficiently "aware of itself."

One thing conspicuously absent from American discussions of the imagination before 1825, as compared with the other side of the Atlantic, is the painful examination of the choking effect of refinement and civilization on the artist. We often analyze and praise something when we feel that it is just beginning to stultify us, or to slip from our grasp. There was no cause for such analyses in America. Its inhabitants, too, perhaps knew the state of nature well enough not to turn to it for an answer to the question where imagination had fled after Shakespeare and Milton. Besides, the burden on the writers of the fledgling nation was not so much one of the past; it was then, as in large part it remains today, uniquely a burden of the future, the burden of a country destined to create wonderful ideals for the world that it could never quite live up to itself, a never-ending optimistic tragedy. The great split between man and nature, the dualism that scarred so much European thought, simply was not a large factor in America before 1820 or 1830, and so the imagination was not required to stitch it up.

### THE AMERICAN MAINSTREAM

Yet the interest that was directed toward the imagination from about 1770 until the first few decades of the next century was considerable. Kames's *Elements of Criticism* (1762) went through thirty-one American editions by 1883, almost one every four years. Blair's *Lectures* (1783), complete or abridged, enjoyed fifty-three editions, and students at Harvard and Yale used Blair as a standard text. By 1835 thirty-nine of these editions had been printed, and ten other colleges were assigning the *Lectures.** John Quincy Adams, as Boylston Professor of Rhetoric and Oratory at Harvard, based his *Lectures on Rhetoric and Oratory* (1810) on Blair. Although it was rhetoric, not the imagination, that became a focus of interest in the college curriculum, the approach to rhetoric by the Scottish critics was basically psychological, with the premises of eliciting and cultivating emotional and imaginative response.

Shortly after 1800, interest in the association of ideas burgeoned, stimulated first by Alison's *Essays on Taste* (1790) and then magnified by Francis Jeffrey's popularization of Alison's theories in his article on "Beauty" in the *Encyclopedia Britannica* (1816). Typical of the inroads made by associationism is Samuel Gilman's appreciation of Thomas Brown published by the *North American Review* in July of 1824:

> By imagination, in the common use of the word, is meant the *creative power* of the Imagination. But is even *this* a separate and peculiar faculty of the mind? . . . First there arises . . . some conception, or simple suggestion of a particular subject; next, this subject excites in him a *desire* of producing by it some beautiful or interesting result . . . and our judgment, all the time, approving and rejecting, according to . . . relations of fitness and unfitness.[12]

Another contributor to the *North American Review* was William Cullen Bryant, whose 1825 *Lectures on Poetry* (pub. 1884) echo Brown, the associationists in general, and late eighteenth-century criti-

* See William Charvat, *The Origins of American Critical Thought* (Philadelphia, 1936), pp. 30–31. On the influence of Scottish associationism, see J. W. Rathbun, "The Historical Sense in American Associationism," *PQ* 40(1961): 553–568.

cal theory. But Bryant applies these points directly to poetry and criticism. Poetry is not an imitative but a *suggestive* art, as Bryant explains in his first lecture "On the Nature of Poetry." The "very limitation" of language forces it to address the mind, not the senses, and as Reynolds pointed out, the best art pleases the mind—the imagination. Suggestive touches, adds Bryant, "act like a spell upon the imagination and . . . fill it, perhaps, with greater delight than the best defined objects could do. The imagination is the most active and the least susceptible of fatigue of all the faculties of the human mind."

Bryant stresses that poetry should not excite the imagination alone. A train of nothing but "striking images" will not do. Sounding like Hazlitt, Bryant calls for poetry to excite pathos and the passions, to involve understanding and reason. In an unusual anticipation of what would a generation or so later become a popular critical term, Bryant attacks "pure poetry" as "mere imagery, with the least possible infusion of human emotion." The closest combination of imagination with passion and with figurative language is to be valued most highly. The union of imagination with passionate sympathy is exemplified by Ophelia who, with "the wildness of frenzy in her eye, dressed with fantastic garlands of wild flowers, and singing snatches of old tunes," presents

> a picture for the imagination, but it is one which affects the heart . . . when, in the midst of her incoherent talk she utters some simple allusion to her own sorrows, as when she says, We know what we are, but know not what we may be, this touching sentence, addressed merely to our sympathy, strongly excites the imagination. It sets before us the days when she knew sorrow only by name, before her father was slain by the hand of her lover, and before her lover was estranged.

Also like Hazlitt, Bryant champions the importance of feeling in critical judgment, noting that "strong feeling is always a sure guide." Gerard had made similar comments on the passionate association of images in Shakespeare's *Tempest*. Bryant notes that oratory is, except for metrical arrangement, based on the same principles of passion and imagination as poetry, which again shows the influence of textbook Rhetorics that permeated American education.

Stepping back to 1800, we get another glimpse of the general foundation of the idea of imagination that was laid in the early part of the century. In that year appeared John Witherspoon's *Lectures on Moral Philosophy and Eloquence*. Witherspoon, born in Scotland, was ordained there and did not leave until 1768, when at forty-five he became president of Princeton. He was also the only clergyman to sign the Declaration of Independence. His posthumous *Lectures*, published six years after his death, reflect courses he taught at Princeton as well as his earlier studies at the University of Edinburgh. His view of the imagination typically combines the Scottish School and a broadly classical, moral aesthetic that has its roots in Addison and Hutcheson. Witherspoon identifies four innate senses as those for beauty, pleasure in imitation, harmony, and order or proportion: "the whole of these senses may be considered as belonging to one class, and to be the particulars which either singly, or by the union of several of them or of the whole, produce what is called the pleasures of the imagination."[13] These pleasures are "applicable to all the fine arts."

Addison's "pleasures of imagination" and Shaftesbury's and Hutcheson's "senses" enumerated by Witherspoon were part of America's habitual thoughts about the imaginative power. To these were added the psychological and critical observations of later eighteenth-century associationists, all of which culminated in remarks like those of Bryant in his first lecture on poetry. In 1803, for instance, Joseph Dennie's important weekly, the *Port-Folio* (Philadelphia, 1800–1827), carried the comment: "The accuracy, learning, and acuteness of a Gerrard [sic] has developed the various sources of the pleasures of the imagination . . . [Addison] has the merit of commencing the inquiry, and of affording, though not all, at least the principal materials."[14]

The *Port-Folio*, for which Dennie was called by the *Monthly Review* of Charleston our "American Addison," published, among numerous reviews, biographies, and reprints of British and Continental authors, part of Coleridge's translation of *Wallenstein*, poems by Cowper and Chatterton, letters of Johnson, and comments on Wolff, Gray, Joseph Warton, Samuel Bowles, Hartley, and Priestley. Because of its readership throughout the country and its literary and philosophical interests, the *Port-Folio* is broadly representative of American thoughts on the imagination in the first quarter of the nineteenth century. Its pages of "Original Poetry" include poems dedicated to "The Powers of Genius" and others dealing with the effect of "fancy" on the heart's desires ("Creative Fancy's magic power/Shall gild the remnant of my day" and "Amusing fancy here shall come,/And paint the past in colors strong"). Taken as a whole, the verse shows something curious. The American attitude toward the imagination is generally more cautious than the British or German one of 1800. There is hesitancy about what Shakespeare calls "the food of sweet and bitter Fancy." Again typical is this quatrain from the *Port-Folio:*

> I guard my heart, lest it should woo
> Unreal beauties that Fancy drew,
> And, disappointed, feel despair,
> At loss of things, that never were.

One article, sounding like Johnson or Hume, discusses the relation of imagination to "illusion," a relation unfortunately necessary for "the business of human life." Imagination leads us to intense personal attachments, but if we could pierce through our illusions, the author remarks with a wry distance, we could foresee "the sad seasons and corroding cares of matrimony" and "the population of the world would suffer a diminution."[15]

The *Port-Folio* featured several articles on sympathy as a product of association and imagination. There were calls in reviews, too, for a more imaginative and "genuine language of nature and of passion."[16] Adam Smith was a dominant influence on discussions of sympathy; Blair and Priestley, now an American, on those of impassioned speech. Though some of the *Lyrical Ballads* were reprinted, no mention seems to be made of their Preface.

One American essay is characteristic of interest in the subject as a whole. Entitled simply "On Fancy," it appeared in the April 1807 issue of the *Monthly Register* of Charleston. Written by "a young gentleman of South Carolina," it sums up a bundle of related concerns. First, like most Americans at this time, the author prefers "fancy" to "imagination." Many, perhaps following Addison, used the two words synonymously. But even in the United States in 1807 there was awareness of a possible difference between the terms, as the editor of the *Monthly Review* reveals in introducing the essay: "We take it for granted, that the young gentleman uses the word *"Fancy"* as synonimous with *Imagination;* if not, the whole of his reasoning rests upon a false foundation, and consequently . . . must hasten to swift decay."[17] The two terms were obviously being used with distinctly different connotations by some, or else the editor's note would have been unnecessary.

The essay, which harkens back to Hobbes's apostrophe to fancy in his "Answer to Davenant," claims that fancy may "devise theories of philosophy, or inspire the offerings of the muse." The writer echoes Gerard and Ogilvie in calling for the "mutual and cooperative" influence of fancy and judgment. In a remarkable coincidence, the essayist, employing a metaphor similar to Shaftesbury's and anticipating a somewhat different use of it by Keats in his letters, says that "he, who pretends to be enamoured of the scenes of fancy, will be viewed as a cameleon, living on air." But then, swinging in mood like Keats's *Ode to a Nightingale*, the essayist concludes that "To possess a fancy vigorous and elastic . . . is to command happiness." Furthermore, "The influence of fancy cherishes and expands the germs of religion and patriotism," not to mention the fine arts, where we may give it freer rein. The author also quotes Akenside's *Pleasures*. Jejune though it is, the essay reveals a considerable range in its rapid summary of multiple ideas and attitudes converging to one large concept.

### FRENEAU AND THE POWER OF FANCY

It seems at first odd that Philip Freneau's "The Power of Fancy" appeared when it did, in 1770. In America this is a singularly early claim for the imaginative faculty. Yet the poem comes directly from a tradition established by Warton, Gray, and Collins, poets whom Freneau might well have read while at Princeton, where he graduated with Aaron Burr, James Madison, and H. H. Brackenridge, and where he heard Witherspoon lecture. (Madison was Witherspoon's pupil for a year.)

"The Power of Fancy" is a progress poem in reverse, a stunning redirection of the usual British theme of the progress of poetry westward from Greece to Rome and then to Hibernia's shore. Freneau instead traces Fancy from Arcadia back eastward to the Hebrides, to the home of Ossian, then to "Britain's fertile land," on to "Tempe's verdant wood" and Hector's tomb, until she leads Freneau "over Ganges' streams" and places him on Tinian. Then he pleads with Fancy:

> Farther, farther in the east,
> Till it almost meets the west,
> Let us wandering both be lost
> On Taitis' sea-beat coast,
> Bear me from that distant strand,
> Over ocean, over land,
> To California's golden shore—
> Fancy, stop, and rove no more.

The reverse progress has been a continuous eastering, an "orienting," until fancy returns to the New World on the California coast. Fancy has thus left and returned to the American continent and been everywhere, from Arcadia east and farther east to California, except in America itself. Is it possible that Freneau meant to leave this break in Fancy's global circuit, this final three-thousand-mile stretch, because its promise was as yet unfilled, yet definitely there?

The answer appears in part in Freneau's preface to a satiric piece, titled "Advice to Authors," that he wrote eighteen years later in 1788 under the name of "The late Mr. Robert Slender." These comments also throw light on the question whether America at this time may have been without the literary self-consciousness and over-refinement necessary for any close formulations of the idea of imagination. Freneau begins the piece:

> There are few writers of books in this new world, and amongst these very few that deal in works of imagination ... In a country, which two hundred years ago was peopled only by savages ... it is really wonderful there should be any ... original authors at all ... especially when it is considered, that according to the common course of things, any particular

nation or people must have arrived to, or rather passed, their meridian of opulence and refinement, before they consider the professors of the fine arts in any other light than a nuisance to the community ... I mean to say, in plain language, that you may make something by weaving garters, or mending old sails, when an Epic poem would be your utter destruction.

Freneau, who twice went to sea for extended periods and may himself have mended old sail, had epic ambitions, but his declining years were blighted by poverty and the loss of his home. In 1832, his eightieth year, he died in a blizzard.

"The Power of Fancy," written when he was eighteen, displays a sense of imagination as a cosmic power of ideas and of divine-human creation, "A spark from Jove's resplendent throne." All creations—all things no matter how solid—are but "Fancies of the Power Divine," divine imaginations. There is a generally transcendental feeling here, as there is in his mention of "Ideas of the Almighty mind!" These lines suggest some of Herder's poetry, or German *Frühromantik* effusions, fed by Platonism, on the power of God living in man's creative imagination. Freneau connects the strength of fancy not only with the cosmic-religious sense in Herder and Akenside but with art and human happiness in general: "Fancy, to thy power I owe/Half my happiness below."

But this line, "Fancy, to thy power I owe," will return to Freneau in a disturbingly transposed key. In "The Power of Fancy" this ubiquitous and inventive force descends "like lightning" to "the prison of the fiends," where Freneau objects to any further downward direction: "But, O never may she tell/Half the frightfulness of hell." The possibly disturbing consequences of fancy evaporate into the bright air again. But then in "The House of Night" (1779)—written during the Revolution, in which Freneau was made prisoner by the British—the fifth stanza begins immediately to dwell on wild and frightening effects of imagination. Instead of "Fancy, to thy power I owe ... happiness," Freneau strikes an ominous and almost helpless note:

> Fancy, I own thy power—when sunk in sleep
> Thou play'st thy wild delusive part so well
> You lift me into immortality,
> Depict new heavens, or draw scenes of hell.

Freneau recounts "fancies of malignant power!" and "A fearful vision at the midnight hour." His phrasing recalls Coleridge's *Dejection*. The power of fancy in "The House of Night" suffers under a dark and horrible tinge. The poem could well be a scenario for a frightful tale by Poe. "Fancy, I own thy power," becomes a sinister and haunting admission. Freneau, who earlier had seen Fancy where "innocence reclines her head," now surveys a "horrid form": *"Fancy, I own thy power—Death* on the couch,/With fleshless limbs, at rueful length, was laid." Now he hears "howling dogs" and on the "wide extended Chesapeake" he sees, "by pictures fancy formed, The black ship travelling through the noisy gale." America had, by the late 1700s, essentially experienced what both Emerson and Poe would later find in the imagination: the highest confidence and also a curious, preternatural fear.

# 15

# ORGANIC SENSIBILITY: HAZLITT

*T*he development of William Haz-
litt's career mirrors the growth of the eighteenth-century associationist
tradition from which he emerges. He begins, as did most early and mid-
eighteenth-century critics, with premises of moral thought based on
psychology. After expanding this stance in his first book, *An Essay on
the Principles of Human Action* (1805), he shifts to a deeper consideration of the human psyche, its processes of association, its active and passive confrontations with the world, and its imaginative shaping of experience. As his second book, he abridges the seven volumes of Tucker's
*Light of Nature Pursued* (1807). Then, having disengaged himself
from a mechanical associationism, Hazlitt turns, as the mid and late
eighteenth century before him had turned, to the uses of sympathy,
imagination, and a more fluid and coalescing associationism in the criticism of the arts, especially poetry.[1]

Hazlitt's forte as a critic is an unerring eye for the passage or phrase
that reveals the character of a work or of its author, or, as he often says,
which exemplifies the process of imagination. His own writing has unusual flair and verve, and he tinges his prose with pungent metaphors.
Although often unequivocal, he is remarkably sensitive. Extending the
approaches of Gerard, Priestley, Smith, Beattie, Tucker, and Alison,
Hazlitt enriches the background of psychology by reemphasizing the
classical concept of art as *mimesis,* an imitation of nature. After 1807, he
turns his theory (if it can be called such) directly to the concrete.
Others had done this, but their criticisms of literary passages appear
more as appendices to their analyses of ideas. Hazlitt places his criticism
directly in front and is suspicious of system, definition, and what
Wordsworth calls "meddling intellect." This attitude leads Hazlitt to a
looseness in his use of terms; contradictions readily appear. He even
places his theoretical convictions in the context of the vivid image: once

suggestive detail is by-passed in favor of a general rule, the arts begin "to resemble Antaeus in his struggle with Hercules, who was strangled when he was raised above the ground, and only revived and recovered his strength when he touched his mother earth."

Hazlitt's approach can be called "organic" or "Romantic" in a way that does not apply to Reynolds or Stewart. Yet the incremental step from such writers as Tucker, Priestley, Gerard, Stewart, and Reynolds to Hazlitt is not large. At the Unitarian College in Hackney, Hazlitt personally studied under Thomas Belsham and Priestley. It is typical of Hazlitt that, in remembering "The Late Dr. Priestley," he praises Priestley's union of "metaphysical refinement" and "experimental [empirical] philosophy." Indeed, the union of these *"almost* incompatible faculties" became for Hazlitt, as for many of the later associationists, one of the acts of the imagination. Hazlitt represents a complete blending, or what the Germans might call a *Verschmelzung*, of the British traditions of empirical psychology, associationism, intuitionalism, common sense, sympathy, moral thought, and interest in genius. The blending is so thorough that when Hazlitt comes to define the highest artistic and creative power, he honestly balks: "This power is indifferently called genius, imagination, feeling, taste; but the manner in which it acts upon the mind can neither be defined by abstract rules, as is the case in science, nor verified by continual unvarying experiments, as is the case in mechanical performances."[2]

Yet from the earliest stage of Hazlitt's writing, the imagination occupies the highest place. It is the mainstay of his moral speculation, just as it becomes the focus of his criticism. Hazlitt's career developed as it did because, as he progresses through these various concerns, he begins each stage with the idea of the imagination.


### IMAGINATION AS A GENERAL POWER

In its broad sense "Imagination is another name for an interest in things out of ourselves." It permits us to act sympathetically, to turn away from ourselves by substituting a concern for others. We imagine ourselves in their situation, and our capacity for direct feeling moves in their behalf. When thinkers had stressed the importance of sympathy, as Adam Smith had done in his *Theory of Moral Sentiments*, they had done so, according to Hazlitt, by making it a heartless and automatic association produced by "an unmeaning game of battledore and shuttlecock kept up between the nerves and muscles." Hartley was the most glaring example. The theory of "blind impulses of associated mechanical feeling," when "made to explain everything . . . becomes merely a confusion . . . and a handle for quackery and paradox."* The "modern philosophy" simply left "natural impulses of passion and imagination out of the account."[3]

Only twenty-seven when he formulated his view of the connection between sympathy, morality, and the imagination, Hazlitt would later say, "The only thing I ever piqued myself upon was the writing the *Essay on the Principles of Human Action.*" His most systematic work, it established a psychological framework for his criticism: our senses put us in direct touch with present reality, and memory gives us an awareness of the past. But neither the senses nor memory can convey what has yet to happen. "That which is future, which does not yet exist, can excite no interest in itself, nor act upon the mind in any way but by means of the imagination." Only when we identify with our future selves does it take on an apparent reality and "presentness" with which we can sympathize. A child nearing a fire does not feel his present and future selves as two distinct things. He fears *becoming* burned. He "projects himself forward" and "identifies with his future being."[4] In this way both Johnson and Hume discussed the extrapolative or *projecting* power of imagination.

By the same process that we project and identify with our own future, we also enter into the feelings of others. The imaginative act has simply turned to a new object. In ethical terms, imagination and the sympathy it excites are neutral. Self-love and disinterested benevolence stem equally from the imaginative capacity for sympathy. "I could not love myself, if I were not capable of loving others." Selfish people steer their sympathies only inward, to their own future. Yet if our minds dwell on another person—and Hazlitt believes this is a natural impulse—his situation begins to enter and dominate our consciousness. Then a steady stream of impressions will collect and reinforce our habitual interest in him. The more we know, the more we become involved. Our reaction is "excited in proportion to our knowledge of the pain, and of the disposition and feelings of the sufferer." We remember how *we* have felt in the past, and this helps to indicate how the person feels with whom we identify. The imagination extends our "original passive impressions" into an active sense of what another person experiences. Of course, each individual "is a world to himself."[5] His motives are complex, in flux and half-hidden, as Hume stressed. But the imagination is a cumulative power, and once it turns to another person, it accelerates in activity: each new impression mixes with and helps to interpret all those before

* For a similar objection raised by Coleridge, see below, pp. 331–332.

it, so that a suggestive momentum or direction is built. The imagination works throughout each second of life; like breathing, it is involuntary and even unnoticed, but necessary for the health and life of the mind.

The imagination, then, is essentially a potential energy in the mind, a capacity that uses and is not formed by sense impressions. In contrast, many associationists had concluded that the mind itself was wholly empirical in its operation. But their method of examination had rubbed off onto the clues. Those who had assumed a *tabula rasa* found on it only their own fingerprints. One could say that the intellect as pictured by empirical psychology is curiously fit to practice only empirical psychology. It works piecemeal, relies on the senses, develops generalities by linking small units together, and forges its final conclusions into a protective armor of rules and abstractions.

The fact that Locke and many "half metaphysicians" discounted what they vaguely called "innate ideas" did not prove that the mind lacks innate capacities, which exist before any phenomena are impressed on them. Hazlitt essentially expands the meaning of "experience," which he says had been confined "to a knowledge of things without us." He divorced it or, as Coleridge would say, "desynonymized" it from sensation: "Purely sensational knowledge is not the key." The mind, in its imaginative grasp, reaches "either within or out of" itself so that consciousness combines external objects with internal ways in which the mind registers, associates, adds to, and transforms these objects. For this reason, Hazlitt feels Locke neglected "the *internal* principle of all thought."[6]

The main liability of the empiricist was the ease with which he slipped into "abstraction," while believing he avoided or opposed it. When empiricism lumps together concrete impressions, it tends not to see them in their mixed totality and interconnection but to over-refine them, to produce abstract ideas, such as "substance" or "ratiocination," whose umbilical cord with experience has been pinched. This abstraction had too long passed for "reason," as Reynolds and Coleridge said. The interplay and internal process of life had boiled away until only a dry powder remained: "The instant we begin to refine and generalize beyond a certain point, we are reduced to abstraction ... The habit, too, of detaching these abstract species and fragments of nature, destroys the power of combining them in complex characters, in every degree of force and variety." Hazlitt agrees that abstraction is necessary and useful, but as the final goal of synthetic thought, it is too rarefied and dessicate. Even Kant—though it is not clear that Hazlitt knew much about him—ended with too much "artificial and arbitrary" system. Abstraction provides helpful "short-cuts," but it limits comprehension by ignoring particulars.[7]

Kant's statement, which Hazlitt was fond of quoting, that "The mind alone is formative," has meaning only if one recognizes that the mind first collects materials to form. Otherwise, "it is having to make bricks without straw." These materials come not only by direct sense experience but also by the internal sensations and processes of mind, one of which is association. What Tucker, Belsham, and Priestley had started Hazlitt extended. He removed completely the discrete intervals and step-like nature of the associative process. "The imagination is an *associating* principle," but it suspends ideas and compound associations in a solution where they freely move, interacting with each other. These ideas are then ready to form around and encrust any new object or experience with which they have an affinity. As a result, a new concept or idea is formed. Each time the mind perceives something new, the process repeats, and its store of associations grows. The process is fluid. In the "pervading and elastic energy" of imagination, associations are not fixed in a sequential order. From an internal fund, ideas and feelings rush to surround any object that presents itself to the mind. This fund brings "all nature and all art to bear on a particular purpose, on continuity and comprehension of mind." That Hazlitt still maintains the imagination is an "*associating* principle" sets him apart from Coleridge, Blake, and Shelley, who rather stress that association is a principle which contributes to a higher, more comprehensive power of creative imagination. The object, according to Hazlitt, becomes the center of a whole intellectual world. Association thus forms conscious, realized patterns and works toward a unified design.[8]

But the external world, in all its concreteness, is never static, and no still-life can capture its reality. The imagination perceives not only that patterns in the world often are not patterns for long but, more important, that there are patterns of change itself, that there is process. An imaginative mind can telescope time, see the cause and effect of a thing, and associate it with another event or object not immediately present. Original impressions become combined "in all possible forms," which, with a sense of design and unity, approximate the metamorphosis of nature. Like Goethe, we can pick up a handful of dry seeds and say, "These are roses, and they shall bloom." In Hazlitt's words, "We see the *process*" of things. Imagination creates a sensitive analog in the mind to what alters and moves around it.[9] Much later, in 1876, Emerson would state the position with a finality that is not closed but suggestive: "The endless passing of one element into new forms, the incessant metamorphosis, explains the rank which the imagination holds in our catalogue of mental powers. The imagination is the reader of these forms."[10]

In time, the imaginative power develops a ready response and intelligence, called by Hazlitt "common sense." In the totality of mind, objects and experiences fuse into larger wholes that "you may not be able to analyze or account for . . . in the several particulars." The result is a body of response that informs and guides all actions.[11] Here Hazlitt is building not only on Scottish intuitionalists but on Hobbes, whom he studied carefully, and on Tucker and John Fearn. All impressions "coalesce and act in unison . . . that is, without our being conscious of anything but the . . . settled result."[12] The ideas of this "habitual reason" are superior to abstraction. Particulars are neither isolated nor whisked away; in coalescing, they become living and vital, as they are in nature.

In this synthetic and cohesive process of mind there are no partitions. Each thought and association acts as a relay in "the unity of thought and consciousness." The concept is similar to Herder's *Besonnenheit*, or total awareness. The best word Hazlitt found for this process was "imagination." Working by intuition and analogy, it carries a built-in power to design and to judge ideas and actions, a power that recalls Hobbes's *sagacitas*. People who "trust to their imagination or feelings, know how far to go, and how to keep within certain limits." The *"instinct of imagination"* is an unconscious power, first absorbing experience, then giving out "what it had attracted and moulded into itself by elective affinity, as the loadstone draws and impregnates iron."[13] This image was used in a similar context by Akenside, Gerard, Tucker, and even Fichte. In one of Hazlitt's best passages on the organic unity of mind provided by imagination, a unity that extends from remembered "objects" to the "I" who invents new ones and blends them with "thoughts and feelings," he comments:

> Thus the poet is not a being made up of a string of organs—an eye, an ear, a heart, a tongue—but is one and the same intellectual essence, looking out from its own nature on all the different impressions it receives, and to a certain degree moulding them into itself. It is *I* who remember certain objects, who judge of them, who invent from them, who connect certain sounds that I hear, as of a thrush singing, with certain sights that I see, as the wood whence the notes issue. There is some bond, some *conscious* connection brought about between these impressions and acts of the mind; that is, there is a principle of joint and common understanding in the mind, quite different from the ignorance in which the ear is left of what passes before the eye, &c., and which [is an] overruling and primary faculty of the soul, blending with all our thoughts and feelings.[14]

### INTENSITY OF FEELING

The sagacity of the imagination does not wait on the page-turning, slow progress of deduction. It darts at once, as Reynolds said, "by what appears a kind of intuition, to the conclusion." The phrase Hazlitt uses to summarize this intuitive power that draws particulars into a purposeful whole, "organic sensibility," has passed into the language; Wordsworth had, in his Preface to *Lyrical Ballads* (1800), remarked that a good poet is "possessed of more than usual organic sensibility." The organic growth of works of imagination, says Hazlitt, can be seen in Milton's description:

> So from the root
> Springs lighter the green stalk; from thence the leaves
> More airy; last the bright consúmmate flower.

Passion and feeling had become important elements of the imaginative process for Kames, Priestley, Gerard, Duff, and Tucker, but Hazlitt makes passion and feeling the most important. What resulted was the "association of *feelings.*" What we think and what we are "is got at solely by *feeling*, that is, on the principle of the association of ideas." The power and consistency of imagination depends more on "an ebullition of feeling" than on "remote and abstract principles." The degree to which a philosophy takes this into account is crucial for its success. "In art, in taste, in life . . . you decide from feeling, and not from reason." We judge actions more fairly if our conclusion comes from the heart as well as the mind. From his point of view, Hazlitt had overturned the "cool" analysis of empiricism on even more direct and purely empirical grounds. He spoke for the *Zeitgeist* when he remarked, "Without the inward sympathy to impel us forward, the indifferent observation of the outward signs" cannot "attain to the truth of nature." Sympathy, and "the root of our imagination," depend on feeling—on the heart. "Passion, in short, is the essence, the chief ingredient in moral truth; and the warmth of passion is sure to kindle the light of imagination on the objects around it."[15]

Passion and feeling alone, however, are not sufficient; they can be present at a low temperature; it is their warmth or intensity that makes the difference. The mind naturally desires strong excitement. Burke had graphically explained this need, saying that if the audience watching a tragedy heard that a public execution was about to take place outside, they would rush out, leaving the theater empty. Even when danger or fear acts as a deterrent, the power of hypnotic feeling often overcomes it: "It is a well-known fact that few persons can stand safely on the edge of a precipice, or walk along the parapet wall of a house, without being in danger of throwing themselves down; not we presume from a principle of self-preservation; but in consequence of a strong idea having taken possession of the mind, from which it cannot well escape, which absorbs every other consideration, and confounds and overrules all self-regards."[16]

The instance that entered Hazlitt's mind had provoked Horatio, too (*Hamlet* I.iv):

> the dreadful summit of the cliff
> That beetles o'er his base into the sea
> . . . . . . . . . . . . .
> The very place puts toys of desperation,
> Without more motive, into every brain
> That looks so many fathoms to the sea
> And hears it roar beneath.

The mind latches onto the object or action that is before it and, soon mesmerized, desires to be enthralled. Conceiving the situation so forcefully, the mind admits no thought or object that is alien to the pattern of events and passion. The mind gains "a more intense perception of truth . . . calling out the powers of observation and comparison." Strong feeling organizes this more accurate imitation of nature. It gives the mind a force-field that admits and orders ideas and arranges them according to their importance. Intensity never lets go of its subject until it forms "a certain graceful consistency." Feeling provides harmony of form in art as well as in experience.[17]

## GUSTO

Hazlitt's wonderful term, which attracted Keats, for the intense feeling and awareness associated with a particular object or idea is "gusto." The mind does more than examine an object, it embraces it until the last iota of pleasure and pain is wrung from the embrace and its associations. This feeling conveys the total *Inhalt* and essence of a thing, placing it in the universal scheme of nature. Gusto "is power or passion defining any object." Distinction between object and subject blurs as the mind fuses itself with the thing at hand. Sensual and intellectual faculties work together. The intensity and truth of feeling we develop about an object and bring to it repay us with the true nature and character of that object. The two are inseparable. Gusto is a speeding up of the metabolism of the mind and stimulates its powers into extra alertness. We see more externally, feel more internally, and the two experiences join and magnify each other until a "more striking degree" of feeling awakens.[18]

I saw a thrush, says Hazlitt, fly from a cold barren hill, coming from his warm wood shelter, whistling distantly. "A mingled feeling of strangeness and joy" accompanied these connected experiences and combined with them to form one total impression. In art, for example, "There is a gusto in the colouring of Titian. Not only do his heads seem to think—his bodies seem to feel."[19] Similarly, "Milton has great gusto. He repeats his blows twice; grapples with and exhausts his subject. His imagination has a double relish of its objects, an inveterate attachment to the things he describes, and to the words describing them." This double blow and relish of gusto characterizes Milton's description of the Chinese and their "cany wagons light." Chaucer catches "the very *feeling* of the air, the coolness or moisture of the ground. Inanimate objects . . . have a fellow-feeling in the interest of the story; and render back the sentiment of the speaker's mind."[20]

In gusto, a strong central feeling excites all the senses at once, by affinity, from inward. We "interpret one sense by another." The five senses work together like fingers on a hand and grasp the object in its totality. Smells and tastes, says Hazlitt, remain in our minds because we do not encounter them as often as we are bombarded by visual images. "The taste of barberries, which have hung out in the snow during the severity of a North American winter, I have in my mouth still, after an interval of thirty years." Mixing and exciting the senses, gusto recreates the "internal character, the living principle" of an object. As the mind's keenest involvement with the external world, it produces a "deep, sustained internal sentiment."[21] Hazlitt would have been delighted with the kind of gusto in Proust. The psyche develops an "*internal* design" corresponding to the natural world.[22]

Gusto is the Latin ablative of the word meaning "taste," and Hazlitt's idea of taste is a way of organizing into general aesthetic categories, such as "beauty" or "the sublime," the individual impressions of gusto. For instance, a beautiful statue and a beautiful sunset leave different impressions, but both objects excite a common and intense core of feeling. This is what Hazlitt means by the observation that personal reactions to beautiful objects are never identical, but that they meet "in the extremes" of feeling. They "form an ideal class" of taste. "The IDEAL," however, is the *one* particular object that within its own class "expresses most completely . . . a given character of quality, as of beauty, strength, activity, voluptuousness . . . and preserves that character with the greatest consistency throughout." In its general and ideal sense, taste is rooted in gusto, the "concentration" we feel for concrete nature, and shows "entire sympathy with the finest impulses of the imagination."[23]

POETRY AS THE HIGHEST IMAGINATIVE LIFE

For Hazlitt, poetry imitates nature, "but the imagination and the passions are a part of man's nature." Poetry imitates nature as seen through and colored by the passion and involvement of the psyche. The highest forms of art express a nature not only perceived but half-created by the feelings ("gusto") of heart and mind. "Poetry acts by sympathy with nature, that is, with the natural impulses, customs, and imagination of men." Objects themselves take on human interest, which poetry magnifies until nature is by association imbued with an extra meaning, one that resonates with the purposes and experiences of human life.* "Neither a mere description of natural objects, nor a mere delineation of natural feelings, however distinct or forcible, constitutes the ultimate end and aim of poetry." Imagination mingles the two. It represents objects as they are molded by thoughts and feelings "into an infinite variety of shapes and combinations of power." If imitation means a simple representation of objects as they seem, this is diametrically opposed to the power of imagination, which presents an object with all its associated feelings and ideas. "We do not see nature with our eyes, but with our understandings and our hearts."[24] As early as 1750, Johnson had remarked that nature's general effects on the eye and ear are uniform and incapable of much varied description, but "philosophically considered," nature is inexhaustible (*Rambler* 36).

The artist should reveal nature, then, through the medium of sentiment and passion. He can awaken in each natural object the slumbering power to become a symbol of our affections and a "link in the chain of our endless being." Uniting imagery and feeling, poetry speaks the language of the imagination more than any other art form. "It describes the flowing, not the fixed." It is more flexible in engaging the senses and can suggest any feeling. Painting, sculpture, and music run against nearer limits. Pictures focus too sharply on objects or faces, as Claudius implies when he taunts Laertes: "Or are you like the painting of a sorrow,/A face without a heart?" The visual arts freeze things in time. Music is temporal but excites only one sense. In fact, all the arts except poetry essentially engage a single sense or at most two. But entering the mind in an intelligible as well as sensual way, poetic language stimulates all feelings and senses from the inside. Poetry leaves some work of the imagination to the reader.[25] As in sculpture, some of Michelangelo's most beautiful and suggestive works are those he left unfinished.

Poetry, as well as the arts in general, must keep a strong grip on the particulars of nature and the nuances of human behavior and feeling. Fact and feeling go hand in hand; the one implies the other, in a relation-

* Cf. Wordsworth and Coleridge on the same subject, below, chs. 18 and 21.

ship that Hazlitt, anticipating T. S. Eliot, prized in English literature of the seventeenth century. Poetry is passion speaking eloquently. The genius lets each passion speak for itself as deeply and strongly, though not necessarily as violently or excessively, as possible, because he wants to make the reader feel that way himself. "The very intensity and truth of feeling" pushes the poet into fiction. Put another way, imaginative poetry falls in with the language of power. It magnifies its objects; "it admits of no medium. It is every thing by excess." Hazlitt turns to *The Tempest* for an example: "So (as it has been ingeniously remarked)* when Prospero describes himself as left alone in the boat with his daughter, the epithet which he applies to her, "Me and thy *crying* self," flings the imagination instantly back from the grown woman to the helpless condition of infancy, and places the first and most trying scene of his misfortunes before us, with all that he must have suffered in the interval."[26]

The range and power of poetry come from a pattern of words. Figures of speech and phrases become identified with a pattern of feelings and ideas. "Words are a measure of truth. They ascertain intuitively the degrees, inflections, and powers of things in a wonderful manner." They are the atoms of a second universe in which the psyche has touched, sympathized, and associated itself with part of the natural creation. Words become objects and feelings themselves. A figure of speech requires no proof: "It gives *carte blanche* to the imagination" and encourages us to think of the connections between facts and feelings, the journey of the mind as it considers nature in relation to its own experience. Great poetry, like Shakespeare's, becomes "hieroglyphical. It translates thoughts into visible images." These images are figurative truths that produce complete awareness of a whole, dramatic situation. In *Macbeth*, Malcolm calls to the grief-stricken Macduff: "What! man, ne'er pull your hat upon your brows." The action could be anyone shading his eyes from the sun, but the suggestive power of language is so fitted to the immediate situation that it vents a sorrow that would be cheapened by mere description. Hazlitt believes French classical drama falls short of the golden age of English theater because it is removed from the union of feeling and thought. Characters describe their feelings, they do not speak directly. We sense that someone has interposed between us and the object or character at hand. Images should not be the adornments or examples of thought, something thrown in to add a comparison. In the best poetry, forms of speech are "the building, and not the scaffolding to thought."[27] A phrase touches a whole web of action, which in trembling with it is also imitated by it.

---

* Hazlitt is probably referring to Coleridge's fine analysis of the same passage; see below, ch. 21.

Hazlitt reverts to a popular theme of Shakespearean criticism in the 1770s and 1780s. Shakespeare's images and characters are true imitations, not descriptions of passion and nature (Hazlitt's "building, and not the scaffolding"), which is related to Coleridge's distinction between imitation and copy. Coleridge used the question in *Lear*, "What, have his daughters brought him to this pass?" as an example of imagination catching a whole situation at once, through simple words.[28] There is the same power in Lear's cry, repeated by Burke and flung at the House of Commons when, feeling betrayed by his supporters, he cried, "The little dogs and all, Tray, Blanche, and Sweetheart, see, they bark at me!" As Hazlitt explains this cry, it is:

> no old Chronicle of the line of Brute, no *black-letter* broadside, no tattered ballad, no vague rumour, in which this exclamation [of Lear's] is registered; there is nothing romantic, quaint, mysterious in the objects introduced: the illustration is borrowed from the commonest and most casual images in nature, yet it is this very circumstance that lends it extreme force . . . by showing that even the lowest things in creation . . . had in his imagination turned against him . . . It is the depth of passion . . . or of the poet's sympathy with it, that invests them with corresponding importance.[29]

In addition, the names of the dogs, Tray, Blanche, and Sweetheart, have the reverse association expected. They essentially mean truth (or loyalty), purity, and intimacy. This reverse association of ideas heightens the working of the imagination and helps to explain Hazlitt's remark that Lear's cry comes "by the force of contrast."


### MODERN PROBLEMS

Hazlitt, like William Duff and like Lycius in Keats's *Lamia*, felt it could not be concealed "that the progress of knowledge and refinement has a tendency to circumscribe the limits of the imagination, and to clip the wings of poetry."[30] But admitting that many undefined and uncommon objects and feelings which gave "birth and scope to the imagination" had become outworn, he turns not only to the question of the artist seeking new objects and actions but also to the change in the audience and taste of an age and a society already bombarded with masterpieces and, more perplexing, with a profusion of less-than-masterpieces. The present age talked; it failed to act. It lived on retrospect. People flocked to see Greek tragedy and perhaps felt their own lives tragic, but no great poetry came of it. Shakespeare "could not have written as he did, if he had lived in the present time."

Taste, in an absolute sense, had not grown better or worse, but was more fixed; bad taste had grown more universal and consequently harder to budge. Diffusion of taste never guaranteed improvement. Too often it stifled what was good or promising by introducing too many competitors, mostly poor ones. Men of imagination had as much genius as ever, but now when they turned to a subject, the public was indoctrinated and expected something of less than imaginative genius: "When 10,000 boarding-school girls, who have learnt to play on the harpsichord, are brought out in the same season, Rossini will be preferred to Mozart, as the last new composer."[31]

A contagion of mediocrity was just one problem confronting the modern imagination. Another was its own tendency, perhaps in defense against the sheer numbers, to indulge in self-centeredness or "egotism." Keats's phrase describing Wordsworth, "the egotistical sublime," was undoubtedly inspired by Hazlitt. As Keats was himself to realize, Wordsworth was a great poet of a new kind; Hazlitt even called him the greatest one living. Yet the temptation of the modern, "romantic" imagination was to be too subjective. There is "in Mr. Wordsworth's mind," notes Hazlitt in reviewing *The Excursion*," an evident repugnance to admit anything that tells for itself, without the interpretation of the poet,—a fastidious antipathy to immediate effect,—a systematic unwillingness to share the palm with his subject." Wordsworth sympathizes only with feelings that easily mingle with his own identity. Here was a case where the "channels" of the imagination had been grooved inward instead of turning to others and to "immediate effect" or "gusto." Wordsworth "sees nothing but himself and the universe."[32] Hazlitt makes him sound like the kind of poet Fichte would have been had he been endowed with more literary gifts and a love of nature.

Too much pathological cult of the self infected the present time. Anything, it seemed, could be turned inward. Too many people traversed exotic worlds, rummaged about the ruin of civilizations, crossed stupendous mountains, seas, and deserts and then, like Childe Harold, proceeded to see everything as a mirror for themselves. At best, they presented a story like Manfred's but were always on the verge of plunging off the mountains into extreme self-centeredness.[33] In the end, the spasmodics' cult of feeling-for-feeling's sake would become transparent and pathetic rather than heroic: they lamented that their feelings failed to be misunderstood. Commenting on a popular spasmodic-like play, the tragedy *Bertram, or the Castle of St. Aldobrand* (1816), by the Irish dramatist C. R. Maturin,* Hazlitt put his finger on a key distinction. "Mere sentiment," as opposed to that sentiment with an object of sufficient importance and value, is nothing but "self-created, beginning and ending

* The play was very popular and a financial success. For Coleridge's critique of it, see ch. 23 of the *Biographia*.

in itself." Ideas that come out of our own heads are "soon exhausted, and we recur to tiresome, vapid imitations of ourselves." Hazlitt, Keats, and Goethe (the most prominent examples) knew, often through personal experience, that Romanticism must wrestle with its own bad "egomorphic" impulses. A poet, said Goethe, does not deserve the title when he voices subjective feelings, but does only when he appropriates to himself the world and expresses it: "A subjective nature has soon talked out his little internal material, and is at last ruined by mannerism"; in other words, "Every healthy effort . . . is directed from the inward to the outward world."[34]

Hazlitt pinpointed the major fault of modern poetry as an experiment to reduce verse "to a mere effusion of natural sensibility," which lets imagination pervert itself into egotism; Johnson had made a similar remark in *Rambler* 154. Much of the writing of his own generation irked Hazlitt. Byron (and *Le Byronisme*, as Hazlitt would be quick to point out, became a French idol) showed "an unaccomodating [*sic*] selfishness," which "is like a cancer, eating into the heart of poetry." Byron "locks himself in the Bastille of his own ruling passion." One of Hazlitt's favorite passages in literature is *"Ah, voilà de la pervenche!"* But in the end, Rousseau's self-interest, though he might feel delight at seeing a periwinkle, suffocated his imaginative faculty. Nothing could be further from the truth, thought Hazlitt, than Madame de Staël's opinion that imagination was Rousseau's strength. Instead, he had "the most intense consciousness of his own existence."[35]

Hazlitt reasserted the classical belief that some subjects are more suitable for imitation than others. If the imagination becomes enmeshed in a minor topic, it grows "fickle and fastidious." Like Coleridge, Hazlitt denied that rural life was "manly" or "poetic" and criticized Wordsworth for making "pedlars and ploughmen the heroes and the interpreters of his sentiments." The cult of self and the proud cultivation of rustic subjects were the least imaginative efforts possible. German writers suffered a similar fault. They believed the "paradox" that all subjects are equally fit or, worse, that the more mean and unpromising a topic, the greater play it gave to creativity and imagination.[36] Passion is genuine only when it springs from "powerful causes" and is directed to "the highest subjects." What Hamlet meant when he told the players to hold the mirror up to nature was "to embody a distinct interest out of ourselves by the force of imagination and passion." The greatest philosopher, the best poet, forgot himself, or else stood in danger of being forgotten by the world.[37]

## FANCY AND IMAGINATION

Probably recalling remarks he had heard Coleridge make, Hazlitt distinguished fancy from imagination in 1815. But Hazlitt, unlike Coleridge, continues to see imagination as an associative principle, and fancy as one too, only less synthetic. Imagination enlarges and connects ideas while fancy separates and compares them, finding only one point in which they are similar. Wit acts on the most superficial level. It notices slight resemblances or binds together two surprisingly different things in "pretended union." Wit and fancy play with what is at hand, but imagination can bring the whole mind to bear on a single experience. Wit tends to diminish one's interest in all possible meanings and feelings associated with any one object. Imagination "enforces and aggrandises. It would be hard to shut up Homer and Waller in the same pew or compartment of the brain. The latter would be squeezed to death."[38]

Hazlitt often singles out the French as illustrating the presence of wit and fancy without imagination. Their vanity and self-centeredness proceed from "want of all real imagination." They lack an emphatic sense of nature because they do not identify with anything outside of themselves. The French mind "has always its own consciousness," "a glittering halo of personal conceit." It runs too rapidly through sensations to connect them into larger units. Hazlitt cites Coleridge, who thought that Molière's delightful sympathy with his characters and his sense of a dramatic whole rather than of a linked series of scenes could only have been possible if his father had been an Englishman![39]

## DRAMA, TRAGEDY, AND MYTH

The "strong-hold" of poetry is not the general or the ideal, in which one feeling or characteristic is captured and preserved as in formaldehyde, but an ability to portray individuals and events in vital interconnection. "It is the business of poetry, and indeed of all works of imagination to exhibit the species through the individual." The form of poetry that best escapes abstraction, permits the writer to express the feelings of others, and has a natural focus on the individual is the drama. Hazlitt prizes it above all other genres: "It is essentially individual and concrete, both in form and in power. It is the closest imitation of nature; it has a body of truth; it is 'a counterfeit presentment' of reality; for it brings forward certain characters to act and speak for themselves, in the most trying and singular circumstances."[40]

Epic poetry never escapes the voice of an intervening narrator. And lyric verse often ends in the tedium of personal sensibility; the poet gives only "the idle effusions of his own breast." But the playwright can turn invisible and mute. Consequently, the sympathies of the audience are engaged directly by the characters and action. No other art makes us feel more that we are looking at and participating in life. No other art strikes so close to home. It was perhaps under Hazlitt's influence, as well as under Shakespeare's, that Keats felt one of his greatest ambitions was the writing of "a few fine plays." Whereas comedy or farce undercuts sympathy, tragedy "substitutes imaginary sympathy for mere selfishness. It gives us a high and permanent interest beyond ourselves, in humanity as such."[41]

Although for Hazlitt tragedy is the highest form of dramatic art, our sympathies and souls can be engaged outside ourselves in two other ways. The gods and goddesses of myth provide personal and individual forms with which to identify fundamental human feelings and archetypes. Various sides of the psyche assume an external, concrete form that never dies, an immortal form that is not human, but humanized. Hazlitt perceives the need for myth in terms of sympathetic identification. "Men will have some idol, some mythology of their own—the *dii majores* or *minores*—something . . . they would wish to resemble." The genial gods, the deities of particular place, are born by an habitual association of ideas. "I have once enjoyed," says Hazlitt, "the cool shade of a tree, and been lulled into a deep repose by the sound of a brook running at my feet." Soon the grouping of pleasant associations came to personify a friendly power that inhabited the place, and Greek myth must have originated in a similar way. The imagination attaches real feeling to a certain name, so that myths may go for centuries inert, buried in books, then revive simply because we come to have "the same associations with them."

Beyond myth, yet subsuming it, the imagination extends our views of consequences into another state of being. It is a key to religious sensibility. Like Coleridge and Blake, Hazlitt found in the language and power of the Bible a poetry that combines imagination and faith. The deepest human feelings and beliefs are expressed in the most intense and boldly figurative way. Hazlitt loved the story of Ruth (which Keats used in his "Ode to a Nightingale") for its natural affection, and the book of Job for its imagery—"more intense in passion, than any thing in Homer."[42] In religion, the imagination not only gives us the power to look into the puzzle of creation but, once we take the leap of faith to accept the unknown and to explain it by a holy presence, the imagination forms, in symbolic poetry, the most powerful expression of belief.

Like so many of his predecessors in psychology and critical writing, Hazlitt regards the imagination as the basic characteristic of genius. Genius, for Hazlitt, does not possess special powers that other minds lack completely; there is no quantum jump into creativity. A great artist exercises a greater degree of sympathetic power, not "acuteness of organs or extent of capacity . . . but an *intense* sympathy with some beauty or distinguishing characteristic in nature." For this reason, Hazlitt prefers Shakespeare to Wordsworth; Shakespeare is ready to dwell on the subject itself, to identify with it, and to present it with gusto and passion; Wordsworth is the egotistical genius. In direct contrast to the "ordinary . . . exclusive and self-willed" genius of Wordsworth, Shakespeare's identity is a product of his own disinterested sympathies for nature and his identification with individuals. Hazlitt characterizes Shakespeare in his own words: "my nature is subdued/To what it works in, like the dyer's hand."[43]

Hazlitt strengthens the Romantic premise developed during his childhood and adolescence by critics like Maurice Morgann, William Richardson, and Elizabeth Montagu, the premise that now pervaded the attitudes of Keats and Coleridge to Shakespeare. Keats called it "negative capability." It is the power of the dervish, the chameleon, the Proteus who can assume all forms and all passions. Hazlitt expresses the nature of Shakespeare in a new simile: "By an art like that of the ventriloquist, he throws his imagination out of himself, and makes every word appear to proceed from the mouth of the person in whose name it is spoken." Shakespeare is the anti-egotist. Thinking of an object or of another person, he instantly becomes it.[44]

Like one soul successively animating different bodies, Shakespeare's imagination worked most strongly in character portrayal. One of Hazlitt's favorite examples is Cleopatra: "Few things in Shakespeare . . . have more of that local truth of imagination and character than the passage in which Cleopatra is represented conjecturing what were the employments of Anthony in his absence—'He's speaking now, or murmuring—*Where's my serpent of old Nile?*'" "How fine," says Hazlitt, "to make Cleopatra have this consciousness of her own character."[45]

Shakespeare caught the modifications of feeling, the plastic nature of sentiments and behavior. Going out of himself by the force of imagination, he could peer into "the connecting links of the passions, and their effect upon the mind." He saw everything, by intuition and instinct, as a process, a drama. Each action, each telltale hint of passion, is in a state of metamorphosis, becoming whole by its affinity or antipathy to every other speech and act brought near it. Everything flows by the force of natural association. A train of thought suggests various inflections of one feeling, all of which melt into and heighten one another, "like chords in music," a phrase that recalls Hume's statement that the passions act like a stringed instrument, setting up sympathetic vibrations in each other, and not like a wind instrument that produces only single notes.[46]

On a higher level of generality, Hazlitt believes Shakespeare's imagination imitated the process of nature. It created another, "imaginary reality" or second world, a sister planet no astronomer could find, but one populated to such a faithful degree that we take it for our own. Preeminent in Shakespeare was "imagination, that is, the power of feigning things according to nature." Following the lead of Morgann's *Essay on Falstaff*, Hazlitt calls Shakespeare's characters "historical." We speculate about what they say and do off-stage. In his truth to nature, Shakespeare is no moralist; that is, he draws no morals in the conventional sense. But he shows reality in its truth and complexity by showing it through many human lives. In this respect he is the greatest of all moralists.[47]

The poetry of sympathy, passion, and imagination—three words packed with meaning for Hazlitt—grows from both the moral and intellectual part of human nature. The works of imagination, as he calls them, embrace the world in its relation to the desire to know, the will to act, and the power to feel. Their expression appeals to every facet of experience; they come the nearest to truth and nature. In fact, because of their passion and intensity, their distillation in time and harmony of impact, the imagination in them "is, in this sense, sometimes truer than reality."[48] There is no more powerful parable of the spirit than *Lear*.

In its moral scope and sense of totality, the greatest poetry (and for Hazlitt this means Shakespeare) is endowed with "all the forms of the imagination, and with the deepest workings of the heart." It has a depth and harmony of mind that imitates; but more, it holds communion with the soul of nature. In his full power, the poet identifies with and is able "to foreknow and to record the feelings of all men at all times and places."[49] He is a prophet. Hazlitt's concrete associationism, his psychological interests and stress on sympathy or "gusto" of the particular realized as part of a larger process, and his romantic, "organic sensibility" lead him to the prophetic and the visionary. In his love of the imagination he attempts to understand, without abstract theory or oracular spiritualism, the how and the wherefore of what, after all, had always been a "classical" attribute of the poet imitating nature,

the prophetic soul
Of the wide world, dreaming on things to come.

# PART FIVE

# *Literary Explorations*

# 16

# THE NEW PHILOSOPHERS' STONE
# AND THE NEW PIERIAN SPRING

*W*e have discussed Kant's concepts of the imagination and how he mediates between several traditions. He variously presents the imagination as one element in faculty psychology, as an empirical power of perception, as a transcendental power able to form images of complex ideas, as an aesthetic or artistic force related to genius and *Geist*, and as the "blind power hidden in the depths of the soul," responsible for all synthetic and creative acts of mind. But Kant had difficulty in drawing together and reconciling these notions, and so did both his followers and detractors. As the 1790s progressed, the idea of the imagination reemerged in several shapes. In Kant, all the grains of sand were momentarily held together in one giant grasp, but with no mortar to secure them, they sifted out again through different fingers.

Herder represents an intuitive view of the imagination embracing myth, prophecy, religious enthusiasm, and the Shaftesburian, neo-Platonic idea of man as a Promethean creator. Goethe expresses some of these interests, as does Schiller, and Goethe shows a well-rounded literary view of the imagination without operating from a narrow critical procedure. His vision of the faculty is nimble and multi-sided; he is aware of its uses in many fields, especially in art, but is committed to no one system and wary of speculation without the addition of personal character and experience.

Fichte represents a more specialized and philosophical approach. He, like Reinhold and Maimon, wanted to purify and correct Kant, especially the first *Critique*. For Fichte, the imagination is a key to the act of philosophizing, the highest of endeavors. Close to Schiller in the mid 1790s, Fichte follows the line of Schiller's *Ästhetische Erziehung* (1795) in his own *Über Geist und Buchstab in der Philosophie* (1798, written four years earlier), which discusses the imagination as it governs aesthetics and the fine arts. When Fichte tries to explain how the self relates to the external world, he concludes that the imagination is the only answer. Schiller sees the imagination more as the heart of an aesthetic approach to art and, beyond this, to experience and to the whole of human life and conduct, an approach that will fulfill and integrate human nature. Taking the same general attitude as Fichte to the effect that one must mediate between the formal or ideal impulse of the self (*geistlich*) and the sensuous, real world of nature, Schiller sees this mediation not in philosophically speculative terms but as an act of aesthetic perception and creativity.

The Schlegels and Novalis then took for granted that the imagination was of supreme worth: they came to the idea with the philosophical groundwork already largely laid, and they were familiar with it. Their mission was not so much to define or analyze the imagination as to use the idea in remolding the direction of art, in poeticizing the world, and in bringing the unifying, ideal powers of imagination to actuality through new poetic creations designed to transform dull and sensate life into a transcendental, romantic kingdom, and to reform the corrupt world into a moral, liberated Eden. Yet their views are not hermetically sealed. These writers keenly interested themselves in each other's work and enjoyed, with rewards and frictions, what Johnson had lamented was rapidly vanishing from the learned world, a true "community of mind."

## HERDER'S INTUITIVE APPROACH

As a young man in Königsberg, Herder attended Kant's lectures. Kant likely introduced him to a principle that remained strong throughout Herder's life, that all things in existence are connected by Law to one ground of being. But Kant inclined to an analytic and metaphysical exploration of this concept, especially in its relation to human consciousness, and in 1766, when Herder was twenty-two, Kant published his *Träumen eines Geistersehers erläutert durch Träume der Metaphysik*, showing the shaky foundations of enthusiastic, spiritual explanations. Herder, increasingly drawn to studies in anthropology, myth, and language, soon found he had stronger affinities with Hamann, now a customs official in Königsberg. With respect to the idea of the imagination, Herder offers several possibilities, but his sympathies are obvious.

One of Herder's ideas recapitulates Hamann's critique of Kant (*Metakritik über den Purismum der reinen Vernunft*, 1788) and appears in Herder's own *Metakritik zur Kritik der reinen Vernunft* (1799). It is dry and skeletal, a simplified outline of Kant's idea of the imagination as expressed in the early and mid 1780s. Herder uses the term *Einbildungskraft* and stresses that the imagination receives and creates sense impressions and joins the senses to the understanding. His routine thinking ignores the idea of imaginative synthesis in the way Kant explains it. For Herder, *Einbildungskraft* has little or no connection with the ideal or spiritual world. But these thin comments in the *Metakritik* are not what Herder means by the imagination at all.

For Herder a second and far more meaningful concept of the imagination helps to reveal religion, establish the true cosmology, and purify man's soul, whose creative acts actually are a part of the absolute power that creates nature. This creative drive permeating nature and art, present in and joining together God and man, Herder calls by several names and phrases: *"Kraft Gottes in der Natur," "Kraft des Lebens und der Bildung," "eine sehr wirksame Kraft, die Bildnerin der Gestalten," "dies Bilderschaffende Vermögen die Dichtungskraft unsrer Seele, Phantasie,"* or simply *"Trieb"* or *"Bildungstrieb."*

Apparently after 1781 *Einbildungskraft* had for Herder too close a connection with Kant and the first *Critique*. The names and phrases Herder uses for what can only be called "imagination" represent a universal creative force. In *Adrastea* (1801), Herder gives a clear explanation of the universal flux and human reflex of this power. Significantly, the section in which this appears is entitled *"Früchte aus den sogenannt-goldnen Zeiten des achtzehnten Jahrhunderts,"* and he considers the discovery and explanation of this imaginative force to be an achievement, albeit in the midst of many errors, of the eighteenth century.

Herder asks the essential question: how do ideas or spirits, or what might be called the Word of God, attain material reality? The answer lies in a shaping power, which in its simplest, unwilled form in man surfaces in dreams and visions. Recalling Tetens' and Sulzer's explanations of the imagination, Herder describes this power in its highest capacity: "So this wizardress calls forth not only the forms of things buried inside of us as they appeared to us once in the past; she also causes forms never seen before to appear; she creates and generates." As far as the divine creative power is concerned, "The Poet imitates this divine formative power; or more, he works under its influence with understanding and intention."[1] Herder repeats the notion, which he may have received most directly from Breitinger, whose works he admired, that poetry, by imitating *den göttlichen Bildungstrieb* (the divine creative instinct) shapes a new and higher world.

*Bildungstrieb* had not previously been seen as a synonym for the imagination. Originally a physiological term, it appears in J. F. Blumenbach's *Ueber den Bildungstrieb und das Zeugungsgeschaft* (1781) and in his *Über die natürlichen Verschiedenheiten im Menschenge-schlechte* (published in 1798 in Leipzig, about the time Herder was writing *Adrastea*, also published in Leipzig). Kant mentions *Bildung-strieb* in the 1799 edition of the *Critique of Judgment*. By the late 1790s, then, the word had expanded in usage from developmental biology to a more general sense of an inner drive by which a living form or entity attains the material completeness of the genetic or "spiritual" content contained within itself. Schiller uses *Bildungstrieb* in *Die Ästhetische Erziehung*. In letter IX, for example, he says that the impatient creative force may try to impose an order on the moral or spiritual world: "Far too impetuous to proceed by such unobtrusive means, the divine im-pulse to form often hurls itself directly upon present-day reality, and upon the life of action, and undertakes to fashion anew the formless ma-terial presented by the moral world."[2]

A more important use occurs in letter XXVI, where Schiller makes *Bildungstrieb* an indispensable part of the imaginative process of artistic imitation. "*Der ästhetische Kunsttrieb,*" the aesthetic drive of art, inevi-tably involves *Bildungstrieb*. As soon as the even wider power of aes-thetic appreciation of life, *der Spieltrieb*, comes into play, it too is fol-lowed by the *Bildungstrieb*, which creates "*etwas Selbständiges,*" something autonomous, like Herder's "*neue Welt*" fashioned by the imitative, formative drive. Schiller thus makes it impossible to separate art and an aesthetic life in general from the concept of *Bildungstrieb;* the *Spieltrieb* is always accompanied by the imitative *Bildungstrieb*, and in this sense the two may be considered as one whole power: "And as soon as the play-drive begins to stir, with its pleasure in semblance, it will be followed by the shaping spirit of imitation, which treats semblance as something autonomous."

Schiller's, and possibly Schelling's and Herder's, use of the term *Bil-dungstrieb* reinforced Coleridge's interest in both the word and the concept, an interest that could have begun as early as 1799, when Coleridge attended Blumenbach's lectures at Göttingen. Blumenbach's *Institutiones physiologicae*, which mentions the concept, was used as a text in the course of lectures; and Coleridge annotated Blumenbach's *Über die natürlichen Verschiedenheiten*. Coleridge's own tentative ex-planation of *Bildungstrieb* is "Imagination=imitation or repetition of an *Image,*" a definition that also uses "repetition" in a sense similar to the "repetition" in his remarks on the primary imagination.[3]

The poet, according to Herder, imitates God's creative power; "*oder vielmehr, er wirkt unter ihm mit Verstand und Absicht.*" The creative power of God is itself in and works through the poet; it is actually mag-nified and nuanced by the poet's understanding and intention. In a short essay of 1787 , "*Über Bild, Dichtung, und Fabel,*" Herder explains this process: "Divine nature has painted images for us on a huge, illuminated canvas; from it we seize these images and paint them in our souls with a brush finer than one made from rays of light."[4]

His explanation is typically metaphorical. It shuns the metaphysical and avoids abstract aesthetic theory. But when Herder's comments on the imaginative power are combined with his faith in myths of creation and in the truth of religious prophecies, especially the Old Testament, his total view, in its pantheism, is a modified form of Spinoza's or Shaftesbury's thought. To the teaching of Spinoza, which Herder helped to popularize but somewhat misrepresented, Herder adds some of Leibniz's monadology and, most importantly, a fervent belief in Jesus as the symbolic being in whom meet God, matter, spirit, man, and the transforming creativity dwelling in them all. Jesus becomes a "middle point," a "mediating center," and in this respect Herder resembles Blake.

Herder's poem *Die Schöpfung, Ein Morgensang* (1773) summarizes in lyric form several of his attitudes. He speaks of *"Gottes reger Kraft/Kraft, durch die er Alles Schafft!"* Midway through the poem he turns from the Genesis-like story of cosmic and earthly creation to the position of man himself. He proclaims that man represents *"Was Geschöpf und Schöpfer ist,"* a sentiment later echoed in *Adrastea.* Then he suddenly rhapsodizes:

> And so I am, I am it, yes,
> What this god-like form appears!
>
> I—like God! So moves in me
> Creation's plan.

Here again the English parallel is Blake. Herder envisions Christ as the nexus where all converges:

> The Form of God in Word and Act,
> The form of man in God's own way,
> Mediator, creator, guardian are
> You in All, Jesus Christ!

Christ is then addressed not as the Spinozistic one and all (*en kai pan*) but as the one in all, the all in one:

> One in All, All in One,
> You were and are and yet will be,
> You, from whom creation springs,
> You in all God's forms.

For Herder, as for Blake, Coleridge, and Schelling, Christ symbolizes the creative force in God and in man, the unity of the two. In the last line of the poem, Christ is the *"Mittelpunkt in Gottes Ruh!"* that is, the mediating figure, the central point between nature, God, and man, where creative power radiates out to all three from Christ's one recognizable and inclusive form. This is not, strictly speaking, pantheism or Spinozism; but it is a blending of these with the idea of the imagination and the figure of Christ. Herder's use of Christ as the *"Mittelpunkt"* occurs several times in his works and has an important bearing on the idea of the imagination.[5]

Christ is the *"Mittel . . . und Prototyp der Schöpfung."* He is *"das Schöpfungswort Gottes."* In a commentary on the New Testament published in 1775, Herder states that Jesus *"ist der Mittelpunkt und Eckstein des Ganzen, das Mittelglied der Berechnung,"* the central point and touchstone of all, the mean of reckoning.[6] Coleridge, as he approaches his treatment of the imagination in the *Biographia*, quotes from the hymns of Synesius in which God is implored to descend to some *middle* ground, to some standard, some mean, or some means by which to embrace all. Furthermore, Coleridge connects the ideas of the imagination with the *Logos* of the new Testament, especially with St. John. Herder's comments on Christ as the middle point and as the true standard and representative of the creative power of God and man invariably come in either the context of the *Logos* or in commentary on the gospel of St. John. Herder's *Aus der unveröffentlichen Schrift: Johannes* (1773–1774), *Ankündigungen Johannes und Jesus* (1773), and *Erläuterung zum Neuen Testament* (1775) are just three examples.[7] For Herder, Christ is the incarnate center of the imaginative and creative power. This is what Blake was saying, almost simultaneously, and what Coleridge later envisioned as a general topic of his *Magnum Opus*. These views show why, for many Romantics, salvation and imagination became virtual synonyms.

The imagination as a means or middle ground drawing all to one point also has implications outside the Christian context. It was, in fact, in the mid 1770s that Tetens observed how associated ideas, while having several points of connection, nevertheless tend to cluster around *one* predominant point, a central middle point. This clustering about one point is achieved by the work of the imagination. (*"Welches ist nun der Punkt, um den herum die Phantasie, als um einen Mittelpunkt wirket?"*) The presence of such a central image or idea around which many others group themselves led Tetens to conclude that this point is a vital nexus fusing all the ideas associated through it "as one." (*"In dieser Hinsicht ist die Verknüpfung der Ideen in der Seele eine durchgängige Verbindung singularum cum singulis."*) This thoroughgoing joining or fusion of ideas occurs especially in individuals of large and rich imagination (*"in einer grossen und reichen Einbildungskraft"*). And it is exactly the presence of a "middlepoint" (*Mittelpunkt*) that permits the imagination to operate in an intuitive and immediate (*unmittelbar*) fashion.[8]

The imagination thus might easily be conceived of as a middle or central agency. This may be what Schiller has in mind when he refers to a synthetic *Mittelkraft* joining man's ideal and sensuous natures into one.[9] Furthermore, the imagination as a "middle" makes it the perfect union of polar opposites, a concept that fascinated Bruno, Hamann, Coleridge, and Schelling. Schelling's "*Indifferenzpunkt,*" the one point mid-way between two poles or forces, as in a magnet, thus becomes connected with the imagination. And when Coleridge says in the *Biographia* and elsewhere that the imagination reconciles opposites and smooths away contradictions, he is reiterating a quality of the imagination discussed for well over thirty years. The concept is in Schelling, Kant, Schiller, Hamann, and Herder; and its general basis, though not the specific connection with the idea of the imagination, can be traced to Plato. Coleridge says the poet's imagination "reveals itself in the balance or reconciliation of opposite or discordant qualities." Even Longinus, in his treatise *On the Sublime*, praised Sappho because "at one and the same time she calls up soul—and body, ears, tongue, eyes, and color . . . uniting opposites, she freezes while she burns, is both out of her senses and in her right mind." Fichte, in his deduction of the general meaning of *Geist* in *Über Geist und Buchstab in der Philosophie*, asks where is this elusive unity of the *middle* that unites art, the artist, his subject, and the audience in one: "Where does the incomprehensible connection of this mediator with [its] goal lie, and by what art has it divined what it could not possibly find through any conscious reflection?" The answer is that this reconciliatory unity rests in a cetain *Geist*, which Fichte equates with *Einbildungskraft*. In *Über Geist und Buchstab* he partially explains *Geist* in the appreciation of inspirational art, where "our imagination creates from itself in a way like the artist's."[10]

When we talk about the imagination as a middle point, we are inevitably speaking of it as a point of unity, what Fichte calls the "*Vereinigungspunkt.*" This unity and reconciliation becomes essential to Schelling and Coleridge; in Herder we sense it, though in a less encompassing manner. Perhaps influenced by Tetens' *Versuche* (1776), Herder in 1778 presented his *Vom Erkennen und Empfinden der Menschlichen Seele*, wherein he attempts to explain imagination in a psychological-physiological fashion, and relies in part on a theory of nerve impulses and reactions. But what is more important, as early as 1778 he suggests, as a result of his interest in language and its origins, that *Einbildungskraft* means the general power to shape into one, to form a unity. This is twenty-five years before Schelling's statement of the same idea in a more general application. (Also, this is three years before Kant's first *Critique* would spoil the word *Einbildungskraft* for Herder.) Herder discusses not the "polar opposites" of a philosophical system but the mother's effect, or humanity's effect, on a child, which is an imaginative effect in the sense not of being imaginary but of tending to produce a unified result from all constituent relations between the self and the outside world that occur as early as the womb. The human being even in infancy begins to sense life as a totality, a unity of consciousness:

> But now, since by all our experiences we are each full of impulse and life, and since our respective lives are, in such a wonderful way, one unity in us each [*ein Eins in uns sind*], one human soul, which all mechanical connections and limbs willingly serve; and that even this coalescing, soul-bestowed unity in us is called an image [*Einbildung*] if we take that word in its true extent, what is absurd in the thought that this world of the soul in the midst of which, as it were, the child is suspended—this whole psyche of humanity that holds the child in its arms—participates with him in each impression and with each of his impulses?[11]

This idea recurs in the 1805 *Prelude* (II, 232–265) in which Wordsworth speaks of the mother's care of the infant as life's first touch of love and imagination.

A similar sentiment of unity, but carried to the highest reaches of art and human achievement, occurs in Schiller's *Die Künstler*. Here the power of art unifies all sensibility and intelligence "in *one* magic bond," "in *one* bond of truth, in *one* stream of light." As in Herder, the final role of "*die schöne Bildkraft*," as Schiller calls it, is to bring life into unity, which anticipates not only Schelling but Coleridge's "esemplastic,"—to shape into one—and his remark that the poetic imagination struggles to idealize and to unify. There is a parallel, too, between Herder and Schiller's progression from a human awareness of divine creation to "*eine zweite höhre Kunst*" of the poet and Coleridge's progression from the primary to the secondary level of the imagination.

Herder's network of ideas concerning the imagination combines religion, myth, and poetry with a dash of psychology. He uses a wealth of terms and phrases to identify the imaginative power in its various guises, and this multiplicity of views would soon form part of what thinkers immediately after him wanted to establish by one term and by one systematic outlook, if that were possible without violating the truth of constituent parts. Referring to Herder's view of history, Isaiah Berlin pays significant tribute to his perception

> that the task of integrating disparate data and interpretations of events, movements, situations, and synthesizing such heterogeneous material into a coherent picture, demands gifts very different from those required for rational methods of investigation or formulation and verification of specific hypotheses: above all, the gift of breathing life into the dead bones in the burial ground of the past, of a creative imagination."[12]

That Herder could perceive the necessity of "a creative imagination" for all his tasks, including historical research, stemmed not from an automatic exercise of such imagination but from his discovery of the very nature and working importance of that creative imagination, which he could then turn to any endeavor.

## FICHTE AND SUBJECTIVE IDEALISM

Johann Gottlieb Fichte (1762–1814), born into a Saxon farming family, made his own way when young and first achieved prominence by applying Kant's philosophy to religious questions. Kant had not yet made this connection in an orderly fashion, and when Fichte's *Versuch einer Kritik aller Offenbarung* appeared anonymously, many attributed it to Kant himself. By the early 1790s Fichte, as only a contemporary disciple can do, was bending the still-hot bar of Kant's doctrine into a new curve. A generation later the bar might be stronger but, in that odd tempering process of intellectual history, it would have cooled enough to resist hammering or recasting.

Fichte snatches the idea of the imagination from Kant and increases its importance. He also tries to unify the many ideas of the imagination in Kant, but falls short. The essential problem in Fichte's system is the nature of the border or point of intersection between the self, called the *Ich*, and an external reality, which Fichte defines in terms of the self, his starting point, and calls the *Nicht-Ich*. Fichte concludes that only the imagination can act as negotiator between the self and the outside world. But his stance leaves him open to misunderstanding. He is to the transcendentalists, in a way, what Berkeley is to the empiricists. Everything seems to be defined only in terms of the self, which suggests a thoroughgoing, self-indulgent subjectivism. Coleridge satirizes Fichte in the *Biographia* and attacks the "crude egoismus" into which Fichte descends. But in letters and notebooks Coleridge states, "my faith remains with Fichte," who is described as creeping toward the very altar of the godhead and as even having got his trembling hands upon the horns of it!

The fact is that in Fichte's system the *Nicht-Ich* is an ungrounded postulate of the *Ich*, something hard for anyone with a mainly empirical sense to accept, whereas the *Ich* itself belongs to a larger being, an *absolute Ich*. There is no cult of personality, no laissez-faire capitalism or Hobbsean morality, all of which Fichte has been accused of propagating. As in the case of Coleridge, religion seems to be at the bottom of everything. Fichte was remarkable for memorizing sermons as a boy. He wrote extensively on the moral life and is frequently considered one of Germany's first socialist writers.

Fichte conceded nothing to the empiricists or, as he called them, *"die Dogmatiker."* Even the *Ding-an-Sich* was anathema to him. He considered it a concession to the outside world, a usurpation of the power of the *Ich*. Transcendentalists who believed in it were *"transzendentale Dogmatiker."* But Fichte at first followed Kant concerning the activity of the imagination. Both the synthesis of pure forms as well as the synthesis of sensuous experience take place in the imagination, which is thus connected to both reason and the senses and brings them together in the understanding. Fichte echoes Kant, quoting him in several places without reference, and identifies *Einbildungskraft* as *"ein Kraft, der wir uns selten, oder nie bewust werden,"*[13] a power we are seldom if ever conscious of. In the *Transscendentale Elementarlehre* (1790–1791), the imagination acts as a nexus between the senses and pure forms, which later becomes one basis for Schiller's *Spieltrieb*.

But by the middle and late 1790s Fichte concentrates more on the ideal side. In the *Versuch einer neuen Darstellung der Wissenschaftslehre* (1797–1798), an important supplement to the *Grundlage der gesammten Wissenschaftslehre* (1794–1795), Fichte amputates any vestige of objective reality outside the self, at least as far as that reality is believed to have its own characteristics instead of being determined by the *Ich*. *"Das Princip des Dogmatikers, das Ding an sich, ist nichts, und hat . . . keine Realität."* He dismisses anything that is not a product of the imagination, and in doing so, he turns the psychological basis of the critical philosophy into the imagination alone, de-emphasizing the stature of pure reason and of the psychic unity of faculties. Every thing is determined by imagination, which synthesizes and unifies all relationships perceived in time and space: "the thing is none other than all these relationships gathered together by the imagination, and all these relationships taken together with one another are the thing."[14]

Fichte cannot "prove" this in the same way as "proving" the existence of a transcendental number like *pi*. He maintains that his system has no other weapons to combat the dogmatists than faith and self-assurance. This assurance balances on the imagination, for imagination alone creates reality and is the working power behind the *Ich*. In the *Grundlage der gesammten Wissenschaftslehre*, Fichte stresses, *"Es wird demnach hier gelehrt, dass alle Realität . . . bloss durch die Einbildungskraft hervorgebracht werde."* This must be accepted as the exclusive groundwork of all transcendental philosophy worthy of the name. By the same token the *Ich* in all its activity, its consciousness, and its life stands or falls as the imagination acts between the self and the world: "the possibility of our consciousness, of our life, of our being for ourselves, that is, of our being as individuals [*als Ich*], is based on that activity of the imagination." In a note of 1795 (*"Erklärung: Ich sehe mich genöthigt"*), Fichte says that these truths about the absolute shaping power of the imagination appear in the spirit and direction of Leibniz's philosophy and are unmistakably contained in Kant's. Fichte feels he is completing a journey, one started a century before, toward the true value of the imagination.[15]

## "ICH UND NICHT-ICH ZU VEREINIGEN"

Having described imagination as the creatrix of consciousness itself (*"Schöpferin des Bewusstseyns selbst"*), Fichte sets forth on a more difficult task, to unify the opposites inherent in the confrontation between the self and the world. These opposites or "contradictions" may consist of a sense of finite self versus an endless world of experience, or the friction of an ideal or general moral law as it faces a tricky personal situation, or the form that the mind tries to impress on an intractable tableau of changing words and perishable matter: "The problem is to unify the opposing *Ich* and *Nicht-Ich*. It is through the imagination, that unifies the contradictory, that they can be most perfectly united."[16]

The union of the two opposites that occurs through the imagination happens exclusively within the *Ich* itself. This is not only because the *Nicht-Ich* is a postulate of the *Ich* but also because everything must be brought back to the understanding and to the reflection of the self if it is to have any effect on practical life. Fichte stresses that the *Nicht-Ich* is a necessary postulate of the *Ich*, because the idea of opposition and struggle is necessary to life. Otherwise there would be no creation and no death, only an eternal presence that is divine and boring. As Goethe says in *Faust*, error was created to keep the angels awake.

Fichte describes the action of the imagination when it binds and unites the self with the outside world, the subjective with the objective, as a "hovering" or "oscillating," *"Schweben der Einbildungskraft."* In other words, the imagination becomes the catalyst in a dialectic process. It permits the thesis of the *Ich* and the antithesis of the *Nicht-Ich* to fuse in synthetic unity. This concept comes from Kant, but Fichte outlines it more clearly. In altered modes and applications this dialectic process, which in Fichte is instigated and governed by the imagination, becomes central in Schelling and Hegel. Schelling turns the dialectic to his *Philosophie der Kunst*, and Hegel applies it to history. Yet looking at Kant and Fichte, we see that the intellectual power and first birth of the modern dialectic springs from interest in the imagination.[17]

### IMAGINATION AS MAN'S HIGHEST SPIRIT

Fichte, in an audacious move, equates man's spirit with his imagination, *"Geist"* with *"Einbildungskraft."* Almost simultaneously Kant was suggesting connections between genius, spirit, and the creative imagination, but Fichte moves the pawns out more quickly and gets his big pieces onto the board. Having distinguished between the ordering and rearranging power of the reproductive as opposed to the creative work of the productive imagination, Fichte identifies the searching spirit of man, through which all great accomplishments emerge, with the creative imagination. *"Geist überhaupt ist das, was man sonst auch produktive Einbildungskraft nennt."* He uses *productiv* and *shaffend* synonymously as they modify *Einbildungskraft;* "spirit" is, generally, what we also call productive or creative imagination.

By presenting new images and concepts that do not normally punctuate experience, the imagination, or spirit, elevates all human endeavor. It facilitates true progress—not material or technological advances, though these may be by-products of the spirit, but novel patterns of looking at and investigating the cosmos and man's position in it: "This power of imagination ... insofar as it raises into consciousness higher images, ones not forthcoming in the course of usual experience, is called spirit. Without spirit the elements of philosophy are not even possible."[18]

Fichte thus turns his discovery into a way of looking at the well-springs of philosophy, at what Coleridge and earlier Gerard called the "philosophical imagination." All philosophy relies on the creative imagination. This is a stunning conclusion because it means that the fine arts and philosophy are grounded on precisely the same faculty. This realization would set Schelling on a course to reveal the inherent relationships between philosophy and artistic genius.

On the whole, however, Fichte's interest in art finishes second-place to his enthusiasm for philosophy. All ideas, images, representations, mental constructs, and schema that we do not encounter in experience through our senses, and, more important, the transcendental philosophy itself are products of the creative imagination. Just as all truths, including the inner spirit of transcendentalism, are formulated by the creative imagination alone, so they can be fully grasped by it alone:

> This, then, is the work of *the creative imagination* ... On this faculty depends whether we philosophize with or without spirit ... because the fundamental ideas [of any approach to or system of knowledge] in one who studies them must be presented by the creative imagination itself ... The whole operation of the human spirit proceeds from the imagination, but an imagination that can be grasped no other way than through imagination.[19]

It was this proposition of Fichte's, rather than the *Ich*, that attracted Coleridge and Schelling. Although both in their own ways were "followers" of Fichte, they preferred a subjective view that rested directly on God, on a divine and absolulte *Ich*, a view more easily fused with a sense of the external world not as a postulate of the self but as God's creation. In one light, it is just a matter of emphasis, though one that could be important. Fichte's subjectivism, while recognizing an absolute *Ich*, centers about the self; and while in the end Coleridge and Schelling are "subjectivists" too, their belief more directly embraces the primacy of one creating intellect, an archetypal subjectivity, an absolute, a personal God.

In Fichte, however, no concept, not even the *Ich* itself, is at the mercy of the imagination. Nothing comes about, no matter how the imagination operates, unless there is action: the self must *act*. This action is different from either empirical sense or ideal realizations. Action is a special property of the self, connected with the struggle of human freedom.

Moreover, imagination cannot supply what Fichte calls *Gefühl*, namely sensation, feeling, sensibility, or passion. The imagination is thus a means, an agency, a conductor of the self, a shaper of the raw material of experience, and an instigator of new ways of looking at life. But the imagination, just as it is not the beginning of the self, is not the end. It is a means to an end, which Herder called *"das Mittel."* Fichte explains, *"Die schaffende Einbildungskraft bildet nur insofern, in wiefern im Ich Gefühl vorhanden ist,"* the creative imagination shapes only insofar, and as far, as the self is suffused with passion. The imagination is a means of using and elevating the feeling within the self to a new state. The creative imagination is thus *"das Vermögen Gefühle zum Bewusstseyn zu erheben,"*[20] the power to raise passions into consciousness.

### ARTIST'S FANCY AND PHILOSOPHER'S IMAGINATION

Fichte deals with the imagination as a means to a higher aesthetic life and artistic productivity, even though his tone is not as affirmative or as adventuresome as that of some of his German contemporaries. For one thing, Fichte, in speaking of art and the artist's imagination, almost invariably uses the word "fancy" (*Phantasie*), indicating a wild and often unconscious miscarriage of the more philosophic "imagination" (*Einbildungskraft*). Fancy is in the artist's realm because it is empirically oriented and deals with the concrete. By the same token, empirical philosophy, which includes Kant's *Ding-an-Sich*, is *"das abentheuerlichste*

*Misgeburt, welche je von der menschlichen Phantasie erzeugt worden,"*
a reckless miscarriage fashioned from man's fancy. This statement
comes from perhaps the best introduction to Fichte's system, the Introduction to the *Versuch einer neuen Darstellung der Wissenschaftslehre*
(1797–1798).[21]

Elsewhere Fichte identifies fancy as a purely associative power exemplified by the way we connect the hum of a bee with the flower into
which it flies, even though we may never see the two together. Fancy,
working on an empirical level, impresses itself on the artist and makes
the artwork an involuntary production. Fancy is also less regulated than
imagination. Whatever enters the mind by suggestion, fancy can fabricate into a seeming reality. There are few controls to shape its power.
*"Es ist der Phantasie Wohl möglich, so etwas als denkbar zu denken,"* it
is entirely possible to the fancy thus to think of anything as conceiv-
able.[22]

Finally, however, Fichte sees in the poet or artist something more
than philosophic or aesthetic power. An individual may have the potential to become an aesthetic philosopher, but as soon as he becomes that
alone, the nature of poetry is somehow closed to him: "He who is a poet
may also be an aesthetician; but the poet is never an aesthetician
[alone], or else he is not a poet at all."[23]

Fichte never identifies "spirit" with fancy in the way that he does
with imagination. But there is another exception to his seeming prejudice against art at the expense of philosophy, his *Über Geist und
Buchstab in der Philosophie* (1798), three letters similar in content to
Schiller's *Ästhetische Erziehung* (1795). Fichte here includes imaginative art, the highest "spiritual" quality in art, within that sphere occu-
pied by the highest philosophy. This view is an exception to his general
stress on speculative philosophy, but it shows his awareness of important issues concerning art and the imagination. Fichte himself translated
sonnets from the Portugese and Spanish; he also wrote a novella, *Das
Thal der Liebenden. Über Geist und Buchstab in der Philosophie*,
which never proceeds to a discussion of philosophy and dwells for the
most part on literature, may have been an attempt to ingratiate himself
with Goethe.[24]

At any rate, Fichte finds that imaginative art joins the sensuous world
to aesthetic form. Through our imaginative spirit we attain a creative
faculty (*"dieses freie Schöpfungsvermögen"*), which enables us to see
human life itself as an artistic product of the imagination: *"Der Mensch
ist ein seltsam Kunstprodukt."* Fichte, however, sees the highest spirit of
art emerging from the philosophically ideal and transcendental. The artistic imagination is not, as in Schiller and Schelling, a unity of ideal and
real but, true to Fichte's general tendencies, an ideal, almost abstract

force that impresses itself on the artistic medium and even on the mind of the individual artist.

### SCHILLER: *SPIELTRIEB* AS AESTHETIC IMAGINATION

Schiller's aesthetics mediates between the enthusiasms of Herder and the theoretical background supplied by Kant and Fichte. Born in 1759, the year in which *Rasselas* and *Candide* appeared, but later influenced by Baumgarten, Lessing, Mendelssohn, Winckelmann and more directly by Rousseau, Goethe, and Kant, Schiller offers his view of the imagination most explicitly in *Die Ästhetische Erziehung* (1795) and to some degree, as we have seen, in his poem *Die Künstler* (1789). Schiller felt the tug of both poetry and philosophy, and from the two he tried to breed a vigorous cross, combining artistry with speculative and moral thought. By placing the aesthetic imagination at the top of man's faculties, Schiller paved the way for Schelling who, though traveling by a different route and trying to include more in his system, would reach the same conclusion about the supreme importance of aesthetic education. *Die Ästhetische Erziehung* is really a study of the education of man's imagination.

In the *Aesthetic Education*, *Spieltrieb* is usually translated as "play-drive," a unique term which has since been made more popular (though somewhat trivializing and distorting Schiller) in the phrase "art as play." While Schiller uses *Einbildungskraft, Kunsttrieb, Phantasie*, and *Imagination* elsewhere, his idea of *Spieltrieb* parallels the idea of imagination in other major figures. *Spieltrieb* can be taken to stand for the imagination when it operates in an aesthetic context that includes not only art but perception and the conduct of life. One reason Schiller employs *Spieltrieb* and places less emphasis on more traditional terms is that, like Herder, he was deterred by the use of *Einbildungskraft* in Kant, Fichte, and Maimon. In the 1780s and 1790s these thinkers often used *Einbildungskraft* in a strictly philosophical and purely speculative sense.[25] Like Herder, Schiller turns to *Bildungstrieb* as the "imitative and shaping power" of art habitually associated in British thought with "imagination."

*Spieltrieb* unifies two other drives or principles found in the psyche as it confronts the world, both of which correspond to the two poles between which the imagination mediates in Kant, Coleridge, Fichte, Schelling, Herder, and at moments in Keats. The first principle or drive is that of the real world, the condition of matter and the senses, which is outside the self. Schiller describes this pole first as *"Zustand,"* roughly equivalent to Fichte's *Nicht-Ich*. This pole represents the empirical and the "objective," which Schiller also refers to as the "external." The mind associates sensuous forms in a *"Phantasiespiel,"* a play of fancy similar to the association of ideas, where "idea" means a sensuous object, image, or memory. For Schiller, human receptivity to this principle is based on the senses and is fundamentally passive. "The first of these drives, which I call the sensuous," is also referred to as *"Stofftrieb,"* the apprehension of matter and substance.

The human psyche has another basic drive or principle: "The second drive, which one calls the formal." This *Formtrieb* represents the activity of the self in a realm of ideas and forms, mental or transcendental exercises. The *Formtrieb* is identified with what Schiller, like Fichte, calls the *"Ich."* For Schiller, just as the sense drive is anchored in the senses, the drive for form and ideas is attached to reason, more in its Platonic implications than in its logical and deductive sense. The *Formtrieb* is an active principle. It is subjective, *"geistlich"* and *"innerlich."* Thus, the two drives that Schiller posits correspond to essential divisions made by Kant, Fichte, Jacobi, Coleridge, and Schelling, which they, like Schiller, announce (often at the beginning of important works or at a crucial place in them) as a prelude to a "deduction" of the imagination.

In Schiller the *Spieltrieb* is the mediating and unifying drive, the *"tertium aliquid"* that creates final harmony. The *Spieltrieb* unites the permanence and self-sustaining identities of the ideal world with the individual process and flux of material existence: "That drive, therefore, in which both the others work in concert ... the play-drive, therefore, would be directed toward annulling time *within time,* reconciling becoming with absolute being and change with identity."[26] The *Spieltrieb* brings sense impressions, feelings, and passions (*Gefühle*) into harmony with the ideas of reason. In its total capacity it effectually serves the same *kind* of purpose as *Einbildungskraft* does in Kant, Schelling, Fichte, and Goethe, or as "imagination" does in Coleridge.

Although the *Spieltrieb* unites the two basic drives or circumstances of existence into a single play of aesthetic appreciation and creativity, it is a mistake to translate *Spieltrieb* simply as "imagination." *Spieltrieb* or *aesthetic* imagination should not be equated with the more general sense of imagination or *Einbildungskraft,* unmodified by any reference to art or aesthetics, also found in Schiller. In effect, as with Tetens, Sulzer, Kant, and Schelling, Schiller posits different levels of imaginative power. *Spieltrieb* is his highest level of the imagination. In this sense, as an aesthetic unity of the psyche that produces a whole view of the world, it foreshadows Schelling's *"ästhetische Anschauung,"* an aesthetic intuition that brings "the whole man" into harmony with nature. Art is a result of this aesthetic outlook, an inevitable and glorious byproduct, but the *Spieltrieb* should not be identified with the productive power of art alone. The *Spieltrieb* first creates a broader world-view, saturating the way in which we experience and act. And it is this aesthetic world-view that in turn fosters imaginative art. In short, the *Spieltrieb* is the imagination understood in its full aesthetic life, which initiates the artistic impulse (see diagram).[27]

In letter XI, Schiller notes, *"Der Gegenstand des Spieltriebes, in einem allgemeinen Schema vorgestellt, wird also lebende Gestalt heissen können."* This sense of living, active form is similar to Coleridge's *forma informans* and anticipates Herder's statement in *Adrastea* (1801) that, *"In unserer Seele ... schläft unter andern Eine sehr Wirksame Kraft, die Bildnerin der Gestalten."* This power to form and shape is Herder's *Bildungstrieb*. Like Schiller's *Spieltrieb*, its duty is to shape experience and the various powers of the psyche into a unity (*"ein Eins zu finden und sich auszubilden aus Vielem."*) Just as Schiller claims that only when man plays is he truly human, so Herder notes that this production of living forms is what fulfills man: *"Und in dieser Gestaltenbildung, wenn sie guter Art ist, sind Menschen so froh und selig!"*[28]

At a crucial juncture in letter XV, Schiller explains the main reason for his new terminology of *Spieltrieb:* "This term is fully justified by linguistic usage, which is wont to designate as 'play' everything which is neither subjectively not objectively contingent, and yet imposes no kind of restraint either from within or from without."

In effect the *Spieltrieb* unifies the subjective and the objective, the inner and the outer, until neither can be said to exist in its own right. This is the same unification of opposites we have witnessed in many other writers, often performed under the name of "imagination" or *Einbildungskraft*, or occasionally under one of the *Dicht-* terms.

Schiller tried to clarify the scene with yet another term (*Benennung*) despite the fact that so many terms as to be confusing were already at hand. For one reason, Kant and Fichte had recently given *Einbildungskraft* and *Phantasie* connotations with a philosophical outlook that seemed to choke feeling, the arts, and any psychic unity other than a theoretical one. Schiller wanted an aesthetic term, or one easily tailored to an aesthetic use. But the *Dicht-* terms were too specific in their reference to the fine arts, especially poetry. Although Tetens, following Gerard, had originally conceived of *Dichtungskraft* as a psychological term explaining the quality of genius and creativity in general, in the twenty years since Tetens that term and its cognates had acquired a flavor that was too dependent on literary criticism alone. Schiller wanted a term that implied a way to look at the world, a way to act and to experience as well as to create art.

The word *Spiel* already had good connotations, some of which al-

# The Dialectical Play of Imagination

Schiller: *Stofftrieb*
 *Zustand*
 real
 sensuous, *sinnlich*
 passive
 objective
 external
 association of sensuous
 images
 *Ideenfolge, Phantasie-
 spiel*
Tetens: *Phantasie*
Kant: empirical imagination
 reproductive
Fichte: material or dogmatic
 imagination
 *Phantasie*
Schelling: *sinnliche Anschauung*
Coleridge: association of ideas
 fancy
 the objective
 *principium cog-
 noscendi*

Schiller: *Formtrieb*
 *Ich*
 ideal
 spiritual, *geistlich*
 active
 subjective
 internal
 free motion of forms
 *freie Bewegung, erhebt
 sich der bildende Kraft
 zum Ideale*
Tetens: *Einbildungskraft*, in
 broad, ideal sense
Kant: *transzendentale Einbildungskraft*
 productive
Fichte: *Einbildungskraft*, especially in philosophy
Schelling: *intellectuelle Anschauung
 Einbildungskraft*, in
 ideal sense
Coleridge: philosophic or transcendental imagination;
 the subjective
 *principium essendi*

Schiller: *Spieltrieb*
 an aesthetic life
 *lebende Gestalten
 die bildende Kraft
 ästhetische Einbil-
 dungskraft
 Bildungstrieb
 Kunst, Schönheit*
Tetens: *selbstätige Phantasie
 Dichtungskraft, Genius*
 (from Gerard)
Kant: *Einbildungskraft*, in highest
 aesthetic and synthetic
 sense; *Geist, Schönheit,
 Kunst*
Fichte: *Geist, Einbildungskraft*
Schelling: *ästhetische Anschauung
 Einbildungskraft*, in
 highest sense
 *Kunstprodukt, In-Eins-
 Bildung*
Coleridge: imagination, poetic or
 secondary, the fine arts,
 especially poetry
 beauty, esemplastic

ways included the idea of the imagination. For one thing, *Spiel* implied real activity and process, a moving and a mingling that was missing from Fichte's more limited and static-sounding *"Schweben der Einbildungskraft."* *Spiel* suggested active friction and the interplay required for a final harmony, as in Schelling's *"Wechselspiel"*). In the *Critique of Judgment* Kant had spoken of the "free play of the imagination," a common phrase which he employed in the context of aesthetic judgment. Goethe would in 1827 say of the Elizabethan stage, *"Die Einbildungskraft hat freies Spiel,"* and he would remark on *"ein freies Walten der Einbildungskraft."* But there are also significant uses of *Spiel* before Schiller's. In *Laokoon* (1766), Lessing explains that the moment the artist selects to depict or to imitate must be when the situation is somewhat developed, but not completely; room must be left for suggestion:

> Now that only is fruitful which allows free play to the imagination [*was der Einbildungskraft freyes Spiel lässt*] . . . But no moment is so disadvantageous in this respect as the culmination of a course of action. There is nothing beyond, and to present the uttermost to the eye means to bind the wings of fancy and force her . . . to employ herself with feeble images, turning from the given fullness already expressed as her limit.

Here the "free play of imagination" captures a ripe moment when the tension and process between sensuous tumult and final form are most evident. In that moment there is a mediation between the material reality and its ideal shaping spirit; neither dominates, and we see their interplay most clearly.

Wieland also used play and imagination, the bridge between spirit and matter, to depict the broadest activities of life and art. In his *Etwas von den älteseten Zeitkürzungs-Spiele* (1785), he claims:

> Man is then only healthy in body and soul, fresh, brisk, and powerful, feels himself happy in the enjoyment of his being, only when all of his concerns, spiritual and bodily, are caught up in *play*. The most beautiful arts . . . are *play* . . . Take away from life whatever is the servant of iron-handed necessity and what is all that is left over but *play?* Children play with nature, poets with their imagination.[29]

The play of the imaginative act, moreover, seems to be a natural, even a universal concept. It was not restricted to eighteenth-century Germany. In the *Advancement of Learning*, Bacon remarks that "as for poesy it is rather a pleasure or play of imagination, than a work or duty thereof." Bacon uses "poesy" to imply creative and aesthetic acts of the mind in general, a usage echoed in Coleridge's "On Poesy or Art."

*Spieltrieb* was a natural choice for Schiller. It had a favorable history, the kind he wanted, positive and broadly aesthetic. The *Trieb* added a sense of innate urgency, similar to Aristotle's observation in the *Poetics* that human beings have basic drives or instincts for imitation and for harmony. *Spieltrieb* escaped the more purely psychological and philosophical usages of *Einbildungskraft* in something like Maass's *Versuch über die Einbildungskraft*. Yet Schiller could now enrich his ideas by employing *Einbildungskraft* and *Phantasie* in addition to *Spieltrieb*. With *Spieltrieb*, Schiller makes a frontal assault on the whole question of imagination and aesthetic life, implying perception of nature, action, moral ideas, ideal forms, and imitative art. Also there was the pleasant rhetorical shock produced by saying that play, not reason, duty, or religion, was the highest fulfillment of humanity.

## OTHER TERMS

Taking *Spieltrieb* as the aesthetic and the highest level of imagination, Schiller, along with Tetens, Platner, Kant, and Schelling, sees one or two additional levels. For these lower levels he uses *Einbildungskraft*, *Phantasie*, *Phantasiespiel*, and *Imagination*. These terms refer to the activities of the imagination in general—to perception, the association of ideas or *Ideenfolge*, and the enthusiasm for purely ideal creations—that are more or less enclosed within either the senses or the form drive, and which are therefore "incomplete" and below the totality of the *Spieltrieb*. One way to interpret the additional terms is that *Einbildungskraft* usually stands for a general, not a final unifying play of imagination, while *Phantasiespiel* refers more to fancy or the association of empirical, sensuous images without the actual creation of new ones:

> Like the bodily organs in man, his imagination, too, has its free movement and its material play, an activity in which, without any reference to form, it simply delights in its own absolute and unfettered power. Inasmuch as form does not yet enter this fantasy play at all, its whole charm residing in a free association of images, such play—although the prerogative of man alone—belongs merely to his animal life, and simply affords evidence of his liberation from all external physical compulsion, without as yet warranting the inference that there is any autonomous shaping power within him. From this play of *freely associated ideas*, which is still of a wholly material kind, and to be explained by purely natural laws, the imagination, in its attempt at a *free form*, finally makes the leap to aesthetic play. A leap it must be called, since a completely new power now goes into action; for here, for the first time, the mind takes a hand as lawgiver in the operations of blind instinct, subjects the arbitrary activity of the imagination to its own immutable and eternal unity, introduces its own autonomy into the transient, and its own infinity into the life of sense.

The unification of material fancies and ideal imaginings into a new aesthetic whole—the "leap" required for this—is, as Schiller explains, a process that demands blending, balancing, and cultivation. It is an education in itself, nothing less than the whole education of the human imagination, which is the real subject of Schiller's book, and the imagination is an obstreperous power, always derailing and heading off into either fantastical or imaginary vagaries.[30]

The *Spieltrieb* (or *Einbildungskraft* understood in an aesthetic, artistic sense) serves to unify the imaginative life in general. Schiller's plan for the cultivation of the imagination may be seen as an attempt to solve, once and for all, the nemesis of Cartesian duality. One of the main reasons that the idea of the imagination hypnotized thinkers and critics who had any philosophical background is that it promised to heal the troubling dualism. The imagination becomes the psychological and aesthetic realization of a pre-established harmony. Or the harmony does not even have to be pre-established; the imagination may create and establish its own.

Whichever the case, the cultivated and unifying imagination leads us to imitate nature. But the beauty of the fine arts is just one product of the *Spieltrieb*. However grandiose it sounds, the fullest object of the *Spieltrieb*, of the educated imagination, is an aesthetically beautiful and artistically enriched life. Now in this kind of life, art is not only an imitation of nature but also an imitation of the larger aesthetic and moral state of the human psyche as it confronts nature. Thus the highest art involves a transformation of nature and a transformation of the self in living, and the work of art symbolizes this new life. Schiller stresses this point in his essay *On the Sublime*.

The beautiful in art, the *Schöner Schein*, is the ideal as it is cast in the garment of the real. It is not to be mistaken for reality itself but is a calling on reality to attain a higher state. Schiller's message is similar to Shelley's in the *Defence*. Art for Schiller, as it becomes for Schelling, is the highest *tangible* expression of aesthetic life. Just as Blake insists that "the Poetic Genius is the true Man," Schiller argues that "the poet is the only true *human being*."[31] Only when man plays is he truly human, fulfilling all human potentialities, and only art brings the whole man into play.

In Tetens, Kant, Herder and Fichte, the will works intrinsically with the highest level of imagination. This concept appears in English thought as well and can be found in Burke, Gerard, and Coleridge, especially in his definition of the secondary imagination as "co-existing with the conscious will" and in his remark in the *Biographia* that imagination is first set in motion by the will and the understanding and should be kept under their "irremissive, though gentle and unnoticed controul." Schiller does not stress the connection between will and imagination, but he remarks on the absolute necessity of this bond. Will, which for Schiller might be described as the primal life-force or power to exist, to adapt, and to act, which is not the same as hard work or consciously applied "will power," is the ground of personal being. It is present in every act and human drive. Referring to the sense and form drives, Schiller finds that "the will maintains a perfect freedom between the two." He then concludes: "It is, then, the will which acts as a *power* (power being the ground of all reality) *vis-à-vis* both drives; but neither of these can of itself act as a power against the other . . . There is in Man no other power than his will."

If the *Spieltrieb* is the sole harmonizer of the two drives, then the *Spieltrieb*, or aesthetic imagination, becomes the only true expression and working out of man's will, the utmost effort of his being and potential. This underlying theme in Schiller is found in every significant thinker on the imagination. Although separated neither from spontaneity nor from reason, the imagination also emerges as the drama of the will struggling to fulfill itself. The imagination generates our sense of becoming and elevates us above a naturalistic existence, an elevation that reason can not accomplish nearly as well. In *On Naive and Sentimental Poetry* Schiller reveals this idealistic bias: the "fundamental wealth" of the poetic imagination resides not in "the sensuous features" but in the "mind and idea" of art.

## TRANSCENDENTAL POETICS

There are two kinds of learned sages, says Blake in his *Descriptive Catalogue of 1809*. One is the philosophic and the other the poetic. By 1795 in Germany the two had begun actively to fuse. To this combination was added a third element. The new sage of the transcendental era was also a kind of priest. It was above all the poet himself, not the cleric or the philosopher, who could hold all three functions within the unity of his soul. Art and the artist expressed the divine best. To be a poet was to be sanctified. Wackenroder, the Schlegels, Novalis, Schleiermacher and others shared this ideal. The artist, said Schleiermacher, is "a true priest of the Highest" who "presents the heavenly and the eternal."[32] The poet was not only to offer his own credo but prophetically to lead the nation, the whole of humanity in a new creed, the basis of which would be the poet's imagination. So Novalis stated that "Knowledge is only one half" of what we require: "belief is the other." And although he formulated knowledge cryptically as a combination of reason and understanding, he considered the object of true belief, the new religion, as a compound of reason and imagination (*"Vernunft und Phantasie ist Religion."*)[33]

What poets and artists actually were writing or producing was just one side of the new view of the imaginative creator. Another, perhaps more important side was that the poet inwardly possessed a metaphysics of art and a religious depth of insight that was the supreme, though sometimes unspoken, poem of a higher life. Mankind was making a conscious evolutionary step in the life of the spirit; the very name that Friedrich von Hardenberg chose for himself, Novalis, implied this evolution. In *Gespräch über die Poesie*, Friedrich Schlegel envisioned, as others did, a new mythology to carry out this program of the new poet. In 1798 Schlegel wrote Novalis that he hoped to follow Mohammed and Luther by writing a new Bible! Novalis himself made the observation, perhaps prompted by Schlegel, that "The history of each man should be a Bible, it comes to be a Bible . . . a Bible is the highest product of all writing."[34] Here the hope and conviction strike consonances with Blake.

Novalis, however, felt that his talent lay more in the direction of a symbolic, archetypal story in which imaginative vision transforms earthly life into a new world, a higher and happier transcendentalized existence. This kind of story, easier and less imposing to write than a new Bible or holy book, was the *Märchen*. Its ultimate philosophic and religious purpose helps explain why it gained such importance for Novalis and other German Romantics. The *Märchen* was to unify mundane folk experience and elevate it to an ethereal plane. In one of his late prose fragments Novalis writes: *"Poetics.* In the *Märchen* I believe myself best able to express the voice of my heart and soul. (Everything is a *Märchen*)."[35] His words recall Addison's plea for a return to the "fairy way of writing," a critical hope reflected in Bodmer and Breitinger. Novalis felt empowered to put this kind of imaginative experiment into effect. The *Märchen* might best be described not as a story about fairies, nor as a fairy-tale as such, but as a story predicated upon imagination, built and constructed according to the dictates of the imagination, of its leaps, inventions, and unifying powers. It is a story in which imagination predominates and the secondary touches are provided by reason and understanding, not the other way around. Coleridge's *Christabel* might be seen as a *Märchen* composed in English verse.

No matter what the form of literary espression, the new metaphysics and new religion of art placed upon poetry and, more important, upon the poet himself a great burden of expectation and revelation. As Collins and Shelley soon would reiterate, the poet lifts the veil from the face of the eternal and beautiful. He was to create the universe anew. The image of lifting the veil we find also in Novalis and Schelling. Schleiermacher implies that we all create veils inside ourselves; for the poet to lift the universal veil and reveal the divine, he must first lift the inner veil from his own perceptions and soul. He must wipe off the film of familiarity that clouds his vision. He must discover within himself a quality Blake and others stressed, the indwelling divinity, *Est Deus in nobis*. For Friedrich Schlegel, too, the artist's imagination alone could part and see behind the mortal veil that hides the secret of a more profound existence.[36]

Naturally there was a dream-like quality to this enthusiasm. But the hope was expressed well by Keats, who said that the imagination is like Adam's dream: he awoke and found it truth. For centuries the different worlds of dreams, prophecies, and actual events had been seen in close relationship, as indeed, with a psychoanalytic twist, they still are. But Novalis wanted to identify the dream of the imagination with life. There would be a complete transformation. Experience was not simply to be interpreted or connected or understood through the imagination; it was to be wholly predicated on and dictated by the disposition of imaginative vision and faith. "Love and faith," remarks Novalis, "will make our life eternal poetry." The vision of transformed reality becomes complete in Novalis' *Heinrich von Ofterdingen* (1802), a *Märchen*. The poem introducing the second part proclaims, "The World becomes the Dream, the Dream the World." Novalis was speaking for a poetic spirit that conceived its mission not only as an imaginative expression of philosophy and religion but also as an actual discovery of them. "This," he writes, "is the kernel of my philosophy. The more poetic, the truer."[37]

A symbolical language was needed to convey the newly created imaginative realm. "Language," observes Heinrich in Novalis' *Märchen*, "is really a small world in signs and sounds." This compressed world was to mirror symbolically the world at large. In fact, it was therefore not to "mirror" it at all but to reshape it. Hazlitt, Coleridge, and Goethe used the image of a hieroglyph to catch this sense of poetic power. Friedrich Schlegel does also, declaring that art "is nothing other than the hieroglyphic expression of external nature in its clairvoyant transfiguration by the imagination."[38] Wolff had spoken of the ability of the *Facultas fingendi* to produce "hieroglyphs" and "symbols." Novalis, Wackenroder, and August Schlegel championed the necessity of presenting the poet's vision in symbolic language. This meant that the poet was to create the scriptures, symbols, and poetry of a new faith from scratch, without the aid of actual martyrs or popular religious cults. So the poet naturally turned to one or two convulsive events, such as the French Revolution, or more often to his inner vision, the transformation of his own experience.

There are numerous ways to look at the higher calling of poetry demanded by Novalis and the Schlegels. One way is to judge whether or not the artists and poets ever attained, in poems and productions themselves, their metaphysical ideal of art, an ideal set not only by themselves but by philosophers like Schelling. Such a judgment may be largely a matter of personal taste. But we should look at themes in the new poetic movement that reflect topics we have already discussed, for the "new" movement enjoyed a number of connections with what preceded it. Most obvious is the development of the transcendental philosophy in Kant and Fichte, which Schiller then applied to aesthetics. Novalis, for instance, studied Schiller and Fichte thoroughly, Kant less so. The prose fragments of Novalis contain notes primarily on philosophers and scientists, not poets and critics. Typically, he claims that the artist is a transcendental creature (*"Der Künstler ist durchaus transzendental"*).[39]

The romantic goals of Novalis and the Schlegels are to a large degree the outgrowth of transcendental philosophy which, especially in Fichte, Schiller, and Schelling, posited a transcendental realm and a corresponding region of the mind with the imagination supremely important. All these writers stress the unity of mind and aesthetic response attained through the imagination. Novalis seems to paraphrase Fichte when he says, "All our inward and outward faculties and powers are to be deduced from the productive imagination." Novalis reduces this proposition to one even more elemental. There are many functions in the psyche, such as emotion, understanding, and reason, but only one *power*, or way of effecting change and movement, and that is the imagination. Aesthetics belong wholly to psychology; that is, if aesthetic values are determined by psychology (*"Die Ästhetik dürfte wohl ganz zur Psychologie gehören"*), then the productive imagination becomes the supreme arbiter of aesthetics.[40] This conviction recalls not only Schiller, Fichte, and Kant but also the Enlightenment's preoccupation with the link between psychology and aesthetics, which was explored by the associationists and led directly to the idea of the imagination in Gerard, Tetens, Priestley and Hazlitt.

Novalis also picks up the pantheistic strain of Herder, the ideal of romantic Spinozism built on the connecting force of imagination. In *Heinrich von Ofterdingen* the poet is again the middle point and holy source of a pantheistic universality (*"Ich bin der Mittelpunkt, der heilige Quell... Es bricht die neue Welt herein... Eins in allem und alles in einen, / Gottes Bild auf Kräutern und Steinen / Gottes Geist in Menschen und Tieren"*). The totality and unity of the world are seen from the mediating perspective of the poet and are actually a product of his imagination.[41]

### IMAGINATIVE SYMPATHY AS A TRANSCENDENTAL ACT

Novalis makes the enigmatic remark that "The poet is thus the transcendental physician" ("*Der Poet ist also der transzendentale Arzt*"). The statement is similar to Keats's observation that the poet is a physician "to sooth the cares, and lift the thoughts of man." But why is Novalis's poet "transcendental"? The context of his remark reveals an even deeper connection between Novalis and a concept of long-standing importance in the Enlightenment, sympathy. For Novalis speaks of the necessity of the artist to identify himself with the inner spirit of whatever he imitates. "There is a symptomatic and a genetic imitation [*symptomatische,* imitation of outward appearance or idiosyncracy, versus *"genetische,"* imitation of true form and inner spirit]. The latter alone is vital. It presents the innermost unity of imagination and understanding." This distinction sounds similar to August Schlegel on mechanic versus organic form, Coleridge on copy versus imitation, or Schelling on imitation of outward particulars versus indwelling natural spirit. But Novalis continues in a vein that sounds like a combination of Hazlitt's definition of gusto and Keats's speculation that the poet identifies completely with his subject and has no character of his own. Of the ability to imitate the essence of an object or another person, Novalis says: "This power of truly awaking in one's self a foreign individuality—and not to be deceived by an imitation of superficialities—is still wholly unfamiliar and rests on the most extremely wonderful *penetration* [of the object], on a spiritual mimesis. The artist conforms himself to all he sees and wishes to be."[42]

Novalis has a keen sense of an imaginative imitation based on sympathetic identification, of the poet altering himself into what he sees. The poet thrives in a protean fashion. Novalis thus enters the considerable line of eighteenth-century thought on the power of sympathy. Schlegel used the image of Shakespeare as a protean deity, common in English criticism by the end of the century. In the twenty-third of his *Lectures on Dramatic Art and Literature,* he remarks that by the diversity of tone and color which Shakespeare employs in imitating the "quality of the subjects he assumes, he is a very Proteus."

Exactly at the point where Novalis states that the poet conforms himself to what he sees and wishes to be, he continues, "Poetry is the great art of construction of transcendental health. The poet is thus the transcendental physician." In other words, Novalis is indicating that the act of sympathetic identification, of the going out of one's own nature to penetrate and to imitate other natures and natural objects, is actually the transcendental act by which the poet ministers to the health of mankind. The "inmost sympathy" that Novalis mentions in the poetic Preface to the second part of *Heinrich von Ofterdingen*, which elsewhere he calls the "greatest sympathy and interactivity" of poetry, becomes the goal of transcendentalism.[43] To pierce through the phenomenal world by a sympathy that permits knowledge of the thing-in-itself, bringing the senses and the intellectual intuition into unity (*"innigste Vereinigung der Einbildungskraft und des Verstandes"*), uniting phenomenon and noumenon, subject and object, and breaking the bounds of time and space by identification with other individuals, leads to the conclusion that sympathetic imagination is the greatest transcendental act of both art and knowledge.

Perhaps Novalis gleaned the idea of sympathy from the Schlegels or from any number of translations and discussions of English critics who stressed the concept. Although this young transcendental poet was reaching some of the same conclusions as British writers were, he expressed them in a slightly different vocabulary. Hazlitt said that imagination is another name for getting out of ourselves, the supreme moral good, and Novalis states at the close of his fragment on the poet as transcendental physician that, "Poetry mixes all to its great goal of goals: *the elevation of man above himself*," the reaching out of the psyche in sympathy. This is the greatest good, and "the greatest good rests in the imagination."[44]

# 17

# THE PROPHETIC AND VISIONARY:
# BLAKE AND SHELLEY

*P*ossessing an almost dogmatic faith in the imagination, Blake believed in its promise of liberty and salvation with greater militancy than any other British Romantic. For him imagination is the sole way to create art and to reveal religion, two acts existing in and through each other. He builds his own mythology on imaginative vision, and obscure though his prophetic books may seem, he is the only English Romantic to realize the critical hope of the later eighteenth century, that the new idea of the imagination would produce an original series of myths rather than reinterpret classical ones. He practiced and lived out the message of Schelling's theoretical statement that "Mythology is the necessary condition and the first material of all art." Compared with Keats or Schiller, Blake approached a kind of fanaticism; but as Keats, Coleridge, and Meister themselves recognized, a thin line, if any, divides the "poet's" vision from the "fanatic's."

Blake champions the freedom of the creative mind and has no doubts what purpose that freedom should serve. The imaginative life is the only real life, for man's imagination fully creates reality through an interpretative perception of it. "All things Exist in the Human Imagination," states Blake, and "Mental Things are alone Real . . . Where is the Existence Out of Mind or Thought?"[1] The universe is a construct of the imaginative power that is in both God and man, and when man realizes this, he has taken the first step to truth and salvation. Similar ideas appear in Akenside, Tucker, Thomas Brown, and Coleridge, but Blake is categorical: "Imagination is My World; this world of Dross is beneath my Notice." His religious vision is attained and reaffirmed—as in the Bible—through symbols and mythopoesis. Christ becomes God's attempt to be man and attain man's vision, and it is in Christ that the imaginations of God and man become one. Taken by itself, imagination is "the Divine-Humanity," and as "Man is All Imagination," so also "God is Man & exists in us & we in him." Not only is "The Eternal Body of Man . . . The Imagination, that is, God himself," but more symbolically, the body of man is "the Divine Body of the Lord Jesus" and "we are his Members."[2]

Blake is separated from his contemporaries by, among other things, the thoroughness and individuality with which he completes his vision of creation, life in a fallen world, salvation, and the apocalypse. He turns the imagination to a frankly Christian view, but one that also embraces psychology, history, and cosmology, seeing each of these as an image or matrix reflecting the others on a different scale of magnitude or order. Blake's symbols, language, and idiom set him apart from many other poets, but the staunch single-mindedness of his poetic practice should not cloud the fact that he shares basic premises about the imagination with other Romantics. Because of Blake's extremity and fervor, the outlines of the idea of the imagination and the uses to which it can be put are often more clear-cut and definite in him than in poets who write a more open idiom. In some respects, Blake is an easier poet to understand than Byron or Keats.

Blake's idea of the imagination has roots in philosophical and religious traditions that include both esoteric and popular elements and which extend back through the eighteenth century, the hermeticists of the sixteenth and seventeenth centuries, the Renaissance, medieval and ancient philosophy, and sacred Hebrew poetry. Blake is the English vice-regent of one of the long-established provinces within the larger idea of the imagination, the province of the religious visionary or prophet whose divinely inspired, and hence imaginative, utterances become the *ne plus ultra* of symbolism in poetry. In Blake's concept of the imagination we recognize similarities with and at times direct influences of Boehme, Paracelsus, Meister, Pico della Mirandola, Swedenborg, Agrippa von Nettesheim, Kant, and Schelling. English poets and thinkers who in one or more of their views prefigure Blake include Milton, Bunyan, Shaftesbury, Akenside, Joseph Warton, Collins, and Christopher Smart. The eighteenth-century traditions of dissenting preachers, millenarianism, and commentaries on the books of the prophets and Revelation are firmly in Blake's background. Blake took elements of the idea of the imagination that were readily available to him and which had become or were becoming major forces in religion, philosophy, and poetry. He rejuvenated and fused these elements into the theoretical basis of his own idea, and from this he elaborated his myths and prophetic voice.

Under the aspect of eternity to which Blake constantly felt himself subject, his idea of the imagination is not really original. It is, by his own credo, an effort to restore and revive the older imaginative examples of the biblical prophets and of the great symbolic poets Homer, Pythagoras, Socrates, Euripides, Virgil, Dante, and Milton.[3] Blake is trying to recapture a mythopoeic and symbolic approach to the imagination and to the arts in general, an approach he believes now moribund. "The Nature of Visionary Fancy, or Imagination, is very little known," but by a conscious effort we can retrain ourselves in its practice. Just as the oak dies but returns by its seed,

> so the Imaginative Image returns by the seed of Contemplative Thought; the Writings of the Prophets illustrate these conceptions of the Visionary Fancy by their various sublime & Divine Images as seen in the Worlds of Vision . . . The Nature of my Work is Visionary or Imaginative; it is an Endeavour to Restore what the Ancients call'd the Golden Age.[4]

The notion of a "revivalist," one engaged in an endeavor to restore true meaning or faith, conjures up a picture of a naive preacher warning against sin and drink and extolling Christian virtue in general terms. But true revivalists, like Jonathan Edwards, George Whitefield, and Blake, want to restore the living spirit, language, and way of thinking represented by Noah, Daniel, Ezekiel, and John. For Blake this spirit and language, and the poetry it produced, could best be summed up by the word "imagination." Blake is a Protestant revivalist in the radical sense of the word.

To summarize the leading features of Blake's symbolic system, already the subject of brilliant, full-scale interpretations, could usurp a third of this book. Besides, Blake regarded his own mythology as only his individual stamp or tool, which is different for each person. All such mythologies work from a more fundamental and generic structure of the imagination, one that is straightforward and common to all men, if only they would seize and put it to use.

### THE IMAGINATION AS REALITY

With numerous Enlightenment and Romantic thinkers Blake shares the sense that imagination is an energy or force that creates and transforms as it perceives. His concept recalls Leibniz's *vis activa* and stresses the active side of the imaginative power, while nevertheless recognizing its passive or resting contemplation. Unlike many others Blake does not distinguish between levels of the imaginative power. For him, there is only one operation and essentially only one degree of it. It blends together the various levels discussed by other thinkers. This is one of the reasons that the word becomes so big for Blake and implies so much. In addition, he puts his notion into rather cryptic or terse statements.

Berkeley's belief that the mind alone creates reality appealed to Blake, and although opposed to Blake and Berkeley in other respects, Hume had said essentially the same thing: the imagination alone creates our picture of reality. Blake argues that it conditions our experience of space and time rather than submitting to their abstract domination and "immutable" rules. We are "Creating Space, Creating Time according to the wonders Divine of Human Imagination."[5] Kant seriously considers this idea, too, in some of his later writings.

From another angle, the sense of a shaping activity in Blake's view of the imagination closely approximates what Coleridge and Schelling, reviving a term employed by Spinoza and common among the Schoolmen, particularly John Scotus Eriugena, refer to as *natura naturans*, the forming or plastic spirit that works in God and in the human mind. Blake, in conscious contrast to Wordsworth, emphasized both that the mind alone is formative—which unconsciously echoed Kant and Hazlitt—and that nature by itself is not, as Wordsworth implies, "fitted" to the mind, but is "fallen" and dead. But seeing nature with imaginative vision, we enliven and rescue it, and also save our own souls. Shaftesbury and Leibniz emphasized this point, which Leibniz reiterates by quoting Ovid and Seneca, *"Est Deus in nobis."* For Blake, imagination is this very God in us: "God is Man & exists in us & we in him."

When Blake says that the imagination creates reality, he is voicing the same kind of attitude found in Keats as well, who remarks that certain ethereal things gain their worth by the "ardour of mental pursuit" we invest in them. For Keats, "mental" here means "imaginative," as it does everywhere for Blake, who believes that imaginative pursuit redeems the fallen world and elevates what Keats calls "nothings," like poetry, to shape, to meaning, and to supreme worth.[6] Art is the idea of mental pursuit, the "mental fight" of the prefatory lyric to *Milton*, and taken in its broad concept, as it is in that lyric, it leads to salvation.

Imaginative art also guarantees individual freedom and liberates the mind, preventing enslavement to static systems of government and the fashionable, shallow *dicta* of "art" that simply decorate or rearrange earlier productions. Gray, Herder, Coleridge, Shelley, Wordsworth, and Keats likewise perceived that the ideal of freedom must constantly feed on a creative vision of things as they should be. Blake's plea for art as the guarantor of free expression, besides echoing Milton, anticipates the philosophical argument in Schelling's *Über das Wesen der menschlichen Freiheit* (1809). It is a direct result of the view that imagination and freedom are bound together that Blake, Shelley, Coleridge, and Wordsworth were definite and heated in their political actions and opinions, especially during the early phase of the French Revolution. And Blake, like Hazlitt, retained a fiery and vocal liberalism throughout

life, despite the irony that in France its radical exercise resulted in Napoleon, who said himself, "The world is ruled by imagination."

Along with Hazlitt, Wordsworth, and Coleridge, Blake climaxes a
line of thinkers from Hume to the 1820s. And there are earlier connections, too. For instance, Blake read Paracelsus and Boehme. "The whole
heaven, indeed, is nothing but an imagination," and "Even as [man]
imagines himself to be, such he is, and he is also that which he imagines." These sentences sound like Blake, but they are in *Paracelsus his
Archidoxies* (1661), a book Blake read. Blake aims a heavy verbal artil-
lery on the earlier eighteenth century, on Locke and Newton, but he
finds few major enemies in English thought after the 1740s and 1750s
when it comes to the idea of imagination. His intellectual quarrel with
Reynolds is based on a partial reading of Reynolds, a quarrel further
complicated by questions of artistic technique and audience. Blake is not
a stray outsider on the idea of the imagination. He is, in some respects,
very much the insider, attempting to restore what he considers to be an
age-old conception of prophecy and imaginative art.

## SUBJECTIVE AND OBJECTIVE

Since the meaning of the world is predicated on our individual imaginations, any border between the object and the subjective self dissolves,
and the self—creating the world by its own vision—assimilates the
world into itself as a part of itself, and consequently becomes its own
object. This process is what Coleridge and Schelling, who culminate a
philosophical movement of at least two generations, were also fervently
preaching as a corollary to the imaginative power. The idea is neo-Platonic and appears in Thomas Taylor's *Restoration of Platonic Theology*
(1788–1789), with which both Blake and Coleridge were familiar. Taylor elucidates the commentaries of Proclus on Euclid's *Elements*. In the
case of perceiving beauty, for instance,

> the spectator is no longer external to the spectacle; but he who acutely
> perceives, contains the object of his perception in the depths of his own
> essence . . . It is requisite we should transfer the divine spectacle into our-
> selves, and behold it as one, and as the same with our essence . . . But it is
> requisite that the soul . . . should profoundly merge itself in contempla-
> tion, till instead of spectator, it may become another specimen of the ob-
> ject of its intuition; such as it came from thence, abundantly shining with
> intellectual conceptions.[7]

In Blake, the object becomes part of the subjective self because the
imagination makes the object into what it is in the process of perceiving
it. Although this merging or identification of the subjective and objec-

tive in Blake is not the same thing as the concept of empathy or sympathetic identification developed in the later eighteenth century and perfected by Hazlitt, the imaginative eye is for Blake always turned outward, away from the selfish. Blake conceives of an "antithesis of imagination and Selfhood."[8] The freedom of the self to create something eternal means the opposite of self-involvement and self-concentration, the lowest and worst form of living hell (Ulro), where the individual psyche splits into specters and devours itself in self-cannibalizing solipsism. The unity of subjective and objective carries with it, for Blake as for many others from Arbuckle and Smith through Shelley and Coleridge, a moral dimension. The imagination becomes in effect the "moral sense."

Blake's view about the union of the subjective and objective differs in at least one important way from most other critics and poets concerned with the subject. Identification and empathy with objects or people had, in other writers, resulted in a stress on the power of "suggestiveness" to capture the essence or implications of a character or situation. But Blake emphasizes the clearly defined and sharply outlined particular. Art is meant not to suggest a particular personal trait or object, as these should be made specific, but rather to suggest a larger vision and order of reality as a whole. In one respect, Blake feels that the kind of suggestiveness that plays on our senses is not worth pursuing. What is wanted is the kind of suggestiveness found in a long poem—a total view of the world, of a whole society, of a religious myth, or of all these interwoven. Thus, in Blake's shorter lyrics the suggestiveness is never primarily of a sensuous nature. The intention and result are more intellectual, and many of his lyrics have to be read together to get an overall picture of what he is saying. The same is true of his proverbs and aphorisms. Each one is concrete and well-defined. But when they are taken as a whole or in a group, they become intellectually suggestive.

### THE MEANING OF NATURE

Blake accepts innate ideas, or innate capacities to create certain perceptions, as part of a large connection between the material form of nature and the ideas or activity of the divine-human imagination. In nature, man's creativity meets with God's. Nature is "fallen"; that is, it remains imperfect and beneath paradise, cut off from a direct communion with God where eternity and permanence reign. But man's imagination can regenerate nature and raise transitory forms to the symbolic level of "ever Existent Images" and ideas. There is, in Blake, a kind of pre-established harmony between the psyche and nature. This is not to say that Blake believes in what he called the "fitted and fitting" of Wordsworth, the equivalency of nature and the mind. Rather, the mind has the creative potential to mold nature to something amenable and meaningful. Man's imaginative vision—by referring to a higher spiritual and divine truth—works to create this harmony; it is not an automatic reflex. Yet angered by the "pure" empiricists who trivialized Locke, and angered somewhat unjustly by Locke's own position, Blake puts it more extremely: "Innate Ideas are in Every Man Born with him. They are truly himself. The Man who says that we have No Innate Ideas must be a Fool & Knave."[9]

God has placed in man at least the potential to create a harmony of mind and nature, and in that sense the harmony is pre-established. It is destroyed if we fail to engage our imaginations. The forms in nature can thus become symbolic, in the sense implied by Goethe's remark that nature is God's poem, characters written in a huge size, secret hiero- glyphs to be deciphered by the poet. Of all the passages in Wordsworth, Blake most admired the one in *The Prelude* where Wordsworth's imagi- nation, in a flash of perception, sees the woods and waters of Simplon pass in the Alps as the types and symbols of eternity and the apocalypse. Nature is one step in bringing man closer to God and to the apocalypse; Christ—who is man, nature, spirit, and God as one—is the highest step.

Blake's sense of nature imaginatively perceived, a nexus for the imagi- native power in God and man, is actually a *Naturphilosophie*, and like Schelling's, it fits into a larger scheme, existing side by side with a phi- losophy of ideas and subsumed by a religious or mythological view. Four stages are involved, Blake's "four-fold vision," which can be com- pared with the four recognized, chronological stages of Schelling's phi- losophy:

| *Blake* | *Schelling* | *Shared Vision* |
|---|---|---|
| Ulro, the self and its specters | Influenced by Fichte, the "*Ich bin*" stage | The self divided from the world, the subjec- tive |
| Generation, the "fallen world," nature | *Naturphilosophie;* the "*Es gibt*" stage, the ma- terial world | The self perceives na- ture, the subjective meets the objective |
| Beulah, love and recon- ciliation of the self and nature, of male and fe- male | *Identitätsphilosophie,* "*Ich bin*" resolved with "*Es gibt*," both part of a larger whole | Unity of self (ideal or intellectual world) and material world, of sub- jective and objective |
| Eden, eternity and di- vine truth, vision and myths free man | Mythological and theo- logical interests, *Über ... menschlichen Frei- heit* | Unity of self, nature, and the divine, the mythopoetic, panen- theism |

There is no question of influences, but the parallels are striking. They again illustrate that Blake, in his own way, is in the vanguard of contemporary philosophy. For man's creative energy or imagination to merge with God's through the medium of nature is to see, according to Blake, that "Nature is a Vision of the Science of the Elohim."[10] This, as Schelling tried to show, is the kind of credo that belongs to the highest *Naturphilosophie*. For Blake, nature becomes subservient to a revealed faith. At the apocalypse we realize that nature is a necessary but interim stage to a higher reality. Blake's "four-fold vision" could also be compared with the four stages of poetry that Keats describes in "Sleep and Poetry." Although the one-to-one correspondence is not exact, the direction of the stages is again remarkably similar.

When Blake says that "to the Eyes of the Man of Imagination, Nature is Imagination itself," he is again speaking of what Coleridge and Schelling mean by *natura naturans*, the forming power or "connatural" energy working in the mind and in nature alike, an energy available for man's enlightenment if only his imagination has the courage to use it properly. An earlier example of this view of nature is found in Thomas Burnet's *Telluris Theoria Sacra* (1681), translated as the *Sacred Theory of the Earth* (1684–1689), which Coleridge considered translating into blank verse. Blake contrasts this idea with the dead forms of nature—Coleridge and Schelling's *natura naturata*—which in Blake are often represented by mechanical or mineral images.

Finally, Blake envisions God's archetypal act of creation as welling up from a deep abyss, which may be associated with an ocean or sea. This image also occurs in Wordsworth, Coleridge, Shelley, Schelling, Tucker, Akenside, and Milton. It can be traced back through Boehme and Paracelsus to Plotinus, the Bible, and Thales. The divine-human imagination, as Blake calls it, is working with the deepest universal secret (Paracelsus' *"Mysterium Magnum"*) and with an original unity, a region of depth and awful force where spirit and idea are directly converted into matter and matter "decays" or is reborn into energy.

### A VISION OF UNITY: LOVE AND CHRIST

What God creates through the imagination remains part of an overall unity, and the diversity of matter and spirit points back to one source. Blake's religious view may seem pantheistic, but in fact Blake is more of a "panentheist," as are the younger Wordsworth, Coleridge, and Schelling. They all believed during at least one important stage in their lives in the *en kai pan*, the "one and the all," whose two elements form the word panentheism. This view recognizes the inviolable unity of God as one separate being yet sees him simultaneously as a presence dwelling in each part of his creation. The idea of the creative imagination rekindled a full-blown panentheistic religion and cosmology in many Romantics. To the extent that they departed from orthodox Christianity it was because they thought it could not express the active force, the art, and the organic flux within a large cosmological unity. Yet for Blake, as for Herder, Coleridge, and Schelling, Jesus remains the central focus. Put one way, he is the imaginative conjunction of the "One and the all."

If the universe were "split" between the creator (the One) and the creation (the all), then what would hold the two together? God and the "fallen world" are the original and archetypal "subject" and "object." Yet what is the ground of their unity? If nothing, then what is created or "fallen" from God must remain eternally separated from Him. This, and not "sinful" in the usual personal and guilt-ridden sense, is what "fallen" means in Blake. Poetry, man's own imaginative creation, is one attempt to regain the unity of subject and object, the oneness with God; it is an attempt to restore the Golden Age before the fall. But poetry is not really enough. There is a greater tendency toward union in nature, God, and man. The answer for Blake—as for Shelley, Coleridge, Wordsworth, Baader, Schelling, and perhaps even Keats—is love, the kind of love, as Dante says, that moves the sun and stars. Love and desire become the hope to regain an original union in God. Art and poetry are merely a step to the block, as Eliot says, a step toward that timeless moment when the rose and the fire are one. Imagination and love, as Blake argues and Wordsworth affirms, cannot exist without each other. For as imagination is the power that creates something new, so love binds the creator to his work and brings the universe in sympathetic harmony. This Shaftesburian idea becomes one of the mainstays of Shelley's *Defence*.

In Blake there is, as Northrop Frye states, "the struggle to create, and the loving contemplation of what has been created." The idea was not new. A basic Judeo-Christian belief, it is mirrored in the first chapter of Genesis, where God not only creates but after each creation sees or perceives that the creation is good and that it is worthy of love. In the Koran, we find God becomes known as *ar-Rahman*, "the Compassionate," because every act of creation proves not only his power but his beneficence. The creative art and love of the human imagination participate in God's creation and love.[11] Blake's belief in periods of creative expansion followed rhythmically by contemplation or rest is another way of representing the active and the loving, or the active and the passive, sides of the imagination. It prefigures Matthew Arnold's belief that a period of true criticism, or of the loving contemplation of art, can be followed by a time of great creations themselves.

If we look at fallen man and fallen nature as God's creation, then by what specific act of love—by what specific act of the imagination—does God bind Himself to his own creation? In St. John, the gospel that Coleridge intended to use in his *Logosophia* as part of a commentary on the imagination and communicative intellect in God and man, the answer is simply, "For God so loved the world, that he gave his only begotten Son, that whosoever believeth in him should not perish, but have everlasting life" (3:16). Jesus becomes the Logos, the act of love incarnate, and for Blake, as for Coleridge and Schelling, Jesus is the imagination in divine-human form. In the Preface to *The Cenci*, Shelley also says that imagery and passion "should interpenetrate one another, the former being reserved . . . for the full development and illustration of the latter. Imagination is as the immortal God which should assume flesh for the redemption of mortal passion." Jesus and the love that is Jesus become, for Blake, the imaginative connection of the "One and the all." Jesus' love, man's love, is more important even than the gift of prophecy: "And though I have the gift of prophecy, and understand all mysteries . . . and have not charity, I am nothing" (1 Corinthians 13:2).

Jesus, understood as the completing and all-penetrating bond of love and imagination, changes the character of the Trinity for Blake, as Christ does in a similar way for Coleridge and Schelling. The idea of a holy number or figure of four appears in Blake's four-fold vision as well as in the Pythagorean Tetractys, the Hebrew Tetragrammaton (the four consonants representing the "incommunicable name" of the Supreme Being), Masonic symbolism, and the works of Paracelsus, Boehme, and Tucker. Blake, Coleridge, and Schelling connect a four-fold figure with both Christ and the idea of the imagination. Earlier thinkers, especially Tucker and Boehme, associated the holy Quaternary with God's creative and imaginative force. Schelling and Coleridge both seem to discern a fundamental and meaningful similarity in all interpretations of the holy Quarternary, the Tetractys, and the Tetragrammaton taken together. To these they add the Trinity, giving it, as it were, a fourth dimension. So does Blake.

At bottom, these holy "fours" represent the same thing—the unity and connection of God the creator, the world of flesh and matter, and the world of spirit and ideas, all joined through a fourth element, the transmuting and loving power of the imagination, which to Christian and Jew comes in the person of the Messiah. Blake recognizes this loving power as the highest reach of the imagination, and Jesus is for him the symbol of symbols, where love and imagination are drawn into unity. Frye puts Blake's view succinctly:

The three persons of the Trinity are to be connected by ors rather than ands, and the real God is fourfold, power, love and wisdom contained within the unity of civilized human imagination.

God is Father, Son, and Spirit: the imagination tries to see this Trinity in the fourfold unity of Jesus.[12]

## "AN ENDEAVOUR TO RESTORE"

These religious and philosophical issues explain why Blake's idea of the imagination insists on prophetic vision. He wants to revive the work of the Hebrew prophets and of St. John. The kind of imagination that produced the book of Ezekiel or Revelation is the imagination Blake wants to re-establish. He felt that inspired poetry such as we find in the Bible should not be looked upon as an historical event centuries old. If God lives in human hearts and minds, and if his truths are eternal, then faith and truth should continue to express themselves in symbolic art. Without a living voice to transform the particulars at hand, faith will petrify. For Blake, each truth or holy image is a type of other truths; the eternal and godly live in the moment and must not hesitate to proclaim its truth. And so Israel becomes England. Israel *is* Albion. The poet's power of metaphor will devise archetypes like these into larger visions and myths, and those into scriptures or a holy book. "The Hebrew Bible & the Gospel of Jesus," notes Blake, are "Eternal Vision or Imagination of All that Exists."[13]

A long tradition unites prophecy with the concept of the imagination. It includes Plato's *Timaeus* and the works of Maimonides, Pico della Mirandola, Francis Bacon, Spinoza, and at least one of the Cambridge Platonists, John Smith.[14] The tradition was perhaps strongest during the medieval period. From the time of Aquinas and William of St. Thierry to the Renaissance, the imagination had two roles, a conventional one as mediator between the senses and the higher power of reason, but also a prophetic one linked directly to God. Occult or magus-like overtones sometimes colored this prophetic power, but the Bible remained as its essential basis.

Blake believed that poems such as *Paradise Lost* continued the prophetic strain. The great sway of Milton had, throughout the eighteenth century, kept the prophetic mode alive. Gray, the Wartons, and Collins saw in Milton a heaven-descended power of imagination differing in kind from Shakespeare's. Blake was ready to snatch up and champion this tradition.

Smart, Gray, and Cowper had ventured on this same path. And although Tucker claims to be a follower of Locke, his chapter titled "The Vision," which concludes *The Light of Nature Pursued*, is in some respects the eighteenth-century work most similar to Blake's prophetic books. Tucker speaks of emanations; he tracks his own path through space; and much of the imagery anticipates the cosmic and religious considerations in Blake's *Milton*. In "The Vision" Tucker also remarks on the "Holy Quaternion" and on the character of "Psyche," which he uses in somewhat the same way Keats was to do more than forty years later.

Blake himself was trying nothing less than to revive symbolic poetry in the manner of the Hebrew prophecies and St. John. His attitude is anticipated in Hosea 12:10, which Bunyan places at the beginning of *Pilgrim's Progress*: "I have used similitudes." Bunyan's poetic "Apology" to the book makes a case for the kind of imagination Blake was trying to rescue. To Blake's way of thinking, the imagination had suffered a general fatigue, especially since the Renaissance and during the eighteenth century. The imagination could never be restored to its full power except by the frank use of myth and symbols to represent the interworkings of religious faith, psychic states of the individual, cosmological mysteries, and current events, all transposed into metaphors and symbols as they are in the Bible. Blake hoped that the imagination could again directly elevate the five senses and the human need for storytelling into the service of spiritual faith.

### AN "ANACALYPTIC POET"

An apocalyptic poet literally uncovers the truth and prophesies the future. He is the poet who reveals. But the imagination, as the instrument of all prophetic writers, is paradoxically not a literal power at all. In fact, the apocalyptic poet employs numerous symbols and metaphors and, like Blake, his own complex and even obscure system of myth. He expresses his vision symbolically; after "seeing" or experiencing it directly himself, he covers it in a language that must be deciphered. But this recovering of his vision he hopes will be a true recovery, a regaining of the original truth ("an endeavour to Restore . . . the Golden Age"), which is the only way that truth can be revived and communicated.

The paradox that the imaginative poet, to reveal or to uncover his vision, must encode his message in an original or even personal idiom, led Coleridge to describe Blake as an "apo- or rather anacalyptic Poet, & Painter."[15] The anacalyptic poet (from Greek *ana-* up, back, again, excessively + *calyptein*, to cover, conceal) literally re-covers in order to recover and restore; only when we become initiated to his symbols can he be called "apocalyptic."

Blake uses an image that itself represents the kind of imagination and poetry he champions. Several times he suggests the vision of a chariot with four wheels that turns into a throne, just as the chariot in Ezekiel becomes the throne of God later appearing in Revelation. Blake calls on this chariot in the lyric preface to *Milton:* "Bring me my chariot of fire," suggesting too the fiery wheels of Ezekiel's chariot. The image becomes associated with the four-fold, highest imaginative life.[16] It is the moving mediator between heaven and earth. In a parallel passage Coleridge in his *Statesman's Manual* describes the imagination as:

> that reconciling and mediatory power, which incorporating the Reason in images of the Sense, and organizing . . . the flux of the Senses by the permanence and self-circling energies of the Reason, gives birth to a system of symbols, harmonious in themselves, and consubstantial with the truths of which they are the conductors. These are the *wheels* which Ezekiel beheld, when the hand of the Lord was upon him, and he saw visions of God . . . *Withersoever the Spirit was to go, the* wheels *went, and thither was their spirit to go:—for the spirit of the living creature was in the* wheels *also.*

This kind of symbol appears in Keats's "Sleep and Poetry" (ll.122–80) and in Shelley's *Prometheus Unbound* (II.iv. 110ff.), where the chariots are connected with love, the psyche, and "deep truth." The chariot of Ezekiel also appears earlier in Gray's "Progress of Poesy" (ll.95–101), where it is associated with divine poetry and Milton, with the "secrets of th'Abyss" (as are the chariots in *Prometheus Unbound*), and with the "flaming bounds of Place and Time," suggesting Blake's Sea of Time and Space and what lies beyond it. Blake is always—as these other poets are sometimes—trying to reintroduce the oldest and most mysteriously resonant idea of a divine-human imagination.

### SHELLEY

Much of what Shelley says explicitly about the imagination is a ringing of the changes, in a high and impelling rhetorical mode, on ideas evolving and intertwining since Adam Smith and Alexander Gerard began to explore the concepts of sympathy and genius in the 1750s and 1760s. The *Defence of Poetry* (1821) can be seen as a great aesthetic peroration on many themes concerning the imagination developed in the two generations preceding Shelley. Nothing quite so sweeping about poetry and society had been written in England since Sidney's *Apology.* The work arrives—as Shelley said of the "intellectual philosophy" and the revolution it was accomplishing—"on that verge where words abandon us."[17]

In one of the most famous passages in the *Defence*, Shelley says: "The great secret of morals is love; or a going out of our own nature, and an identification with the beautiful . . . not our own. A man . . . must imagine intensely and comprehensively; he must put himself in the place of another and of many others . . . The great instrument of moral good is the imagination; and poetry administers to the effect by acting upon the cause. Poetry enlarges the circumference of the imagination."

We can now see this in perspective as an epitome of the whole idea of sympathy and sympathetic imagination and their expression through poetry—an idea that began with Shaftesbury then moved with Arbuckle and others in the 1730s and passed through Adam Smith to the associationists and Hazlitt. Shelley states the concept of sympathy in its bare essentials, coming close to a terse abstraction. He comments on Wordsworth in *Peter Bell the Third* (IV.36–40):

> He has as much imagination
>    As a pint-pot;—he never could
> Fancy another situation
> From which to dart his contemplation
>    Than that wherein he stood.

Shelley makes explicit what had shimmered beneath the surface in the criticism of the associationists: poetry is the best teacher of morals because it is the greatest sympathetic exercise of imagination. Like Hazlitt, Shelley points to the engagement of moral imagination in drama, a major reason for the Romantic popularity of Shakespeare. In drama, says Shelley, "The imagination is enlarged by a sympathy with pains and passions so mightily, that they distend in their conception the capacity of that by which they are conceived." Our essential humanity is enlarged.

Sympathy engages us too in a larger, harmonious universe of interrelated beings and events. The tone of Shaftesbury and of the neo-Platonists in this respect is here vibrant. Shelley's use of "love" as a synonym for the sympathetic imagination is paralleled by Keats, Blake, Schelling, Wordsworth, and Coleridge. Love becomes another name for the individual imagination as it turns outward and sympathizes with the world and with other human beings: "*Thou* demandest what is love? It is that powerful attraction towards all that we conceive, or fear, or hope beyond ourselves . . . and seek to awaken in all things . . . a community with what we experience within ourselves."[18]

Beyond ourselves there is a larger "Power," as Shelley expressed it in *Adonais*, "Which wields the world with never-wearied love."[19] As Keats's "Ode to Psyche" ends by invoking the power of love, so does

Shelley's "Epipsychidion" (162–168), in which, once again, love and imagination are closely identified:

> Love is like understanding, that grows bright,
> Gazing on many truths; 'tis like thy light,
> Imagination! which from earth and sky,
> And from the depths of human fantasy,
> As from a thousand prisms and mirrors fills
> The Universe with glorious beams and kills
> Error.

We have seen how the perceptive and ordering power of imagination had, by the latter half of the eighteenth century, come to mean the ability to shape reality in full. Berkeley, Blake, and Fichte are extreme proponents of this notion. Shelley repeats it, along with the idea of merging the internal with the external, of the subjective with the objective. "I confess," he says, "that I am one of those who am unable to refuse my assent to those philosophers who assert that nothing exists but as it is perceived." In the *Defence* he simply states that "All things exist as they are perceived; at least in relation to the perceiver." And in his *Speculations on Metaphysics* Shelley puts the crux of his "intellectual philosophy," of his subjective transcendentalism struggling to join the outer world through the power of love, by saying that man is "*pre-eminently an imaginative being.* His own mind is his law; his own mind is all things to him." Shelley is expressing what he conceives as the major development in philosophy from Berkeley to his own day: "The view of life presented by the most refined deductions of the intellectual philosophy is that of unity. Nothing exists but as it is perceived."[20] As in Blake, Kant, Fichte, and Schelling, time and space become constructs of the imagination.

Yet Shelley turns to the "intellectual philosophy" without discarding the empirical power of association. As Earl Wasserman points out, the poetic imagination for Shelley works by "unifying associative laws." Shelley notes in *Speculations on Metaphysics* that "the most astonishing combinations of poetry . . . are no other than combinations which the intellect makes of sensations according to its own laws."[21] The duty of each generation of poets, he goes on in the *Defence*, is to offer metaphors and symbols that will "create afresh the *associations*" of integral, concrete thoughts and preserve them from abstraction. Shelley here appropriates into a larger schema one of the associationists' essential points about the imagination. He recognizes that associations are often most natural and lively "in the infancy of society," as William Duff had maintained in the last part of his *Essay on Original Genius* (1767), a theme that would continue to haunt the rest of the eighteenth and early nineteenth centuries.

Shelley's concept of a universal "Power" working through the individual imagination goes even farther back—to Leibniz and Shaftesbury with their stress on power or *Kraft* in the act of creation. "Power," remarks Shelley, is one of the "modes in which thoughts are combined" by the imagination.[22] This power is not a strictly personal attribute. It has pantheistic implications. It is the wind that fans the fading coal of the creative mind. It can be interpreted in part as what Shelley in *Queen Mab* calls the "universal mind." In his essay "On Life," he states that once we accept the mind or intelligence as formative of all that exists, then "Pursuing the same thread of reasoning, the existence of distinct individual minds, similar to that which is employed in now questioning its own nature, is likewise found to be a delusion." The phrase "which . . . nature" implies that the individual self needs to establish an identity and to affirm its own nature. But if the self is indeed part of a larger mind, as Shelley conceives it, then the same thing must be true of this larger, supra-personal being or intelligence. It, too, must need to establish its own identity and to affirm itself. This concept becomes vital to Coleridge ("self-affirmation") and to Schelling ("*Selbstaffirmation*"). There is a parallel between Shelley's "individual" and "universal mind" and Fichte's "empirical" and "absolute *Ich*."

In short, if there was, and remains, one original Being and creative imagination, then we are still part of It and must recognize our essential unity with It—and hence with each other. This is one of the great themes of "Ode to the West Wind," especially at its climax. The program for realizing this unity, for feeling it "on our pulse," as Keats says, is rigorous, but the reward is great. In the "Essay on Christianity," Shelley observes simply that "Whoever has maintained with his own heart the strictest correspondence of confidence, who dares to examine and to estimate every imagination which suggests itself to his mind, who is that which he designs to become, and only aspires to . . . the divinity of his own nature . . . has already seen God."

Here again is the theme that the imagination discovers "the divinity in man," Shelley's phrase in the *Defence* for the idea of *Deus in nobis*. The power that moves the aeolian lyre of our imaginations is a larger "all-penetrating spirit" by which we attain a "consentaneity of powers" that, however briefly, illuminates the abode of the eternal.* In *Adonais* (XLIII), Shelley describes Keats's dying into life:

> he doth bear
> His part, while the one Spirit's plastic stress
> Sweeps through the dull dense world, compelling there,
> All new successions to the forms they wear.

* For the phrase "all-penetrating spirit" in Coleridge, see below, p. 365.

The poet becomes a genius when he "dares to examine and to estimate every imagination which suggests itself to his mind," for then he attains, as Blake says, the "divine-humanity."

Gerard, Akenside, and Fichte used the image of a magnet for the power of the individual imagination, a force above the level of the senses yet with strong, concrete results. According to Fichte, for instance, both magnet and iron must contain "something" that causes them to act on each other. In his *Grundlage der gesammten Wissenschaftslehre*, he concludes that if the magnet represents the self or the ego and the iron stands for the external world or the non-ego, then the mutually attracting force between them is *"ein Schweben der Einbildungskraft,"* an unseen force that hovers above, oscillates between, and unites the self and nature. The force is selective, ordering—creative at its highest level—and mysterious.[23] Shelley expands the image of the magnet as imagination, perhaps using as a source Plato's *Ion* (533–536), which would also have been familiar to Gerard, Akenside, and Fichte. "Descending through the minds of many men," Shelley explains, the force of poetry and imagination "is attached to those great minds, whence as from a magnet the invisible effluence is sent forth, which at once connects, animates, and sustains the life of all."

Besides making the well-known argument in the *Defence* concerning the poetic imagination and the striving for a higher and more civilized life, Shelley puts his point in *A Treatise on Morals:* "Imagination or mind employed in prophetically bringing forth its objects is that faculty of human nature on which every gradation of its progress, nay, every, the minutest, change depends."[24]

When Shelley insists on this prophetic nature of the imagination, he, like Blake, does not mean "fortune-telling," as he carefully points out, but an apprehension of truths and ideas, or of ways to attain them, a vision of how they will or can act in the future.

If—aside from Blake—we ask who shares with Shelley his premise that imagination and poetry are creators and shapers of society, the answer is Hobbes. For Hobbes maintained that "Fancy" gives birth to all the arts, decoration, and culture, which together make up what is meant by civilization.* The *Defence* is saturated with this message. Poets are "the institutors of laws, and the founders of civil society," or civilization; they are "the unacknowledged legislators of the world." The remarkable thing is that Hobbes reaches this conclusion from a supposedly pure empiricism. Shelley arrives at the same point from the "opposite" stance of the "intellectual philosophy," which for him means a transcendental world in which the individual mind is itself part of one

---

* See above, pp. 16–17.

"universal mind." For Hobbes the imagination works from the material toward the spiritual and ideal. For Shelley, the path works backward. The two views can also join to form the third and more encompassing path that Coleridge and Schelling blaze.

There are several reasons for the conjunction of one of England's hard-line empiricists, Hobbes, and one of her allegedly "unworldly" idealists, Shelley, who stand respectively at the beginning and end of the rise of the idea of the imagination from 1660 to 1820. But the main reason is the interest that Shelley and Hobbes shared in the Greek poets, historians, and philosophers. In them could be traced how the creative and philosophic imagination built one of the prototypical cultures of Western civilization and how, at every turn, the literature and the poetry of the Greeks determined their moral, political, and civil character from Homer to Alexander. In a love of Greek culture and an interest in the relationship between creative imagination and society, Sidney and Arnold throw even wider brackets in time.

## A CALLING TO THE UNAPPREHENDED

Aside from varying and repeating, however unconsciously, themes about the imagination already current for two generations, Shelley quite drastically deviates from some of the established concepts. Each time he takes a new path, he tends to reduce the role of the will, consciousness, deliberate choice, and concrete fact. This is partially due to his stress on the impelling force of one "universal mind" or power working through all individuals, and it recalls the old bond between dreams or divine visitations and the imagination. But although, like Yeats, Shelley minimizes a conscious control of the imaginative process, he simultaneously increases the amount of belief or faith that should be placed in imaginative creations. These creations are "true" or believable, as Coleridge says, insofar as we are able to suspend our disbelief. Shelley envisions a new and higher belief springing from this suspension of mere verisimilitude. We can recall how Reynolds, Kames, Reid, Stewart, and Alison began to see imagination as the "residence of truth" providing an "ideal presence"; Shelley is carrying their contentions to the bourne of heaven.

Poetry, says Shelley in the *Defence*, "acts in a divine and unapprehended manner, beyond and above consciousness." The poet becomes an instrument of a higher melody. "Poetry is not like reasoning, a power to be exerted according to the determination of the will." Most English and German thinkers had come to see imagination as a conflation of willed and unwilled, voluntary and involuntary, but Shelley sees it as an unpredictable, even sudden inspiration over which we exert little control. In a way, the individual imagination becomes more passive because it is transmitting something deeper and more meaningful, yet doing so without any conscious will or control. Whereas Coleridge, participating in a long line of English and German critics, stresses the role of the will, as in his definition of the secondary imagination, Shelley says that the "birth and recurrence" of poetry "have no necessary connexion with consciousness or will."[25]

While Fichte believes deeply in the value of the will for the philosopher, his concept of the artist's imagination (*Phantasie*) and will, as well as his extreme idealism, make him parallel to Shelley in several instances. When Fichte describes the poet in his *Ich will untersuchen, wodurch Geist vom Buchstaben* (1794), he says: "*Seine Phantasie treibt ohne alle sein Zuthun ihr Spiel. Der Geist treibt ihn; der Geist redet aus ihm.*"[26] The poet's will has been superseded by an unconscious spirit of force, which operates "completely without his help." Similarly, Shelley's concept of the universal mind or Absolute finds a parallel in the absolute *Ich* of Fichte as well as in the dialectic of Schelling. The attempt to regain this Absolute, to recapture a clarity of thought that sees harmony in the relationships of the universe, which Shelley expresses at the beginning of the *Defence*, has an analogy in Blake's endeavor to restore the Golden Age. Shelley's last lyrics in *Hellas* express this idea, defining the permanent calling of poets as the struggle to grasp again the true and original knowledge of the secrets of cosmos and creation, to strip things and ideas to their elemental natures until they are seen in their basic connections, causes, and effects.

But poetry, the highest act of the imagination, is never in certain possession of the Golden Age. There is always a struggle to capture the "unapprehended," to hear the music of the spheres, what Keats calls the "melodies unheard." This is the goal of an imaginative becoming, which returns to the primordial state of unity. Poetry is an attempt to rebuild the Tower of Babel, to eat of the Tree of Knowledge a second time. When Shelley observes that the secrets of the abysm remain hidden and has Demogorgon say that "the deep truth is imageless" (*Prometheus Unbound*, II. iv, 116), we might ask what it is that has no image of itself. The answer seems two-fold: either nothing, a complete vacuum, or else a truly all-encompassing unity, which can have no true image of itself because it is nothing less than the grand total of all images in their interaction and interrelation.

"Unapprehended" or "imageless" become key words in the imaginative process. We glimpse a higher realm, but only briefly, and then we are back in the magic shadow-show of present reality. Poetry "creates anew the universe" and, as Sidney says, offers us a golden instead of a brazen world. But the new world is fleeting, and imagination must not only create or perceive this higher world but also bolster our belief in it because the creation itself is ephemeral.

In the *Defence*, "reason" means the calculating faculty, that which Reynolds had forty years earlier referred to as fostering principles falsely called rational—the deductive, step-by-step, logical process.[27] "Reason is to imagination as the body to the spirit, as the shadow to the substance." In *Prometheus Unbound* (II. iv, 10–11), Asia reports that the living world contains "passion, reason, will/Imagination," and the order here seems to be roughly ascending. In *Hellas* (795–797) a similar list appears. The "quick elements" of "Thought," of the mind in general, appear as "Will, Passion,/Reason, Imagination," the list again building to its climax. Shelley in effect replaces the Platonic *nous* with the imagination.

### PARADOXES OF THE IMAGINATION

Shelley's idealistic faith in the imagination presents several paradoxes that weighed heavily on him and were perhaps a cause of the sense of burden that colors part of his life. First, if the imagination is inspirational and unwilled, the poet may become an automaton. But if the poet is really struggling to attain an "unwilled" moment of inspiration, then the will does seem to be involved up to the time of that transient flash of insight when the veil falls away from his eyes.

Second, Sidney had observed that while the poet "never lieth," he "never affirmeth" either. Shelley has put himself in the position of believing that the poet does affirm something, a higher world, but there is no way to prove that it exists or what it is like. It must be taken on faith. "We know nothing. We have no evidence; we cannot express our inmost thoughts. They are incomprehensible even to ourselves."[28]

Shelley also faces the paradox that a faith in something naturally uncertain and hidden leads him in his poetry to create a world that itself is diffuse, sometimes abstract. He hesitates to offer something concrete and permanent, for that might be a permanently false guess. Above all, Shelley's higher world is "unapprehended," a recurring word in the *Defence*. True meaning, true reality, is "veiled" and ineffable, which puts a seemingly impossible barrier in the way of poetry. "How vain is it to think that words," exclaims Shelley, "can penetrate the mystery of our being!" The poet never secures his own greatness, "and the most glorious poetry that has ever been communicated to the world is probably a feeble shadow of the original conceptions of the poet."[29] Because of this built-in frustration, "the created poem is," as Milton Wilson notes, "the purgatory of the imagination." Shelley admits that we are left with "the inmost naked beauty of the meaning never exposed." Again, there is a parallel with the inner-directed idealism of Fichte who, in describing the operation of the productive imagination (*produktive Einbildungskraft*), remarks that, *"der Maler aus seinem Auge die vollendete Gestalt auf die Flache hinwirft, gleichsam hinsieht, ehe die langsamere Hand ihre Umrisse nachmachen kann."*[30] For Shelley, the moment between the immediate eye of the imagination and the slower execution of the hand is that time when the true essence of the vision partially evaporates and becomes irredeemable.

The final paradox for Shelley is that the creation of a diffuse, even abstract higher world—one that can never be accurately expressed in words—places a hazy and receding goal before the poet. In approaching this mirage-like vision, any organic progress is in danger of disintegrating. The tension between ideal and real sublimates into the ideal alone, and organic movement, as Hazlitt would conceive of it, is forestalled. The result can be a return to abstraction, something Shelley abhorred in the language and concepts of the eighteenth century. But in Shelley, as in Keats and most of the high Romantics, "love," "beauty," "truth," and similar words are becoming too crammed with meaning. Even "imagination" begins to have this difficulty.

With Shelley, the imagination has plumbed mortality and is anxious to go beyond. It is not that Shelley was, in Keats's phrase, "half in love with easeful death," but—and it is quite a different thing—that Shelley, like Antony and Cleopatra, must "needs find out new heaven, new earth."

# 1 8

# WORDSWORTH

*B*y the 1790s the imagination had become, indirectly if not directly, the central theme of poetry itself, and to explore it in detail would be to recapitulate the history of Romantic poetry. Our concern with the background and growth of the concept and with its more philosophical underpinnings leaves us able to touch on poetry as it reflects or extends these major issues. We should glance at Wordsworth, however familiar much of what he says is, if only because no other poet—in his own work—offers a more explicit concept of the imagination. To discuss the ramifications of the subject in his poetry would fully re-interpret it. With a few exceptions, therefore, we shall confine ourselves to what he says or suggests directly about the imagination. His poetry has been written about so extensively that to quote and remark about it runs the risk of cliché, but the hope is that what he says can be seen in the light of figures discussed in previous chapters. Wordsworth reflects and rephrases thinkers in the latter half of the eighteenth century, including Hartley, Gerard, Tucker, Reynolds, Reid, Stewart, Alison, as well as writers who, since the 1770s, had been calling for a "natural language of passion."

In one respect, Wordsworth was carrying out theories and values prized by many of the associationist critics he read. Not only did his stress on natural and passionate language belong to a critical program under way while Johnson was still alive, but so did his view of the imagination, at least as he conceived of it as an excited power of association involving ideas and emotions, stirred and compounded by memory with an energy that could result in an intense contemplation of the endless or the infinite. Coleridge, in fact, thought that Wordsworth failed to distinguish imagination sufficiently from a keen or heightened association. Although the *Lyrical Ballads*, according to Wordsworth's 1800 Preface, propose incidents over which is thrown "a certain colouring of imagination," they make the incidents "interesting" by tracing them through "the primary laws of our nature: chiefly . . . the manner in which we associate ideas in a state of excitement." This is close to a paraphrase of convictions voiced by Gerard, Priestley, and Alison.

As with Coleridge and Schelling, discussion of Wordsworth's idea of the imagination—and, not independently, of its relation to Coleridge's—becomes enriched and complicated by the flux and inconsistencies that evolved during more than fifteen years. What Wordsworth thought about the imagination in 1798 or 1800 is not exactly what he thought about it when he wrote the 1815 Preface. Coleridge charged, in fact, that Wordsworth expressed critical "sentiments" rather than stable principles. There is the further caveat, again stressed by Coleridge, that as with most poets (Coleridge would include himself), Wordsworth's poetry does not always square with the opinions expressed in his prose.

Yet with *The Prelude* we encounter a poem that is itself a *Bildungsroman* of the imagination, a story of its development in the poet's maturing mind, and that story seems always to have been more important to Wordsworth than theoretical reflection on any change in his own critical ideas, or any attempt to correct them. "Imagination having been our theme," says Wordsworth near the end of *The Prelude*, "This faculty hath been the moving soul/Of our long labour." It is as if two characters act in the poem, Wordsworth and Wordsworth's concept of the imagination, which shapes his being as much as a teacher or close friend. Wordsworth is convinced that the imagination is a varied power allowing us to perceive nature and also to infuse our deepest feelings, sympathy, and religious faith through the material forms and experience of the world. He himself best describes and exemplifies that type of imagination which he calls "meditative," as opposed to the "dramatic" kind he finds supremely exemplified in Shakespeare.

Wordsworth extricates the idea of the imagination from a philosophical and critical atmosphere and joins the intellectual content of the idea to a moving narrative. This fusion of poetry with ideas, or with the central, ideal force behind the creation of poetry, prompted Coleridge to remark that Wordsworth was uniquely capable of producing "the first geniune philosophic poem." *The Prelude* is a vindication of the attitude that imagination permeates life. And without this personal testament we would miss a closing link in this history of the idea. *The Prelude* does not, in a specifically philosophical or critical sense, say much more about the idea of the imagination than Akenside's *Pleasures*. But the individuality and the connected experiences in *The Prelude* are among the reasons why it is far greater. The idea becomes humanized. Akenside's poem is an understanding and rather abstract portrait of the imagination; *The Prelude* is an imaginative treatment of it.

## PERCEIVING NATURE

We might expect Wordsworth to leap directly into the poetic and artistic role of the imagination and elaborate little about it as a perceptive power. But he feels that the perceptive power is crucial and forms the basis of the poetic imagination. And for Wordsworth, the perceptive imagination is nearly equivalent to Coleridge's primary imagination, the ability to form a coherent vision of the world from a jumble of sense impressions. This power of perceiving has "first-born affinities that fit/Our new existence to existing things."[1] In the second book of *The Prelude* he explains this awakening. Speaking of the way in which an infant begins to experience the world, he relates how the young mind coalesces feeling, impressions, and objects into larger wholes until, re-creating the *"active* universe" within itself, the growing mind becomes "an *agent* of the one great mind." This is close to Coleridge's description of the primary imagination as the "prime *Agent* of all human *Perception,"* which in the finite mind repeats "the eternal act of creation in the infinite I AM."[2] Wordsworth and Coleridge are squarely in the eighteenth-century tradition of viewing the imagination on several levels.

In the 1815 Preface, Wordsworth refers to "one of the earliest processes of Nature in the development of this faculty." Guided by his own *"primary* consciousnesses," he undertakes to show how internal feelings cooperate "with external accidents to plant . . . images of sound and sight, in the celestial soil of the Imagination."[3] The child who experiences this awakening in the first exercise of the imaginative faculty "is surprised into a *perception"* of images, which the poem describes. And this perception is also an act of creation, "the first Poetic spirit of our human life." Tracing this process in *The Prelude*, he speaks first about an infant:

> his mind
> Even in the first trial of its powers
> Is prompt and watchful, eager to combine
> In one appearance, all the elements
> And parts of the same object, else detach'd
> And loth to coalesce.
> . . . . . . . . . . .
> . . . his mind
> Even as an agent of the one great mind,
> Creates, creator and receiver both,

Working but in alliance with the works
Which it beholds.—Such, verily is the first
Poetic spirit of our human life.[4]


## NATURE AND SELF ENTWINED

Perceiving nature as both "creator and receiver," the mind associates the particulars of the world with inner feelings and sentiments. In the passage quoted just above, the infant is resting in its mother's arms, and from her "his soul/Doth gather passion."[5] Her "feelings pass into his torpid life/Like an awakening breeze," or like that "corresponding mild creative breeze," that "vital breeze" which Wordsworth invokes at the beginning of the poem. These feelings and emotional attachments the infant passes on to his perception of the world; he feels at one with nature. The association of ideas or aesthetic values with nature becomes, as with Hazlitt, an association of feelings. The bond between feelings and the "beauteous forms" of nature is intrinsic. There are

first-born affinities that fit
Our new existence to existing things,
And, in our dawn of being, constitute
The bond of union betwixt life and joy.[6]

In the passage where Wordsworth steals a skiff on Ullswater and rows out into the lake, the huge crag that looms up and seems to stride after and rebuke him takes on a living force. At the end of the passage he addresses the "Wisdom and Spirit of the Universe," saying that not in vain

didst Thou intertwine for me
The passions that build up our human Soul
. . . with high objects, with enduring things,
With life and nature, purifying thus
The elements of feeling and of thought.[7]

Nature becomes more than the physical object of perception; there is, in "all the mighty world/of eye and ear," not only "what they . . . perceive" but "what they half create." The mind becomes aware of a higher spirit that communes both with all "thinking things" and with all "objects of thought." So the bond of associated feelings between the soul and the forms of nature embodies those feelings in those very forms and discovers a spirit and creation that underlies both man and nature. As Wordsworth puts it in the 1800 Preface, "The passions of men are incorporated with the beautiful and permanent forms of nature."[8] The imagination is here "endowing and modifying" nature; it is humanizing nature. While Wordsworth was in his teens, his imagination attained a self-conscious power to mingle the forms of nature with passions, a self-consciousness absent in the infant:

A plastic power
Abode with me, a forming hand . . .
A local spirit of its own . . .
. . . but for the most
Subservient strictly to the external things
With which it commun'd. An auxiliar light
Came from my mind which on the setting sun
Bestow'd new splendor . . .
. . . and the midnight storm
Grew darker in the presence of my eye.[9]

Here the imagination acts as "an auxiliar light," intensifying what is seen, "Coercing all things into sympathy," so that "To unorganic natures," says Wordsworth, "I transferr'd/My own enjoyments."[10]

This modifying and humanizing power simultaneously lends to and finds in nature a moral sense, which Wordsworth recognizes as:

The anchor of my purest thoughts, the muse,
The guide, the guardian of my heart, and soul
Of all my moral being.[11]

Here he is rooted directly in the eighteenth-century associationist and sympathetic tradition, but expressing it in an urgent and personal voice. Shaftesbury, Hutcheson, Burke, Smith, and Priestley had never offered such a particular and local testimony:

To every natural form, rock, fruit or flower,
Even the loose stones that cover the high-way,
I gave a moral life, I saw them feel,
Or link'd them to some feeling.[12]

We also receive and give back again in mutual flow with nature, the poetic power being active and passive alike.[13] One of Wordsworth's great contributions is to show that even as our imaginations create and interpret nature, so in a simultaneous reciprocity nature channels the force of our imaginations. Nature is like the imaginative mind in that it, too, becomes active and passive. The human mind and human form, as well as the forms of nature, become capable of a mutual spirituality. This is achieved essentially by the sympathetic power of the imagination, by "primal sympathy." One of the recurring words in Wordsworth's poetry and criticism, the "forms" of nature, had been used significantly not only by Burke and early associationists but by Alison in his *Principles of Taste* (1790). There Alison stated that in perceiving natural and aesthetic "forms," we sympathize with them, and they become beautiful "because we identify" with their shape and motion. In addition, Alison noted that the natural world, "by leading our imaginations," encourages us to associate immediate sensations with earlier experiences. These psychological and aesthetic observations emerge as major principles of organization and meaning in poems like *Tintern Abbey* and *The Prelude*. Wordsworth emphasizes that the process of inwardly creating and receiving natural forms becomes habitual. Through it the poet finds what is most affecting and "really important to men." Thus, "by the repetition and continuance of this act feelings connected with important subjects will be nourished, till . . . by obeying . . . the impulses of those habits *we shall describe objects and utter sentiments . . . in such connection with each other*, that the understanding . . . must necessarily be . . . enlightened . . . and . . . ameliorated."[14]

Later, in his 1815 Preface, Wordsworth mentions more specifically how individual images become symbolic and laden with a felt meaning: "O Cuckoo! shall I call thee Bird,/Or but a wandering Voice?" In these familiar lines the imagination formulates such a question because it remembers constantly hearing the bird in spring but seldom seeing it. Such "processes of imagination," which lead to calling the bird "a wandering Voice," are "carried on either by conferring additional properties upon an object, or abstracting from it some of those which it actually possesses, and thus enabling it to react upon the mind which hath performed the process, like a new existence." Imagination, in this sense, "has no reference to images that are merely a faithful copy . . . but is a word . . . denoting operations of the mind upon those objects."[15]

On a higher plane, Wordsworth conceives of the imagination as working upon several objects or characters in combination, connecting and opposing them even as it alters them singly. "Take . . . images separately, and how unaffecting the picture compared with that produced by their being thus connected with, and opposed to, each other!"

"As a huge stone is sometimes seen to lie
Couched on the bald top of an eminence,
Wonder to all who do the same espy
By what means it could thither come, and whence,
So that it seems a thing endued with sense,
Like a sea-beast crawled forth, which on a shelf
Of rock or sand reposeth, there to sun himself.

Such seemed this Man; not all alive or dead
Nor all asleep, in his extreme old age.
. . . . . . . . . . . . . . . . . . . .
Motionless as a cloud the old Man stood,
That heareth not the loud winds when they call,
And moveth altogether if it move at all."

In these images, the conferring, the abstracting, and the modifying powers of the Imagination . . . are all brought into conjunction. The stone is endowed with something of the power of life to approximate it to the sea-beast; and the sea-beast stripped of some of its vital qualities to assimilate it to the stone; which intermediate image is thus treated for the purpose of bringing the original image, that of the stone, to a nearer resemblance to the figure and condition of the aged Man; who is divested of so much of the indications of life and motion as to bring him to the point where the two objects unite and coalesce . . . After what has been said, the image of the cloud need not be commented upon.[16]

## VISIONARY POWER

After this last example in the 1815 Preface, Wordsworth abruptly asks, "Thus far of an endowing or modifying power" in one or several images, "but the Imagination also shapes and *creates;* and how?" Architectonic and planning, the highest poetic power brings all things to bear on one, "consolidating numbers into unity, and dissolving and separating unity into number," phrases similar to those in Coleridge's definition of the secondary imagination. For Wordsworth, the "visionary power" is a symbolic picture of life, feelings, and nature as they are in sympathy with each other. It is connected, in unbroken progression, to the original and simple act of perception, the primary or "first/Poetic spirit of our human life." The creative power is not different in kind from our waking power of perception that already "half creates." Wordsworth approximates Coleridge's remark that the secondary imagination is different not in kind but only in the degree and mode of its operation. In Book XIII of *The Prelude* Wordsworth describes the perceptive imagination, which "even the grossest minds must see and hear" and which "Nature . . . Thrusts . . . upon the senses," as

> a genuine Counterpart
> And Brother of the glorious faculty
> Which higher minds bear with them as their own.

This glorious faculty of the poet deals with "all objects of the universe" as an aesthetic, human, and emotional experience. Those who possess this faculty "for themselves create/A like existence" in their own works of art.[17]

Coleridge (among, as we have seen, others) states that the poetic or secondary imagination is "co-existing with the conscious will." Similarly, relating how his own poetic power grew and how he became conscious of "the works of art," Wordsworth speaks of the images and "shapes of human life" and explains that "A wilfulness of fancy and conceit . . . gave them new importance to the mind." Then

> that first poetic Faculty
> Of plain imagination and severe
> . . . . . . . . . . . . . . . . . . . .
> Began to have some promptings to put on
> A visible shape, and to the works of art,
> The notions and the images of books
> Did knowingly conform itself.[18]

Like Coleridge, Schelling, and Gerard, Wordsworth uses as one criterion for distinguishing the primary from the secondary level of imagination the fact that the secondary or poetic power is "knowingly"guided, at least in part, and has a "wilfulness" grafted upon it.

But how, in more specific terms, does the imagination *"create?"* As Wordsworth says, "From touch of this new power/Nothing was safe." It intensifies and endows every situation with feeling and drama. It magnifies and joins perceptions into new life; it creates actions more distilled and concentrated than those which actually occur, yet the actions it creates are plausible. There is a sense now that the imaginative power is of a different kind than heightened or intensified association. The visionary power *transforms* a character or an object. "Then common death was none," continues Wordsworth, and the "tragic" was "super-tragic, else left short." Imagination builds the thick texture of one powerful experience, which touches on and draws from myriad circumstances:

> Then, if a Widow, staggering with the blow
> Of her distress, was known to have made her way
> To the cold grave in which her Husband slept,
> One night, or haply more than one . . .
> . . . . . . . . . . . . . . . .  . . . . . . . .
> The fact was caught at greedily, and there
> She was a visitant the whole year through,
> Wetting the turf with never-ending tears,
> And all the storms of Heaven must beat on her.[19]

Catching the widow's plight "greedily," the creative power becomes obsessed and is engaged completely and willfully. It magnifies the situation and makes her mourn each night "the whole year through," not just the one or two nights she did. It adds the touch of her "never-ending tears" wetting the grave, suggesting an infinite and bottomless grief, which is immediately echoed by a harmonious action of nature when "all the storms" of wind and rain must *"beat* on her," with the added hint—by the word "Heaven"—that a terrible omnipotence is witness to and part of this suffering. The woman, her actions, the natural and the spiritual worlds, all become symbolic and archetypal in one scene and one expression.

The visionary power "attends upon the motions of the winds/Embodied in the mystery of words." Words alone shape formless ideas into objects and motion—the explanation goes back to Theseus' "lovers, lunatics, and poets" speech, which Wordsworth paraphrases in the 1815 Preface. Words are a mysterious force approximating Coleridge's laboratory of the imagination where essence is elaborated into existence. Of this mystery Wordsworth says:

> There darkness makes abode, and all the host
> Of shadowy things do work their changes there
>
> . . . . . . . . . . . . . . . . . . . . . . . . . . . .
>
> Even forms and substances are circumfused
> By that transparent veil with light divine;
>
> And through the turnings intricate of verse,
> Present themselves as objects recognis'd,
> In flashes, and with a glory scarce their own.*

In the 1815 Preface Wordsworth explains this effect of single words and of their larger composition, citing the simile from *Paradise Lost* (II, 636–643):

> "As when far off at sea a fleet descried
> *Hangs* in the clouds, by equinoctial winds
> Close sailing from Bengala, or the isles
> Of Ternate or Tidore, whence merchants bring
> Their spicy drugs; they on the trading flood
> Through the wide Ethiopian to the Cape
> Ply, stemming nightly toward the Pole: so seemed
> Far off the flying Fiend."

Here is the full strength of the imagination involved in the word *hangs*, and exerted upon the whole image: First, the fleet, an aggregate of many ships, is represented as one mighty person, whose track, we know and feel, is upon the waters; but, taking advantage of its appearance to the senses, the Poet dares to represent it as *hanging in the clouds*, both for the gratification of the mind in contemplating the image itself, and in reference to the motion and appearance of the sublime object to which it is compared.

But not only does the word "hangs" carry special power, the whole passage vibrates with an interwoven use of language, in which Wordsworth sees the technical mastery of imagination in the creation of specific effects:

When the compact Fleet, as one Person, has been introduced "Sailing from Bengala," "They," i.e. the "merchants," representing the fleet resolved into a multitude of ships, "ply" their voyage towards the extremities of the earth: "So," (referring to the word "As" in the commence-

---

* This passage (V, 598–605) may be compared closely with the letter from a friend in Chapter 13 of the *Biographia*, the paragraph beginning "The effect on my feelings."

ment) "seemed the flying Fiend:" the image of his Person acting to recombine the multitude of ships into one body,—the point from which the
comparison set out. "So seemed," and to whom seemed? To the heavenly
Muse who dictates the poem, to the eye of the Poet's mind, and to that of
the Reader, present at one moment in the wide Ethiopian, and the next in
the solitudes, then first broken in upon, of the infernal regions![20]

## FANCY AND "MEDITATIVE" AND "DRAMATIC" IMAGINATION

Wordsworth adds little to the distinctions between fancy and imagination mentioned above in chapter 13. He stresses that fancy deals with
the fixed and unmodified (Coleridge's "fixities and definites"), while
imagination creates from "the plastic, the pliant, and the infinite." But in
the 1815 Preface, where his remarks on fancy and imagination mainly
appear, he does make one interesting point. The effect of fancy is largely
one of "rapidity and profusion." Its power is a sparkling surface play,
transient and "evanescent." Whereas fancy works with this "temporal"
succession, imagination guides us to the "eternal." Thus, imagination
"leaves it to Fancy to describe Queen Mab as coming 'In shape no big-
ger than an agate-stone/On the fore-finger of an alderman.' " Fancy cir-
cumscribes; imagination expands. Imagination "does not tell you that
her gigantic Angel was Pompey's Pillar ... or that his dimensions
equalled those of Teneriffe or Atlas;—because these ... are bounded:
The expression is, 'His stature reached the sky!' ... When the imagination frames a comparison ... it ... grows—and continues to grow—
upon the mind."[21]

Just as important as these remarks on fancy and imagination is
Wordsworth's division of poetic genius. In the one category of "enthusiastic and meditative Imagination" he puts Hebrew Scripture, Milton,
and Spenser. "Of the human and dramatic Imagination," on the other
hand, "the works of Shakespeare are an inexhaustible source." Then
Wordsworth asserts somewhat defensively, perhaps smarting from
Hazlitt's criticism of him, that he has tried to turn the imagination
"upon its worthiest objects, the external universe, the moral and religious sentiments of Man, his natural affections, and his acquired passions." But he does not volunteer to place himself in either of his own
two categories, perhaps because his contemporaries were already drawing the conclusion for him.[22]

## THE SPIRITUALLY SYMBOLIC: LOVE

Late in life, on July 1, 1845, Wordsworth wrote to Henry Reed, a
Philadelphian who edited Wordsworth's poems for American publica-

tion, that "what I should myself most value in my attempts" is "the spirituality with which I have endeavoured to invest the material Universe, and the moral relation under which I have wished to exhibit its most ordinary appearances." This comes in the context of a long retrospect on English poets since the later eighteenth century. Investing the material universe with a spirituality was, for Wordsworth, a unique calling of the imagination. This calling, and the pantheistic sensibility it produces, animate those two sublime moments in *The Prelude*, crossing the Alps at Simplon Pass and climbing Mt. Snowden. After he describes crossing the alpine pass, Wordsworth launches into the apostrophe, "Imagination!"

> In all the might of its endowments, came
> Athwart me . . .
> . . . . . . . . . . . .
> . . . in such visitings
> Of awful promise, when the light of sense
> Goes out in flashes, that have shown to us
> The invisible world, doth Greatness make abode.

He turns to the most concrete things and sees them as symbols of spiritual feelings. The woods, waterfalls, and winds, the torrents, crags, and rocks—all, "As if a voice was in them," are

> like workings of one mind, the features
> Of the same face, blossoms upon one tree,
> Characters of the great Apocalypse,
> The types and symbols of Eternity.[23]

And in this vision the self is lifted to the divine because man and a holy spirit are merging in nature, in what Wordsworth elsewhere calls this "new world" that the imagination creates, perhaps echoing Shakespeare's "brave new world," a new world in which we experience a unity of "action from within and from without," where one power dwells in both "the object seen, and eye that sees." Here is the complete union of the internal and subjective with the external and objective, the deepest sympathy.[24]

Ultimately this is not a power of knowing, in the sense of knowing the laws of chemistry or of the marketplace. It is the power of moral faith and passion reflected in that last line of the sonnet concluding the series on the River Duddon: "We feel that we are greater than we know." Wordsworth links the imagination with reason and passion until the three become one:

> Imagination, which, in truth,
> Is but another name for absolute power
> And clearest insight, amplitude of mind,
> And Reason in her most exalted mood.

>      . . . truth
> By reason built, or passion, which itself
> Is highest reason in a soul sublime.[25]

But at the mystic height of the imaginative power, it becomes so all-binding in its religious, sympathetic, and moral character that it can be compared with and can stand with only one other human and divine quality, love. The same transformation into or identification of the imagination with love occurs in Shelley, Schelling, and to some extent in Keats and Coleridge. This final reach of the imagination, long suggested by eighteenth-century thinkers who trusted the role of the imagination in faith (Arbuckle, Akenside, Hartley, Hutcheson, Gerard, Priestley, Duff, Reynolds, and Brown) is now expressed without reservation. Our "spiritual Love," says Wordsworth, "acts not nor can exist/Without Imagination." In mankind we find "an object . . . Of pure imagination, and of love."[26] The strongest statement about imagination and love comes when they are envisioned as merging into one:

> Imagination having been our theme,
> So also hath that intellectual Love,
> For they are each in each, and cannot stand
> Dividually.[27]

Imagination is the perceiving and creating of whatever is outside the self, and love is our attachment to those perceptions and creations—and both love and imagination, as one force and one feeling, are necessary if life and being, whether Supreme or human, are to find hope and joy. This ineffable benevolence of "Imagination—here the Power so called/Through sad incompetence of human speech,"[28] represents the upward limit of the idea as a theme for both philosophy and poetry.

# 1 9

# GOETHE AND KEATS

*A*lthough Goethe was forty-six years old at the time of Keats's birth in 1795 and lived for eleven years after Keats's death in 1821, it was in the space of only five years that the young Keats began to discover and treat the imagination in a way remarkably similar to the one pursued by Goethe for over fifty. Though a man's years be short, remarks Bacon, his hours may have been long. There are naturally great differences between the two poets, differences in temperament, talent, and style, which cannot be explained by nationality or simply by Goethe's longevity contrasted with Keats's premature death. Apparently, neither read anything the other wrote. To place them together may seem a capricious or violent yoking, but in their hope and regard for the imagination we find an uncanny correspondence, a set of elective affinities.

Keats and Goethe share an inescapable and powerful attraction to the imaginative life, to the life of poetic creation, which Goethe, as had many before him, calls a "divine gift." But co-existing with their trust and enthusiasm is an intense and even painful awareness that instead of reconciling the poetic or ideal world with reality, with what Keats calls "the van of circumstance," the imagination can further separate the two and deceive the psyche. Perhaps no one since Johnson better expresses this combined love and suspicion of the imagination than Goethe and Keats. Their wary attitude is heightened by the presence of their own massively powerful imaginative minds, their ability to create a passionate vision. We see this even in their early works. Endymion seeks the unattainable—as we all seek "to burst our mortal bars," and finds that this can be done only by accepting the "real" of the world. Young Werther likewise pursues an impossible object, one that he frankly admits he has magnified in his own imagination, and ends in a mixture of joy and triumphant hope, riddled at last with despair, paralysis, and

277

suicide. Had Werther and Endymion lacked imagination, the drama and tension in the two works would evaporate. Goethe and Keats are pre-eminently poets of the drama of experience treated imaginatively, the polarity of a life shaped ideally by the imagination but one that also senses it cannot flee reality "on the viewless wings of poesy."

A central theme in both poets is the individual imagination caught in the intractable conditions of a fallen world, a theme that includes the involvement of the poet in his art and the struggle of his self-conscious imagination to escape its own subjectivity, so tempted by the ease of self-expression in poetry, and to attain some sort of objectivity or truth. But this "escape" may be only part of a larger and more sinister artistic illusion or escapism. Keats and Goethe affirm that one of the great debates expressed by art and art alone is the debate between life and art itself, that is, the strife and creative friction generated by the encounter of the creative imagination with experience, and literally the danger (*ex-periculo*) of facing life devoid of art. To a large degree, works like Goethe's *Faust* and Keats's *Lamia* and *The Fall of Hyperion* are efforts in which the poets displace themselves and introduce characters, such as Faust or the poet-dreamer in *Hyperion*, whose imaginative inner life confronts the inevitable realities of death and cold fact. To this end Keats and Goethe use myths—Faust, Psyche, Hyperion, Iphigenie, Lamia, Endymion—in dramatizing what Keats calls the debate between "damnation and impassioned [imaginative] clay." Both poets choose to revive and transform myths, not to create new ones in the manner of Blake. Perhaps this approach stems from a conviction that all lasting myths have as their basis not primarily an original narrative or new characters but an archetypal significance that endures because it represents a deep-seated truth about human nature. Thus, there are no new or old myths as such, but only those that carry greater or lesser archetypal weight.

When Keats expresses belief in nothing but the "holiness of the Heart's affection and the truth of Imagination," when he calls for a "regular stepping of the Imagination towards a Truth," and when later he questions the value of poetry as anything but an ornament, a "Jack o lanthern"—and if this is so, that "it is not so fine a thing as philosophy—For the same reason that an eagle is not so fine a thing as a truth,"* he is touching on the core of Goethe's own life-long debate and

---

* Keats, *Letters* (ed. Rollins) I, 242; II, 81. On the characterization of poetry or the imagination as a "jack o' lantern," cf. Coleridge to Josiah Wedgwood (*CL* I 646, Nov. 1, 1800): "Your late Governess . . . interested me a good deal; she appears to me to have been injured by going out of the common way without any of that Imagination, which if it be a Jack o' Lanthorn to lead us out of that way is however at the same time a Torch to light us whither we are going. A whole Essay might be written on the Danger of *thinking* without Images.—"

self-evolution that led him to call his autobiography *Dichtung und Wahrheit*. The tone and more serious observations of Keats's letters often sound like Goethe's conversations with Eckermann. And when Keats is puzzled by a reliance on "consequetive reasoning," since it is imagination that can pierce to the essence of a thing in a concrete way full of gusto (as he heard his friend Hazlitt describe it), and when he praises Wordsworth's imagination for proceeding down the darker corridors of experience and touching on "the burden of the mystery," he is voicing the same concern we find in Goethe's remark that a man "who has been brought up in the so-called exact sciences will, from the height of his analytical reason, not easily comprehend that there is something like an exact concrete imagination."

Goethe lived long enough to become a sage and, as George Santayana points out in the Introduction to his *Three Philosophical Poets*, Goethe's poetry of experience becomes philosophic, just as philosophy becomes poetic, because they have together reached a level of shared imaginative vision that not only results from—but extends far beyond—individual systems of philosophy and schools of poetry.[1] Keats realizes this, too, when he speculates that "a fine writer is the most genuine Being in the world" excepting the "human friend Philosopher," but the poet also remains "a friend/To sooth the cares, and lift the thoughts of man." Something more than the dreamer who is but a "fever of himself," the poet-philosopher has the ability, the "negative capability" to create and lose himself in a vision and an achievement greater than himself.

### GOETHE

Goethe did not construct a formal theory on the imagination, but his scattered opinions, avoiding what he might consider the quagmire of formulas and cumbersome system, strike at important issues. His thoughts on the imagination cannot be called original, though by now we can see how hard this would be to say of anyone. Many of his views have a flavor of the second half of the eighteenth century, his earlier years, and when he voices them in 1815 or 1825, there is nothing novel in their drift. But it is Goethe's expression of the complexity of imagination, and of its elusive nature, that we value most highly. Although he at times dredges up a rationalistic skepticism about the imagination, which Schiller shares and which recalls Johnson and Hume, Goethe realizes that a balance of enthusiasm and circumspection is often the wisest course in any human undertaking. He keeps something of a *via media* about the imagination, from which he surveys the borders and extremes of the surrounding countryside.

On the subject of the imagination Goethe is a dilettante in the early meaning of the word, namely a lover of the fine arts, who prefers not to embroil himself in the professional, specialized bustle and debates that are often unworthy of the effort invested in them. In the end, Goethe's idea of the imagination carries an earned and practical weight; it is a good ballast, not so heavy that the course of the idea, which by Goethe's youth was already moving with strong momentum, slows or sinks. Quite the contrary, a certain stability is added.

Goethe sees the imagination as a potentially split faculty. Nothing can match its creative power or its grasp of the flow of experience, but when it is unregulated and estranged from reality, it becomes the greatest source of terror and even despair. No wonder young Werther, hopeful but half mad at the possibility of rejection by Charlotte, cries out when she sends a note for him to come, *"Was die Einbildungskraft für ein göttliches Geschenk ist!"* For Goethe, the imagination is not the supreme faculty but is first among equals, if only because in its central position it calls on all other faculties at once. In a note, apparently written about 1828, he remarks: "The imagination actually appears to have no rules . . . But in possession it becomes regulated in the most manifold way through feeling, through moral considerations, through the need of action, and most happily, however, through taste, in which reason itself takes hold of each matter and element involved." This is all even-handed, and the tone here, calling on reason, feeling, taste, and moral sensibility to aid the imagination, takes us back to Burke, Gerard, Reynolds, Tetens, and the kind of analysis common before 1790. Goethe's point is that the imagination cannot regulate itself unless we expand its definition beyond all reasonable bounds. In a sense, this is the conclusion reached by Coleridge and Schelling, too. For them, imagination becomes subsumed by reason, for reason contains all faculties. For Goethe, the "regulated" imagination stands behind Homer, Sophocles, Pindar, and Shakespeare. Their work is organic and whole. A "romantic" and "unregulated" imagination, however, throws out its phantasies in a more effusive poet like Klopstock.[2]

To recognize the unique law of the imagination is to understand the unique value of poetry. In one of the conversations with Eckermann (July 5, 1827), Goethe finds the French unable to grasp that the law of the imagination differs from that of the understanding in the same way that poetry differs from prose. Goethe takes much for granted; although he goes no further in his analysis of the poetic imagination and the prose understanding, he suggests the whole question of style, language, diction, rhythm, subject-matter, and expression to have a psychological basis. This same psychological stylistic haunts Coleridge, for the idea of imagination, as a controlling and controlled faculty, stands behind his attempts to define poetry and what sets it apart from prose.

Although Goethe is far from breaking new ground, he beautifully re-states essential considerations. The same is true of his long description of the imagination, appearing in a letter of 1817 to the Grand Duchess Maria Paulowna, where Goethe remarks on Kant's *Critique of Pure Reason:*

> Paragraph three seems to harbor a major deficiency which makes itself felt in the whole development of that philosophy. Here the major facul-ties of the mind are listed as sensation, understanding, and reason. But the imagination is overlooked, causing an irreparable gap. Imagination ... supplements sensation in the form of memory . It submits a pattern of the world to the understanding in the form of experience. It creates or finds sensuous shapes corresponding to the ideas of reason. Thus it gives life to the totality of the self, which would otherwise stagnate.
>
> Whereas imagination performs such services for its sister faculties, it is only through these dear kinfolk that imagination in turn is introduced to the realms of reality and truth. Sensation presents to it shapes of clear and definite contour; the understanding regulates its productive energy; and reason provides it with complete assurance that it is not playing with dream phantoms but is founded on ideas ...
>
> ... Imagination hovers above sensation and is attracted by it. But as soon as imagination spies reason above, it attaches itself firmly to this highest guide. And thus we see the sphere of our modes completely rounded but infinite nevertheless, because one faculty always has need of the others and they all supplement each other mutually.[3]

Goethe probably did not get much beyond the first part of the *Critique*, whether he was reading the first edition of 1781 or, more likely, the sec-ond, 1787 edition where the imagination diminishes in importance, be-cause no one familiar with the *Critique* would make this kind of sweep-ing statement about its shortcomings on the imagination. More important, Goethe describes a multiple power. The stress on memory and on "a pattern ... of experience" recalls Hume, Johnson, and the mid-century psychologists. Goethe also characterizes the imagination as productive and creative, connected to both the sensuous real and the immaterial ideal. The imagination gives the psyche an organic unity, "rounded" yet "infinite" in its constant inner working and communica-tion. The "totality of the self" is created by imagination. Any unity of human life must pivot around it. By focusing on the imagination, Goethe, perhaps even better than Hume or Coleridge, elevates faculty psychology to a formidable and sophisticated picture of the mind, of life itself. Kant himself never made such a clearly rounded statement about the imagination.

Yet even in its potential for harmony the imagination hides something self-destructive. It extrapolates hopes beyond the ability of events to realize them. The imagination can *"ins Leere schwärmen,"* rhapsodize in emptiness. As it jumps back and ahead in time, it may act on foolish desires and try to preserve what must crumble or attain what can never be. In this sense, its "mastery " of time makes us slaves of delusion. Young Werther's opening letter of May 4, 1771, laments how stubbornly the imagination magnifies human sorrows and how vulnerable it is to them: "the pains of man would be less if they were not—God knows why they are made that way—involved with so much restless activity of imagination, recalling memories of past evils before bearing an indifferent present."

But while the past imprisons us through the imagination, the future does, too. In *Dichtung und Wahrheit* Goethe describes the natural human temptation to entertain hopeful projections that may be foiled: "Our desires are premonitions of powers that lie within us, forerunners of those that we shall be in a position to carry out. What we can and might do, our imagination presents outside ourselves and in the future; we feel a longing for that which we already quietly possess. Thus a passionate apprehending of what truly may be transforms it into a dreamt reality."[4] And sometimes, a hope connecting past and future, or a symbolic image of that hope, hypnotizes the imagination and cannot be escaped.

Midway in his trial of love and spirit Werther exclaims prophetically: "I have no other prayer than to her; no form appears to my imagination other than hers, and I see everything in the world around me only in relation to her . . . I often do not know whether I'm living in this world or not . . . I see no end to this suffering but the grave."

The real balance of the imagination is upset by its unreal extrapolations, its tragedy, and its unregulated power then wobbles off in a collision course with personal disaster. A delicate balance must be maintained between awesome psychic forces, for the imagination deals with the inevitable, the probable, the possible, and the improbable all at once, and it must fuse these into a picture of reality that is the only basis for happiness. The imagination becomes "errant" in all senses of the word: adventuresome, bold, wandering, lost, thoroughgoing, treacherous, low, and noble. No matter what it presents—and we cannot afford to ignore what it presents to us, that is the catch—it blurs and fuzzes the edges: "Our imagination is not able even once to give the form of something seen truly, or to conjure up beautiful objects faithfully; always the presentation will contain something misty and indistinct."[5]

This essential message is similar to what Keats says about the life of the imagination in *Lamia* and the odes. Art is a mixed blessing, what Goethe calls "an illusive waking dream, hovering back and forth." The phrase recalls Keats's mention of Adam's "waking dream," which he woke to find true. With luck we can arrive at "a truthfulness of the imagination," a state in which imagination goes beyond the mere reordering of facts but, in its transformation of them, never forgets the principles and laws upon which those facts are built.[6] The imagination can extend reality into the realm of the possible; it can realize the potential of ideas and of desires if it is willing to cast an eye on what determining laws and experiences have already shaped and must continue to shape, on what Keats calls "the van of circumstance." The imagination thus acts both as an emissary between the empirical and the concrete and as an ideal vision of the future, of new knowledge that might be revealed. In a conversation with Eckermann on January 27, 1830, Goethe describes this kind of imagination as it applies to scientific and natural studies, to the *Naturforscher*, but the implication of his statements can be broadened to every endeavor: "I do not mean the imagination that wanders in a vague state and concocts things that do not exist; but . . . the imagination that . . . anticipating the measure of the real and of what is known, proceeds to probable things. Thus it may test whether this anticipation also be possible . . . Such an imagination assumes, however, a broad and even-tempered mind disposed to a large overview of the living world and its laws."

The danger is that in everyday life, especially in contacts with other people, the imagination will rush to paint what we do not have in rosy colors, as if what we are not and what we lack would be, if only *we* had them, a source of happiness. Goethe, in this particular angle of his vision, illuminates, with Hume and Johnson, the heart of human psychology. There is one kind of imagination that projects itself outward, believing that if only its present state were changed, then pleasure would result. This kind of imagination can ignite envy, covetousness, or the canker of dissatisfaction. The creative imagination of art, often fashioning a pleasant, escapist world, can actually intensify this tendency. "Our imagination," says Werther "fed by the fantastical images of poetry, constructs an order of being in which we are the lowest and everything outside of us appears more noble, everyone else of more scope . . . We feel so often that . . . what we lack appears to us to be possessed by another, to whom we then give everything we have for it, and, on top of that, a certain ideal comfort."

But we can escape such subjectivity and see the world and ourselves for what they are, according to Goethe, only through art itself. But the art must draw on the other kind of imagination that opens us to experience, that informs our hearts and minds with truth. Art based on this kind of imagination reaches our "inner sense," Leibniz's "*sens interne*," and exposes us completely to the outside world. This is the familiar theme of fusing subjective and objective, releasing the self from the pit of its own experience, opening it to other experiencing natures.

Goethe, like so many British writers, turns to Shakespeare for this consummate and freeing act of artistic imagination. Shakespeare offers, as Johnson said, "the stability of truth"; that is, he presents people and things as they are, even if they are changing and in flux. And Shakespeare offers this truth to our inner being, our inner sense, through the imagination. Just as the imagination may be the most misleading and seductive of powers, so it can be the most delightful and attractive in presenting truths that would otherwise be lifeless and lacking in that dramatic human interest which makes us want to apply them to our own conduct. Just as Goethe's poetry was described by himself as "occasional," that is, prompted by his own experience, so the imagination is not an abstract but an occasional faculty prompted by experience, but able to extend and transcend it: "Now all throughout, Shakespeare speaks to our inner sense; through this [sense] likewise exists the metaphoric world of the imagination, where consequently there arises an integral work about which we are unable to give ourselves a proper reckoning."[7]

Goethe distinguishes between the imagination and two other qualities. One is *Gefühl* (passion or feeling) and Fichte stresses the difference between imagination and feeling or emotion even more than Goethe; it is even possible that Goethe took the idea from Fichte. The other distinction Goethe makes is between imagination and fancy (*Phantasie*). Although Goethe sometimes uses *Einbildungskraft* and *Phantasie* synonymously, at other times he emphasizes a difference between them. In all of these instances fancy is a more general and unregulated power, incapable of the unifying and productive strength of imagination. Goethe, in a conversation of 1817, speaks of "Fancy, which binds together the most unlikely things and magnifies one circumstance by another." This follows earlier German discussions and many English definitions in attributing to fancy an associative or connecting power, but not the highest power to blend images into new wholes. *Phantastisch* (fantastical) for Goethe has the connotation of something completely unreal, a figment of the imagination. In another context, he clearly intends a difference between fancy and imagination. Art that is bad is not just a product of fancy; it is a twisted use of the stronger power of imagination and thus something that must be attacked and criticized intelligently because of its perverse unity. "There is a uniqueness of the worst kind," says Goethe about Auguste Jacobi's work, "owing to fancy or, even more, to imagination."[8]

Goethe, like Fichte, does not really oppose feeling to imagination. They work to one end. Perhaps because Kant and Tetens had not dealt much with the passionate side of the imagination, and perhaps because Tetens and other Germans, even Herder, had not emphasized the emotionality of the imagination, this "split" was bound to come about. But Goethe is essentially trying to heal it. Most of his references to the two together view them as allies, working in tandem.[9] This line of thought may be behind Coleridge's attempt to formulate a new German word, *"Einbildungsgefühl,"* a power of feeling that unifies what it creates.

## KEATS AND "THE AUTHENTICITY OF THE IMAGINATION"

By the last half of the century, critics had renovated the belief that the poet could produce another world, a re-creation of experience, a "higher" realm of overflowing riches, symbols, and mystery, where myths are born to ravish the sensuous mind. But the Enlightenment had added a new dimension to this belief. Responsibility for creating this other world was now falling exclusively to the imagination. Among English writers in the succeeding generation, Keats seemed pre-eminently gifted to shape this poetic world and to transform the critical hope of the Enlightenment into a tangible accomplishment. His richness of phrasing, sensuous density, and power to surprise and gratify the imagination could seduce both thought and feeling and carry them to "magic casements, opening on the foam/Of perilous seas, in faery lands forlorn."

Keats felt that the overwhelming concern of the modern poet was to find new ways to pry open and exploit new opportunities. The persistent and major concern of Keats's poetry becomes the imagination itself, its uses and pitfalls. We cannot condense the development of his own imagination here, but we shall look at four different themes concerning the imagination that jostle and mix in his thought in a self-transforming process.

The first theme is sympathy or empathy, which for Keats is an imaginative identification so intense that the essence or being of a thing suddenly comes upon us with wonder, as if we were seeing it for the first time and beholding its multiple relations to the universe at large all compacted and implied almost instantaneously. Yet Keats wonders whether this fine energy is a sufficient goal for poetry, and whether the imagination should rather seek truths to lighten and guide the life of the individual heart.

The second major theme is that even as the power of identification produced striking effects, it brought Keats to question—especially with the example of Wordsworth in front of him—the nature of individual identity and of the inner, dramatic life of the psyche, as opposed to the poet who identifies with so many subjects so intensely that his own character is neutralized or "annihilated." Influenced by Hazlitt, Keats realized that the power of identification and the energies it captures, however "fine," are morally neutral. The imagination gives an artist freedom but does not define what he shall serve. The poet's imagination ought to become wise and "philosophic." It should explore all avenues of experience, including the one where we can no longer identify with each person and each thing but must settle on some ideas or "truths," some guides for conduct in life that sift and judge experience and that note the qualities of people beyond their raw energy and immediate fascination.

The third theme is the dangers of the imagination. Keats was supremely talented and bravely committed to earn his livelihood by writing poetry. His personal risk and insight add weight to his treatment of the pitfalls of the imagination in a way no mere theorist can duplicate. In his great odes he creates symbols that the imagination can use to debate with itself its own value, to represent the creative process as art itself, and to engage its own powers in a quest for self-justification. Keats returns to a concern with illusion and reality. He contrasts the pure dreamer who is but "a fever of himself" with the wise poet who becomes "a friend/To sooth the cares, and lift the thoughts of man."

The fourth theme is the several ways in which, Keats hoped, the imaginative power can wrestle down its own darker side and reconcile the opposites and contrarieties of experience. In this category are the poet's own evolution, a sense of organic process, myth, and the hope that writing poetry might actually be the best way for the imagination to work out its own salvation and to purify human motives at large.

### SYMPATHY AND INTENSITY

Keats had himself a vigorous sympathetic imagination and immediately recognized and prized this ability in other poets. His evocative and suggestive language and his vivid concreteness facilitate and express a sympathy with the natural world and, to a lesser extent because of the genres in which he wrote, with the characters he creates. His sympathetic imagination surfaces habitually in descriptions loaded with a Shakespearean weight of phrase and epithet. After all, even when it transcends the sensuous, the imagination must bring sense images into play and appeal to the ear and the inner eye. The force and sudden wonder of poetry, its delight and grasp of reality, depend on "intensity," or what Hazlitt called "gusto." Cowden Clarke describes reading the *Faerie Queene* with Keats, then still in his teens. A line excited him, reports Clarke, and "He *hoisted* himself up and looked burly and dominant, as he said, 'what an image that is—"*sea-shouldering whales!*" ' " In playful "concerts" with friends, Keats delighted in mimicking the low and melancholy sounds and the ungainly shape of the bassoon. He once remarked that "if a Sparrow come before my Window I take part in its existence and pick about the Gravel." At another time, according to his friend Richard Woodhouse, Keats might feel himself a billiard ball and get "a sense of delight from its own roundness, smoothness, volubility, & the rapidity of its motion."[10]

In the intense and immediate act of reaching out of the self, the poet's words capture the naturalness of things and unobtrusively entice the mind to relish them. In a passage from his letters, reminiscent of Wordsworth's Lucy poems, Keats's own imagination seems to feel nature directly and translate life into a universe of open possibilities: "The roaring of the wind is my wife and the Stars through the window pane are my Children ... I feel more and more ... as my imagination strengthens, that I do not live in this world alone but in a thousand worlds."

The imagination can identify with ideas and events, too; it leaps the barriers of time and space. Keats expresses this adventure for himself: "Now to me manners and customs long since passed ... among the Babylonians or the Bactrians are as real, or even more real than those among which I now live."[11]

Shakespeare was for Keats the supreme example of sympathetic imagination. "He has left nothing to say about nothing or any thing," complains Keats in something between jovial mock-despair and real worry. "For look at Snails, you know what he says about Snails ... this is in the Venus and Adonis:

> As the snail, whose tender horns being hit,
> Shrinks back into his shelly cave with pain,
> And there all smothered up in shade doth sit,
> Long after fearing to put forth again."

And a few months later Keats, transferring the image to an aesthetic idea, speaks of a "trembling delicate and snail-horn perception of Beauty." Only with "gusto" or "intensity" can the imagination achieve the breathless astonishment of its greatest effects. The poet "lives in gusto," for intensity or power of presentation elevates even the painful and tragic to a vital energy and provides a cathartic effect. "The excel-

lence of every Art is its intensity, capable of making all disagreeables
evaporate ... Examine King Lear & you will find this exemplified
throughout."[12]

Keats realizes that imaginative identification can nullify his own character in a way similar to Shaftesbury's ideal poet. "Men of genius," he
says in a letter of October 27, 1818, "are great as certain ethereal Chemicals operating on the Mass of neutral intellect—but they have not any
individuality, any determined character." The identities of other people
"pressed" upon his own. The real poet is a "chameleon"—an image
Hazlitt also used—changing to fit his surroundings, "the most unpoeti-
cal of all God's creatures." This is one possible gift of the imagination:
that it merges the self in the world so fully that the self may cease to
exist, and the resulting vision become infinitely more clear, having lost
the sullied accidents and inevitable restrictions of the ego. "It is a
wretched thing to confess," Keats writes, "but is a very fact that not one
word I ever utter can be taken for granted as an opinion growing out of
my identical nature—how can it be, when I have no nature?" The dramatic poet especially has no identity. Living individually and *sub specie
genera*, objective through the sum total of all subjective possibilities, his
imagination can create and assume any identity. In this frame of mind
Keats looked to "a famous gradus ad Parnassum altissimus— ... the
writing of a few fine Plays—my greatest ambition."[13]


## NEGATIVE CAPABILITY AND THE QUESTION OF IDENTITY

Keats maintains that as soon as we lose our identity, we lose our
world-view; our established picture of reality slips away, and poetry
simply generates a series of intense moments. This approach to art affords the mind intellectual and aesthetic freedom. No subject is rejected
out of hand. Each idea conjures up its opposite, and we need not decide
between the two. We probe all explanations for what goes on in the
world, which is more educational in the true sense of the word. We are
thrown, as Keats said, into life's fluid "uncertainties, mysteries, doubts,
without any irritable reaching after fact and reason."[14] No formulas or
analytic molds, none of what Reynolds referred to as "principles falsely
called rational" and what Keats calls "consequitive reasoning," can then
warp our outlook. Truth is so elusive that an *irritable* reaching after it, a
hot pursuit of certainty, only estranges what we seek and crushes what
we grasp for too tightly.

But Keats, being utterly true to this attitude of "Negative Capability," begins to wonder whether it really is the best course for the imagination. One could perhaps be too positive about *it?* The imagination,

after wandering in delightful regions and intense feelings, often of its own making, might grow jaded and cut off from a balanced overview of life. It might enjoy an absolutely unconfined scope, but to what end? A lifetime of such an existence could terrify the soul, which would still face only doubt and uncertainties at death. To give the imagination free reign to annihilate values and identity was to slide toward nihilism. Even Shakespeare's sonnets brimmed with a sincere self—sonnets that Wordsworth called the "key" with which "Shakespeare unlocked his heart."

Although Keats looked askance at the pompous certainties and smug prejudices of some, the fetishes they carried to ward off troubles and even truth, he also recognized that philosophic wisdom was necessary and that the imagination must seek out and incorporate it. He does not perceive "how any thing can be known for truth by consequitive reasoning," but he nevertheless admits, *"and yet it must be."*[15] In fact, it was largely "consequitive" reasoners like Gerard and Kant who had established and elaborated the idea of the imagination to the point where Keats and the Romantics could develop and extend it. Keats felt sure that the imagination should explore and assimilate that quality of thought called wisdom. His first test of this hope is a period of limbo when the imagination has come "beyond its proper bound," beyond the narrowly fictive and the self-indulgent, but has not yet secured a definite guide or even rule of thumb for its own activity:

> to philosophise
> I dare not yet! . . .
> . . . is it that imagination brought
> Beyond its proper bound, yet still confin'd,
> Lost in a sort of Purgatory blind,
> Cannot refer to any standard law
> Of either earth or heaven?[16]

"Intensity"—the kind of feeling roused by "the anxiety of a Deer"—and the immediate energies of imagery may be "the very thing in which consists poetry." But "if so it is not so fine a thing as philosophy—For the same reason that an eagle is not so fine a thing as a truth." Keats also remarks that a "fine writer is the most genuine Being in the world," "excepting the human friend Philosopher," a use of the word "friend" in connection with the life of the philosophic imagination that would have pleased Coleridge.[17] Keats was beginning to see that the imagination must weave itself in the mingled yarn of life. It must enter the "van of circumstance" that brings change, pain, and sorrow. An enclave of imagined luxury fails in the long run. If nothing else, we would rebel against its eventual boredom. More likely, some event would break into our lives and dissolve our castle-building. This is one theme of the "Ode to Melancholy," where a sad, strong passion lies side by side with dying beauty and with joy, "whose hand is ever at his lips/Bidding adieu." If the imagination carries us to a sweet refuge and bower as in the beginning of *Endymion*, it simultaneously imprisons us in a graver and sadder realm:

> Ay, in the very temple of Delight
>   Veil'd Melancholy has her sovran shrine,
>     Though seen of none save him whose strenuous tongue
> Can burst Joy's grape against his palate fine;
>   His soul shall taste the sadness of her might,
>     And be among her cloudy trophies hung.

Keats speaks of the years that bring the philosophic mind, and again echoing Wordsworth, he hopes that "Knowledge" may "ease the Burden of the Mystery: a thing I begin to understand a little." What he had once called "the authenticity of the Imagination" must now taste a bittersweet fruit, not treat life's "wakeful anguish" with narcotics, but with a more pungent corrective.[18]

If what is important is the way in which the individual imagination perceives and shapes reality, then this inner process of mind, with the personal identity it constructs, should become a subject for poetry. Wordsworth seemed to think so, and Keats looked to him as illuminating the darker corridors of experience and leaving "the chamber of Maiden Thought" behind. So many things seemed to derive their worth from the "ardour of mental pursuit" spent on them—meaning by the word "mental," as Blake does, *"imaginative"* pursuit.[19] That is the whole idea behind sympathy. As a result, the most worthwhile subject to examine is the inner life of the mind and spirit. The imagination can trace the development of the self, what Coleridge and Schelling called the mind in its "process of self-construction," a phrase that has rough analogies in Keats's "vale of soul-making" and "system of Spirit-creation." This turning of the imagination to its own identity helps to explain what the "Ode to Psyche" is all about. The individual heart and mind become their own subject, and through their activity the world becomes "philosophically considered," to use Johnson's phrase, and can be expressed by an infinite number of images.

Poetry need no longer rely exclusively on the simple appearance or "gusto" of external nature. This self-examination is not a retreat into the subjective ego but a movement toward the drama, "the greeting of the spirit" as Keats put it, that goes on between the self and the world. Keats was reaching the same point of view arrived at by Leibniz and Shaftesbury and echoed down through Kant, Fichte, Schelling, and Coleridge.

In fact, many important philosophers from 1750 to 1820 either end their careers or occupy themselves throughout their careers with an increasing focus on aesthetics, art, poetry, and even myth. This was the case with Kant, Hume, Schelling, and with the associationists. Conversely, many poets discovered the zest and importance of philosophic or religious ideas to their art—not abstract ideas but ones that affect how we perceive the world and conduct ourselves in it. Keats, Shelley, Schiller, Goethe, Blake, and Wordsworth are examples. Someone like Coleridge, "poet, metaphysician, bard," fits both ways. As Leonhard Meister put it, the imagination of the poet or of the religious fanatic must get in touch with philosophy. The reason for this marriage of philosophy and poetry, which Keats was realizing, has to do largely with the rise of the idea of the imagination. Rarely since ancient Greece had poetry and philosophy enjoyed such an entwined growth in so much literature and thought, produced by so many individuals.

In the self-construction of the imaginative process as Keats heralds it in the first of the great odes, the "Ode to Psyche"—the first poem, he says, in which he really took "pains"—Cupid or Love is present at the end of the poem not only as the traditional partner of Psyche but also as an expression of the notion, found as well in Coleridge, Blake, Wordsworth, Shelley, Baader and Schelling, that love is the bond between the self and the world, the way that the imagination cares for what it has perceived and created. The whole tenor of the poem indicates that the imagination is questioning itself, trying to direct and reveal its own power and pry open its own secrets. So Keats addresses Psyche: "And pardon that thy secrets should be sung/Even into thine own soft-conched ear."

Even as the poet's imagination turns to the outside world, it is also turning to the inner self, to the soul, and this necessary turning of "a working brain" is the ultimate act of the imagination, for now it can begin to reconcile the self and its own "shadowy thought" with worldly substance. Coleridge, too, remarks that the best part of language is derived from a "reflection on the acts of the mind itself . . . formed by a voluntary appropriation of fixed symbols to internal acts, to processes and results of imagination." Keats chooses Psyche as a fixed symbol of all internal acts of the mind and therefore as a symbol of the mind's reflection on its own acts and imagination. Psyche, thus seen by Keats as the "latest born and loveliest vision far/Of all Olympus' faded hierarchy," subsumes and transforms nature. Introduced by Apuleius' *Golden Ass* in the second century A.D., Psyche was in fact the last goddess to enter the pantheon. Schelling, too, in his oration *Concerning the Relation of the Plastic Arts to Nature* (1807), had seen that "by virtue of the pre-eminence" which the fable of Psyche gave "to the soul," the story concluded the cycle of the old stories of the gods; *it closed an imaginative circle* and permitted art "to attain a new, if higher, level."

Describing his own commitment to his new emphasis on the life of the individual imagination and its artistic treatment, Keats transforms images of nature into mental images, nature "philosophically considered" as Johnson had said seventy years before:

> Yes, I will be thy priest, and build a fane
> In some untrodden region of my mind,
> Where branched thoughts, new grown with·
> pleasant pain,
> Instead of pines shall murmur in the wind.

Since exploration of the psyche performed (as it was) by the imagination was a form of self-exploration, then all the better, provided it did not become solipsistic and provided it remained open to other created objects and kept that "casement ope at night,/To let the warm Love in!"

By undertaking this new course, the poet would acquire a personal identity. Perhaps that was necessary. As Keats said in a different context, which nevertheless applies to the new direction of the imagination and the psyche, poetry "must be kept up." The ideal of the characterless poet might not work now. To use Schiller's distinction, Keats saw that the creative imagination, attaining a sophisticated consciousness of itself, might have to be "sentimental" rather than "naive" in order to accomplish anything new. Keats also sensed that not only does the individual poet grow and evolve in his own career, but art and poetry have a collective imagination which evolves through history and can "subdue" individual intellects to the course of a collective imagination.

### THE TREASON OF THE IMAGINATION

One pitfall remained ever-present. Keats knew, from personal achievement, how beauty of language and escapist charm can outshine other poetic considerations. *The Eve of St. Agnes* could, in one light, be looked on as a charming but vapid indulgence. Like Shakespeare and, later, Thomas Mann, Keats became profoundly aware how the great artist's vision can teeter on the verge of a convincing illusion and how a master of the imagination can contrive specious comfort through dreams, even in the guise of rejecting them. The retractions of Chaucer, Boccaccio, and Tolstoy come to mind. Few since Johnson, and no one in the Romantic period with the possible exceptions of Coleridge, Byron, Goethe, and Schelling, examined the treacheries of the imagination with more honest scrutiny than Keats, although on the surface, the theme of delusive, restless imagination was common. Keats puts it in a light mood in *Fancy:*

> Ever let the fancy roam
> Pleasure never is at home
> . . . . . . . . . . . . . . . . .
> Where's the cheek that doth not fade,
> Too much gaz'd at?

And Cowper in *The Task* (I, 537–543) shows that fancy is "Delusive most where warmest wishes are." Still, Keats trusted the imagination as the only way out of its own labyrinth; his suspicions are therefore not rationalistic but spring from an imaginative stance that struggles to be self-corrective.

Keats knew he had little solid religious or philosophic background on which to base the quest of the imagination. The "holiness of the heart's affections" and a regular stepping of the imagination toward truth were not clearly defined ideals nor ways, in and of themselves, to produce good poetry. They were not complex enough, not tempered adequately. And if the imagination turned to itself both as its own subject and as a self-corrective, this offered not only hope but an easy chance for self-deception. The imagination might spiral downward into illusion. Each attempt to escape would then add to the unreality and increase the poet's isolation, making his inner mind and judgment like a carnival house of mirrors.

Much of Keats's greatest poetry is concerned with art in general, but more specifically with the creative imagination itself and how it not only promises the clearest vision of life but also operates with a terrible inner vulnerability to deception and weaknesses. Once its judgment or gyroscope goes kilter, whether this standard is called "beauty," "truth," "goodness" or "greatness," the imagination falters blindly.

The symbols of art in two of Keats's odes, the nightingale and the urn, offer hope that the imaginative life, able to create other worlds and to luxuriate in both history and faery lands, might reconcile humanity to the pain and transitory pleasure of earthly life. But the last stanza of the "Nightingale," where the bird fades away and the narrator is left doubting the nature of the whole experience, severely questions the ultimate stamina and worth of the imagination: "Forlorn! the very word is like a bell/To toll me back from thee to my sole self!" The stanza has earlier, though weaker, counterparts. Cowper in *The Task* (IV, 302–307), for instance, speaks of being "reclin'd at ease" until "the freezing blast,"

> snapping short
> The glassy threads, with which the fancy weaves
> Her brittle toys, restores me to myself.

The individual heart remains in puzzlement where, as Keats says, "but to think is to be full of sorrow." Although the resolution offered by the Grecian urn seems more secure, the urn also freezes life in a tragic as well as a beautiful pose. Its unheard melody mediates between real events and an eternal, imaginative realm, but nothing ever happens. The comfort that the urn offers is nothing more than the affirmation that life is hard and that great poetry yields something like what Keats got from *King Lear*: "The bitter-sweet of this Shakespearean fruit." If the goal of the imagination is simply to report on what experience is, it must then give up the transforming and magical power of art and abandon the attempt to "burst our mortal bars" for fear that any result is bound to be unrealistic and deceptive. Both odes catch the imagination as it is questioning itself. Keats knew that the imagination could not continue to be its own subject forever. A dangerous artistic incest, such action would lead to no resolutions at all. But he nevertheless tried, through the use of poetry itself, to discover what relationship between life and art constitutes "the authenticity of the Imagination."

*Lamia* darkly suggests that wisdom and knowledge may be at odds with a certain kind of imagination. Although the poem ends ambiguously, it denies imaginative art as an exclusive ideal; it ends in the sorrow and destruction symbolized by Lamia's serpent character and her crown of willow and adder's tongue. But with all the gifts of imagination on her side, she manages to appear genuine to almost everyone. The false imagination may be as strong or stronger than the helpful and truthful one. Keats senses a danger in what had been urged since the 1760s, the placing of judgment completely within the bounds of imaginative power.

The *Fall of Hyperion*, the last of Keats's longer poems, exposes the inner tensions and motives of the poet's imagination in a more personal voice. Six months before he died, Keats wrote to Shelley that, "My Imagination is a Monastry, and I am its Monk." The *Fall of Hyperion* asks whether the poet's seeming withdrawal from life is a crazy dream or something of real worth. In the poem, the idea of the imagination remains two-edged, but the debate broadens to ask what end or purpose the imagination should serve. Identifying such an end as clearly as possible is the way to proceed, since like all human capacities, the imagination can be turned to ends both good and bad:

> Whether the dream now purpos'd to rehearse
> Be poet's or fanatic's will be known
> When this warm scribe, my hand, is in the grave.

The poet (or visionary) and the dreamer are "sheer opposites" and "antipodes" because they employ the one thing they have in common, a lively imagination, in opposite directions. The dreamer, admonished as "a fever of thyself," must rechannel his imagination in order to become a humanist, a sage, and a physician to the spirit. Without this higher calling and change of identity, the dreamer's "beauty" or "intensity" is counterfeit.

TENTATIVE ANSWERS

The themes of the imagination intermingle during Keats's rapid development of four or five years. These include "intensity" and sympathetic identification, with their accompanying receptivity, speculation, and "Negative Capability"; "philosophy," or a belief that the poet should embody wisdom and knowledge and explore the individual psyche even at the risk of endangering the ideal of a characterless poet; and the treasonable side of the imagination, or the inability of art to be trusted to purify the imagination and to conduct life. The question was how to resolve these concerns.

Keats developed several tentative answers. Throughout his poetry we meet with the idea that the imagination can fuse the material and real world to spiritual or "ethereal" truths and elevate the mundane without indulging in a dream world. This union of corporeal and ethereal had become a major theme of the imagination in the eighteenth-century. In his own way Keats is trying independently to bring together the empirical and the Shaftesbury-Platonic traditions. He characterizes the imaginative genius as an ethereal chemical transforming "the Mass of neutral intellect." Using Adam's dream (which Adam awoke to find true) to symbolize the essential identity of the life of spirit and ideas with its counterpart on earth, Keats describes the dream as "a conviction that Imagination and its empyreal reflection is the same as human Life and its spiritual repetition."[20] The complex self-scrutiny of the imagination becomes a question of waking and dreaming, as in the close of *Ode to a Nightingale*: "Was it a vision, or a waking dream?/Fled is that music:—Do I wake or sleep?"—Or the conclusion of "What the Thrush Said": "And he's awake who thinks himself asleep." The phrase "waking dream" occurs in Cowper's *Task* (IV, 286–290), which also has some affinities with Coleridge's *Frost at Midnight*. Cowper confesses:

> Me oft has fancy, ludicrous and wild,
> Sooth'd with a waking dream ...
>                    ... while with poring eye
> I gaz'd, myself creating what I saw.

In *Endymion* Keats asks Pan to

> be still the leaven,
> That spreading in this dull and clodded earth
> Gives it a touch ethereal—a new birth.

Here is the "greeting of the spirit" in action, the spiritual or transcendental which rescues the "dull and clodded" even as the concrete rescues the spiritual and permits it to enter our lives in tangible form. This imaginative act is the interest, the *inter esse,* of poetry. As the spiritual or ethereal shapes and informs the concrete, symbols or "hieroglyphics" are being created. Keats explains that "The spiritual is felt when the . . . letters and points of charactered language show like the hieroglyphics of beauty;—the mysterious signs of an immortal free-masonry!"[21] These, in the *Fall of Hyperion,* are

> symbols divine,
> Manifestations of that beauteous life
> Diffus'd unseen throughout eternal space.

Yet this speculation about symbols had more to do with the way in which the imagination works than with specific spiritual values. The question remained whether spiritual truth was simply "to envisage circumstance, all calm," and regard that as "the top of sovereignty."

Another guide for the imagination might be "beauty," but "beauty" wobbles in meaning for Keats. Early in his career it tends to equal "intensity." Later, as the urn seems to say, it is something larger called "truth," which Douglas Bush has suggested might better be taken to mean "reality." This is the stark "Real of Beauty" Keats apprehends during his visit to the tomb of Burns. Or then again, "beauty" may be a shorthand term for the unity of real and ethereal, or it may be some intuitive standard of judgment. The word hampered Keats, as it did many Romantics. It was at once too open and too liable to be restricted. The word gave room and leeway but failed to preserve the original meaning intact.

Yet the change alone in the meaning of beauty for Keats indicates something vital. In the two *Hyperions* "beauty" changes into "a fresh perfection" brought by the new deities, "a power more strong in beauty." The imagination must work through a process in time; it is self-transforming. The poet must develop in stages, the imagination working out its own salvation. In a fluid world, which, as Prospero said, will one day dissolve and leave "not a rack behind," the imagination must move, too, and change its stance. As early as "Sleep and Poetry " Keats had outlined a process or program for the imagination. It begins with pastoral imagery and nature seen in its intensity, then proceeds to "a lovely tale of human life." This is not the end, however, for the poet must pass on to a deeper, more tragic sense, a third level, where we find "the agonies, the strife/Of human hearts." Finally, on a fourth level, all is subsumed into a mythic and symbolic stage where life is seen "most awfully intent" through the creation of visionary figures, who redeem everything into an eternal present and themselves dissolve into the light of heaven. These stages represent more than an organic process in nature; they give a sense of the organic and developing process of the individual imagination as it matures.

Keats's search to unfold the imaginative life also starts to develop a path atypical of British thought at that time. It would usually be thought of as German. In the two *Hyperions* a vast historical movement and shift of power rumbles around the poet. It catches him in the twilight of one race of gods and the rise of another. There is a collective imagination of civilization that changes and carries the poet with it. Keats thought Wordsworth a more timely example to follow than Milton because Wordsworth was reacting and contributing to the present state of the collective imagination. Yet Milton "had sure as great powers." Keats therefore infers that a "general and gregarious advance of intellect . . . really a grand march of intellect . . . a mighty providence subdues the mightiest minds to the service of the time being."[22] This idea appears in Coleridge's Philosophical Lectures of 1818–1819, which center on "the gradual Evolution of the Mind of the World, contemplated as a single Mind in the different successive Stages of its development." The idea may be inferred from Hazlitt's "Spirit of the Age" and also from Shelley's *Defence of Poetry*, which refers to the "all-penetrating spirit" of poets as "less their spirit than the spirit of the age."

Keats saw this idea in a new way and put it into mythic shape in his poetry. Herder, the Schlegels, Schelling, and Goethe also explored this collective evolution of the artistic and imaginative mind. Schelling, in his *Oration Concerning . . . the Plastic Arts*, had spoken about "the oldest and most powerful epoch of liberated art," which occurred, "according to the poetic myths of the allegorical primeval world, after the embrace of Uranus the earth first brought forth Titans and heaven-storming giants, before it produced the gentle realm of tranquil gods." Keats tries to recapture in the second *Hyperion* that puzzling but undeniable change from the oldest epoch of art to the "tranquil gods," the shift to a "new beauty" challenging the poet. There is a *Geistesentwicklung* or spirit-evolution of the imagination, what Hegel called the "*Entwicklungsgeschichte des Geistes*," the evolutionary history of the spirit.

There are, then, no permanently frozen guides for the imagination.

The fluid, organic universe of things, of ideas, and of the mind itself will not permit it. There is, as Coleridge said, an eternal act of creation. It seems to Keats that one of the important ways to keep the imagination aware, alive, and responsive to personal changes and to changes in mankind at large is poetry itself, which

> alone can save
> Imagination from the sable chain
> And dumb enchantment.

# PART SIX

# *Harmony of Being*

# 2 0

# SCHELLING

*O*ptimistic and visionary, Friedrich Schelling (1775–1854) united transcendental philosophy with a philosophy of nature. He wanted to show that these two general systems are merely different ways of approaching one world-view, which ultimately relies on "an aesthetic act of the imagination." As part of his "New Philosophy," he developed a concept of the imagination as a manifold power. At its most general level, imagination interfuses and joins the "transcendental" philosophy of mind with the "nature philosophy" of physical reality. Without this umbilical cord of imagination, these two elements in Schelling's thought would separate and die. In the course of thrusting forward the idea of unity, Schelling progressed through three or four major stages. After his rejection of Fichte's subjective idealism, he went on successively to the *Naturphilosophie*, then to an objective or transcendental idealism, thence to the *Identitätssystem*, finally ending his career with work on myth and theology, a theistic or "existential" phase. His thought evolved naturally and was progressively inclusive. His trek through various and ever more encompassing systems exemplifies his own contention that all intelligent life, including God, struggles to fulfill its own potential through the process of "self-construction."

The creative imagination climaxes Schelling's New Philosophy, which includes all but his earliest Fichtean and last "existential" phase. Part of this philosophy, the Philosophy of Art, tries to bind together the philosophies of nature and of mind by seeing in works of art, in their highest and best sense, a unity of man's self-conscious and free intelligence with nature's material and objective reality. Through creative imagination the mind affirms its own existence by joining its subjective impulses and perceptions with the particulars of nature. The resulting work of art, or *Kunstprodukt*, is itself real and objective, a token and a promise to man; it *symbolizes* the union of the mind's free and willful consciousness with the independent and given nature of the cosmos. The power to produce this unifying symbol is the power of *"In-Eins-Bildung,"* or *Einbildungskraft,* imagination. As the dialectic between self and nature, the imagination reconciles and fuses the transcendental intelligence with the material system of nature. The living symbol and talisman of this union is, Schiller contended, an aesthetic perception, the work of art itself. Art has a vital epistemological function. Art is a dialectic: *"Ohne dialektische Kunst ist keine wissenschaftliche Philosophie."*[1]

Schelling believed that in the philosophies of the late seventeenth and eighteenth centuries a dualism had split man from nature and cut the human psyche from its moorings in physical and spiritual realities. The self could no longer trust its own knowledge; the ego languished in subjectivity. Descartes had widened the gulf between the self and external reality by placing the burden of self-affirmation, the proof of self-existence, on nothing but the ego's own power: *cogito, ergo sum.* Kant showed how impossible it is for the mind to verify its own knowledge and thereby aggravated the split between man's intelligence and the laws of the universe.[2]

Schelling takes the problem of the subjective *"Ich bin,"* as opposed to the objective universe, the *"es gibt,"* and attempts to resolve their dualism. Consonant with his hunger for synthetic unity, he sees the two premises as polar opposites contained within one approach. What he now requires is some force or creative power to transform the "subjective," transcendental pole into the "objective" pole of nature and the cosmos. This power of transformation must also reverse itself, carrying on a two-way commerce between the ideal realm of thought and the real realm of tangible bodies, time and space. Imagination, the power of *"In-Eins-Bildung,"* becomes this productive and creative power in the universe. It changes thought into substance and finds in each individual thing the inner, formative spirit of its creation.[3]

Schelling uses many pairs to clarify the nature of the two poles connected by the imagination. On the one side are finite form, matter in its particular and concrete manifestation, the individual, nature, and works of art. This pole includes a beautiful tropical fish, Saturn's shadow cast on its own rings, and the Apollo Belvedere. On the other side are infinite being, spirit in a universal or abstract mode, the race or type, the mind of God, and the mind of man. This is where God broods over the face of the waters, where the Logos of St. John speaks, and where souls feel what Buddha calls Nirvana. The "productive power," apparently no thing in itself, is the power that creates all things. More dramatically, it is the power to make galaxies out of a seeming vacuum, worlds out of stellar dust, and the *Last Supper* from dyes and wet plaster. Only by exercising this pervading creative spirit in both man and nature, only by re-attaining a pre-established harmony, can perception and reality, the ideal and the real, work through each other and become one.

## THE KEYSTONE OF THE IMAGINATION

Schelling's philosophy and sense of the imagination are fundamentally ideal. Like concepts of modern physics, his philosophical concepts are unusually difficult to picture concretely. He appeals to a transcendent idea of the universe and of the universal creative power. He formulates his idea of art in philosophical terms. At times he is excessively abstract, even murky. Frequently a term or category runs riot, as if he were keeping a cross-referenced file on the universe. The appeal is often to speculation rather than to empirical concreteness or psychology. He possesses the curiosity and imagination of the greatest scientists, but his scientific knowledge is naive. He is not a strong and practical critic of art, and he wrote little criticism. But Schelling's strengths and virtues capture those fresh and wonderful years of philosophy, science, and art when the Enlightenment flowered into Romanticism. He combines the best of both worlds. He attempts what every great philosopher must: he confronts the basic puzzles of life. He asks why there is something instead of nothing. He combines science, philosophy, religion, and art. Without substituting art for religion, he makes high claims for art. Passion galvanizes his articulate pleas.

His style sparkles, his lectures entranced audiences. Even while juggling philosophical terms, he never forgets that philosophy is a human pursuit. His philosophy searches for and explores "totality," a meaningful grasp of the universe. He seeks for the truth not of an isolated formula but of a new philosophy that would rejoin man with nature and realize both as one life whose form and identity are shaped by that imaginative power which springs from the ground of all being and which inevitably leads man, in his own highest imagination, to return to that ground of being.

Schelling is difficult. He offers a plethora of definitions and terms. To arrive at an understanding of him is like navigating through the Nile Delta to the sea. Main channels disappear. The current loses force and direction. But at the end there is the sea, as surely as there is the snow on the inland mountains.

Like Coleridge, Schelling sees reason, in its broadest sense, as the inclusion of all faculties—understanding, imagination, and the senses—as these are governed and informed by the realm of ideas. "But reason contains within itself sense, understanding, and imagination as just so many distinctivities, without itself being any one of these in particular." Imagination differs from reason by actually forming a perception, image, symbol, or work of art that embodies concretely what in reason remains as a potential, something ideal and purely intelligential. Imagination gives the "clarity" and "fullness" of reason a concrete form, a finite representation in the cosmos. Imagination reveals the connection of these particulars to the universal forms of reason. "Thus imagination is related to reason as fancy is to the understanding. The former is productive, the latter reproductive . . . Outside reason there is nothing, and all is contained in it."[4]

God's divine imagination, *"die göttliche Einbildungskraft,"* is the generating power of the universe. The word "nature," after all, means what is generated, and the imaginative or artistic person is a "genius," which has the same word origin as both "nature" and "generate." *Der Weltsystem*, the complete organization and purpose of the universe, is God's reason. Its material form exists through the power of divine imagination saturating the cosmos:

> As the sun stands freely in the heavens, joining and uniting all in the power of its clear light, so the soul of eternal nature stands in the interlinkage [of being] itself as the unity and, so to speak, as the divine imagination of that linkage, free and unbounded, as the origin of all feeling existence, which in visible nature pulsates as the heart. And, moving and circulating everything in nature's holy body, it gives rise to each impulse and to the intimacy of all creation.[5]

Imagination is both a divine and a human attribute. God's imagination shapes man and the universe. Man's imagination, with its highest activity as art, is an analog, on a smaller scale, of this holy power of eternal creation:

> Through art, divine creation is presented objectively, since it rests on the same idea of the infinite ideal dwelling in the real on which the creation of art rests. The exquisite German word *Einbildungskraft* actually means the power of forming into one, an act on which all creation is founded. It is the power through which an ideal is also something real, the soul the body; it is the power of individuation, which of all is the truly creative one.[6]

This definition dwells on an important meaning of the word as not only Schelling but also Tetens, Herder, and Coleridge understood it: the power of shaping into one: Coleridge's "esemplastic." Schelling means *Einbildungskraft* to carry the weight of *"In-Eins-Bildung."* The

Absolute, or God, is itself *"die ewige In-Eins-Bildung des Allgemeinen und Besondern,"* the eternal forming-into-one of the universal and the particular, and art is the human reflection of this unity. Living in each creature and image of the real world is an idea that is continually being brought to fruition. The ideal lives in and through the actual. Imagination creates the real image, the living language and symbol of ideal reason. Imagination potentizes reason, releases its potential, and makes ideas productive: they appear in material form. Only imagination, then, can direct us to the highest calling of philosophy—the Absolute, or God. And since art is that activity of man which most closely resembles the creative imagination of God, the highest philosophy is the philosophy of art. Art represents the mind's informing ideas as well as the presence of nature. It symbolizes the two as one in the work of art itself: "Each true work of art created by the imagination is the resolution of the contradiction similar to the one that in ideas is presented as a unity. The mere reflective understanding grasps only simple series and hence grasps an idea, as the synthesis of opposites, as a contradiction."[7]

In each object or work of art it creates, the imagination fuses a universal form, the infinite or *"Unendliche,"* and a finite, individual manifestation. The idea of form, and form's concretion as matter, become indivisibly one and exist in and through one another. In the imaginative act two unities are formed, each of which is really the other. Form becomes being and being becomes form. Thus, in the imaginative creation of the universe at large, there are *"Natur und Gott, in gleicher ewigen Durchdringung,"* nature and God, forever passing through one another.[8]

Since *Kraft* means power or force, imagination for Schelling is an immaterial and even mysterious energy. It exists only as it charges and guides, like magnetism, electricity, or gravity, the making of a new relation or work of art. Imaginative creation presupposes a dialectic between what is infinite or ideal and what is finite and real. Nature itself is the differentiation of the Absolute into many forms of matter. The forms of nature as they appear to us are each "only one moment or point of process in the eternal act of the realization of identity from opposites."[9] The particular objects in nature, *"die Naturseite,"* express only one side of things. The other side is the "idea of multiplicity in unity, of the finite in the infinite." This is the ideal or spiritual realm, the realm in which things first existed as ideas, and to which they finally return. Imaginative creation thus involves both a centripetal force of unification and a centrifugal force of differentiation. The presence of God and the static existence of ideas are at the center of these forces. Coleridge expresses a similar concept.

In these two actions of the real becoming ideal and the ideal shifting into the real, there is a point of intersection much like the point equidistant between magnetic poles. Here the creation appears simultaneously real and ideal, "*beides in Eins gebildet sein.*" This process exemplifies the polar logic, the "dynamic process" that also entrances Bruno, Jacobi, and Coleridge. All creation and productivity has at its heart the opposition, the mutual interchange and working through to a final identity, of the universal or ideal and the particular. In this process they build a point of unity (*Indifferenzpunkt*), which represents both concrete nature and the heaven-descended law. This is, in a sense, the middle ground that Synesius mentions in his prayer as quoted by Coleridge in the *Biographia*. The result of the two forces, or the dialectic of *Einbildung*—of the real and the ideal, the natural and the transcendental—is a third force, "*eine dritte.*" This is what Coleridge refers to as the *tertium aliquid*, a third element which is the synthesis of the dialectic.[10]

### LEVELS OF THE IMAGINATION

In his *System des transzendentalen Idealismus*, among other places, Schelling uses *Einbildungskraft* to describe that power mediating between the ideal and the real, the ego and nature, the theoretical and the practical. First he uses *Einbildungskraft* as a shorthand or "common" term without quibbling about its connotations. In our perception of the world we have a faculty that both vacillates between and joins the ideas of reason and the particular qualities of objects that are sensed directly. But in order to mediate between reason and understanding, this faculty must produce something that is neither an idea nor an object—something in between. This *produktive Anschauung* or productive intuition connects the senses, understanding, and reason. It permits the mind to operate as an integral unit. This form of imagination is creative not in the artistic sense but in the sense of presenting to the self a meaningful and related vision of what it perceives in the external world. This activity of imagination is allied more with perception and reproduction than with artistic creativity.[11]

Some confusion arises, because *Einbildungskraft* thus takes on more than one meaning. Schelling hesitates to use *Einbildungskraft* only in connection with perception or productive intuition, which hobbles the term. Following the practice of others, including Kant, Tetens, and Fichte, Schelling holds in reserve what he believes to be the highest and fullest import of *Einbildungskraft*, presenting this meaning in the last chapters dealing with art in the *System*.

Schelling, like Coleridge, gives imagination at least two functions in the human mind. We receive elementary stimuli from the outside world, such as noise, light, color, hardness, stench, and sweetness. These are the stuff of Schelling's *ursprüngliche Anschauung* or original sensory perception, and he calls this stage of mind the first potential or power: "*erste Potenz.*" But these stimuli are then grouped, ordered, and arranged into objects, and these groupings have a connection with the world of forms and ideas. We do not see just light and color, but a painting: we do more than sense sweetness, we taste sugared tea. We compare the passive perceptions in ourselves with our active ordering of them. The two, active and passive, interplay in an unending dialectic. This process Schelling calls, somewhat ambiguously, "*produktive Anschauung,*" or productive perception or intuition. It might be better called *re*productive, because he stresses that the mind is building up a comprehensive picture of what is already in the world. This *produktive Anschauung* is the second power or "*zweite Potenz*" of the imagination. The perceiver and what is perceived struggle to become one. They merge, then a new perception must be assimilated, and they separate, then merge again. The imagination here is that kind exercised in reading a book but not in writing it. The process goes on and on. In this sense, it is the mind's "eternal act of creation," striving to contain the world within itself, as part of its own identity. However, the result is never satisfactorily objective. The assimilation is always directed inward and forms a purely mental or subjective synthesis, an intellectual perception or intuition ("*intellektuelle Anschauung*"). This is as far as transcendental philosophy can go, as far as Fichte went. It cannot put the mind's own images and ideas into an objective and real form that is outside the mind itself.

For this, the imagination must work in its highest potential or power ("*höchste Potenz*"), and this is the creative power of art. Schelling calls this power *Kunstvermögen* or *Dichtungsvermögen*, terms favored by Sulzer and Tetens, who was indebted to Gerard. This is the normal meaning of creative or productive power and should not be confused with Schelling's *produktive Vermögen*, which is of lesser power. Imagination in this highest level, as *Kunstvermögen* or *Dichtungsvermögen*, yields *Kunstanschauung* or "*eine ästhetische Anschauung,*" the artistic or aesthetic intuition. It creates a definite new form, the work of art, which expresses the mind's relationships to its own perceptions and to the external world. What is more, the work of art is external and objective. The mind has created something that releases itself from a neverending series of perceptions and self-perceptions. The work of art is unmistakably a part of the world, a part of nature, yet also a part fashioned by a free act of mind.[12] Schelling's view of the imagination may be charted:

| | |
|---|---|
| *erste Potenz* | without consciousness; original perception of the senses |
| *zweite Potenz* | consciousness; *Einbildungskraft* as intellectual intuition or perception |
| ↓ *dritte oder höchste Potenz* | self-consciousness; *Einbildungskraft* as *Kunst-* or *Dichtungsvermögen;* aesthetic or artistic perception[13] |

The intellectual perception becomes objective only through the aesthetic perception or work of art. Philosophy itself can stand on objective grounds only when it embraces the productive power of art. The highest power, or *Kunstvermögen*, subsumes and incorporates the two lesser ones; the scale is progressively inclusive and all of it may be called "imagination." Near the end of the *System*, Schelling says of this power: "As yet we have not been able to grasp this process fully because only the artistic power [*Kunstvermögen*], can completely reveal it ... It is the creative imagination [*Dichtungsvermögen*], what in the first potentiality is original perception [*ursprüngliche Anschauung*] and, conversely, in its highest potentiality is simply the repetition of productive perception [*produktive Anschauung*], in which case we call it the poetic imagination [*Dichtungsvermögen*]. That power which is active in both, the only power by which we are able to conceive of and to unite the contradictory, is one and the same—the imagination [*Einbildungskraft*]."[14]

Schelling explains the highest level of imagination, the power of *Kunstanschauung*, as "*die in der höchsten Potenz sich widerholende produktive Anschauung,*" a repeating or echoing in a higher sense of the lower power of *produktive Anschauung*, or productive perception. Here, as in his whole scheme of the imagination, there are parallels to Coleridge's remark on primary and secondary imagination. Coleridge's primary imagination corresponds to that level required for the *productive* or *intellectual intuition;* the secondary imagination is like Schelling's *Kunst- oder Dichtungsvermögen*. Coleridge considers the secondary as "an echo" of the primary, similar in kind but differing in degree. This is similar to Schelling's description of *Dichtungsvermögen* as "*die in der höchsten Potenz sich widerholende produktive Anschauung.*" Whereas Schelling's *productive intuition* is not creative or artistic, the *Kunst-* or *Dichtungsvermögen* is. What Schelling calls the second power or potential (*die zweite Potenz*), Coleridge calls primary. He, unlike Schelling, does not give a level of power to the merely sensory or *ursprüngliche Anschauung*. Schelling's *dritte* or *höchste Potenz* is therefore like Coleridge's secondary imagination.

In his remarks on the primary and secondary imagination Coleridge also had an eye to Tetens, who preceded Schelling by twenty-five or thirty years. Tetens and Schelling use similar terms and break the imagination down in similar ways. Coleridge read both their discussions relevant to arranging the imagination into separate levels of power. Chapter 12 of the *Biographia* relies to some degree on Schelling's *System des transzendentalen Idealismus* with respect to the levels of imagination; on this subject, the progression in the two books is similar. Thus, Schelling re-enforces Tetens' contribution to Coleridge's distinction. Although there is no proof, it is extremely likely that Schelling read Tetens, for Tetens had a wide influence. Tetens, moreover, praised and used the work of Gerard on genius, and Gerard seems to have suggested to Tetens, as well as to Kant, his categories of the imagination. Although Gerard is not as detailed as his German admirer, he separates the creative imagination of genius from the common or perceptive imagination. Schelling likewise believes that only genius can express the highest power of imagination, *Kunst-* or *Dichtungsvermögen*. Thus, at least four figures—Gerard, Tetens, Schelling, and Coleridge—and five if Kant is included, are interrelated in their attempt to separate the imagination of art and genius from that lesser form required in the acts of sensory and intellectual perception. This split between creative imagination and a perceptive or common imagination possessed by all individuals gained increasing currency from 1760 on.

Schelling often uses the now archaic German word *"Imagination"* with a meaning different from *Einbildungskraft*. In these cases *"Imagination"* indicates the mind's ability to reflect on or to speculate about reality in a free, almost dream-like state. *"Imagination"* considers the nature of infinity: it thirsts to see the cosmos as a unified whole but lacks power to make these mental activities anything more than a perpetual possibility. Schelling also employs the Latinate term to stress the dangers or even the evil inherent in the mind's free power of creation and will.[15]

## A HIGHER UNITY AND PANENTHEISM

From a union of the nature and transcendental philosophies, Schelling developed his *Identitätssystem* or *Identitätsphilosophie*. The essential feature of this system is the concept of the Absolute. This postulate undergirds his whole thought starting 1798 or 1799. The Absolute is a philosophical assumption, but it reveals deep religious implications, too. Schelling pursued theology ardently from 1803 on, and his researches have had impact on theologians in the nineteenth and twentieth centuries.

The Absolute, or Absolute Identity, is the ground of all being, the creative source of everything in the universe. It is both transcendent, as one being or intelligence, and immanent, as the sum of all created things. Each thing partakes of and is a manifestation of the Absolute. Schelling, wishing to avoid pantheism, identifies the Absolute with God, who is not merely the sum of all his material or spiritual creations. God dwells in all things and in all forms of spirit, but is fundamentally and originally one as well: the source and unmanifested Being itself, Coleridge's "I am that I am." This is not the same position as pantheism; Schelling's *Identitätsphilosophie* in fact plunges into panentheism. God is not only the animated sum of things but is also the being who creates and animates: "This God, in whom the being of all things is, who however himself remains in unpolluted unity, still places over and above particular things the ultimate image of his inexpressible identity [*das potenzlose Bild seiner potenzlosen Identität*]."[16]

In his *Privatvorlesungen*, Schelling differentiates his viewpoint from pantheism, which does very little to account for the fact of creation: "The common pantheistic attitude towards this leaves God with no particularity or uniqueness for his own existing Being; it leaves him more in a general substance, which is simply the medium of things."

Schelling believes that God is not only a kind of carrier-wave on which all things are transmitted but is also the single source of all transmission and all being: "God is both; he is first the Being of all being, but as such He must Himself also exist independently; that is, he must, as the Being of all being, possess a fundamental ground or consistency for Himself." God has two principles, the one *and* the all: "The first principle or the first originating power is the one through which the particular, unique, and individual exists. We call this power the Self; in God we call it the I am [*Egoismus*]. If this power were the only one, then God would be merely an alienated, separate, removed Being."[17]

In other words, this first principle explains the oneness, the individual God, but it cannot account for the created world or for any existence outside of this one being of God. The second principle, the principle of the all, grapples with individual things and life; this is the power of divine imagination or, as Schelling came increasingly to call it, the power of love. It is through this creative power that "*Gott eigentlich des Wesen aller Wesen ist.*"[18] Neither principle alone—neither the concept of God as one nor the concept of God as creating, animating, and existing in all things—can fully clarify the nature of the Absolute.

These two principles, when taken together, suggest the famous phrase *en kai pan*, the one and the all. A subtle slippage of mental gears often takes place when this phrase is heard. Frequently the conjunction "and" is taken as an equal sign. The three words then mean that God is equal to the all, that God is one only and simply as the sum of all things. But *en kai pan* can be interpreted to mean that God is the union of the one with something else distinct, the creating and informing power found within all individual existence. God subsumes these two different qualities. Both are necessary to the Absolute; each is sufficient only if accompanied by the other. This position is a genuine pan*en*theism. It explains the possibility of a God who is one and individual, who creates the universe, yet who also pervades it. Although it does not explain exactly why God created the universe, it is also a step in that direction.

Schelling, Hölderlin, and Hegel had used *en kai pan* as a watchword during their student days at Tübingen. But for about seven years afterward Schelling assumed a general pantheistic approach and adopted the commonly accepted, Spinozistic view of the phrase, that God is simply all things *in toto*, conceived as a vague unity. Schelling's writings from about 1800 reveal a shift, an effort to assert a truer sense of that magic formula. According to Schelling, *Dieses "Geiste der Ein-und-Allheit"* was not fully and correctly explained by Fichte, who mistook it for the pantheistic idea of all funneled into one ego or self. Neither the one nor the all is to be stressed at the expense of the other, in Schelling's view: *"Aber nicht nur das Ganze als Ganzes ist Göttlich. Auch der Theil und das Einzelne ist es für sich."* If one side seems to get the upper hand and manifestations of God claim that they alone are God, Schelling reasserts the balance: *"Aber die Einheit Fehlt."* Two cryptic pronouncements of Schelling now come sharply into focus. He guarded against the idea of the universe as simply a theater for the comings and goings of material things—*"Universum nicht = das materielle"*—because the universe is, actually, in its totality, all things material and spiritual. That is, the universe is the equivalent of God both manifested and unmanifested—*"Das Universum an sich = Gott."* The Absolute "is not the cause [alone] of the universe, but the universe itself." There is, in other words, a true symbiosis between the dual principles of God. These principles are mutually interdependent, like two racers who, holding hands as they cross the finish line, are allotted only one place: "God has in himself an inner Ground of his existence that, insofar as He is existing, precedes Him; but even so, God is nevertheless the priority [*das Prius*] of the Ground in which the Ground, even as such, could not be if God did not exist as a Being who acts."[19]

In God, then, there are no polarities. Subjective and objective, universal and particular, merge into one. The Absolute contains the pre-established harmony and unified source of everything in the realms of matter and spirit. This identity is vital to Schelling's thought. It is the "eternal

and living copula," which unifies all polarities. The center of all knowledge and reality knows within itself no contradictions. All branches of
science and experience stem from this one point. At this "central organ"
toward which philosophy strives, all knowledge becomes objective and
is transformed back into the being of God, its original source. This philosophy becomes, inevitably, theology. From God come all things, by
his power of imaginative creation. And by the power of imaginative vision all things return to him. The Absolute exists in reason but also acts
and lives by creative imagination; God is at once eternal and dynamic.
He is self-sufficient even and only as He manifests his own potential. In
one respect the dual nature of God as one and all represents a combination of the philosophy of nature, which accounts for the all or plenitude
of creation, and the transcendental philosophy, which deals with the nature of the single intelligent self.[20]

Another way to view Schelling's idea of the Absolute is that it embodies both reason and imagination. Reason is the self-sufficient principle of God as one, and imagination represents the power of God to
manifest himself in all forms. God, then, is himself the great Proteus.
With this idea of the Absolute Schelling hoped to solve that old paradox:
God is one and self-sufficient, yet He found it necessary to create the
plenitude of forms and life filling the universe. Many other philosophies
were good as systems, but they could not answer the riddle of creation.
They could not explain why there is something instead of nothing. For
Schelling, the key to the answer was not only divine reason but divine
imagination.

### THE FIRST STEP: THE NATURE PHILOSOPHY

Schelling develops his "New Philosophy" in stages. At each plateau
of development he seeks to include what has gone before it. And as his
thought evolves, the concept of imagination becomes increasingly important. It acquires powers both cosmic and human until it suffuses the
universe and man's soul with cohesive strength.

Schelling takes the first step in his grand synthesis with the *Naturphilosophie*. His purposes here are multiple. He wants to show that
matter is everywhere informed by divine imagination, by a creative
spirit working continually to shape and alter everything. Consequently,
the nature produced by this shaping force is itself productive, restless,
and dynamic. It evolves new forms that interact and whose identities are
determined in part by their myriad relationships with each other. Yet
each thing also represents the one idea or impulse responsible for its

creation. In this sense, all forms of matter are symbolic. Objects in nature are like works of art. Their substances are ideas made tangible.

For Schelling, spirit is pregnancy of matter, and matter is the concretion of spiritual and imaginative force. This force does not work only at the moment of God's first creation; it is ever-present, intertwined and involved with its material manifestation. It is the eternal creative power of God. "Through the creative power of a divinity the whole system of nature comes into being, and with it the entire plenitude of things, each suitable in its place, that exist apart from us." Matter alone cannot explain how matter came into being. There is a higher principle that creates, orders, and connects all. "To the inspired investigator Nature itself is the world's holy, eternal creating primal energy, which engenders and actively brings forth all things out of itself." This creating and unifying spirit, God's imagination, permeates the fabric of nature. "Born of that spirit, nature is always drenched with it."[21] This idea even prompted Schelling to write a poem, sounding very much like Herder, that ends:

> I am the god you nourish in your heart,
> The spirit that moves in everything
>
> . . . . . . . . . . . . . . . . . . .
> Where force in force and matter in matter in-weave
>
> . . . . . . . . . . . . . . . . . . . . . . . . . .
> Is One Pow'r, One playing back and forth and weaving,
> One drive and striving t'wards an ever higher life.[22]

Nature has two qualities—one of shaping imaginative force, the other of tangible symbols, things touched and seen. The imaginative power, operating to create these symbols, Schelling calls *natura naturans*, a scholastic and Arabic term he may have gotten from Jacobi. The sensible object itself, the body or *form* created, is *natura naturata*. The *natura naturans* "is nature creating," and Schelling equates it with "the divine imagination." *Natura naturans* is the force responsible for an object's *being*. The concept is Platonic. By the power of God's imagination, the eternal being or essence of a thing becomes one and the same with its own real and temporal manifestation. But in the object itself, the idea is *potentized;* its potential for real existence is fulfilled through the imagination. The *natura naturans*, which is divine imagination turned to a particular idea and its object, provides a bridge (*"das ewige Copula"*) between the real and ideal realms.[23] The nature we perceive is the material side of a grand dialectic. It is actually part of an ideal world. Consequently, nature is as meaningful as any mind; it is as meaningful as the ego or self. It is a huge arena in which the individual human mind can seek the moving spirit of the world, and in which we learn to imitate the divine creative force.

In the *Naturphilosophie* Schelling was trying to correct errors or im-
balances that he believed had split apart man and nature. The culprit
was seventeenth and eighteenth century scientific rationalism; man had
become too much the object of his own reflection. As a result, he saw
nature as completely external and material. This created a sense of alienation, a crevice between man's mind and nature which pure doses of empiricism only served to widen: Hume ended in a chasm of skepticism.
Images were no longer trusted to carry the force of ideas; real circumstances were separated from appearances, and nature took on the aspect
of a great illusion or cruel joke. This alienation from nature soon became
an alienation from the self; the mind found that if it could not trust its
perceptions of the world, then it could not trust its perceptions of its
own self either. The endless circle of reflection could not be broken, and
a spiritual sickness set it. Man's inner harmony was out of kilter: "However, as soon as I separate myself from nature, and with myself all that is
ideal, then only a dead object remains for me, and I cease to comprehend
how life outside myself can be possible." But "the creative imagination
at last discovered the symbolic language that one only needs to interpret
in order to find that nature speaks to us all the more understandably the
less we are merely considering her reflectively."[24]

Spinoza and Leibniz had recognized the realms of matter and spirit.
But while they connected them, which was more than Descartes did,
their connections were lopsided. In Spinoza everything became swal-
lowed in the vague idea of God as all things. Any sense of matter being
transformed into spirit was lost. Leibniz "came and went the opposite
way": all was brought to bear, in the end, on the individual being or intellect. This was Fichte's error, too. In Spinoza all was *"es gibt,"* in
Leibniz and Fichte all *"Ich bin."* No true dialectic was established. Nature was either God or simply a construct of the mind.[25]

For Spinoza, imagination was always directed to the real and material; for Leibniz, toward the perceiving intellect. This dualism challenged Schelling, and at times he saw the whole of his own endeavor as a
solution to it. He underscored his effort by classifying all previous systems as either Spinozistic or Leibnizian, the kind of remark that appealed to Coleridge (*"Unter allen bisherigen Systemen nun kenne ich
nur die beiden—das Spinozische und Leibnizische"*).[26]

Schelling's answer to the split was to use the imagination as a two-
way power. He would rescue, renovate, and combine Spinoza and Leibniz with an eye to Plato and the Platonic ideas.[27] In the creation of nature the divine imagination forms specific material things as symbols of
the ideal world, things which in themselves contain the ideas, the *natura
naturans*, that inform them. In the perception of nature as symbolic,

man's imagination sees at once the ideal and the real inherent in the universe.

For Schelling, God's creative imagination makes the universe dynamic. It is like the laboratory or atom-smasher where spirit and matter are mutually interchanged in individual things, but also where individual things and forces affect each other, either directly or through intermediaries. Each thing that comes into existence does so by paying a kind of homage to the things surrounding it. For example, a rose bush wrenched absolutely from its environment cannot live. It cannot be. There is no water or air to nourish it, no ground to be fertilized by its eventual decay, no soil to serve for its roots, no sun to fuel its metabolism. Alone, the rose is absurd. It can never be the rose of love, or the rose of the world. Brittle, lifeless, it will disintegrate, disperse, and return to those nebulous molecules of deep space to which it owes its distant ancestry and in which is also found the ancestry of everything it needs—water, oxygen, and light. Everything in the cosmos interconnects with its immediate surroundings, and those surroundings with wider environs, until the world, the solar system, and more are included. Things necessarily exist through and by other things. The rose bush needs air and moisture far more than, say, the starlight of Vega Lira, but all connections continue on until a universe of related things and motions is formed. This universal ecology has a dynamic character. Even time and space are functions of energy, motion, and matter.[28]

The identity of everything is thus in relationship to everything else. "There is no isolated Being or isolated thing-in-itself." In positive terms, the whole of nature works through each thing. Complete process and interdependence govern: "No phenomenon in nature is . . . fixed, but in each bat of an eye it is reproduced through the power of all nature." This recalls Hazlitt's remark that poetry imitates the flowing not the fixed. By this principle, according to Schelling, the universe evolves and changes through a series of infinitely small and rapid movements. There is no rest, no still point in the turning world except the Absolute, God, the creating intelligence itself. To reach this point is the highest goal of the *Naturphilosophie.*[29]

Nature, then, consists of particulars, of spirit differentiated into objects. Behind these objects is the realm of ideas and creative force. Nature is the birth of ideas. Every natural object is thus potentially a symbol of the spirit or of *natura naturans*, a meeting point of the eternal and the temporal, the universe and the particular. This means that science ultimately asks the same questions that philosophy asks; the two disciplines are forks of one road that rejoin. Schelling brings science under the umbrella of philosophy: they have the same end; their studies are animated by the same creating force. The highest presence in the material world is "that of the imagination of nature" (*Einbildungskraft der Natur*). The goal of Schelling's "speculative physics," natural symbols form a "new mythology" representing the world-system and reason of God.[30]

Schelling's scientific knowledge was incomplete and crude by modern standards. He could not reach the goal he set for it, or even prove his own speculations. His attempt to be a factual polymath seems as remote as Plato's in the *Timaeus*. But anyone familiar with the progress and puzzles of modern science, with the questions it poses and the answers it suggests, can only be amazed by Schelling. The moving force behind the *Naturphilosophie* is *the divine imagination* or *the imagination of nature*, one and the same. It is the force and phenomena, spirit and body. It is man's highest goal, as both philosopher and scientist, to fathom, and as artist, to participate in this imagination: "What is all the renown of the most clever skeptic against the life of one man who carries a world in his head and the whole of nature in his imagination?" Perhaps this search of philosopher and scientist, and the hope it implies, is what Einstein had in mind when he said, "Imagination is more important than knowledge."

### THE SECOND STEP: THE PHILOSOPHY OF MIND

The *Naturphilosophie* starts from the real and proceeds to the ideal. Then, on the ideal side there is a new and more direct study of mind and intelligence itself. This quest for intellectual consciousness or the transcendental philosophy is seen by Schelling as pointing with the nature philosophy to one Absolute Identity of real and ideal, the *Identitätssystem:* "In the eternal activity of the Absolute we comprehend two necessary sides, one real and one ideal; thus, from the perspective of the forms philosophy can take, it has been necessarily divided into two camps." In the opening of his *Darstellung meines Systems der Philosophie* (1801), Schelling constructs his new philosophy on these two bases: "The system . . . is the same that I . . . have oriented consistently in the transcendental—as well as the nature philosophy."[31]

Since the real tends to return to the creating or the perceiving intelligence, what needs ultimately to be explained is consciousness or intelligence itself—in man, the subjective self or ego. To probe what is not grounded in the material world, to reach the basis of man's knowledge, only transcendental philosophy will serve. It explores the phenomenon of self-consciousness and the ground of man's being. As Coleridge observes, this philosophy explains the very process of being and intellection; or put another way, it is the philosophy of becoming. Schelling's most thorough treatment of it is the *System des transzendentalen Idealismus.*[32]

The nub of Schelling's transcendentalism is that the conscious self will always be lost in a dark house of subjectivity unless it affirms the nature and potential of its own existence by creating something objective and real, which is outside of itself. If the self succeeds in this creative act, it will perform the task of objectifying itself. Schelling calls this act *Subjekt-objektivirung*, the process of subject-objectivization. Its product unifies the mind's subjective and internal consciousness with the external world's objectivity and lack of consciousness. This act of self-affirmation (*Selbstaffirmation*) produces something real and objective, which nevertheless originates in the subjective mind and the mind's ideas. This product is the ideal union or idea (*Einbildung*), the identity of subjective and objective, internal and external, consciousness and absence of consciousness. The free activity of its creation is harnessed to and harmonized with the necessary presence of an external world. The dialectic of nature and mind, real and ideal, at last produces a synthetic third, identified with both, which reconciles man's creative freedom to the necessity of what has already been created. For God, this product is nature; for man, it is art. And the power by which the mind or intelligence creates this product is *Kunstvermögen* or *Dichtungsvermögen*, the highest level of *Einbildungskraft*, the force of *In-Eins-Bildung*. The person possessing this highest power of imagination is called a genius. Genius is "a portion of the Absolute nature of God."[33]

The transcendental philosophy, with its resolution in the creative act, reflects back on nature. It answers the question of why there is a creation and a universe. God's ideal being, his oneness, was not self-sufficient. As an intelligence himself, He formed nature as his own act of self-affirmation. Thus He became self-sufficient only at that moment when he started to create something external to his original being through the power of divine imagination. "Why is there not nothing; why, moreover, is there something? Is not the All or God, and not the something, the only valid answer?" God and nature stand in special relationship as the one and all. Nature is God's artwork. "What we call nature is a poem that lies locked up in a secret and wonderful writing." Nature fulfills the eternal act of God's self-perception and self-affirmation, in which both ideal and real participate. The temporal progress of nature and life, or history, is an epic composed by God's spirit. He is thus inextricably present in nature and history. They are actually part of his being, and necessary to it.[34]

Only the artistic or creative imagination both solves the questions of transcendental philosophy and explains the presence of nature. Through the act and product of its own creativity, the ego or intelligence actually sees itself becoming objective and real. Imagination frees man from the closed circle of self-reflection and subjectivity.[35]

For man, imaginative art transforms his subjective being. As Hazlitt noted, imagination is another name for getting out of ourselves. It affirms the self, along with the self's relationship to nature, in an objective form. Art does more than mediate. It joins man and nature with the closest intimacy. The work of art is a kind of wedding ring. The creative imagination produces this aesthetic symbol in which man and nature, internal and external, the mind's free consciousness and nature's lack of it, the ideal and the real, the universal and the particular, no longer contradict each other. They fuse into one entity. This work of art is outside the self. It is the self having made itself an objective part of the cosmos: "To the philosopher art is the highest pursuit because it unlocks to him, as it were, the holy of holies, where what in nature and history are torn asunder—and what in life and action (even as in thought)—must be eternally fleeting, now burn together, as it were, in one flame."[36] Hazlitt similarly remarks in "On Genius and Common Sense, The Same Subject Continued," that "Originality is the seeing nature differently from others, and yet as it is itself . . . It is only minds on whom she [Nature] makes her fullest impressions that can penetrate her shrine or unveil her *Holy of Holies* . . . Whoever does this is a man of genius." Schelling's tone also has strong affinities with Shelley's *Defence* and with those two famous paragraphs of the conclusion to Pater's *Renaissance* that begin with the short quotation from Novalis. To the artist, according to Schelling, nature is no longer a version of the ideal world compressed and restricted into real images that must be reproduced within the psyche. To the artist, nature is part of his own being, and he becomes part of nature as well.

Schelling had separate stages but not separate systems. His thought coheres and is the grand exposition of a dialectic and its synthesis. His end was encompassing unity. He posited several stages because experience itself, and the universe, is manifold. He never disowned the *Naturphilosophie*, transcendental idealism, or the *Identitätssystem*. Each one is a rung on the same ladder, a refracted image of the same object. As soon as Schelling dropped Fichte's subjectivism in 1795 at the age of twenty-three, he was on a singular mission that demanded several landing places. He refers to the transcendental even when he speaks of nature. He reflects on nature even as he explores the transcendental. And the Absolute Identity, living through the power of imagination, is the apex and copula of both.

### IMAGINATION AND ART

When Schelling attempted to explain the precise nature of imaginative or "organic" art, his critical eye was duller than Coleridge's. However, at least three concepts in Schelling became earmarks of romantic art and bywords of its criticism. These are "genius," "beauty," and the idea that art, calling on the whole man, affords him a union with God and a form of salvation. The three concepts are connected. For example, given the religious aspects of salvation, the genius assumes a prophetic voice, and the beautiful in art becomes an expression of God's truth, the best symbol of man's place in nature.

After some fashionable protests against "mechanical" art, the art of copying and rearranging without transformation, Schelling makes an extreme and rather militant point about "organic" art and the genius who can create it, which departs markedly from the German rococo and the aesthetics of Baumgarten and Winckelmann. Art seeks to imitate the productive force found in nature, in such a way that the work of art lacks all appearance of artifice and confronts us, as do Shakespeare's characters, with the surprise of a new reality. The secret of art is not method, but spirit. Only by capturing the working spirit of nature's creative power, the *natura naturans*, can the artist imitate nature truly:

> Only mighty movements of the feelings, only profound convulsions of the imagination by the all-animating, all-governing forces of nature could have imbued art with the indomitable vigor with which, from the rigidly enclosed earnestness of the constructions of early times to the works of overflowing sensuous charm, it remained ever faithful to truth and begot in the spirit the loftiest reality it is granted mortals to look upon.[37]

Art should emulate the "eternally creating primal energy." The secret of the best art is internal process: it shapes and generates form from within; it unifies all parts. It is not the imposition of form on a heterogeneous mass or the external manipulation of surface effect. In other words, creative imagination, not fancy or reason, is the secret of art.

The genius captures this secret, and his imagination imitates God's creative power. In this, Schelling follows Gerard and Tetens. But for Schelling, true genius is necessary only for the arts; science and learning may be helped by it, as in the case of Newton's gravitational system, but when it is absent, only the arts necessarily suffer. In the middle and late decades of the eighteenth century genius was not exclusively assigned to art, but Schelling pushes it there; genius, in its popular sense, was becoming synonymous with art, originality, and creativity. A genius is, above all, a creator more than a thinker, discoverer, or investigator. And the *sine qua non* of genius, without which genius falters into artifice, is imagination—the only productive and unifying power.[38]

Imaginative genius, the artist, is the immediate and participating divinity in man:

> This eternal idea of man in God as the immediate cause of his creations is what we call . . . genius, the indwelling divinity in man. It is, so to speak, a portion of the absolute nature of God. Each artist is accordingly able to produce only so much as the perpetual conception of his own being is bound up in God. Now the more he already perceives the universe in this manner, the more organically he proceeds . . . the more prolific he is.[39]

No other romantic thinker more cogently backed his plea for the divine nature of imagination and art. It was not a new idea, but Schelling's claim has an added dimension: for him, art is the pursuit of objectivity. Imaginative genius does not seek a personal or idiosyncratic vision, but one, like Shakespeare's, that embraces all nature. In this general outlook Schelling is close to Keats, Hazlitt, Coleridge, and (though in a different way) Blake and Shelley. Imagination, in the mind of the genius is, as Kant has stated, a faculty *sui generis*. *"Das psychologische Messer"* (the knife of psychology) cannot dissect it; it is free from the labyrinths of faculty psychology, materialism, "rules" of art, and logic. It is spirit, touched by the holy spirit.[40]

Faculty psychology, empiricism, associationism, and transcendental logic had actually nourished and acted as a womb for this romantic idea of imagination and genius. But it is the nature of ideas that, in culminating their progress and establishing a supremacy, they seek to strengthen their identity and position by denying, however falsely, their own ancestry, and by quashing any thought that they owe debts to the past. The new ideal of originality served only to strengthen this impulse. The stress on imagination as intuitive and immediate made it especially difficult for any Romantic to admit that what he professed owed its development to those things he cast off. This is one reason that Romanticism flaunts its difference with the Enlightenment, when, in truth it is the militant but brilliant child of the Enlightenment.

### THE THIRD AND FINAL STEP: ART RESCUES PHILOSOPHY

By making works of art fill such a massive philosophical need, Schelling risked shutting philosophy itself out in the cold, and he knew it. Philosophy yearns for the highest possible knowledge, but to this point it can bring only a part (*"ein Bruchstück"*) of the whole man. "Art brings *the whole man* . . . to a knowledge of the highest, and in this rests the everlasting distinction and wonder of art."[41] Art can secure immediately, in the living and concrete, what philosophy—uninformed by art—strives after vainly. Art solves the dilemma of philosophy, the split between man and nature, the riddle of creation and its relationship to the individual mind.

Since the *Kunstprodukt* or work of art does so much, it might be possible to drop philosophical inquiry altogether and pursue the arts alone, or more specifically, the fine arts, where creative genius holds sway without the help and interpretation of either critic or philosopher. The argument could rapidly decay into a narrow art-for-art's-sake. Yet Schelling pursues something broader that he believes resuscitates the arts, keeps them alive, and brings out their meaning. He wants a way to live, to perceive, and to experience the world in which all things are viewed as an artistic or creative manifestation of either God or man. Poems, plays, and symphonies are wonders; they are the things of art. But people create them in the first place only when they come to envision nature in a certain way. These artists may not be self-conscious about their perspective or vision, or they may come to it in "years that bring the philosophic mind." But only the philosopher in man can analyze, explain, and interpret the artistic vision. This is why Keats restlessly pursued the idea of the poet as philosopher, and why there will always be a profound bond between poetry and philosophy. The conscious realization, unfolding, and interpretation of man's aesthetic or imaginative view of life—a view that is the often unknowing or unselfconscious patron of all artworks—is a philosophy of art (*"Philosophie der Kunst"*). Here, then, is a way to unite art and philosophy. For even as art can give to the eye an image of man and nature in harmony, philosophy holds this image up to the light and presents it to our mind so we may see what ideas and vision of the world make that art possible.

*Die Philosophie der Kunst* is not simply a philosophy or critique of the fine arts, let alone of the arts in general. Like the natural and transcendental philosophies, it is a way to consider the self and the cosmos. But unlike any other philosophy, the *Philosophie der Kunst* sees man and nature under the single aspect of creative imagination and recognizes that the unity of man and nature "is possible only through an aesthetic act of the imagination."[42]

Seen under the aspect of the creative or poetic imagination (*"Dichtungsvermögen"*), philosophy becomes an artistic act and art becomes a philosophic expression. The product of the artistic process is "toward the external," the art work as a real symbol; the result of the philosophy of art is "toward the internal," objective knowledge or true ideas of man and nature. Together, then, art and philosophy complement each other, since at their highest level they are both based on the creative imagination: "Thus philosophy is founded on the productive power just as

firmly as art is, and the difference between them is simply in the alter-
nating direction of that power." Imagination is a two-way power, working between the ideal and real:

> Hence while creativity in art directs itself outward [to the real and indi-
> vidual] ... creativity in philosophy directs itself immediately to the in-
> ward [the ideal] to reflect on it as an intellectual perception. The same
> faculty with which this philosophical act must be apprehended is thus
> aesthetic, and even on this account the philosophy of art is the true or-
> ganon of philosophy.[43]

The philosophy of art subsumes the philosophies of nature and
mind—is really their capstone or joining arch, the *"In-Eins-Bildung"* or
philosophical equivalent of the "eternal copula" of Schelling and Coleridge, and the intended purpose of the incomplete Chapter 13 of the
*Biographia.* Imagination can now be diagrammed in the full context of
art and philosophy:[44]

| | | | |
|---|---|---|---|
| *sinnliche Einbildungskraft* | natural philoso-phy | real | being as physical form |
| *produktive Einbildungskraft* | transcendental philosophy | ideal | being in the pro-cess of self-con-struction |
| *äesthetische Einbildungskraft Dichtungs-vermögen* | *Philosophie der Kunst* | ideal and real | form and being in eternal interpene-tration |

Those who possess the *philosophy of art* enjoy the highest conception of
the world and of man. They perceive all things and ideas in an objective,
aesthetic way. In a work not published until 1917, the *Ältestes Systemprogramm des deutschen Idealismus,* Schelling states this revelation.
The creative imagination alone fulfills reason and releases the power of
ideas: "I am now convinced that the highest act of reason, in which it
comprehends all ideas, is an aesthetic act ... the philosopher must
therefore possess as much aesthetic power as the poet does."[45]

Thus the creative imagination not only permits art but also rescues
philosophy from its personal and metaphysical subjectivity. For Schelling, art and philosophy teeter on the brink unless imagination infuses
them with dynamic vigor. Imaginative art and, more generally, all creative acts of mind may be considered "greater and more worthy" than
"philosophy" itself, including Schelling's own New Philosophy. This
last admission is a great tribute to Schelling's own humility. He was
more concerned with the wonder of life than with his own presentation
of it. This is exactly why his position is inspired; weighed in the bal-

ance, it is selfless. The whole question of art, in fact, becomes so vital that his two most systematic and complete works, *System des transzendentalen Idealismus* and *Vorlesungen über die Methode des Akademischen Studiums,* culminate in sections on art and on the intimate tie between art and philosophy. Schelling's progress is a great drama, for he discovers, like the hero in a Greek play, that his own thought and philosophy are swept up in a larger artistic whole, a vision of life in direct contact with knowledge of the self and cosmos.[46]

In effect, Schelling's philosophy of art elevates philosophy to a broader stage, because the philosophy of art recognizes and includes the power of creative imagination. It catches up the lower levels of philosophy and of imagination, placing them in the highest perspective. In fact, all philosophy can be seen through the eyes of the creative imagination. "We here must remember that the philosophy of art is itself philosophy in general, only presented in the power or potentiality of art."[47] It is astonishing that a philosopher should claim so much for the creative power and for the arts in general. This claim is preeminently for the imagination, the active force of art and philosophy. This claim became the essential principle of all thoughtful Romanticism.

### DIALECTIC OF ART AND PHILOSOPHY

Like Coleridge, Reynolds, Hazlitt, Schiller, Goethe, and so many Romantics not caught up in the whirlwind of personality, Schelling concludes that the highest vision of art and philosophy reaches a summit of truth. The intertwining of art and philosophy (*"diese Verwandtschaft der Philosophie und der Kunst"*) lends philosophy an objectivity it gains no other way. Schelling describes this curious transit of objectivity: "We can say take away from art its objectivity and it ceases to be what it is and becomes philosophy; give objectivity to philosophy and it ceases to be philosophy and becomes art." When philosophy assumes the robes of art, it becomes "objective" and is most properly called art itself.[48]

In arguing that an aesthetic perception is objective, Schelling is stressing not the *Ding-An-Sich*, which for him doesn't exist as such, but an objective interplay of man and nature. The word "aesthetic," after all, comes from the Greek meaning to perceive truly or clearly, and what Schelling means by art is not the fine arts alone but an aesthetic perception, in the most profound sense, of the universal process. Perhaps the closest thing to this sense of art in modern usage is "the faculty of arts" at a university, or phrases (worn thin by use) like "the art of politics" or "the art of thinking." Schelling is specific about the broad sweep of his idea: "Accordingly, in the philosophy of art I take there to be first not art as art [art-for-art's-sake], as such, as it is by itself, but I take the universe in the form of art, and the philosophy of art as knowledge of everything seen in the form or potentiality of art."[49]

But still, no matter how much leeway Schelling gives to "art," he does not place philosophy and thought in general strictly under the aegis of art. Having written from a "philosophic" stance in the first place, he is definitely not downgrading philosophy. In 1812 Goethe, thinking possibly of Schelling, said about recent German philosophers that they assigned art so high a place, *"that they even placed philosophy beneath art."* But Goethe knew that the poetic and artistic surge of his day pushed itself forward because philosophy made room at the top for art and gave it an elevated rank: *"Epoche der forcierten Talente entsprang aus der philosophischen. Höhere theoretische Ansichten wurden klar und allgemeiner."*[50]

Like Arnold's conviction that a critical period, rich in ideas and intellectual ferment, must pave the way for poetic creativity, Schelling believed that, "Only philosophy can once again open for consideration sources of art that have been largely exhausted in their creativity."[51] In the Romantic period, marvelous results followed from this belief. For if struggling artists actually feel that they are witnessing, at first-hand, the igneous streams which are the hottest and clearest sources of art, then those artists can take the *Gradus ad Parnassum.* Their confidence and faith will be their greatest asset. The wonderfully fruitful thing about the development of the concept of imagination was that it concerned the poetic process itself. For Schelling, then, even as art alone completes the philosophic synthesis of mind and cosmos, only philosophy—or criticism—can explain the significance of the artist's imaginative creation. Art's function is promoted to the fuller context of ideas, history, and morality.

Schelling's plea for art is echoed in English by Sidney's *Apology* and Shelley's *Defence.* But where these works approach the philosophic and humane meaning of art from historical examples and the formative effect of the arts, Schelling bases the necessity of art and the characteristics of imagination on a cosmological foundation. In rough terms, Sidney and Shelley defend imaginative literature from the already existing effects and aims of art. Schelling works his way up, philosophically, until he concludes what the very nature and function of art must be if it is to bring the whole man to truth and harmony of being. Shelley and Sidney propagate the *raison d'être* of art; Schelling formulates it and shows its inevitability as part of a universe populated by intelligent life.

The philosopher's reason and the artist's imagination are seen as different sides of the same power. This is a very high, even rarefied level of generalization but, from the standpoint of the philosophy of art, a true one. It explains the stunning remark in the *Vorlesungen* that reason and imagination are, in essence, one: "In the world made concretely manifest, there is from the inner being of the Absolute, which itself is the eternal forming-into-one [*In-Eins-Bildung*] of the universal and particular, an emanation in reason and in imagination, both of which are one and the same."[52] The only difference is that in art the end products are works of art or things, whereas in philosophy the final products are ideas. Philosophy and art together, then, are man's closest approach to the pure identity of the Absolute, or God, who is himself the original mind and the first artist. For Schelling, the power of imagination, art, and religion become confluent. He speaks of *"Der innige Bund, welcher die Kunst und Religion vereint,"*[53] "the inner bond that unifies art and religion." This theme surfaces in Coleridge and later in Arnold, too, though Arnold expresses it in a more cryptic and less profound way. In all three writers the Bible, as imaginative art and as theology, becomes the one central work, at least for Christian theology.

### BEAUTY, SALVATION, AND THE FUTURE

All Romantics inherited the word "beauty," which became something of a deadweight around their necks. With too many common connotations, "beauty" could not convey the combined aesthetic, moral, and philosophic sensibility that was expected of it. Hampered with this unfortunate term, poets and critics attempted repeatedly to explain it until their special meanings, meant to be clarifications, became confused, and people fell back on the lowest common denominator, beauty as something agreeable or pleasing to the senses. New ideas often demand new words, but Herder's *"Besonnenheit,"* Hazlitt's "gusto," and Coleridge's "multëity in unity," all of which were attempts to revamp aesthetic and critical vocabulary and to enrich the depth and nuance of "beauty"—never broke into popular usage.

For Schelling, beauty in an object frees in the psyche a total and harmonious response, a feeling which itself may be called beauty. The idea is similar to Schiller's concept of beauty in *The Aesthetic Education*. All elements of the self, according to Schelling, are called on together and are unified by a corresponding harmony in the external object. The senses, understanding, reason, moral feeling, judgment, and emotion all focus on one end. This end, or beauty, is a cipher or code. Coleridge remarks that beauty is the "short hand hieroglyphic of truth." It reveals the organic interconnection of the universe and symbolizes the world's processes. It suggests, embodies, and reveals these processes and relations in concrete and specific form, so that the psyche can at once be aware of what would otherwise be a multiplicity of experiences.

Beauty focuses, distills, intensifies, and fuses nature with experience. The beautiful object dissolves any barrier between the subjective self and the objective world. Beauty is thus a product of genius and of the creative imagination. It realizes the latent potential for synthesis that is in the psyche. Beauty is economy and shows in the most concentrated way that all things in nature and all faculties in man exist and owe their identities to their many relationships with each other. Schelling was trying to break away from Baumgarten and Kant's aesthetics: the first was too simple, the second too dry. Leibniz helped give him a sense of complete organicism. *Bruno oder über die göttliche und natürliche Prinzip der Dinge* (1802), one of Schelling's major statements on beauty, truth, and an imaginative concept of the universe, reflects the ambiance of Leibniz's *Nouveaux essais*. Later, in 1806, Schelling emphasizes the unity and total awareness that Leibniz taught him to find in beauty: "In each soul we can read the whole beauty of the universe, we can set down and develop all its recesses, for each true perception of the soul locks within itself an infinity of intricate, confused perceptions, which in their development embody the whole universe."[54] Beauty unifies the soul.

The difference between beauty in nature and in art is two-fold. Natural beauty, though powerful, cannot appeal to all the faculties of man. Like nature itself, it cannot resolve and harmonize the split between man and nature. But the beauty of art, even while imitating nature, contains an element of human consciousness. It is beautiful by design and awareness; it engages the psyche more fully than the beauty of nature, which must remain accidental.[55]

The vision of the world awakened by beauty is actually truth in its fullest sense; it is complete awareness. Beauty and truth are one, and both express the objective world. The identity of beauty and truth is the same as the identity of philosophy and art in the *Philosophie der Kunst*. The highest values of each—truth in philosophy and beauty in art—are two sides of the same thing. Truth is ideal, and beauty more real and concrete, but they both are only differing approaches which point to and become the same approach. In his philosophy of art Schelling drives home this point, that "Truth and beauty are simply two differing approaches of the one absolute."[56]

Here again Schelling reaches the Absolute. God is the source of beauty, and it comes from him through imaginative transformation. In the Absolute, beauty is "unborn"; it is ideal and abstract. The "technical side" of art, its "creative science," gives concrete form, body, color, and mass to beauty. In other words, imagination is the highest act of mind because it delivers to the real world what previously was without form and void.[57]

The scheme is Platonic but also Christian. Schelling sees Christ as God's promise of love to man, and God's love is the same thing as God's imagination. This is a religious clarification toward which Schelling struggles from about 1805 on. Increasingly, he identifies the two principles of God no longer as reason and creative imagination, but as reason and love. The oneness of God, working through love, brings about creation itself. Imagination is a form of love because it involves escaping from the self and becoming involved in the world. To this end the whole of creation is God's act of love, Christ is a promise and symbol of that love, and the church is an "artwork" representing the unity of God and man. A remarkable thing in Schelling's *Über das Wesen der menschlichen Freiheit* (1809) is the sense that God's imagination, *die göttliche Einbildungskraft*, is identical with God's love.[58]

Following the implications of this view, Schelling equates sin with false imagination and cosmic evil with a failure on the part of God's imagination. God becomes a being who is not all-perfect but one who, like a great artist, wishes to be perfect and cannot always execute his designs. This false execution of the divine plan and reason—this *"falsche Imagination"*—generates suffering and evil.

Finally, Schelling confronts a dilemma in the nature of man's own imagination and the knowledge it brings. Imagination is a great power; but only an élite, which throughout the *Vorlesungen* he calls an "aristocracy," possesses it. Genius is, by definition, apart from the mass of mankind. Coleridge feared that this stress on the importance of genius and the highest imagination would shut out a vast majority of people and cut them off from the cosmic scheme. But for Schelling, the horizon is brighter. Imagination carries with it freedom but also a vast responsibility, a sense that all individuals in the human race ultimately and historically share a common fate. Real knowledge, true imagination, "can never become really one in the individual, but only in the human race." Even as the act of imagination is an escape from the self, so the benefits of art and the works of genius are given to mankind as a whole. Those who possess imaginative vision, concern, and genius must shoulder the responsibility for leadership and achievement.[59]

# 2 1

# COLERIDGE

*I*n forming his concept of the imagi-
nation, Coleridge draws on nearly every other writer who discussed the
subject. Despite the fragmentary nature of his own statements—it is
hard to find more than a dozen explicit, consecutive sentences at a time
on the subject—he states more about the imagination than any other
Romantic. Others wrote pages on its proper and philosophic definition,
but Coleridge distills, connects, and adds to the background with which
he was so familiar. Assuming the imagination as a fundamental principle
of nature and mind, he pursues it through the details of many fields yet
keeps alive the sense that it remains one principle.

Like Hazlitt and Goethe, Coleridge applies the idea of imagination
directly to "practical criticism," a term he originates. He enters into aesthetics and the theory of language and symbolism and deals with questions raised by Addison, Burke, Duff, Alison, Kant, and Schiller. The
cosmic sense of imagination found in Leibniz, Akenside, and Schelling
resurfaces. The theory that art serves as the crown of philosophy, as in
Schelling's philosophy of art, is shared and rivaled by Coleridge's remarks on the function of the arts and their dependence on creative imagination. Yet Coleridge also dips back into the associationists and psychological critics. Moving away from his youthful enthusiasm for Hartley,
he retains insights from him, as well as from Gerard, Tetens, Stewart,
and even Maass, which add to the working psychological depth he gives
the imagination. He affirms the conviction of Hobbes, Johnson, Hume,
and Keats that imagination, for better or worse, governs the mass of individual experience we call life. With Smith and Hazlitt, he links sympathy and the moral life to the imagination and takes Shakespeare as the
great example of sympathy expressing itself in passionate language. In
the same path as Blake, Shelley, Herder, Novalis, and Boehme, Coleridge holds the imagination to be a prophetic gift; despite his disagree-

ments with Wordsworth over a strict definition of the imagination, Coleridge, using one of Wordsworth's own lines, says that "I reflect with delight, how little a mere theory . . . interferes with the process of genuine imagination in a man of true poetic genius, who possesses . . . 'The vision and the faculty divine.' " The value Coleridge places on the poet's imagination reflects his own experience of writing, yet the philosophical and psychological analyst in him proceeds, like those before him, to explore various "degrees and denominations" of the imaginative power.

Among all these thinkers and writers, nearly all of whom were absorbed, criticized, and used to varying degrees by Coleridge himself, he remains hardest to classify. The range and profundity of his idea of the imagination make it a natural climactic point.[1]

## PHILOSOPHICAL TERRAIN

The central problem of philosophy since Descartes had been the relationship between the individual self and nature, between subject and object. On one side, though in different ways, Fichte and Berkeley stressed the action and innate qualities of the self. Fundamentally opposite in stance, Hobbes, Locke, and Hartley presumed the working effects of nature on an impressionable mind. Leibniz, Kant, Schelling, Jacobi, and to some degree Hume—whom Kant said "woke me from my dogmatic slumbers"—mediated between the extremes. Sometimes it was hard to place a particular thinker in one camp or another, as with Tucker, Tetens, or Gerard. Yet the two basic approaches, easily recognizable in themselves, spawned pairs of labels: materialist or naturalist versus transcendentalist, dogmatic versus spiritual, objective versus subjective, *"Es gibt"* versus *"Ich bin."* By the 1790s, especially in Germany, these common labels were bandied about in compliment and accusation.[2]

Thinkers as widely apart, and as representative in the extreme of these two approaches, as Fichte and Hobbes relied on the imagination to connect the self with nature. As mediating figures, Kant, Schelling, and Coleridge express a multiple and broader view of the imagination, a "dynamic" that comprehends the subjective and objective working organically together, mutually influencing and transforming themselves in one larger system. More than ever the idea of the imagination was crucial because it now was intended not only to explain how the mind makes sense out of nature or, conversely, how nature shapes the mind through the senses, but also to reconcile these two poles in one process.

Coleridge, by the age of forty familiar with the history and intricacies of both British and Continental attempts to solve the basic subject-object issue of philosophy, could turn to the imagination with the hope that at last the true nature of this "synthetic and magical power" might be revealed. He employs various terms to distinguish the two "systems." The "natural philosopher" takes for his object *forma formata* or the "passive" nature of phenomena in themselves.[3] Coleridge roughly groups Aristotle, Locke, and Hartley as representatives of natural philosophy. The subjective system, because it sees self-conscious intelligence as antecedent to all knowledge, he calls the domain of the intelligential or transcendental philosopher. "This is what Leibniz meant, when to the old adage of the Peripatetics, Nihil in intellectu quod non prius in Sensu ... he replied—praeter intellectum ipsum."[4] Kant, Fichte, Schelling, and to some extent mystics like Boehme represent this class of philosophers. Coleridge often speaks as well of the objective system (the philosophy of knowing) and of the subjective philosophy (that of being). "For in this, in truth, did philosophy begin, in the distinction between the subject and the object."[5] In *Aids to Reflection* and the *Biographia*, he affirms, "The very words, *objective* and *subjective* ... I have ventured to re-introduce, because I could not so briefly or conveniently by any more familiar terms distinguish the percipere from the percipi."[6]

Neither system, when taken in any other than its extreme form, denies either conscious mind or matter, but each system makes one dependent on the other. The natural or material philosophers "give the whole to the object and make the subject, that is the reflecting and contemplating, feeling part, the mere result of that." Transcendentalists "give the whole to the subject and make the object a mere result involved in it."[7] These are the "two great directions of man." In one, the mind supplements the experienced world with passion and desires. In the alternate system the "initiative thought," the inherent formation of knowledge, "must itself have its birth-place within, whatever excitement from without may be necessary for its germination."[8]

Turning philosophy since Plato on two hinges, even resurrecting the scholastic Nominalists and Realists under the headings of objective and subjective, Coleridge gives a beautiful image of possible union:

> I have read of two rivers passing through the same lake, yet all the way preserving their streams visibly distinct—if I mistake not, the Rhone and the Adar, through the Lake of Geneva. In a far finer distinction, yet in a subtler union ... are the streams of knowing and being. The lake is formed by the two streams in man and nature as it exists in and for man; and up this lake the philosopher sails on the junction-line of the constituent streams.[9]

As a young man, Coleridge felt enamored with the materialist system and read Aristotle, Locke, Priestley, and the associationists with enthusiasm. He named his first son Hartley. The doctrine of association and the psychology of suggestion fascinated him. But as early as 1797, before his trip to Germany, he became uneasy, saying that, "Those who have been led . . . thro' the constant testimony of their senses . . . contemplate nothing but *parts*."[10] "Constant" empiricism, namely empiricism alone, could not view all parts as they connect to form the whole of experience. Associationism could not eradicate this difficulty. It became like the term "stimulus" in medicine: explaining all, it ended "all-annihilating," becoming a circuitous path explaining nothing. *"The solution of Phaenomena can never be derived from Phaenomena."*[11] Associationism could not account for a theory of perception nor explain the formation, in the mind, of what was associated. Innate faculties and abilities of the mind could not be explained by material impressions made by the senses on the nerves. Following sensations into the recesses of the mind could not explain the very being and inherent nature of that mind. However, Coleridge's early encounters with these thinkers saved him from remote abstractions, the Ptolemaic wheels-within-wheels of logic that sometimes plague Fichte and Schelling. Like Leibniz and Kant, Coleridge found it hard to deny outright any "opposing" view. There must be some value in it.

Associationism was crucial: the poet had to link together ideas, images, and feelings in a lively, unexpected way. It was the metaphysical baggage that went along with associationism as a complete explanation that Coleridge wanted to jettison, for that baggage, the system represented by Hartley, was not "metaphysical" at all. It made each mind the product and prey of atoms vibrating and bouncing into each other. It made a mockery of any "creative" act. It left no room for conscious choice. It was a bow to atheism. The individual possessed "organs of spirit" as well as those of sense.[12] And the poet chose which images were to be associated and created, and in what manner. His will was not like Hartley's theory of the will as described by Coleridge, namely a series of streams, or influences, simply converging into a larger river that takes the path of least resistance. The will of a poet implied spiritual freedom, a desire to create one goal or end in preference to another. And thus the poet had to be a moral agent.

The objective system was a moral and religious failure, for the poet as well as for the philosopher.[13] Filled with deep respect for revealed, even orthodox Christianity, after having repudiated the "errors" of his youthful Unitarianism, Coleridge asks how anyone could read the second chapter of Genesis—" 'And the Lord God formed man of the dust of the ground, and breathed into his nostrils the breath of life . . . *and man became a living soul'* "—and not see that, "Materialism will never explain those last words."[14] The essential motives for Coleridge's philosophical inquiries—motives that remain even when he deals with the imagination—are moral and strongly connected with the Christian religion. Near the end of the *Biographia* he takes an impassioned parting blast at the enthusiasm of his youth and at much of the British tradition since Hobbes and Locke: "the *system of nature* (i.e., materialism, with the utter rejection of moral responsibility, of a present providence, and of both present and future retribution) may influence . . . characters and action . . . to a degree that almost does away the distinction between men and devils . . . and will make the page of the future historian resemble the narration of a madman's dreams."[15]

Coleridge had not turned a facile religious fervor against a major system of philosophy, although he was accused more than once of being a religious "fanatic." He followed that philosophical system to its end and saw it turn from the outward to the inner life. As one delved deeper into individual experience in nature, thought viewed, "as a material phenomenon," could be accounted for only if one were "to refine matter into a . . . modification of intelligence."[16] And if one assumed that the mind works chiefly by associating what it has already appropriated as part of its own being, then activity of mind became nothing but being contemplating its own intelligence, which was an element of the "opposite" subjective system! Coleridge had discovered for himself, as Santayana noted, that "empiricism, understood in this psychological way, [became] the starting point for transcendentalism."[17]

In his mid and late twenties, disenchanted with the objective or natural system, Coleridge pressed on, supplementing his thought with Leibniz, Tetens, Kant, Fichte, Schelling, Schiller, and Jacobi.

As an indication of Coleridge's progression in philosophical speculation, and of his appetite for complete explanations compatible with his own thought and belief, Southey wrote of Coleridge in 1808 that, "Hartley was ousted by Berkeley, Berkeley by Spinoza, and Spinoza by Plato; when last I saw him [1804] Jacob Behmen had some chance of coming in." Later, when Coleridge felt uneasy about the subjective system's tendency to pantheism, he came to believe that Fichte and Schelling erred when they deviated from Kant, and that Schelling's system resolved "itself into fanaticism; not better than that of Jacob Bohme." In a similar way Coleridge earlier pronounced that Hartley erred when he deviated from Aristotle.[18] So many of the essential works here appeared from 1770 to 1795. Hazlitt, in his *Spirit of the Age: Mr. Coleridge*, describes Coleridge's research and omnivorous readings. In a prose ringing out like a Homeric catalogue of the intellect, he follows the trek of mind

Coleridge pursued. Hazlitt's chronology is slightly confused, but its register inspiring.

Coleridge came to accept the postulate of the subjective system, that being or spirit is antecedent to matter or nature, that "all body necessarily presupposes soul." From *natura*, the future infinitive, he reasoned that nature is perpetually becoming and about to be born, and must have originally been spirit itself.[19] The empirical science of materialism would approach "its perfection in proportion as it immaterializes objects" and finds in them their cause, the principle of being and spirit. "This elevation of the spirit above . . . the senses to a world of spirit affords the sole sure anchorage in the storm . . . It is a form of BEING."[20]

Yet even if the better answer to "the whole riddle of the world" were, at heart, being and not matter, then at least one could see that being worked in and through phenomena and was made manifest in material realities. This was the essence of miracles. In art, too, the imagination must work through particular symbols, words, notes, colors, or movements.[21] Gerard, Priestley, Sulzer, and Schelling all stressed this final return to the concrete. Concreteness was Hazlitt's great strength as a critic. Shakespeare said it simply in the line, "A local habitation and a name." All the arteries of life and thought return to the heart after dividing into invisible capillaries. The subjective and objective poles intertwine and fuse, spirit informs matter, and a dynamic synthesis and coalescence of both systems occurs. Nature is then *natura naturans*, and in nature works the informing form (*forma informans*) of the ideal world.

## THE DYNAMIC IMAGINATION

The "Dynamic Philosophy," as Coleridge envisioned it, gives ultimate precedence to the pole of being, taking it as an unconditional postulate, which for him in the end meant God. But the dynamic process in individuals involves all objects of experience until an intimate union of inward intelligence and external substance takes place. "This," Coleridge observed, in contrast to Fichte, "I call *I*—identifying the percipient and the perceived," "a sameness of the conceiver and the conception." The mind lives in the world as the world exists in and for the mind. Coleridge refers to this situation as a *third* philosophical system built on the poles of the first two: "There are therefore essentially but three kinds of philosophers and more are not possible." The first two espouse either the subjective or objective system; the third kind of philosopher includes "those who . . . have attempted to reconcile these two opposites and bring them into one."[22] Translated into poetical practice, this philosophical concept amounted to the same process that Addison, Akenside, Moritz, and Herder had identified as among the highest offices of poetry, especially of myth, namely the communion of corporeal and spiritual, the birth of gods to represent the human perception of nature, or as Keats saw in *Psyche*, the birth of gods to symbolize the inner life of the self.[23] Coleridge even creates a concrete, sensuous image to depict the pure or "abstract self," the self alone:

> All look or likeness caught from earth,
> All accident of kin or birth,
> Had pass'd away. There seem'd no trace
> Of aught upon her brighten'd face,
> Upraised beneath the rifted stone,
> Save of one spirit all her own;
> She, she herself, and only she,
> Shone through her body visibly.[24]

The emphasis for Coleridge was to "make the senses out of the mind—not the mind out of the senses, as Locke did."[25] But the senses are indeed made, and soon much of human life is, in Keats's words, "caught from earth." Thought and reality grow indistinguishable, like two sounds, "of which no man can say positively which is the voice and which the echo." Our intelligent self-consciousness becomes inseparable from our perceptions of the world.[26] Our sympathy and empathy kindle in the presence of personal situations and scenes of nature because our individual identities form themselves by the process of uniting an inherent "abstract self" with objective reality. This was the growth of a poet's mind. In another context it was also Wordsworth's child philosopher growing away form his true self until, after being eloigned from nature, he could again return "In years that bring the philosophic mind." The border between self and nature dissolves: "we receive but what we give/And in our life alone does Nature live."

The Dynamic Philosophy set a framework, not only for philosophy and personal experience but also for science, history, and art, which was at once intellectual and sensual. Coleridge's *Theory of Life* (1816) explains physical and biological processes as the interaction and unification of polar principles. He wrote the piece for James Gillman, a young doctor, for whom in a letter he outlined the basic tenet of the work: "An IDEA therefore contemplates the Alpha and the Omega (one-all; Finite-Infinite; Subject-Object; Mind-Matter; Substance-Form; Time-Space; Motion-Rest; Futuration-Presence; & c & c—and it is indifferent which of the Pairs you take, for they are all Symbols of the same Truth produced by different Positions)."[27]

Nine years later, in 1825, the "Dynamic" appears in *Aids to Reflec-*

*tion,* where Coleridge suggests it is the moving life force, the animating and spiritualizing process of nature.[28] The extent to which the Dynamic had seized his outlook is shown in the fact that he even proposed reform of the grammatical persons: "I" would be the thesis, "it + i = he" the antithesis, and "Thou" the synthesis. The dynamic process worked through both laws in nature and ideas in the mind. It governed science, history, politics and the fine arts including poetry, and had a distinct relation to theology.[29] If we start from a religious assumption that "the mind is beforehand impressed with a belief of a providence guiding this great drama of the world to its conclusion," then it seems inevitable in all forms of life, matter, and spirit "that a certain unity is to be expected from the very circumstances of opposition . . . one point comprising the excellencies of both."[30] Man could feel at home in the creation. Through his imagination, which alone can seize and participate in the dynamic of nature, through what Keats called a "greeting of the spirit," man becomes not an alienated fortress or island but a part of an organic whole, a special creature in whom lives the whole.

### A UNIFIED PSYCHE

Before proceeding to the resolution Coleridge developed for his "system" ("if I may venture to give it so fine a name"), we should examine his vision of the dynamic process in the mind. Here the linchpin or combining nerve of the imagination unifies all faculties within the mind itself. And since the mind images in itself the natural world and its divine scheme, then in integrating the various faculties of the mind, nature itself can be seen as one process connatural to human life, both governed by the same laws of being. The internal and external would become one as seen through the inward "I." Accordingly, Coleridge tried to revamp—he did not reject outright—the scheme of faculty psychology.

Whether the senses receive stimuli from external objects or not, their operation is passive. Nothing originates in the senses; they have no preconceptions, no creative power in themselves. And although the senses can be deceptively literal—as in Blake's "guinea sun" or the boy described by Tucker who, having just gained sight after blindness from birth, climbs a drainspout to take hold of the moon, which looked like a silver shilling—the senses are indispensable. The faculty of understanding includes within itself the receptivity of the senses but adds the power of reflection and judgment. Understanding compares and groups; it orders empirical data, puts them in abstract terms, and generalizes from them. The understanding can distinguish individualities from a class and consequently exercises induction and deduction. It tends to

separate the objective and subjective elements of experience; we are
conscious, then, of being "separated beings, and place nature in antithesis to the mind, as object to subject, thing to thought, death to
life."[31] Truth is known through the understanding, but this is not the
source of truth. The senses alone have direct contact with the purely
objective, and reason alone receives ideas and spiritual truths. "To *think*
of a thing is different from to perceive it, as 'to walk' is from to 'feel the
ground under you.' "[32] Understanding grapples with the polarity or dynamic of experience through words, images, and symbols. By these
alone both sense impressions and ideas are represented. But Coleridge
believes that while the understanding (Kant's *Verstand* and Milton's
"discursive reason") can grasp the two poles of the Dynamic, it cannot
unify them. It cannot create the images on which it depends.

The faculty Coleridge believed held sway in scientific and materialistic researches was not reason, properly understood, but the understanding: "The histories and political economy of the present and preceding
century partake in the general contagion of . . . mechanistic philosophy,
and are the product of an unenlivened generalizing understanding."[33]

Prompted by Kant's example, Coleridge wanted to rescue the original
sense of reason into something more in line with the Platonic *nous* or
Milton's "intuitive reason." Consequently, as early as his mid-twenties,
he—like Leibniz, Tetens, Hazlitt, and Reynolds—deplored the meaning
of "rational" as scientific or empirical. The material or so-called "rational" philosophers, he said, praised lack of imagination as possession of
judgment. As late as 1825 in *Aids to Reflection*, he battled against what
he believed a perversion of the meaning of reason by a succession of
empirical philosophers: "The word *rational* has been strangely abused
of late times." Such rational empiricism could not take in "great things"
or whole conceptions. Its practitioners "were marked by a microscopic
acuteness." They viewed the cosmos as a man examines through his
pocket lens the superficial imperfections in the marble of a large and
beautiful statue.[34]

Returning to the Greek conception of reason and guided by Plato,
Pascal, Leibniz, and "our elder writers" such as Hooker, Bacon, Milton,
Sanderson, and the Cambridge Platonists, Coleridge tries to vanquish
the recent sense of reason as a notion of the "hollow Puppets of an hollow Age."[35] He aims to pierce "the long-neglected holy Cave,/The
haunt obscure of OLD PHILOSOPHY," until its walls sparkle "as erst they
sparkled to the flame/Of odrous lamps tended by saint and sage!" Reason turns directly to ideas and truths which exist in the subjective world
of essence and spirit, without "an adequate correspondent in the world
of the senses."[36] Reason is an immediate and intuitive beholding of es-

sential truths, "having a similar relation to the Intelligible or Spiritual, as SENSE has to the Material or Phenomenal."[37]

Working from this conception of reason, Coleridge then faces "the highest *problem* of Philosophy: whether ideas, as the object of reason, were regulative and only products of the limited individual mind, according to Kant and Aristotle, or whether ideas were constitutive, in the mind and one with the power and Life of Nature, as in Plato, Plotinus and St. John."[38]

If this is the highest problem of philosophy "and not part of its nomenclature," it explains Coleridge's stress on Kant's distinction between reason and understanding. Understanding reflects and generalizes on sense or on symbolic impressions, but it cannot apprehend ideas, whose existence in reason might duplicate laws of the natural world. Because it leads to the "highest problem," the relationship of ideas in the mind to corresponding and constitutive ideas in nature, the distinction between understanding and reason becomes "pre-eminently the *Gradus ad Philosophiam.*"[39]

But Coleridge's reason, unlike the Platonic *nous*, works in and through the senses and understanding. It has full play in a symbiosis with other faculties. Just as understanding includes and subsumes the senses, so reason includes and subsumes understanding. The image of the various faculties is one of concentric circles, each larger one including lesser ones within it. This image accorded, as Coleridge recognized, with the philosophical principle of subsumption emphasized by Leibniz. And the image of reason subsuming all faculties in a larger concentricity elucidates Coleridge's phrase in the *Statesman's Manual*, "self-circling energies of the Reason": "The REASON without being either the SENSE, the UNDERSTANDING or the IMAGINATION contains all three within itself, even as the mind contains its thoughts, and is present in and through them all; or as the expression pervades the different features of an intelligent countenance."[40]

Reason is the highest function of being, itself "the one attribute in which all others are contained, not as parts, but as manifestations."[41] It coalesces with the understanding and the senses but has primacy of truth over them, just as the subjective pole of being coalesces with, but precedes, the objective or phenomenal. Coleridge deviates from this ultimate stress on reason only once, when he calls the imagination, not reason, the "greatest faculty of the human mind."

But the only way to see how ideas as objects of reason inform and work through the senses and understanding is to express the activity of reason in symbols, names, shapes, or images. A truth of the reason, an idea, is "in its own proper form . . . *inconceivable*. For *to conceive* is a function of the Understanding, which can be exercised only on subjects subordinate thereto."[42] Reason must be transformed into a symbolic, sensual language before it can inform other faculties or communicate truth: "All minds must think by some symbols—Yet this a *want*, *pothon*, desiderium, for vividness of *symbol* = which has something that is *without*, that has the property of *Outness* (a word which Berkeley preferred to 'Externality')."[43]

This "vividness" of symbol, recalling Hazlitt, the associationists, Tetens, Platner, Gerard, and Duff, could best be supplied by poetry. Keats came to speculate in *The Fall of Hyperion* (ll. 8–11) that:

> Poesy alone can tell her dreams,
> With the fine spell of words alone can save
> Imagination from the sable chain
> And dumb enchantment.


### THE ALL-CONNECTING NERVE OF IMAGINATION

The imagination gives reason a language and the ability to appear in concrete forms. It mediates between *im*mediate reason and *im*mediate senses and expresses their union to the understanding. This activity is invaluable because "to the forms of the Understanding all truth must be reduced, that is to be fixed as an object of reflection, and to be rendered *expressible.*"[44] The imagination alone permits reason and ideas to inform the whole mind in one interplay of faculties, self-communing, objective and subjective, in contact with the outer world and the inner essence. Imagination is "the laboratory in which the thought elaborates essence into existence."[45] All experience is drawn up under one "living copula." The Dynamic becomes a moving, vital, and all-informing process. The imagination is "that reconciling and mediatory power, which incorporating the Reason in Images of the Sense, and organizing (as it were) the flux of the Senses by the permanence and self-circling energies of the Reason, gives birth to a system of symbols, harmonious in themselves, and consubstantial with the truths, of which they are the *conductors.*"[46]

The imagination is, in the original Greek sense of the word "organic," an instrumentality unifying and touching all parts of a living and autonomous composition. It expresses the highest, ineffable truths as they animate the mind.

The imagination is not, however, simply a messenger emanating from ideas and dictating to our understanding. That would be impossible, because ideas in their immaterial forms are incomprehensible to any faculty except reason; "the higher intellectual powers can only act *through* a corresponding energy *of the lower*."[47] The imagination is protean: it moves through the faculties of the mind and informs each particular faculty in a process and manner not only congenial and immediate to that faculty but also susceptible of receiving influence from that faculty, an influence to be transformed and made immediate to other faculties. Sense, reason, and understanding therefore receive and give their own immediate apprehensions as modified by all faculties. The synthetic process is constant, a "combination or transfer of powers," which involves what might be called continuous feedback.[48] The imagination, as it integrates the whole mind, is "an intermediate faculty, which is at once both active and passive," influencing and influenced by each faculty simultaneously. Then, by translating all mental activity into images or symbols, the imagination produces language that contains the whole potential or "potentized" mind. The understanding grasps this language and uses it for communication. Without our imagination-created language, we are defeated and lost—bereft, as Hobbes said, of civilization. Thus Caliban (*The Tempest* III. ii) advises the drunken sailors conspiring against Prospero:

> thou mayst brain him,
> Having first seized his books . . .
> . . . Remember
> First to possess his books; for without them
> He's but a sot, as I am, nor hath not
> One spirit to command . . .
> . . . Burn but his books.

This explanation of the imagination as one organic and harmonious process helps to clarify Coleridge's short and characteristic descriptions: the imagination is "modifying," "co-adunative," and "fusive"; it is "unifying" and "esemplastic"; it shapes or "forms into one." A lowest common denominator exists in these characteristics: they suggest, either by means of the active present participle or explicitly, a vital and lifelike process. The faculties of the mind affect each other; they mix and transfer power, until they abolish the partitions between them and form one flow of sensation, ideas, reflection, and language.

One immediate consequence of the unifying activity of the imagination is that it no longer becomes possible to talk of subjective and objective facets in the mind. In the mind the Dynamic of the imagination creates unity. The subjective pole of being and the objective pole of natural phenomena "interpenetrate" (a word Coleridge coined) through the imagination, which yields a language capable of communicating and being understood. As Coleridge notes in the *Biographia*:

*In short, what I had supposed substances were thinned away into shadows, while everywhere shadows were deepened into substances:*

> "If substance may be call'd what shadow seem'd,
> For each seem'd either!"
>
> Milton[49]

## NATURE AND CONNATURAL MIND

Coleridge's sense of "primary imagination" as an individual repetition or perceptive duplication of the universe as created by the infinite "I am" indicates that he had given an answer to the "highest problem of philosophy": whether our ideas are regulative and therefore may not be congruent with the laws of nature, or are constitutive and therefore partake accurately of the life and being in the natural world. He became convinced that ideas are constitutive. The imagination not only harmonizes all faculties of mind but is in direct and truthful relation to the dynamic of matter and spirit in nature. Ideas of human reason correspond to those of universal or divine reason.

Yet however much activated by recent German thought, Coleridge drew from Pythagoras, Plato, the Renaissance Platonists, and Leibniz his original notions on the inherent harmony between man's mind and the universal mind revealing itself in the created world. Pythagoras conceived that the inner soul and ideas that are present in reason

> must necessarily be of the same nature and kind with those of the universe which acted upon him and which he alone was capable of beholding . . . He therefore supposed that what in *men* the ideas were, as we should say, those in the *world* were the laws; that the ideas partook according to the power of the man, of a constitutive character, in the same manner as the laws did in external nature.[50]

The Delphic command "Know thyself" Coleridge interprets in the *Biographia* not only as self-knowledge but as consciousness of the world as perceived by the self, "coincidence of an object with a subject"; finally, "Know thyself: and so shalt thou know God . . . and in God all things." Emerson, a Coleridge enthusiast, echoes the sense that nature and the self are one in using the same command to address his audience in *The American Scholar* (1837): "And, in fine, the ancient precept, 'Know thyself,' and the modern precept, 'Study nature,' become at last one maxim."[51]

But as in the case of accepting the antecedence of the pole of being over that of matter, Coleridge knew he could offer no proof that ideas are constitutive. That position was only and forever a postulate. It seemed affirmed by experience and, perhaps more important, by other thinkers. The constitutive quality of ideas was for Coleridge also a result of a religious belief that all creation, including the mind, depends on one absolute being. On the importance of ideas, he had turned directly to Plato. Authorities for his position, he said, "are such that our only difficulty is occasioned by their number." He had not followed Plato strictly in his conception of reason, but he shared with Plato the assumption that a "superessential" source of being had established a harmony between laws of matter and ideas.[52] There was at least no evidence for doubting this assumption. Even science, seemingly concerned with the purely empirical, revealed the conjunction of the mind with the laws of nature. This was the force of Archimedes' cry, *"Eureka"*: his intuitive reason found confirmation in the realm of things. Similarly, Coleridge thought that the Newtonian system triumphed over the Ptolemaic because it was "a yet higher Power, arranging, correcting, and annulling the representatives of the Senses according to its own inherent Laws and constitutive Ideas."[53] Einstein, too, later downplayed his mathematical and experimental abilities, giving greater credit to imagination for the framework of his theories. Coleridge expressed the union of empiricism and true reason in the terse statement, "philosophy becomes scientific and the sciences philosophical."[54]

The constitutive property of ideas leads to a swift conclusion: since the material world and human reason are governed by the same laws or ideas, imagination not only unifies the mind in one process but also *is* (or is at least a part of) the creative force of eternal reason as it works in the universe. This conclusion clarifies the claim that imagination in its highest sense, which for Coleridge would be the secondary imagination, is at one with "the vision and faculty divine." Imagination is the god-like human power. J. P. Collier reported that Coleridge said of the creative power, "The Almighty has thus condescended to communicate to man . . . a portion of his own great attributes."[55] The creative imagination presents nature in its highest sense, identical to the soul of man. The imagination is spiritual even as it works through matter, shaping it organically. In the individual, re-creating mind it is the same impulse of creation that occurs in external nature. The imagination, taken in conjunction with ideas constitutive both in human reason and in the material world, gives a unified perspective on spirit, existence, and matter. So Coleridge argued, like Plato, "that, as there was that power in the mind which thinks and images its thoughts, analogous to this was the power in nature which thought and imagined or embodied its thoughts."[56]

A belief that the imagination is part of the creative and shaping spirit of nature leads to two conclusions. First, the imagination may be said to participate in the power of the original creator, or God. Second, because the answer to the question, "Is not there a *link* between physical Imitation & Imagination?" is affirmative, the imagination plays the most vital role in art, the imitator of nature.[57] The intimacy Coleridge felt between his philosophical system, relying as it does on the imagination, and his religious conviction indicates he believed that even further behind the unity of the polar dynamic there must be one unconditional ground of being, one creator of all ideas. Given the agreement of ideas in the mind with "laws" in nature, and of the human imagination with creative "divine imagination," the only cause for this agreement seemed to rest "in a supersensual essence, which being at once the *ideal* of the reason and the cause of the material world, is the pre-establisher of the harmony in and between both. Religion therefore is the ultimate aim of philosophy." Or as stated in his *Philosophical Lectures,* "it seems to have been the final cause of a philosophy to prepare the way to religion."[58]

As Coleridge sums up the direction of his philosophical system, it includes a belief in constitutive ideas, in the imagination as the sole agency of reason; and in the presence of "one great Being." In other words,

> the mind . . . looking abroad into nature finds that in its own nature it has been fathoming nature, and that nature itself is but the greater mirror in which he beholds his own present and his own past being in the law, and learns to reverence while he feels the necessity of that one great Being whose external reason is the ground and absolute condition of the ideas in the mind, and no less the ground and the absolute cause of all the correspondent realities in nature—the reality of nature forever consisting in the law by which each thing is that which it is.[59]

Touching on the great philosophical issues of his day, Coleridge had given a metaphysical explanation for the age-old saying that the poet, by virtue of his creative power, is divinely inspired; this saying, which had become dangerously close to cliché, he now renovated from the ground up. The key was the imagination in its most complete power. Plato's divine *afflatus,* the *"Est Deus in nobis"* of Seneca and Leibniz, Sidney's poet as vice-creator, Freneau's "spark from Jove's resplendent throne," remarks of Reynolds, Herder, Kant, and Goethe, the "correspondent breeze" Wordsworth felt at the beginning of *The Prelude,* a breeze that seemed like "the sweet breath of heaven," Blake's divine-human imagination—all these and many more may now, by Coleridge's explanation, be seen as affirmations of one truth. And with this renewed confidence, the poet could believe that what Keats calls "guesses at heaven" are true visions.

### LEVELS OF THE IMAGINATION

We have discussed the repeated attempts of Locke, Wolff, Gerard, Platner, Tetens, Sulzer, Kant, Stewart, Alison, Fichte, Schelling, and others to split the imagination into levels or degrees of power. (Most of them also distinguish between fancy and imagination.) Coleridge, fully aware of nearly all these attempts, faced a tangled skein of terms, a Gordian knot of meanings tied up in the single strand of the English word "imagination." His own attempt to define degrees of the imagination culminates a century of interest. Not only are his definitions last in chronology, coming primarily in the *Biographia* of 1817, but Coleridge, though not as exhaustive or as lengthy as others, cleaves to essentials. His hope is to clarify, to simplify, and to join together the valuable contributions of British and German thinkers. Although his analyses remain open to varied interpretations, they shed light on what the imagination meant to him and what it had meant throughout the eighteenth century and the Romantic period.*

In order to distinguish the habitual growth and perceptions of mind from the creative powers of genius, Coleridge scaled the imaginative process in two degrees. The primary imagination is the agency of perceiving and of learning. It is the process of education in the original and general sense: a leading of the mind out into the world. It instinctively forms in itself the knowledge of what nature is and comes to understand phenomena and sense experiences. The symbols created and employed by imagination "are the conductors" of this knowledge. This self-education begins at birth and operates in every human mind by "the spontaneous consciousness natural to all reflecting beings." By means of the senses the mind builds up, or creates, its perception of all phenomena in the external world. The intelligence itself had to exist before it receives sensory information; in other words, "sensation itself is but vision nascent, not the cause of intelligence." The primary imagination must perceive and create in itself the associable before any association can occur. This explains Coleridge's remark that the primary imagination is "but intelligence revealed as an *earlier* power in the process of self-construction," a power which we exercise instinctively before submitting to "*passive* fancy and *mechanical* memory."[60]

We learn the symbols already created in the world, and they become a part of us; their existence is, in effect, *in* us—it is subsumed by our in-

* For further discussion, see my section on this topic in the Introduction to the forthcoming *Biographia Literaria* (*CC*) I, and above, pp. 94–122, 306–309. For distinctions between fancy and imagination, see especially ch. 13 above, but also (for Hazlitt, Wordsworth, and Fichte), chs. 15–16, 18.

telligent self. In the finite mind or "I am," which represents the ground of individual being, the imagination repeats or reduplicates the original creative acts of the universe, itself grounded in and existing as the "choral Echo" of "the great I AM": "The primary IMAGINATION I hold to be the living Power and prime Agent of all human Perception, and as a repetition in the finite mind of the eternal act of creation in the infinite I AM."[61]

The primary imagination or "original unific Consciousness, the primary Perception" is common to all people.[62] In fact, it is taken for granted and not even called "imagination," just as a sense of balance is taken for granted and not mentioned while we are walking. The primary imagination is "the *necessary* Imagination."[63] It automatically balances and fuses the innate capacities and powers of the mind with the external presence of the objective world that the mind receives through the senses.

However, it is one degree to represent and reduplicate the natural world in the individual intelligence and quite another degree to break down what has been perceived in order to recreate by an autonomous, willful act of mind that which has no analog in the natural world. This personal creativity is what we usually mean by the word "imagination": "In common language and especially on the subject of poetry, we appropriate the name imagination to a superior degree of the faculty, joined to a superior voluntary controul over it."[64]

Wolff, Gerard, Tetens, Kant, Schelling, and even Locke with his statement that complex ideas are "made voluntarily," had all stressed this willful control that elevates imaginative power to a creative act. This heightened and extended secondary imagination distinguishes genius.

The function of the primary imagination must precede that of the secondary. Otherwise the higher degree would lack perceptions to recombine and to shape into new relations. Productions of the secondary imagination have roots in common experience: "The secondary imagination I consider as an echo of the former . . . yet still as identical with the primary in the *kind* of its agency, and differing only in *degree*, and in the *mode* of its operation."[65] The adjective "secondary" does not imply a lesser power but signifies that "superior degree of the faculty," much in the way a secondary school advances over but follows and builds on the primary grades.

The "superior voluntary controul" guiding the secondary imagination is "coexisting with the conscious will." A free and deliberate will triggers the secondary imagination. This conscious volition involves consideration of the moral uses of poetry and art generally. The secondary imagination, once activated by the will, "dissolves, dissipates in order to recreate." Coleridge uses the word "recreate" to emphasize that the primary imagination has first formed in the mind the various images of nature. The secondary imagination "dissolves," alters, and reforms these images. It mediates between and *re-conciles* the separate experiences and knowledge perceived in bits by the primary degree. The secondary imagination is part of a self-conscious and willful apperception; the primary degree exercises involuntary or "automatic" perception. The secondary imagination extends and ramifies products of the primary degree. In cases where the secondary imagination cannot dissolve and reform or recreate the perceptions, it at least unifies and groups under the arch of one idea many separate images. Hence "at all events" the secondary faculty "struggles to idealize and unify."[66]

We should be careful not to lose track of Coleridge's usage. When he speaks of the philosophical principle unifying and completing the transcendental or subjective and the natural or objective hypotheses, he uses the word "imagination" or "philosophic imagination." This power is *"esemplastic,"* from the Greek "to shape into one," a word he felt could describe the philosophic and psychological fusion of subjective and objective. The primary and secondary degrees are the two degrees of this activity and share some characteristics: both rely on active and passive qualities in the mind, and both join the world of self and the world of nature. "In philosophical language, we must denominate this intermediate faculty in all its degrees and denominations, the IMAGINATION." Coleridge slightly confuses his distinction of degree, as well as his use of "imagination" to encompass both degrees. But the confusion is easily cleared. In criticism and discussion of the fine arts he uses the unmodified word "imagination" to mean secondary imagination alone. This usage he feels is common, "especially on the subject of poetry." There, when speaking of the imagination, "we appropriate the name to a superior [secondary] degree of the faculty."[67]

We must occasionally decide when he intends "imagination" to mean the philosophical concept as a whole, consisting of both primary and secondary degrees, or he intends the word to stand for secondary imagination alone, that power which we usually call creative. The right choice can be made if it is kept in mind that whenever he discusses poetry, criticism, or the fine arts, as distinct from philosophy or psychology in general, he undoubtedly means the secondary imagination. In these instances he is writing not "in philosophical language" but "in common language, and especially on the subject of poetry." For example, with reference to Wordsworth, he notes, "I challenge for this poet the gift of IMAGINATION in the highest and strictest sense of the word." Coleridge possibly encountered Gerard's terms "primary" and "secondary experience"—the "primary experience" being a perceptive activity that preceeds the more reflective and creative "secondary experience."

The genial or artistic secondary degree of the imagination is what Coleridge implies when he says he will discuss "with it the principles of production and of criticism in the fine arts." It is possible to avoid confusion and employ familiar usage by speaking of the imagination discussed in Coleridge's literary criticism as the poetic or creative imagination, which is equivalent to the secondary imagination as applied to the fine arts. In fact, Coleridge used "poetic imagination" this way. In Chapter 14, he describes characteristics of "the poetic IMAGINATION."[68] And in a letter of December 15–21, 1811, he calls the vital element in literature "a subtle spirit, all in each part, reconciling and unifying all. Passion and imagination are its most appropriate names; but even these say little—for it must be not merely passion but poetic passion, poetic imagination."[69]

### IMAGINATION'S IMAGE OF IMAGINATION

Coleridge's "deduction" of the imagination in the *Biographia* is not quite pinned down nor fully clarified. It remains fragmentary, and the abbreviated thirteenth chapter, with Coleridge's friendly letter to himself excusing the absence of a section of at least one hundred printed pages (presumably never written) and with only the last page on fancy and primary and secondary imagination, seems a brief outline for what could have been. There are superb remarks and examples in other chapters, but nothing protracted.

Coleridge is not alone in this cryptic or gnomic way of handling the imagination. With the possible exceptions of Gerard, Tetens, Kant, and Schelling, who were considerably more confined in their critical use of the imagination for literature, all of the writers who discuss the imagination at length do it either in a restrictive, often repetitive philosophic idiom, as does Fichte, or in the relatively narrow compass of faculty psychology alone, as do Maass and Stewart. In contrast, Coleridge deals with one of the most curious and fascinating properties of the imagination: it is even more powerful as an idea when described in its own terms. Echoing Schelling, Coleridge explains, "An IDEA, in the *highest* sense of that word, cannot be conveyed but by a *symbol.*"[70] And so with the imagination. The symbolic expression of the idea of imagination is, perhaps more than anything else, what the Romantic poets did for the imagination.

If imagination apprehends more than cool reason comprehends, then, as Fichte and even Reynolds argued, reason cannot directly comprehend the imagination; or if it can, according to that principle of subsumption by which every higher power includes the lower ones, then reason cannot express its comprehension of the imaginative power. This requires a symbol, an image. If imagination is a never-ending coalescence of opposites, then words of the understanding only reveal this process by cutting it open. We murder to dissect. A kind of Heisenberg Uncertainty Principle may be at work in attempts to explain the imagination: the very act of observation inextricably alters the nature of what is observed. When the imagination unites the subjective and objective experiences, "There is here no first, and no second," Coleridge remarks; "both are coinstantaneous and one." They "are so instantly united, that we cannot determine to which of the two the priority belongs." Any examination of the process wrenches apart the organic movement and unity. "While I am attempting to explain this intimate coalition, I must suppose it dissolved." Still, this kind of explanation is no more reassuring for Coleridge than it seems to have been for Schelling or Fichte.[71]

Coleridge expresses the elusive, self-transforming power of the imagination in a beautiful image. The point of the image is not merely the ability of the "philosophic imagination" to conceive empathically the active process of nature. Perhaps this is not the point at all. The metaphor seems intended as a symbolic representation of the process of growth in the imagination itself. It is not simply that the imagination perceives the development of nature; it generates a similar process in itself and in the self. This observation reflects one of Coleridge's strengths as a thinker on the imagination, his poetic gift and his willingness at times to use images and symbols, not abstractions and philosophic terms:

> They and they only can acquire the philosophic imagination, the sacred power of self-intuition, who within themselves can interpret and understand the symbol, that the wings of the air-sylph are forming within the skin of the caterpillar; those only, who feel in their own spirits the same instinct, which impels the chrysalis of the horned fly to leave room in its involucrum for antennae yet to come. They know and feel, that the *potential* works *in* them, even as the *actual* works on them![72]

The imagination contains within itself a potential which, uniting with external influences of nature, leads the mind to a new stage of growth.

### ART AND SYMBOLS

The unifying power of the imagination as it reproduces the creation and growth in the natural world holds key importance for Coleridge's comments on the fine arts. His philosophical and psychological tenets form the foundation of his critical principles. He combines the classical concept of art as an imitation of nature with the newer premium on originality and imagination. In imitating nature, the artist imitates and appropriates the *process* of nature. He creates a language, a series of symbols, which reflect and represent this dynamic process. The imagination makes the human affinity to the natural world concrete and recognizable: "The Imagination . . . turns with delight to distinct Images, & clear Ideas—contemplates *a World*, an harmonious System where an infinity of Kinds subsist each in a multitude of Individuals apportionate to its Kind in conformity to Laws existing in the divine Nature—therefore in the nature of Things."[73]

Art embodies particular points of intersection between the imagination of the individual mind and that of the divine power. Art presents "the burden of the mystery" of our being and expresses its otherwise ineffable connection with the universe:

> In looking at objects of Nature while I am thinking, as at yonder moon dimglimmering thro' the dewy window-pane, I seem rather to be seeking, as it were *asking*, a symbolical language for something within me that already and forever exists, than observing anything new. Even when that latter is the case, yet still I have always an obscure feeling as if that new phaenomenon were the dim Awaking of a forgotten or hidden Truth of my inner Nature. It is still interesting as a Word, a Symbol! It is *Logos*, the Creator! and the Evolver![74]

Imaginative art expresses and reaffirms the harmonious human presence in the world. Sympathetic identification with an object, with another person, or with our own future state is much more than emotional response or vague feeling; it is, as Keats wrote in 1819, "a willful and dramatic exercise of our Minds."[75] Art recaptures the harmony between human consciousness and the cosmos. Intensified by passion and excitement, art dissolves the human and the natural worlds into one symbolic language of human import. Coleridge's first important statement in "On Poesy or Art" is that art "is the mediatress between, and reconciler of, nature and man. It is, therefore, the power of humanizing nature, of infusing the thoughts and passions of man into every thing which is the object of his contemplation; Art would or should be the abridgment of nature . . . The object of art is to give the whole ad hominem."[76]

Coleridge wants to infuse the scenes and movements of nature with passions and sensations, with motives and emotions felt in the psyche. This, after all, is how we experience nature. The poet works by "representing external nature and human Thoughts and Affections, both relatively to human Affections."[77] But Coleridge scrupulously avoids suggesting that the poet's personality is the register of what is human.

Collier reported Coleridge's belief that the "crying sin" in modern criticism "is that it is overloaded with personality." Coleridge's stress is not
on self-expression but on the ability to identify with and to feel the object of his verse. He sees the entire cosmos, as it were, *sub specie genera.*
He exercises "that sublime faculty, by which a great mind becomes that
which it meditates on."[78] There should exist in poetry, as in the Dynamic Philosophy, no differentiation between subjective and objective,
internal and external, the human and the natural. So "in every work of
art there is a reconcilement of the external with the internal," of things
and thoughts, such as "to make the external internal, the internal external, to make nature thought, and thought nature—this is the mystery of
genius in the Fine Arts."[79]

   For Coleridge, a great poet implies a profound philosophical basis.[80]
The concept of identity derived from the Dynamic Philosophy fostered
his own poetic "principle of unity," where the poet dwells on his subject, the *object* of his art, so thoroughly that this unity can be seen as
Coleridge's concept of sympathy with a philosophical background. The
result is that Coleridge can describe poetry as

> a rationalized dream dealing . . . to manifold Forms our own Feelings, that
> never perhaps were attached by us consciously to our own personal
> Selves.—What is the Lear, the Othello, but a divine Dream/all Shake-
> speare, & nothing Shakespeare.—O there are Truths below the Surface
> in the subject of Sympathy. & how we *become* that which we under-
> standly behold & hear, having, how much God perhaps only knows,
> created part even of the Form.[81]

The poet employs several tools to achieve the "principle of unity."
Metaphor and simile bind together and equate distinct things, ideas, or
images, which share at least one aspect of similarity. The separate components or images of the metaphor are provided by the primary imagination, while the secondary or poetic imagination works to create the
metaphorical equation as a new perception. The two elements of the
metaphor, one of which ideally has a human import, become each other
even while appearing to maintain separate identities. Through the use of
metaphorical language to describe concrete forms in the natural world, a
poet builds into "each step of nature" a human identity. Shakespeare has
this gift of "humanizing imagery."[82] But the poetic imagination cannot
sift each grain of sand, pick every flower, or depict all wars. To make an
"abridgement of nature," the imagination creates symbols, which give
concrete form to ideas and passions and connect these with the objects
of nature. The artist sees into a "sense of the analogy or likeness of a
thing which enables a symbol to represent it so that we think of the
thing itself, yet knowing that the thing is not present to us." The symbol

so seems to be the thing itself that we give assent and it is. "By more or less mediations," says Coleridge, imitation depends "on this universal fact of words and images."[83]

In poetry, the more kinds of experience and varieties of images drawn into one symbol or metaphor, the more intense and imaginative the writing. If many emotions, thoughts, and sensations focus at once, they intensify each other and form one superadded effect, which was also a basic point of the associationist critics, perfected by Hazlitt. According to Coleridge, symbolic language, grasped by the understanding, presents resonant, not random, groups of figures and images. These groupings are far from accidental: poetry is a *"rationalized* dream."

A symbol is what it represents, but an allegorical image or figure is a replaced identity on a corresponding basis of one to one, or at best of one to a limited number of possible interpretations, an equation and not an identity. Allegory implies equivalency rather than sharing. An allegorical figure, to Coleridge, is essentially a substitute. A symbolic figure individualizes a whole class.

One challenge always faces the poet. He must replace myths and symbols worn out and encrusted with mechanical associations. "Phoebus," observes Coleridge, became objectionable not because it is rare or absent from common language, as Wordsworth argued, but because it is part of "an exploded mythology." No belief, conviction, or actual experience seems related to it. Coleridge reminisces about his teacher Boyer who inculcated distrust of such "poetic" diction: "Harp? Harp? Lyre? Pen and ink, boy, you mean! Muse, boy, Muse? Your Nurse's daughter, you mean! Pierian spring? Oh aye! the cloisterpump, I suppose!" But balanced against this stripping away of shriveled symbols is such a need for symbols themselves that discarded symbols are often reinstated when fresh ones cannot be found:

> The intelligible forms of ancient poets
> The fair humanities of old religion,
> ... all these have vanished.
> They live no longer in the faith of reason!
> But still the heart doth need a language, still
> Doth the old instinct bring back the old names.[84]

## CRITICISM: PRINCIPLES AND PRACTICE

Coleridge views imagination as the life-giving and life-producing force of art, "the SOUL that is everywhere," similar to the idea of *anima* and even to Dryden's *"life-touches"* of "fancy."[85] So essential is the imagination that when Coleridge begins the application of critical principles in Chapter 14 of the *Biographia*, he defines poetry almost exclusively in terms of the imagination. The poet "brings the whole soul of man into activity" because his imagination reconciles "opposite or discordant qualities." It fuses in one the individual and the representative character. It excites emotion and enriches thought. Coleridge quotes, with changes, Sir John Davies' poem "On the Soul of Man," saying that these lines may "be applied, and even more appropriately, to the poetic IMAGINATION," the "she" of the stanzas:

> Doubtless this could not be, but that she turns
>   Bodies to spirit by sublimation strange,
> As fire converts to fire the things it burns,
>   As we our food into our nature change.
>
> From their gross matter she abstracts their forms,
>   And draws a kind of quintessence from things;
> Which to her proper nature she transforms,
>   To hear them light on her celestial wings.
>
> Thus does she, when from individual states
>   She doth abstract the universal kinds;
> Which then re-clothed in divers names and fates
>   Steal access through our senses to our minds.

The lines echo both the letter to himself in Chapter 13, where substance melts into shadow and shadow is materialized, and his statement that imagination elaborates essence into existence. They summarize four crucial aspects of the poetic imagination: it distills and refines nature to essential forms; it embodies these forms by giving each one a concrete, "individual form in which the Truth is clothed"; it unifies all "into one graceful and intelligent whole"; and it transforms the work into human terms, "As we our food into our nature change."[86] Finally, the "celestial wings" of poetic imagination aspire to universal creative power.

Coleridge intends his criticism to rest on "principles of grammar, logic, psychology," and philosophy. Personal "interests" and "taste" spilling over from self-indulgent romanticism he rejects. Even if one could not demonstrably prove the rightness of critical principles, it was far better to navigate with a magnetic north that might not coincide with true north than to have no compass at all. Opinions alone "weigh for nothing"; they serve only as a "taste-meter to the fashionable world." Even Wordsworth's critical theories lacked philosophic depth. Coleridge spoke of "a constitution and code of laws" for criticism. These would have a "two-fold basis of universal morals and philosophic reason" free from all "*forseen* application to particular works and authors."[87] Shared critical principles would lead to similar opinions of the same works. He gave the example of Schlegel and himself. Working from similar philosophic bases, he said they had made independent but nearly interchangeable remarks on Shakespeare's plays as early as 1808.[88]

But the only assay of critical principles built around the imagination is practical and specific application. For Coleridge, the criterion of imagination elevates several authors to a pinnacle. There is Shakespeare's dramatic imagination, Milton's epic one, and Wordsworth's unique kind, "perfectly unborrowed and his own."[89] Genres are not ranked, but certain periods of literature display more imagination than others. French classical theater has little, for example, while the Elizabethan age exhibits much. Coleridge follows no systematic or mechanical outline. He selects one passage, the plan of a work, or a whole literary epoch; but his goal is consistent: to reach what is characteristic and revealing. The idea is that the imagination permeates the overall structure simply because it also operates through the selection of each word, coalescing all into a unified pattern.

In language and what might be called "poetic style," the greater the need to be imaginative, "the more necessary it is to be plain."[90] Obscure or esoteric allusions and phrases foul the immediate apprehension necessary for beauty and pleasure. Yet "plain" does not mean obvious or rustic in Wordsworth's sense; it means readily understood in the context. The result is an open idiom rich in meaning. For imaginative language, *Pilgrim's Progress* was one of Coleridge's favorite books.

In verse, both the origin and the effects of meter derive in part from qualities of the poetic imagination. The voluntary control necessary to each creative act engages deliberate rhythms that order our more spontaneous impulses. Yet the effect of these planned rhythms can be surprising, and attention picks up. Verse is more condensed than prose; more is brought to bear that excites and impassions. Meter, reflecting the volition of the secondary imagination, produces or "superadds" another effect, and the more stimulants poetry unifies, the more of mind it brings into play. Coleridge does not attack free verse, for that form often orders and repeats stress patterns. In fact, he explicitly names prose writings, such as the book of Job, that he considers "poetry ." He simply states that meter orders the creative act at the same time that it stimulates the reader.[91]

Particular words suggest what the mind then completes as a finished picture. In Book IX of *Paradise Lost,* the fig-tree

> spreads her arms
> Branching so broad and long, that in the ground
> The bended twigs take root, and daughters grow
> About the mother tree, a pillar'd shade
> High over-arch'd, and echoing walks between:

> There oft the Indian Herdsman, shunning heat,
> Shelters in cool, and tends his pasturing herds
> At loop holes cut through thickest shade.

This description entices the reader to create in his own mind the literal figure of the landscape. The "echoing walks between" have no sound but represent a series of concentric paths formed by the repeated rising and dipping to the ground of the outstretched branches, their shady canopies diminishing in height as they extend from the trunk. Milton transmits their essence with one word, "echoing," and such words, according to Coleridge, "may be deservedly entitled the *creative words* in the world of imagination."[92]

Too much exactness or "matter-of-factness" forecloses a sense of process. In *The Excursion* Wordsworth writes passages minute and exact, where superfluous details stand out in static clarity. The imagination, however, feeds off curiosity and wonder, when the mind is suspended in eager anticipation:

> As soon as it is fixed on one image, it becomes understanding; but while it is unfixed and wavering between them, attaching itself permanently to none, it is imagination ... The grandest efforts of poetry are where the imagination is called forth, not to produce a distinct form, but a strong working of the mind, still offering what is still repelled, and again creating what is again rejected.[93]

This agility of perception, leaping directly from one vision or image to others, characterizes the portrait of Death in Book II of *Paradise Lost*:

> The other shape,
> If shape it might be call'd, that shape had none
> Distinguishable in member, joint, or limb,
> Or substance might be call'd, that shadow seem'd
> For each seem'd either: black it stood as night;
> Fierce as ten furies, terrible as hell,
> And shook a dreadful dart; what seem'd his head
> The likeness of a kingly crown had on.

A slight haziness or incompleteness of the images keeps the "continuous" mind in a state of uncertainty and prevents it from lapsing into passivity.[94] A thing depicted with the greatest fidelity cannot haunt or allure.

Coleridge contrasts the suggestive, "creative words" of the imagination with

> modern poems, where all is so dutchified, if I may use the word, by the most minute touches, that the reader naturally asks why words, and not painting, are used ... The power of poetry is, by a single word, perhaps,

*to instil energy into the mind, which compels the imagination to produce the picture.* Prospero tells Miranda,

> One midnight,
> Fated to the purpose, did Antonio open
> The gates of Milan; and i' the dead of darkness,
> The ministers for the purpose hurried thence
> Me, and thy *crying* self.

Here, by introducing a single happy epithet, "crying" . . . a complete picture is presented to the mind, and in the production of such pictures the power of genius consists.[95]

The imagination concentrates on the one word "crying." A present participle amid past-tense verbs, it gives a sense of immediacy . It is the only adjective for the rather bland word "self," and so the attribute of crying takes the whole weight of description; except for this pitiful sound, all else is "i' the dead of darkness," unseen. The one word suggests and dominates; it unifies. As Sulzer had noted in his *Allgemeine Theorie,* citing the Virgilian description of young Marcellus as *"Tu eris,"* the imagination of the reader, not the author, now produces the picture, sharing in the creative process.

In *Shakespeare as a Poet Generally,* first published in *Literary Remains* (1836), Coleridge gives his best example of the different workings of fancy and imagination in poetry. Shakespeare, he says,

possessed fancy, considered as the faculty of bringing together images, dissimilar in the main, by some one point or more of likeness, as in such a passage as this [from *Venus and Adonis*]:

> Full gently now she takes him by the hand,
> A lily prisoned in a jail of snow,
> Or ivory in an alabaster band—
> So white a friend engirts so white a foe.

But higher on "the intellectual ladder," Shakespeare proved the indwelling in his mind of imagination, or the power by which one image or feeling is made to modify many others, and by a sort of fusion to force many into one . . . and which, combining many circumstances into one moment of consciousness, tends to produce that ultimate end of all human thought and human feeling, unity, and thereby the reduction of the spirit to its principle and foundation, who is alone truly one . . . [It] acts chiefly by creating out of many things, as they would have appeared . . . [to] an ordinary mind, detailed in unimpassioned succession, a oneness even as nature, the greatest of poets, acts upon us when we open our eyes upon an extended prospect. Thus the flight of Adonis in the dusk of the evening:

> Look! how a bright star shooteth from the sky;
> So glides he in the night from Venus' eye!

How many images and feelings are here brought together . . . the beauty of Adonis, the rapidity of his flight, the yearning, yet helplessness, of the enamoured gazer, while a shadowy ideal character is thrown over the whole!

All of this, done "without any anatomy of description," traces the working of the imagination back to its root in poetry, the image, back to the power of images to form an equation between many images and thoughts and so to join them in one whole. With a more refined, more "armed vision," Coleridge is extending the observations of Gerard, William Richardson, and Priestley, all of whom had prized the imaginative suggestiveness of Shakespere above his "description."

## THE CRITICAL IDEAL OF UNITY

Coleridge marks lines from Wordsworth's "The Mad Mother" for their "disjunction conjunctive of the sudden Images *seized* on from external Contingents by Passion & Imagination."[96] This compares to Johnson's definition of wit in the "Life of Cowley" as *discordia concors*. Coleridge took great wit to mean genius, which in turn subsumes imagination.[97] The imagination at once reconciles contrarieties and is always presenting the results of a polar process. In Hamlet's ghost, for example, Coleridge sees a dialectic working through that apparition, which lends an "accrescence of objectivity . . . yet retains all its ghostly attributes and fearful subjectivity."[98]

Another, more philosophic instance of the imagination's unifying power is Hamlet's soliloquy beginning, "To be, or not to be." In that proposition Coleridge sees an enigma simply and imaginatively expressed, one that directly relates to his philosophic stress on the antecedence of being. If the mind turns "to the consideration of EXISTENCE, in and by itself, as the mere act of existing," it cannot explain its creation, its beginning, or its end. "Not TO BE, then, is impossible: TO BE, incomprehensible." Not only are Hamlet's six words a question of suicide, they echo cosmic mystery. Shakespeare's genius expresses, in so few words, life's unadorned and "sacred horror." The two alternatives are joined suddenly and audaciously by "connecting energy," by the imaginative power of "genial method." Even though Shakespeare's popularity was at its highest point to date, Coleridge could still say that the awareness of such power in the famous soliloquy made it one that "has yet received only the first fruits of the admiration due to it."[99]

Some of Coleridge's most acute critical handling of the imagination as a reconciling power appears in scattered remarks on characterization. Characters conceived imaginatively exhibit distinct personal identity even as they represent a class. They are real people who seem historical rather than literary, but who have impulses and traits of human nature.

Wordsworth's "Michael" depicts true individuals, yet they also embody class characteristics of rural life. Harry Gill and the Idiot Boy, on the contrary, give only eccentric impression. Molière's Don Juan blends perfectly a real and definite man with a general and abstract type.[100] Similarly, Don Quixote has become proverbial yet retains a specific aura about his person because of Cervantes' ability to "combine the permanent with the individual." Ideally, a character seems real and distinctive but also reminds us of people we know in the flesh. This explains Coleridge's remark that Shakespeare's characters "are all *genera* intensely individualized."[101] Jonson's creations, by contrast, are too fixed. Fabricated to represent types, they seldom convince anyone that they actually could be found in life.[102]

The most elusive of Coleridge's critical uses of the imagination appears in his judgments on the overall nature of a work and the quality of mind responsible for it. He often discusses the imaginative conception of a work but then skips the textual explication.[103] However, a number of remarks are penetrating. Although *The Tempest* enchants with its exotic characters, remote setting, and sensual power, the real drama occurs within the mind whose "moved and sympathetic imagination"* creates such a new world and then wanders in it to discover the potential of its own handiwork. The stress always falls on unified structure, where "each part supposes a preconception of the whole," a spirit that controls the work in the way genetic forces move a few embryonic cells to the birth of an individual.[104] Compare *Romeo and Juliet* with any French classical tragedy: the one possesses harmony and interconnection; the other shows only "the shaping skill of mechanical talent" that produces parts like links of chain, touching only sections immediately before and after.

Coleridge repeatedly characterizes great authors as supremely imaginative minds. Among his contemporaries, he finds Wordsworth pre-eminent. Milton's special gift is his attraction of "all forms and things to himself, into the unity of his own IDEAL," coloring them with his own thought.[105] Shakespeare enjoyed the highest and purest state of imagination, which allows him to explore the universe by recreating within himself all existing vantage points of experience. Thus he writes "exactly as if of an other planet, or as describing the movement of two Butterflies."[106] Others, such as Richardson, Montagu, Hazlitt, and Keats, remarked on this power of Shakespeare, but Coleridge placed astonishing emphasis on it. At least four separate times he praises Shakespeare as similar to the god Proteus. Not only did all the workings of imagination find a home in him, but they combined and permitted him to assume

* On "sympathetic imagination," a phrase (but certainly not an idea) that Coleridge originates, see above, ch. 11.

"all forms of human character and passion." In "perfect abstraction from himself" he became all things, yet his images and characters, led in part by his sympathetic identification, were his own willful creation. Thus he also was "for ever remaining himself."[107] He possessed his genius; it did not possess him.

### BEAUTY AND THE IDEAL

In poetry or art, it is the harmonious fusion of many elements into one that Coleridge calls beauty. Art, differing from philosophy in having pleasure, not truth, as its prime or immediate object, affords this pleasure by the presence of beauty.[108] In a fallen world, truth is not identical with beauty. The concept of truth frequently implies what should be rather than what is. Moreover, it is often too general and abstract, or ineffable, and art cannot seize on it as a first goal. Instead, truth is the ultimate end of art. Art presents truth at one remove by the use of harmonious symbols and the beauty these compose. Beauty in art thus serves as truth's "short hand hieroglyphic."*

The definition of beauty and the definition of the sublime had preoccupied aesthetics for a half century or more. Coleridge was now prepared to place at least the definition of beauty in terms of the imagination, though not, like Alison, in terms of associations only. Coleridge stresses that while beauty subsumes the sensual, it "must belong to the intellect"; it involves the whole mind because it reflects the activity of imagination. Beauty does not depend on agreeable feelings, associations, or habits, all of which vary from person to person, as Alison said, and even from one time in an individual's life to another. Beauty brings together things that have a less capricious connection than personal response. In the presence of a beautiful object all human faculties are awakened. We feel "the component parts each in relation to each, and all forming a whole." This kind of coalescence Coleridge describes as "Multëity in Unity." Instantaneously, all powers of the mind and heart interplay together. The true sense of beauty "subsists in simultaneous

---

* Until the deciphering of the Rosetta Stone by Champollion in the late 1820s, Egyptian hieroglyphics, especially brought to the attention of Europe by Napoleon's Egypt campaign, during which the Stone was unearthed in 1799, remained a mysterious set of symbols with hidden meanings of apparent religious, literary, and even governmental significance. Hieroglypic writing was, however, obviously a language of images drawn from visible nature and even from parts of the body and objects such as staffs and flails. Thus "hieroglyphic" itself became a word representing a medium of pure imagination, of pure images, much in the way Chinese ideograms later appealed to Ezra Pound. Not only Coleridge but Wolff, Hazlitt, Keats, Goethe, and Schelling used "hieroglyphic" as an image for the concrete power of imagination carried into a symbolic world where man and nature are united in poetic language.

intuition of the relation of parts, each to each, and of all to a whole; exciting an immediate and absolute complacency, without intervenence . . . of any interest, sensual or intellectual."[109]

In art, beauty is the visible graph of the imagination. It resides in concrete images where the actual process of the connecting and unifying power can be traced. And just as the poet's imagination repeats and partakes of the universal creative power, the beauty he creates imitates the beautiful in nature: "We must imitate nature! Yes, but what in nature,—all and everything? No, the beautiful in nature. What is beauty? It is, in the abstract, the unity of the manifold, the coalescence of the diverse; in the concrete, it is the union of the shapely . . . with the vital."[110]

The forms of natural beauty created by the cosmic imagination are intuitively recognized and imitated by the artistic imagination. Beauty is a "constitutive idea," in harmony with both external reality and the human soul. When hard and fast rules of form are based on an imbalance of human faculties, where either the rational, the emotional, or the sensual holds too much sway, then art cannot adequately depict the flow and interdependent processes of the natural world or of those beautiful forms in it: "The *rules* of the IMAGINATION are themselves the very powers of growth and production. The *words*, to which they are reducible, present only the outlines and external appearance of the fruit."[111]

Ideal form, purified from accidental circumstances, evolves from within, according to the "vital" tendency in the concrete parts and materials at hand to arrange and subordinate themselves even as they are filling the outlines of a larger "shapely" organization:

> If the artist copies the mere nature *natura naturata*, what idle rivalry! If he proceeds only from a given form, which is supposed to answer to the notion of beauty, what an emptiness, what an unreality there always is in his productions . . . you must master the essence, the *natura naturans*, which presupposes a bond between nature in the higher sense and the soul of man.[112]

Each form is the result of some essence or spirit working from within. Here again Coleridge emphasizes that spirit or mind are higher than matter, "that body is but a striving to become mind,—that it is mind in its essence!" All forms in nature, as they should in art, grow out of an internal development where the generic unites permanently with the individual. Universals and genera derive their definition from particulars and individuals; yet each developing particular or individual does not violate but indeed reflects and belongs to a universal or general class already established. Speaking of character in drama, for example, Coleridge states: "The ideal consists in the happy balance of the generic with the individual. The former makes the character representative and symbolical, therefore instructive; because, *mutatis mutandis*, it is applicable to whole classes of men. The latter gives it living interest; for nothing lives or is real, but as definite and individual."

In a larger context, art presents ideal forms as shaping themselves from within and shining through or illuminating the concrete, individual appearance. The artist's imagination alone can imitate that kindred power in a thing or person which, moving from latency to realization, creates and evolves the beautiful and unified form of an object, the whole living character of an individual. A "perfect reconciliation" is effected between the "two conflicting principles of the FREE LIFE, and of the confining FORM":

> the artist must first eloign himself from nature in order to return to her with full effect . . . He must out of his own mind create forms according to the severe laws of the intellect, in order to generate in himself that co-ordination of freedom and law . . . which assimilates him to nature, and enables him to understand her.

The artist becomes something like a keenly ground lens, an "I" focused by the imagination, through which forms of nature are intensified and enlarged while at the same time being refracted according to the index of human experience. The medium of light, common to all elements, comes ultimately from "reason and will, universal reason, and will absolute."[113]

## THE MORAL IMPERATIVE AND FRIENDLY HEART

The poetic imagination exhibits one important characteristic we have touched on briefly: it is morally formative. One of the differentiations between primary and secondary imagination is that the conscious will governs the secondary or poetic imagination. In nature, as in the primary imagination, all process is immediate and unreflecting. However, the secondary imagination, which makes an "abridgement of nature," exercises choice and judgment. Speaking of the artistic process, Coleridge states: "The wisdom in nature is distinguished from that in man by the co-instantaneity of the plan and the execution; the thought and the product are one, or are given at once, but there is no moral responsibility. In man there is reflexion, freedom, and choice; he is, therefore, the head of the visible creation."[114]

The moral attribute of the poetic imagination is not aesthetics in disguise but a genuine concern with the choices of life and with what in nature appeals ad hominem, to the whole and ideal man, not just to certain interests. Each creative act is deliberate and assumes moral responsibility.

Two objections might be raised to Coleridge's insistence on the moral quality of the poetic imagination. The first is, as he himself pointed out, that not all people possess the secondary or poetic imagination. The other objection is more fundamental: nothing really prevents one from denying that our being has any moral aspect. Coleridge answers these two points with the same reply: man's moral sense is based, in the end, upon conscience, faith, will, and belief. Fundamentally and finally, it is religious. One need not attain genial powers or exert creative energy to accept moral beliefs and live by them. Art itself does not dictate or establish the moral life but gives it expression. The poetic imagination does not cater to a narrow morality; it is not moralistic; it combines "thoughts and passions," with "color, form, motion, and sound . . . and it stamps them into unity in the mould of a moral idea." One can certainly deny the moral nature of man, but only by denying God, who is "the *ground* of the universe by his essence . . . its maker and judge by his wisdom and holy will." Denial of man's moral nature would also be the most radical form of self-alienation, Coleridge affirms, for "the free-will," which gives rise to both our moral *and* our poetic natures, is "our only absolute *self*."[115]

Yet Coleridge wondered whether the poetic imagination ensured any personal happiness or salvation. In his philosophic thought he tried to incorporate rather than to deny those who had gone before: "My system . . . opposes no other system." He wanted to include the best of all thinkers, "to reduce all knowledges into harmony."[116] He never lost track of "that profound sentence of Leibniz/that men's errors (intellectual) consist chiefly in *denying*—what they *affirm* with feeling, is most often right."[117]

Even more than honing the mind to a keen edge, Coleridge wanted the heart to be in the right place. For instance, he quotes George Herbert's "Love Unknown" in the *Biographia*. Ostensibly this poem exemplifies a "neutral style," but Coleridge chooses it for its sentiment. The words "friend" and "heart" echo throughout it. He italicizes them for emphasis, and they surface countless times in his own work. One he chose as the title of his best known periodical; it is also the name that Wordsworth gives Coleridge in *The Prelude*. The idea of friendship and sharing mixed so thoroughly with Coleridge's intellectual life that near the close of the *Biographia* he lowers his guard and confronts the question: "Now even my strongest sensations of gratitude are mingled with fear, and I reproach myself for being too often disposed to ask,—Have I one friend?"[118] At age twenty-two, he had written to Southey: "The *Heart* should have *fed* upon the *truth*, as Insects on a Leaf—till it be tinged with the colour, and shew it's [sic] food in every the minutest fibre."[119]

The heart's response and human feelings stand behind or beyond even metaphysics. He could not bring himself to trust the disciplines of philosophy or aesthetics unless they helped to shape the need for guidance, belief, and companionship found in every person. Philosophy and art participate in harmony of being but, by themselves, are hollow manipulations. Along with the imagination, they should be raised to a higher level. It was not enough that a philosophical or artistic system worked; it had to start from pure, human motives, from the conscience, and be built on moral postulates. The creative imagination of the artist was moral, but Coleridge fervently believed all men's morality was at stake.[120] Any "metaphysical Solution," he wrote Southey, "that does not instantly *tell* for something in the Heart, is grievously to be suspected as apocry[p]hal."[121] Regret, and even a desire to reject years of philosophic wandering, tore at his sensitive nature. The "quaint metaphysical opinions" we entertain seem "in an hour of anguish like playthings by the bedside of a child deadly sick."[122] Although he felt addicted to these opinions, he attacked them as "abstruse researches, which exercised the strength and subtlety of the understanding without awakening the feelings of the heart." He had gone "delving in the unwholesome quicksilver mines of metaphysical depths."[123] Gems glistened there, but he wondered what was there to assuage suffering. Even at the time he confessed this (1815), the young man he was to meet walking in Hampstead Heath four years later, John Keats—about whom Coleridge said after having shaken hands with him, "There is death in that hand"—was beginning to explore this same potential treachery of the imaginative and the speculative life.

However, Coleridge could not long remain suspicious or skeptical. Far from turning his back on metaphysics and the imagination, he entwined them with the fabric of morality and religion. In the Dynamic Philosophy, spirit or being was assumed prior to matter. And in all men, though not equally developed, Coleridge saw corresponding "organs of spirit," whose "first appearance discloses itself in the *moral* being." Kant and Schelling reinforced his idea that "philosophy in its first principles must have a practical or moral, as well as a theoretical or speculative side." Coleridge followed Kant's assumption of the moral nature of the will and saw in him a philosopher who, like himself, believed his work stopped only at the verge of religion, that religion "is the ultimate aim of philosophy."[124]

In fact, that which was "the truly *human* in human nature," setting it apart from the animals, was spiritual life. From this internal source sprang will and reason in constitutive harmony with universal reason and absolute will.[125] This inner spirit proved "to be a *deeper* feeling, and of such intimate affinity with ideas, so as to modify them and become one with them." Nothing less than God had established this deeper feeling and harmony, a God "whose eternal reason is the ground and ab-

solute condition of the ideas in the mind, and no less the ground and absolute cause of all the correspondent realities in nature."[126] In a real
sense God, the human heart, and man's moral nature, provide both the
motive and the goal of Coleridge's philosophy.[127]

Before the end of the *Biographia*, he inserts a last definition of metaphysics as, "Know thyself: and so shalt thou know God, as far as is permitted to a creature, and in God all things."[128] In a poem written in 1832
near the end of his life, "Self-knowledge," Coleridge returns to the
maxim, but concludes: "Ignore thyself, and strive to know thy God!"
Only by living in the sense of holy presence can man possess his true
self and reaffirm belonging to a greater being. This is the theme of *Aids
to Reflection*. Those who separate knowledge and philosophic truth
from "the *Heart*, the Moral *Nature*," commit the first apostasy, from
which point it is all too easy to move on to flimsy theological speculation.[129]

## RELIGION, THE ALPHA AND OMEGA OF IMAGINATION

For a time after finishing the *Biographia*, Coleridge felt that the imagination had betrayed him into a mistaken pantheistic attitude. The unity
of the Dynamic, of being and matter, subjective and objective, easily led
to the assumption that the creator or God was in his nature the mere addition of all being and phenomena. God would then not be one being
but wholly immanent instead. Interpreted one way, the systems of
Spinoza and Boehme—both of whom Coleridge admired—were "capable of being converted into an irreligious PANTHEISM." Coleridge affirmed this observation with a personal note: "I well know."[130] Because
of the union of the Dynamic he felt compelled to attack one of Schelling's "fundamental errors" as a notion "of Polarity in the Absolute."[131]
He guarded carefully against any such error seducing him back, un-
aware, into "irreligious" pantheism. Already fascinated by the theory of
polarities, especially while writing the *Theory of Life*, he in 1816 outlined to Dr. Gillman what might be called a panentheistic attitude. God
was unique, one, but also took part in the dynamic union of polarities;
"under the predominance of some One" there was also the "All in
each." Coleridge's conscience always preferred a panentheism that made
room for belief in God as "some *One*." Schelling's system, suggesting a
God formed by the union of two poles "is little more than Behmenism
. . . it is reduced at last to a mere Pantheism." Schelling's "highest" philosophical concept, the unity of polarities, necessitated "the eternity of
the material universe." The ultimate mystery of nature and life was not

in two parts. God was not fissionable. If God were divided once, he could be distributed any number of times throughout the material and spiritual worlds. He would thus cease to be one. In apologizing for having followed Schelling by attributing a polar nature to the godhead, Coleridge explains, "I was myself *taken in*."[132]

God, as the absolute ground of all being, was not himself the unity of natural phenomena and supernatural spirit, but rather "the indispensable CONDITION" of this unity.[133] He was the original identity or self-affirming being. In a direct apprehension of God there could be no sense of process, no need to create or express any unity. Man's imagination was therefore unnecessary, even treacherous, if it created any unity, symbol, or representation and called it God. By revealing and creating harmony between the material and spiritual realms, imagination progressed up *to* the absolute being, but could not synthesize or see a synthesis in God: "The dialectic Intellect by the exertion of its own powers exclusively can lead us to a general affirmation of the Supreme Reality of an *absolute* Being. But here it stops."[134] The God who said, "I am that I am," leaves no room for an accurate human conception or understanding of him.[135] The human consciousness, even as it includes the imagination, is too limited for this task.

Coleridge had scruples about pushing the imagination too far. After 1818, he rarely uses the word. His appropriation of Synesius' hymn in the *Biographia* was just one way of saying he hoped that he had not overstepped the bounds set for man, and that God would have mercy on him if, contrary to his place, he reached out to touch, and thus to pollute, that which was God or of God. God would instead descend and communicate to man, as Coleridge suggests by quoting Synesius again to open Chapter 13: "I reverence the hidden system of noble things which is God. Descend to some middle ground, which I can reach."

In man the deep apprehension of God and of spiritual life has no adequate expression. Symbols and myths cannot fathom but can only approximate a God who is ineffable and whose being is incommunicable. Even the most vivid symbol or figure "is only an approximation to that absolute *Union*, which the soul . . . yearns after."[136]

But in the Scriptures God *has* descended to a middle ground. Here the Logos, or "communicative intellect," of God employs a poetically imaginative language that expresses the effects of God. From these effects it is possible to infer his presence and affirm our intuition of him.[137] In reading Scripture, as in other acts of religious expression, one seeks

> what one had lost on Earth/Eyes—
> Whose Half-beholdings thro' unsteady tears
> Gave shape, hue, distance, to the inward Dream.[138]

The imaginative symbols in Scripture are not in and of themselves God, "to which no Image dare be attached," nor are they the truths of reason; but they partake of and are

> consubstantial with the truths of which they are the conductors. These are the *wheels* which Ezekiel beheld, when the hand of the Lord was upon him, and he saw the visions of God as he sate among the captives by the river of Chebar. *Withersoever the Spirit was to go, the* wheels *went, and thither was their spirit to go:—for the spirit of the living creature was in the* wheels *also.*[139]

In this respect religion, as embodied in the images of Scripture, is the inspired expression of an otherwise ineffable spiritual life and being. Religion becomes "the poetry of mankind."[140] This is the promise of the imagination in Blake's prophetic books, and it is an idea later stressed by Arnold.

During his last fifteen years, Coleridge tried to reconcile the Dynamic Philosophy with traditional Christianity. He concludes that God, as the absolute creator, is found neither in the objective world of phenomena nor in the subjective world of spirit, nor in the union of these two. God includes all three modes and can manifest himself in these three ways; but his absolute being is a fourth mode, "the INEFFABLE NAME, to which no Image dare be attached." The concept of God as one who can manifest himself in three forms suggests the Trinity, a concept especially important to Coleridge: "I affirm that the article of the Trinity *is* Religion *is* Reason . . . & that there neither is nor can be *any* Reasons, any Religion, but what is or is an expansion of the Truth of the Trinity."[141] But the Trinity has no fourth element, unless the three together are considered as a fourth, which Coleridge was expressly trying to avoid.

The Pythagorean Tetractys afforded a better vantage, one that could be "an expansion of the Truth of the Trinity." The Tetractys was a fourth element in the philosophical dialectic. It was the "prothesis" or ground of being for thesis, antithesis, and synthesis, and it provided a format for the synthetic process of the Dynamic Philosophy. This ground of being was "the Subject-Object in absolute Identity neither Subject or Object or both in Combination, but the Prothesis or Ur-ground of both."[142] The fourth point of the Tetractys could also represent "the Supreme Being alone," that absolute God who reveals himself in the Trinity:

> God *is* one, but exists or manifests himself to himself, at once in a three-fold Act, total in each and one in all—
>
> 
>
> Prothesis=God
>
> Thesis=Son     Antithesis=Spirit
>
> Synthesis=Father[143]
>
> 

Expanded to include philosophical and religious meanings, the scheme looks like this:

> God, Prothesis
> Identity, Absolute Being, "Deity as unmanifested"
> Ground of all existence; of subjective, objective, and
>     their union; of material, spiritual, and their union

Son, Thesis                                      Holy Spirit, Antithesis
The flesh, the "filial Word" or          The spirit, "The wind that bloweth
    "only-begotten Logos"                     where it listeth"
Objective manifestation                    Subjective manifestation

> Father, Synthesis
> Union of material and spiritual,
>     manifestation is objective and subjective[144]

This scheme Coleridge calls "the Total Idea of the 4=3=1,—of the adorable Tetractys, eternally self-manifested in the Triad, Father, Son, and Spirit."[145]

Coleridge's chief interest, as far as the imagination is concerned, rests with the Logos or Word, identified with both the Scriptures and Christ. These are symbols of the "communicative intellect in Man and Deity" mentioned in the *Biographia* and elsewhere. The Logos manifests God and communicates his truth and reason to all people, either by the living Word, who is Christ, or by the symbols of the written Word in Scripture. Strikingly parallel to the Logos or Christ is the human imagination that combines and manifests the whole mind and expresses the truth and reason of ideas in a symbolic language grasped by the understanding.[146]

In the *Philosophical Lectures,* a major theme of which is the close connection between philosophy and religion, Coleridge describes Christianity in phrases powerfully reminiscent of the "modifying," "fusing," and "co-adunative" imagination. The working of Christianity is "THE ALL-COMBINING, ALL-PENETRATING, ALL-TRANSFORMING SPIRIT OF UNION AND ENNOBLEMENT."[147]

In one sense, Coleridge's idea of the imagination and his use of it to form critical values and to apply them to particular works is not "original." In every area, whether critical, psychological, philosophical, or religious, numerous thinkers, both British and German, had established the modes, problems, and categories that Coleridge uses in talking about the imagination. And these thinkers were predominantly from the eighteenth century. But Coleridge managed to relate different approaches to one another and to draw connecting lines between them. Perhaps he lacks the truly systematic approach that he found so attractive in Hartley, Spinoza, Kant, and Schelling because one system would have been too confining for him. What Santayana implies about Emerson may be said about Coleridge; if he has any system at all, that system itself should be called "imagination." For the dominant trait of Coleridge's mind throughout seems to be imagination, with all its attendant brilliance and potential treacheries. Imagination is his "method" not in one interest, as for most writers before him, but in several: perceptive, psychological, philosophic, and poetic, all of which he sees together as parts of the greater whole of experience and life.

In another sense, then, Coleridge is one of the most original thinkers on the imagination. In culminating over a century of deepening interest in the idea, he carries it back to the original mystery operating between things, thoughts, ideas, and "creative words," back to the centrality of the imagination in all human achievement. It is natural to turn to him not only for critical insights but for a vital and complete picture, or series of pictures, of what the idea can mean. It had become, in the eighteenth century, a larger part of the collective history and consciousness of the human mind than it had ever been before. Coleridge himself knew this, having studied the history of the idea. As had Prospero and Keats, for whom books at last represented the "stretch of the imagination,"[148] Coleridge surrounded himself with books too—with Locke, Hartley, Akenside, Priestley, the associationists, and Maass; with Leibniz, Tetens, Platner, and Jacobi; with Kant, Fichte, and Schelling; with Aristotle, Plato, and the neo-Platonists; with the Bible, Bacon (the "British Plato"), and the great English divines; with Boehme and Spinoza; with Milton, Wordsworth, and Shakespeare—and with his own experiences and thoughts recorded in marginalia, notebooks, lectures, and poems.

It is a tribute to the power and importance of the idea we have been studying that we can rightly think of Coleridge, drawing so much from his own experience yet from many others as well, as a pioneering thinker on the subject. This recognition of Coleridge as at once a culminating and an original figure reveals that we are still somewhere in the mid-course of discovering all that this idea truly means.

# SELECT BIBLIOGRAPHY
# NOTES
# INDEX

# SELECT BIBLIOGRAPHY

(Articles and some books cited in notes are excluded. Place of publication is mentioned only when it is not London or New York.)

Abercromby, David, *A Discourse of Wit* (1685).
Abrams, M. H., *The Mirror and the Lamp: Romantic Theory and the Critical Tradition* (1953).
Addison, Joseph, *The Spectator* (1711–1714), in *Works*, ed. Richard Hurd (6 vols., 1811).
Aikin, J[ohn], and A. L. [Barbauld], *Miscellaneous Pieces in Prose* (1773).
Akenside, Mark, *The Pleasures of Imagination* (1744).
———, *Poems* (1772)
Albrecht, W. P., *Hazlitt and the Creative Imagination* (Lawrence, Kan., 1951).
———, *The Sublime Pleasures of Tragedy: A Study of Critical Theory from Dennis to Keats* (Lawrence, Kan., 1975).
Alison, Archibald, *Essays on the Nature and Principles of Taste* (Edinburgh, 1790).
Allen, G., *Some Occasional Thoughts on Genius* (1750).
Appleyard, J. A., *Coleridge's Philosophy of Literature* (Cambridge, Mass., 1965).
Arbuckle, James, *Hibernicus's Letters* (2 vols., 1729).
Aristotle, *Works*, ed. W. D. Ross *et al.* (12 vols., Oxford, 1949–1956).
Babcock, R. W., *The Genesis of Shakespeare Idolatry* (Chapel Hill, N.C., 1931).
Bacon, Francis, *Works*, ed. James Spedding *et al.* (14 vols., 1857–1874).
Baillie, John, *Essay on the Sublime* (1747), ed. S. H. Monk (1953).
Baker, Carlos, *Shelley's Major Poetry* (Princeton, 1948).
Baker, Herschel, *William Hazlitt* (Cambridge, Mass., 1962).
Baker, James V., *The Sacred River: Coleridge's Theory of the Imagination* (Baton Rouge, La., 1957).
Baker, Joseph E., *Shelley's Platonic Answer to a Platonic Attack on Poetry* (Iowa City , 1965).
Balfour, James, *A Delineation of Human Nature* (1753).

Balguy, John, *Foundation of Moral Goodness* (1728).

Bancks, John, *Essay on Design and Beauty* (Edinburgh, 1739).

Barfield, Owen, *What Coleridge Thought* (Middletown, Conn., 1971).

Barnes, Thomas, *On the Nature and Essential Characters of Poetry as Distinguished from Prose*, Memoirs of Manchester Literary and Philosophical Society I 1785 (Dublin 1791).

Barth, J. R., *The Symbolic Imagination: Coleridge and the Romantic Tradition* (Princeton, 1977).

Bate, W. J., *Achievement of Samuel Johnson* (1955)

———, *Criticism: The Major Texts* (1952).

———, *From Classic to Romantic* (Cambridge, Mass., 1946).

———, *Samuel Johnson* (1977).

Baumgarten, Alexander, *Aesthetica*, 3rd ed. (Frankfurt, 1758).

———, *Metaphysica*, 3rd ed. (Magdeburg, 1750).

Baxter, Andrew, *Enquiry into the Nature of the Human Soul*, 3rd ed. (1745).

Bayly, Anselm, *Alliance of Musick, Poetry, and Oratory* (1789).

Beattie, James, *Dissertations Moral and Critical* (1783).

———, *Essays on Poetry and Music, as They Affect the Mind*, 2nd ed. (1778).

Belsham, William, "Observations on Genius," *Essays* (1789), pp. 383–398.

———, *Elements of the Philosophy of the Mind* (1801).

Berkeley, George, *Works*, ed. A. A. Luce and T. E. Jessop (9 vols., 1948–1957).

Berlin, Sir Isaiah, ed., *The Age of Enlightenment* (Freeport, N.Y., 1970).

———, *Vico and Herder* (1976).

Blackmore, Sir Richard, *Essays* (1716).

———, *Essay upon Wit* (1716), ed. R. C. Boys (1946).

Blackwell, Thomas, *Enquiry into the Life and Writings of Homer* (1735).

———, *Letters Concerning Mythology* (1748).

Blair, Hugh, *Lectures on Rhetoric and Belles-Lettres* (3 vols., Edinburgh, 1783).

Blake, William, *Poetry and Prose*, ed. David Erdman and Harold Bloom (Garden City, N.Y., 1965).

Blankenburg, Friedrich, *Litterarische Zusätze zu J. G. Sulzers Allgemeiner Theorie* (Leipzig, 1796–1798).

Bloom, Harold, *Blake's Apocalypse* (1963).

Blount, Sir Thomas Pope, *De re poetica* (2 pts., 1694).

Bodmer, J. K., *Critische Abhandlungen von dem Wunderbaren* (Zürich, 1740).

———, *Critische Betrachtungen* (Zürich, 1741).

———, *Von dem Einfluss und Gebrauche der Einbildungskraft* (Frankfurt and Leipzig, 1727).

Boehme, Jakob, *Sämmtliche Werke*, ed. K. W. Schiebler (7 vols., Leipzig, 1922).

Bolingbroke, Henry St. John, Viscount, *Reflections Concerning Innate Principles* (1752).

Boswell, James, *Life of Johnson*, ed. G. B. Hill and L. F. Powell (6 vols., Oxford, 1934–1940).

Bowle, John, *Reflections on Originality in Authors* (1766).

Boyd, John, *The Function of Mimesis and Its Decline* (Cambridge, Mass. 1968).

Breitinger, J. J., with J. K. Bodmer, *Die Discourse der Mahlern* (4 pts., Zürich, 1721–1723).

————, *Critische Dichtkunst* (Zürich, 1740).

Bronson, B. H., *Facets of the Enlightenment* (Berkeley and Los Angeles, 1968).

Brooke, Henry, *Universal Beauty* (1728–1735).

Broughton, John, *Psychologia* (1703).

Brown, John, *Essays on the Characteristics* [*of Shaftesbury*] (1751).

————, *A Dissertation on the Rise, Union and Power, the Progressions, Separations and Corruptions of Poetry and Music* (1763).

————, *The History of the Rise and Progress of Poetry, Through Its Several Species* (Newcastle, 1764).

Brown, Thomas, *Lectures on the Philosophy of the Human Mind* (4 vols., Edinburgh, 1820).

Browne, Isaac Hawkins, *On Design and Beauty* (1768).

Browne, Peter, *Procedure, Extent, and Limits of Human Understanding* (1728).

Brucker, Jakob, *Historia critica philosophiae* (6 vols., Leipzig, 1767).

————, *Kurtze Fragen aus der philosophische Geschichte* (7 vols., Ulm, 1731–1736).

Bundy, M. W., *The Theory of the Imagination in Classical and Mediaeval Thought*, University of Illinois Studies, Vol. 12 (Urbana, Ill., 1927).

Burgh, James, *The Dignity of Human Nature* (1751).

Burke, Edmund, *Philosophical Inquiry into the Origin of Our Ideas of the Sublime and Beautiful* (1757; 6th ed., 1770).

Butler, Joseph, *Works*, ed. W. E. Gladstone (2 vols., Oxford, 1896).

Campbell, Archibald, *Enquiry into the Original of Moral Virtue* (1734).

Campbell, George, *Philosophy of Rhetoric* (Edinburgh, 1776).

Casaubon, Meric, *A Treatise of Enthusiasm* (1655).

Cassirer, Ernst, *Idee und Gestalt* (Berlin, 1921).

————, *The Individual and the Cosmos in Renaissance Philosophy* , trans. Mario Domandi (1963).

————, *Philosophy of the Enlightenment*, trans. F. C. Koelln and J. P. Pettegrove (Princeton, 1951).

————, *The Platonic Renaissance in England*, trans. J. P. Pettegrove (Edinburgh, 1953).

Cavendish, Margaret, *CCXI Sociable Letters* (1664).

Chapman, Gerald W., *Literary Criticism in England 1660–1800* (1966).

Clark, John, *Foundations of Morality* (1728).

————, *Sermons* (1756).

Coburn, Kathleen, *Experience into Thought: Perspectives in the Coleridge Notebooks* (Toronto, 1979).

Coleridge, S. T., *Collected Works* (16 vols., London and Princeton, 1969–   ).

————, *Biographia Literaria*, ed. John Shawcross (2 vols., Oxford, 1907).

————, *Collected Letters*, ed. E. L. Griggs (6 vols., Oxford and New York, 1956–1971).

————, *Miscellaneous Criticism*, ed. T. M. Raysor (Cambridge, Mass., 1936).

————, *Notebooks*, ed. Kathleen Coburn (4 vols., 1957–   ).

————, *Philosophical Lectures*, ed. Kathleen Coburn (1949, rev. 1950).

————, *Shakespearean Criticism*, ed. T. M. Raysor (2 vols., Cambridge, Mass., 1930).

Condillac, Abbé Étienne, *Essai sur l'origine des connoisances humaines* (2 vols., Paris, 1746).

[Cooke, Thomas], *Some Observations on Taste, and on the Present State of Poetry in England*. Prefixed to *An Ode on Beauty* (1749).

Cooper, John Gilbert, *The Power of Harmony* (1745).

——, *Letters Concerning Taste* (1755), ed. Ralph Cohen (1951).

Cowper, William, *Complete Poetical Works*, ed. H. S. Melford (Oxford, 1913).

Cumberland, Richard, *Philosophical Inquiry into the Laws of Nature*, trans. J. Towers (Dublin, 1751).

Darwin, Charles, *Zoönomia* (2 vols., 1794–1796).

D'Avanzo, Mario, *Keats's Metaphors for the Poetic Imagination* (Durham, N.C., 1967).

Dennis, John, *Critical Works*, ed. E. N. Hooker (2 vols., Baltimore, 1939–1943).

Descartes, René, *Oeuvres*, ed. Charles Adam and Paul Tannery (12 vols., Paris, 1897–1910).

deVleeschauwer, H. J., *Development of Kantian Thought*, trans. A. R. C. Duncan (1962).

——, *La Déduction transcendental dans l'oeuvre de Kant* (Antwerp, 1934–1937).

D'Israeli, Isaac, *A Defence of Poetry* (1790).

——, *Curiosities of Literature* (1791–1794, 1793, 1798–1817, rev. 1827).

——, *An Essay on the Manners and Genius of the Literary Character* (1795).

Donaldson, John, *The Elements of Beauty; also Recollections on the Harmony of Sensibility and Reason* (Edinburgh, 1780).

Donoghue, Denis, *The Sovereign Ghost: Studies in Imagination* (Berkeley, 1976).

Dorsch, A. J., *Über Ideenverbindung und die darauf gegründeten Seelenzustände* (Mainz, 1788).

Drake, Nathan, *Literary Hours* (2 vols., 1800).

Dryden, John, *Essays*, ed. W. P. Ker (2 vols., Oxford, 1926).

Du Bos, J. B., *Réflexions critiques*, 6th ed. (3 vols., Paris, 1755).

[Duff, William], *An Essay on Original Genius in Philosophy and the Fine Arts, Particularly in Poetry* (1767), ed. J. L. Mahoney (Gainesville, 1964).

——, *Critical Observations on the Writings of the Most Celebrated Writers and Geniuses in Original Poetry* (1770).

Duncan, John, *Essay on Genius* (1814).

Edgeworth, Richard and Maria, *Practical Education* (1798).

Feldman, Burton, and Robert Richardson, eds., *The Rise of Modern Mythology 1680–1860* (Bloomington, Ind., 1972).

Ferguson, Adam, *Essay on the History of Civil Society* (Edinburgh, 1767).

——, *Fundamental Principles of Virtue and Morality* (2 vols., Edinburgh, 1792).

Feuquières, Marquis de, *Phantasiologie, ou Lettres ... faculté imaginative* (Oxford and Paris, 1760).

Fichte, J. G., *Werke*, ed. Reinhard Lauth, Hans Jacob *et al.* (1961–  ).

Fiddes, Richard, "Imagination," *General Treatise of Morality* (1724).

Flögel, C. F., *Vermischten Beytrage zur Philosophie und den schönen Wissenschaften* (Breslau, 1762).

Fogle, Richard H., *The Idea of Coleridge's Criticism* (Berkeley, 1962).

Fordyce, David, *Dialogues Concerning Education* (2 vols., 1744).
———, *Elements of Moral Philosophy* (1758).
Fortescue, James, *A View of Life in Its Several Passions* (1749).
Freneau, Philip, *The Power of Fancy* (1770).
Fries, J. F., *Von deutscher Philosophie; Art und Kunst* (Heidelberg, 1812).
Frye, Northrop, *Fearful Symmetry: A Study of William Blake* (Princeton, 1947).
Furst, Lilian R., *Counterparts* (1977).
———, *Romanticism in Perspective* (1969).
Gay, John, *Dissertation on the Fundamental Principles of Virtue or Morality*, in William King, *Origin of Evil*, trans. E. Law (1731).
———, *The Present State of Wit* (1711), ed. D. F. Bond (1947).
Gerard, Alexander, *An Essay on Genius* (1774), ed. W. J. Hipple (1963); ed. Bernhard Fabian (Munich, 1966).
———, *An Essay on Taste* (1759).
Gildon, Charles, *Complete Art of Poetry* (2 vols., 1718).
Goethe, J. W. von, *Gedenkausgabe der Werke, Briefe, und Gespräche*, ed. Ernst Beutler (24 vols., Zürich, 1948–1954).
Gore, W. C., *The Imagination in Spinoza and Hume* (Chicago, 1902).
Gravina, Giovanni, *Della Ragion Poetica* (Naples, 1716).
Green, John, *Beauty: A Poem* (1756).
Gregory, John, *Comparative View of the Faculties of Man . . .* (1765).
Hagstrum, Jean, *Samuel Johnson's Literary Criticism* (Minneapolis, 1952).
———, *The Sister Arts* (Chicago, 1958).
Hall, Samuel, *An Attempt to Show That a Taste for the Beauties of Nature and the Fine Arts Has No Influence Favorable to Morals*, Memoirs of Manchester Literary and Philosophical Society I 1785 (Dublin 1791).
Haller, Albrecht von, *Elementa Physiologiae Corporis Humani* (8 vols., Lausanne, 1757–1758).
Hamann, J. G. *Poetische Lexicon* (Leipzig, 1751).
Harpur, Joseph, *Essay on the Principles of Philosophical Criticism Applied to Poetry* (1810).
H[arris], J[ames], *Three Treatises: The First Concerning Art; the Second Concerning Music, Painting and Poetry; the Third Concerning Happiness* (1744, rev. 1765).
———, *Hermes; or a Philosophical Inquiry Concerning Universal Grammar* (1751, 1765, 1771, 1794).
———, *Upon the Rise and Progress of Criticism* (1752).
———, *Philological Inquiries* (2 vols., 1780–1781).
Harte, Walter, *An Essay on Reason* (1735).
Hartley, David, *Observations on Man* (2 vols., 1749).
Hartman, Geoffrey, ed., *New Perspectives on Coleridge and Wordsworth* (1972).
Hazlitt, William, *Complete Works*, ed. P. P. Howe (21 vols., 1930–1934).
Herder, J. G. von, ed., *Adrastea* (6 vols., Leipzig, 1801–1803).
———, *Sämmtliche Werke*, ed. Bernhard Suphan (33 vols., Berlin, 1877–1913).
Hill, Aaron, *Essay on the Art of Acting* (1779).
Hipple, W. J., *The Beautiful, the Sublime, and the Picturesque in Eighteenth-Century British Aesthetic Theory* (Carbondale, Ill., 1957).

Hirsch, E. D., *Wordsworth and Schelling* (New Haven, 1960).

Hissmann, Michael, *Geschichte der Lehre von der Association der Ideen* (Göttingen, 1777).

Hobbes, Thomas, *The English Works,* ed. Sir W. Molesworth (11 vols., 1839–1845).

Hogarth, William, *Analysis of Beauty* (1753), ed. J. Burke (Oxford, 1955).

Hume, David, *Four Dissertations* (1757).

———, *Essays,* ed. T. H. Green and T. H. Grose (2 vols., 1875).

———, *Philosophical Works* (4 vols., Edinburgh, 1854).

———, *Treatise of Human Nature,* ed. L. A. Selby-Bigge (1896; rprt. 1928).

Hurd, Richard, *Q. Horatii Flacci Ars poetica, with an English Commentary and Notes* (1749).

———, *Q. Horatii Flacci epistola ad Augustum, with an English Commentary and Notes; to Which Is Added a Discourse Concerning Poetical Imitation* (1751).

———, *A letter to Mr. Mason, on the Marks of Imitation* (Cambridge, 1757).

———, *Letters on Chivalry and Romance* (1762), ed. E. J. Morley (1911).

Hurdis, James, *Lectures Shewing the Several Sources of That Pleasure Which the Human Mind Receives from Poetry* (Bishopstone, 1797).

Hutcheson, Francis, *An Inquiry into the Original of Our Ideas of Beauty and Virtue* (1725, rev. 1726).

———, *An Essay on the Nature and Conduct of the Passions and Affections* (1728).

———, *A System of Moral Philosophy* (2 vols., 1755).

Jackson, Wallace, *The Probable and the Marvellous* (Athens, Ga., 1978).

[Jackson, William], *Thirty Letters on Various Subjects* (2 vols., 1783).

Jacobi, F. H. *Über die Lehre des Spinoza* (Breslau, 1785, enl. 1789).

Johnson, Samuel, *Yale Edition of the Works of Samuel Johnson* (New Haven, 1958– ).

———*Lives of the English Poets,* ed. G. B. Hill (3 vols., Oxford, 1905).

Jones, Sir William, *Poems Consisting Chiefly of Translations from the Asiatic Languages; to Which Are Added Two Essays: I, On the Poetry of the Eastern Nations; II, On the Arts Commonly Called Imitative* (Oxford, 1772).

Kallich, Martin, *The Association of Ideas and Critical Theory in Eighteenth-Century England* (The Hague, 1970).

Kames, Henry Home, Lord, *Elements of Criticism* (3 vols., 1762).

*Kant, Immanuel, Kritik der praktischen Vernunft* (Riga, 1788), trans. T. K. Abbott (1954).

———, *Kritik der reinen Vernunft* (Riga, 1781, rev. 1787), trans. Norman Kemp Smith (1961).

———, *Kritik der Urteilskraft* (Berlin and Libau, 1790), trans. J. C. Meredith as *Critique of Judgement* (Oxford, 1964).

———, *Menschenkunde oder philosophische Anthropologie,* ed. F. C. Stark (Leipzig, 1831).

Kaufmann, Walter, *From Shakespeare to Existentialism: Studies in Poetry, Religion, and Philosophy* (Boston, 1959).

Keats, John, *Letters,* ed. H. E. Rollins (2 vols., Cambridge, Mass., 1958).

———, *Poems,* ed. J. C. Stillinger (Cambridge, Mass., 1978).

Kinnaird, John, *William Hazlitt: Critic of Power* (1978).

Knight, Richard Payne, *An Analytical Inquiry into the Principles of Taste* (1805).

Knox, Vicesimus, *Essays, Moral and Literary* (2 vols., 1779).

———, *Liberal Education* (1781).

Koyré, Alexandre, *La Philosophie de Jacob Boehme* (Paris, 1929).

Law, William, *Case of Reason* (1732).

Lee, Henry, *Anti-Scepticism* (1702).

Leibniz, G. W., *Nouveaux essais*, in *Opera Philosophica*, ed. J. E. Erdman (1840, rprt. 1959).

———, *Philosophische Schriften*, ed. C. J. Gerhardt (7 vols., Berlin, 1875–1891).

Lessing, G. E., *Laokoon* (Berlin, 1766).

Lindner, Herbert, *Das Problem des Spinozismus im Schaffen Goethes und Herders* (Weimar, 1960).

Lipking, Lawrence, *The Ordering of the Arts in Eighteenth-Century England* (Princeton, 1970).

Lowde, James, *Discourse Concerning the Nature of Man* (1694).

Lowth, Robert, *De Sacra Poesi Hebraeorum praelectiones* (1753), trans. as *Lectures on the Sacred Poetry of the Hebrews* (1787).

Maass, Johann G. E., *Versuch über die Einbildungskraft* (Halle and Leipzig, 1792, enl. 1797).

MacLean, Kenneth, *John Locke and English Literature of the Eighteenth Century* (New Haven, 1936).

Mahoney, John L., *The Logic of Passion: The Literary Criticism of William Hazlitt*, Salzburg Studies in English Literature (Salzburg, 1978).

Mallet, David, *The Excursion* (1728).

Manuel, Frank, *The Eighteenth Century Confronts the Gods* (Cambridge, Mass., 1959).

Marcel, Gabriel, *Coleridge et Schelling* (Paris, 1909).

Marks, Emerson, *The Poetics of Reason* (1968).

———, *Relativist and Absolutist: The Early Neoclassical Debate in England* (New Brunswick, N.J., 1955).

Mayne, Zachary, *Two Dissertations Concerning Sense and the Imagination* (1728).

McCosh, James, *The Scottish Philosophy* (1875).

McFarland, Thomas, *Coleridge and the Pantheist Tradition* (Oxford, 1969).

———, "The Origin and Significance of Coleridge's Theory of Secondary Imagination," *New Perspectives on Coleridge and Wordsworth*, ed. Geoffrey Hartman (1972), pp. 195–246.

McKenzie, Gordon, *Critical Responsiveness: A Study of the Psychological Current in Later Eighteenth-Century Criticism* (Berkeley, 1949).

Meiners, Christoph, *Grundriss der Theorie und Geschichte der Schönen Wissenschaften* (Lemgo, 1787).

Meister, Leonhard, *Über die Schwermerei* (2 vols., Bern, 1775–1777).

———, *Versuch über die Einbildungskraft* (Bern, 1778).

———, *Über Aberglauben, Einbildungskraft, und Schwärmerey* (Bern, 1795).

———, *Über die Einbildungskraft in ihrem Einfluss auf Geist und Herz* (Zurich, 1795).

Melmoth, William, *Letters of Sir Thomas Fitzosborne* (2 vols., 1742–1749).

Mendelssohn, Moses, *Gesämmelte Schriften*, ed. G. B. Mendelssohn (7 vols., Leipzig, 1843–1845).

Moir, John, *Gleanings* (2 vols., 1785).

Monboddo, James Burnett, Lord, *Of the Origin and Progress of Language* (6 vols., 1773–1779).

Monk, Samuel H., *The Sublime: A Study of Critical Theories in Eighteenth-Century England* (1935, rprt. 1960).

Moor, James, *Essays* (Glasgow, 1759).

Moore, T. H., *The Backgrounds of Burke's Theory of the Sublime* (Ithaca, N.Y., 1933).

Mörchen, Hermann, *Die Einbildungskraft bei Kant* (Tübingen, 1970).

More, Henry, *Enthusiasmus Triumphatus* (1662), ed. De Porte (1966).

Morgann, Maurice, *Essay on the Dramatic Character of Sir John Falstaff* (1777).

Moritz, Karl, *Götterlehre oder Mythologische Dichtungen der Alten* (Vienna, 1793).

[Morris, Corbyn], *An Essay Towards Fixing the True Standards of Wit, Humour, Raillery, Satire and Ridicule* (1744), ed. J. L. Clifford (1947).

Muratori, L. A., *Della forza della Fantasia Umana* (Venice, 1740).

Nettleton, Thomas, *Treatise on Virtue and Happiness*, 7th ed., (Edinburgh, 1774).

Neubauer, John, *Bi-Focal Vision* (Chapel Hill, 1971).

Nicolson, Marjorie, *Mountain Gloom and Mountain Glory: The Development of the Aesthetics of the Infinite* (Ithaca, N.Y., 1959).

Norris, John, *Collection of Miscellanies* (1687).

——, *Theory of the Ideal or Intelligible World* (1701–1704).

Nourse, Timothy, *Discourse upon the Nature and Faculties of Man* (1697).

Novalis, *Gesammelte Werke*, ed. Carl Seelig (5 vols., Herrliberg and Zürich, 1945).

Ogilvie, John, *Philosophical and Critical Observations on the Nature, Character, and Various Species of Composition* (2 vols., 1774).

——, *Providence* (1769).

Paley, M. D., *Energy and the Imagination: A Study of the Development of Blake's Thought* (Oxford, 1970).

Park, Roy, *Hazlitt and the Spirit of the Age* (Oxford, 1971).

Parsons, J. W., *Hints on Producing Genius* (1790).

Percival, Thomas, *Moral and Literary Dissertations* (1784).

Perkins, David, *The Quest for Permanence* (Cambridge, Mass., 1959).

——, *Wordsworth and the Poetry of Sincerity* (Cambridge, Mass., 1964).

Pico della Mirandola, Giovanni, *De Imaginatione sive Phantasia* (1533), in *Opera* (Basel, 1573).

Platner, Ernst, *Anthropologie für Aerzte und Weltweise* (Leipzig, 1772, enl. 1790).

Polier, Charles de, *An Essay on the Pleasure Which the Mind Receives from the Exercise of Its Faculties, and That of Taste in Particular*, in *Twenty Essays* (Dublin, 1791).

*Portfolio, The* [magazine], (Philadelphia, 1801–1827).

Price, Uvedale, *An Essay on the Picturesque, as Compared with the Sublime and Beautiful* (1795).

————, *Essays on the Picturesque* (3 vols., 1810).

Priestley, Joseph, *Course of Lectures on Oratory and Criticism* (1762).

————, *Hartley's Theory of the Human Mind* (1775).

Purshouse, A., *An Essay on Genius* (Canterbury, 1782).

Radner, John, "The Sympathetic Imagination: Concepts of Altruism in Eighteenth-Century British Thought," Ph.D. dissertation, Harvard University, 1966.

Randall, Helen, *The Critical Theory of Lord Kames* (Northampton, Mass., 1944).

Reid, Thomas, *Essays on the Intellectual Powers of Man* (Edinburgh, 1785).

[Reynolds, Frances], *An Enquiry Concerning the Principles of Taste, and of the Origin of Our Ideas of Beauty* . . . (1785), ed. J. L. Clifford, (1951).

Reynolds, Sir Joshua, *Discourses* (1769–1790).

————, *Works*, ed. Edmond Malone (3 vols., 1797).

Richards, I. A., *Coleridge on the Imagination* (1934).

Richardson, William, *A Philosophical Analysis and Illustration of Some of Shakespeare's Remarkable Characters* (1774).

Robertson, Thomas, *An Enquiry into the Fine Arts* (1784).

Roston, Murray, *Prophet and Poet* (1965).

Rylands, John, *Select Esssays on Moral Virtue, Genius, Science, and Taste* (1792).

Sachs, Christian, *Der Ursprung des Mythosbegriffes in der Modernen Bibelwissenschaft* (Tübingen, 1952).

Santayana, George, *Character and Opinion in the United States* (1920).

Sartre, J. P., *L'Imaginaire* (Paris, 1940).

Schelling, F. W., *Sämmtliche Werke*, ed. K. F. A. Schelling (14 vols., Stuttgart and Augsburg, 1856–1861).

Schiller, Friedrich, *Ästhetische Erziehung*, ed. and trans. Elizabeth Wilkinson and L. A. Willoughby as *On the Aesthetic Education of Man* (Oxford, 1967).

————, *Sämmtliche Schriften*, ed. A. Ellissen *et al.* (15 vols., Stuttgart, 1867–1876).

Schlegel, A. W., *Vorlesungen über schöne Literatur und Kunst* (1801–1804), ed. J. Menor (3 vols., Heilbronn, 1884).

Schlegel, Friedrich., *Geschichte der Alten und Neuen Litteratur* (Vienna, 1814).

————, *Kritik der Philosophischen Systeme* (Bonn, 1836–1837).

————, *Kritische Schriften*, ed. W. Rasch (Munich, 1964).

————, *Sämmtliche Werke* (Vienna, 1822–1825).

Scott, John Robert, *Dissertation on the Progress of the Fine Arts* (1800), ed. R. H. Pearce (1954).

Shaftesbury, A. A. Cooper, Earl of, *Characteristics* (3 vols., 1711), ed. J. M. Robertson (2 vols., 1900).

————, *Sensus Communis* (1709).

Sharpe, William, *Dissertation upon Genius* (1755).

Shelley, Percy B., *Complete Works*, ed. Roger Ingpen and W. E. Peck (10 vols., 1965).

Smith, Adam, *Theory of Moral Sentiments* (1759), ed. J. M. Lothian (1963).

————, *Essays on Philosophical Subjects*, ed. Dugald Stewart (1795).

Spacks, P. M., *The Poetry of Vision* (Cambridge, Mass., 1967).

Spence, Joseph, *Anecdotes* (1820).
———, *Crito; or a Dialogue on Beauty* (1752).
Spinoza, Benedict de, *Opera* (Stuttgart, 1830).
Spon, Jacob, *Récherches d'antiquités et curiosités* (Lyon, 1683).
Steffens, Henrik, *Beyträge zur innern Naturgeschichte der Erde* (Freiburg, 1801).
———, *Schriften* (2 vols., Breslau, 1821).
Stephen, Sir Leslie, *History of English Thought in the Eighteenth Century* (2 vols., 1876; 3rd ed., 1927).
Stewart, Dugald, *Elements of the Philosophy of the Human Mind* (1792).
Ströhlin, J. F., *Philosophische Rede über die Associationsgesetze unsere Begriffe* (Stuttgart, 1788).
Stubbes, George, *A Dialogue on Beauty* (1731).
Sulzer, J. G. *Allgemeine Theorie der Schönen Künste* (4 vols., Leipzig, 1771–1774).
———, *Theorie der Dichtkunst* (Munich, 1788).
———, *Unterredungen über die Schönheit der Natur* . . . (Berlin, 1774).
Temple, Sir William, *Miscellanea* . . . *in Four Essays* (2 vols., 1690–1701).
———, *Essays on Ancient and Modern Learning and on Poetry*, ed. J. E. Spingarn (Oxford, 1909).
Tetens, Johann Nicolaus, *Philosophische Versuche über die Menschliche Natur und Ihre Entwicklung* (2 vols., Leipzig, 1776–1777).
Thomson, James, *Seasons* (1726–1730).
Thomson, William, *An Enquiry into the Elementary Principles of Beauty in the Works of Nature and Art, to Which Is Prefixed an Introductory Discourse on Taste* (1800).
Thorpe, Clarence, *The Aesthetic Theory of Thomas Hobbes*, University of Michigan Publications in Language and Literature (1940).
———, "Addison's Contribution to Criticism," in *The Seventeenth Century*, ed. R. F. Jones *et al.* (Stanford, Cal., 1951), pp. 316–329.
Tiedemann, D., *Untersuchungen über den Menschen* (Leipzig, 1777).
Trenchard, John, *The Natural History of Superstition* (1709).
Trescho, S. F., *Betrachtungen über das Genie* (Königsberg, 1755).
Tucker, Abraham, *The Light of Nature Pursued* (7 vols., 1768–1777).
Turnbull, George, *Principles of Moral Philosophy* (1740).
Tuveson, Ernest L., *The Imagination as a Means of Grace* (Berkeley and Los Angeles, 1960).
Twining, Thomas, *Aristotle's Treatise on Poetry, Translated with Notes and Two Dissertations on Poetical and Musical Imitation* (2 vols., 1789, 1812).
U[sher], J[ames], *Clio: or a Discourse on Taste* (1767).
———, *An Introduction to the Theory of the Human Mind* (1771).
Vico, G. V., *Scienza Nuova* (Naples, 1725, rev. 1744).
Walcott, D., *Observations on the Correspondence Between Poetry and Music* (1769).
Warnock, Mary, *Imagination* (Berkeley, 1976).
Warren, Howard C., *A History of the Association Psychology* (1921).
Warton, Joseph, *The Enthusiast; or Lover of Nature* (1744).
———, *Essay on the Writings and Genius of Pope* (2 vols., 1756–1782).
———, *Odes on Several Subjects* (1746).

Wasserman, Earl, *Shelley: A Critical Reading* (Baltimore, 1971).
Watkins, W.B.C., *Johnson and English Poetry Before 1660* (Princeton, 1936).
Watts, Isaac, *Logick* (1725).
———, *Improvement of the Mind* (1741).
Webb, Daniel, *Observations on the Correspondence Between Poetry and Music* (1769).
———, *Remarks on the Beauties of Poetry* (1762).
Welch, Livingston, *Imagination and Human Nature* (1935).
Wellek, René, *Concepts of Criticism* (New Haven, 1963).
———, *A History of Modern Criticism* (New Haven, 1955–   ).
———, *Immanuel Kant in England* (Princeton, 1931).
———, *The Rise of English Literary History* (Chapel Hill, N. C., 1941).
Welsted, Leonard, *Dionysius Longinus on the Sublime* (1712).
———, *Epistles . . . A Dissertation Concerning the Perfection of the English Language, the State of Poetry . . .* (1724)
Whately, Thomas, *Remarks on Some of the Characters of Shakespeare* (1785).
[Whiter, Walter], *A Specimen of a Commentary on Shakespeare: Containing an Attempt to Explain and Illustrate Various Passages in a New Principle of Criticism, Derived from Mr. Locke's Doctrine of the Association of Ideas* (1794).
Wieland, Christoph, *Kleinere Prosäische Schriften* (3 vols., Leipzig, 1785).
Wilson, Milton, *Shelley's Later Poetry* (1959).
Wimsatt, W. K., and Cleanth Brooks, *Literary Criticism: A Short History* (1957).
Winckelmann, J. J., *Gedanken über die Nachahmung der griechischen Werke* (Friedrichstadt, 1755).
———, *Geschichte der Kunst des Alterthums* (Dresden, 1764).
Wolff, Christian, *Psychologia Empirica* (Frankfurt and Leipzig, 1732).
———, *Psychologia Rationalis* (Frankfurt and Leipzig, 1734).
Wood, Robert, *Essay on the Original Genius and Writings of Homer* (1764).
Wordsworth, William, *Poetical Works*, ed. Ernest de Selincourt and Helen Darbishire (5 vols., Oxford, 1940–1949).
———, *Prose Works*, ed. W. J. B. Owen and J. W. Smyser (3 vols., Oxford, 1974).
Young, Edward, *Conjectures on Original Composition* (1759), ed. E. J. Morley (Manchester, 1918).
———, *On Lyrick Poetry*, prefixed to his *Ocean: An Ode* (1728).

# NOTES

## 1. THE ESSENTIAL IDEA

1. The most comprehensive discussion of organic theories, in which the plant is the central metaphor, is still M. H. Abrams, *The Mirror and the Lamp*, 2nd ed. (1958), pp. 156–225.

2. Samuel Taylor Coleridge, *Biographia Literaria*, ed. John Shawcross (1907), I, ch. XII, 167. Coleridge identified the butterfly with the human soul through the meaning of the Greek *psyche*.

3. See e.g. René Wellek, "The Concept of Romanticism in Literary History" and "Romanticism Re-examined," in *Concepts of Criticism* (1963), pp. 128–221. Wellek speaks of "one central and valid concept: the reconciling, synthetic imagination as the common denominator of romanticism" (p. 203). Cf. the discussion of "imagination" and "feeling" as central premises in Lilian R. Furst, *Romanticism in Perspective* (1969), pp. 117–275.

4. See Abrams, *The Mirror and the Lamp*; W. J. Bate, *From Classic to Romantic* (1958 repr.). Closely related is the neoclassical concept of art as *mimesis* or imitation and its outcome. See John Boyd, *The Function of Mimesis and Its Decline* (1968); Emerson Marks, *The Poetics of Reason* (1968), pp. 26–38, 78–109.

5. William Richardson, *A Philosophical Analysis and Illustration of Some of Shakespeare's Remarkable Characters* (1774), p. 38.

## 2. EMPIRICISM IN EARNEST: HOBBES AND LOCKE

1. See M. W. Bundy, *The Theory of Imagination in Classical and Medieval Thought* (1927), and his discussion of "Invention" and "Imagination" in the Renaissance, *JEGP* 29 (1930): 535–545. For a brief addendum, especially connecting the notion of *ingenium* to imagination, see W. Wetherbee, *Platonism and Poetry in the Twelfth Century* (1972), pp. 61–63, 94–99.

2. Until the early eighteenth century, *subjectivum* had traditionally applied to the "subjects" of knowledge (now called the "objective"), while *objectivum* meant the concept of the thing in the mind. In short, the meaning of the terms was reversed, reflecting the increased interest in the mind. See Carl von Prantl,

*Geschichte der Logik im Abendlande* (Leipzig, 1855–1870), III, 208–209; Rudolf Ericken, *Geistige Strömungen der Gegenwart* (Leipzig, 1904), ch. 1. The terms *natura naturans* (naturing or creative nature) and *natura naturata* (the world of phenomena, acted upon by the creative) go back to medieval scholasticism, continue in importance through the time of Bacon and Spinoza, and are later given special currency by Jacobi, Schelling, and Coleridge. See *Biographia Literaria*, in *Collected Coleridge*, ed. James Engell and W. J. Bate, I, chs. X, XII (scheduled to appear 1982).

3. See C. D. Thorpe, *The Aesthetic Theory of Thomas Hobbes* (1940), pp. 289–290.

4. Thomas Hobbes, *Leviathan*, in *English Works*, ed. W. Molesworth (1839–1845), III, 15, 11.

5. See Hobbes, *Elements of Philosophy*, in *English Works*, I, 406–407.

6. See Thorpe, *Aesthetic Theory* pp. 80–84.

7. *Elements of Philosophy*, p. 396; *Leviathan*, pp. 4–6. For Vives' distinction, see *De Anima et Vita* in *Works* (1555), II, 497–593.

8. *Leviathan*, p. 6.

9. *Elements of Philosophy*, pp. 396–399, 406–408.

10. *Leviathan*, pp. 11–13, 15.

11. *Leviathan*, pp. 13–14.

12. Thorpe, *Aesthetic Theory* , p. 294.

13. *Elements of Philosophy*, pp. 400–409.

14. See e.g. *Elements*, p. 401: "As appetites and aversions are generated by phantasms, so reciprocally phantasms are generated by appetites and aversions."

15. *Elements*, pp. 408–409.

16. Hobbes, "Answer to William Davenant's *Preface before* Gondibert" (1650).

17. For discussion of the radical effect of Locke in this respect, see e.g. E. L. Tuveson, *The Imagination as a Means of Grace* (1960), ch. 1; and on Locke's popularity among British writers, see Kenneth MacLean, *John Locke and English Literature of the Eighteenth Century* (1936), pp. 1–18.

18. John Locke, *Essay Concerning Human Understanding*, bk. I, ch. 12.

19. *Essay*, bk. I, ch. 12, italics added.

20. *Essay*, bk. I, ch. 12.

21. *Essay*, bk. I, ch. 12.

22. See "Imagination," *Princeton Encyclopedia of Poetry and Poetics*, ed: A. Preminger *et al.* (1974), p. 372.

23. William Law, *Case of Reason* (1732), p. 157.


## 3. CLAIMS OF THE SPIRIT: SHAFTESBURY AND LEIBNIZ

1. Ernst Cassirer, *The Philosophy of the Enlightenment*, trans. F. C. A. Koelln and J. P. Pettegrove (1951), p. 312.

2. Cassirer, *Enlightenment*, pp. 315, 314.

3. Cassirer, *Enlightenment*, pp. 318–319. See Shaftesbury, *Characteristics*, ed. J. M. Robertson (1900), I, 207.

4. Shaftesbury, *Moralists*, pt. 2, sec. 4, in *Characteristics*, II, 65.

5. Charles Gildon, *Complete Art of Poetry*, in *Critical Essays of the Eighteenth Century*, ed. W. H. Durham (1915), p. 56.

6. See Wordsworth, *Prelude*, bk. 8, esp. ll. 249–293 (1850 text).

7. G. W. von Leibniz, *Philosophische Schriften*, ed. C. J. Gerhardt (Berlin, 1875–1890), III, 429–430. See also Thomas McFarland, *Coleridge and the Pantheist Tradition* (1969), pp. 336–337n 5. The translation is McFarland's.

8. Ernest Tuveson, "The Importance of Shaftesbury," *ELH* 20 (1953): 267–299.

9. Leibniz, *Nouveaux essais*, in *Opera Philosophica*, ed. J. E. Erdman (1840, rpr. 1959), p. 196.

10. See e.g. Leibniz, *Nouveaux essais*, pp. 210, 216, 221.

11. *Nouveaux essais*, p. 223; cf. Coleridge, *Biographia*, I, 93.

12. See *Nouveaux essais*, pp. 197, 277–278.

13. *Nouveaux essais*, p. 205.

14. *Nouveaux essais*, p. 273; cf. Coleridge on "organs of spirit" in *Biographia*, I, ch. XII, 167.

15. See *Nouveaux essais*, p. 263.

16. *Nouveaux essais*, pp. 219, 224.

17. *Nouveaux essais*, pp. 352, 407–408.

## 4. THE CREATIVE IMPULSE: ADDISON THROUGH AKENSIDE AND THE 1740s

1. See Clarence Thorpe, "Addison's Contribution to Criticism," in R. F. Jones *et al.*, *The Seventeenth Century: From Bacon to Pope* (1951), 316–329; Thorpe, "Addison's Theory of the Imagination as 'Perceptive Response,'" in *Papers of the Michigan Academy of Science, Art, and Letters* 21 (1935): 509–530. Thorpe substantiates the claim of J. G. Robertson that Addison "laid the foundation of the whole romantic aesthetic in England" (*The Genesis of the Romantic Theory in England* [1923], p. 241), but stresses Addison's background in Hobbes and his value as a brilliant, popular synthesizer of a psychological approach to art and the imagination. See also E. F. Carritt's argument that Addison is a principle influence on Kant's aesthetic, directly and indirectly, *Essays and Studies of the English Association* 12 (1936): 27–35. See also L. A. Elioseff, *The Cultural Milieu of Addison's Literary Criticism* (1963), esp. pp. 145–188; Tuveson, *The Imagination as a Means of Grace*, pp. 92–131. Valuable for the continuity of Addison with Hobbes and Locke is Martin Kallich, "Association of Ideas and Critical Theory: Hobbes, Locke, and Addison," *ELH* 12 (1945): 290–315.

2. *Essays of John Dryden*, ed. W. P. Ker (1926), I, 8, 146.

3. John Dennis, "Advancement and Reformation of Poetry," *The Critical Works*, ed. Edward Niles Hooker (1939–1943), I, 215. Cf. W. P. Albrecht, *The Sublime Pleasures of Tragedy* (1975), pp. 13–24; on the neo-Longinian influence cf. Abrams, *The Mirror and the Lamp*, pp. 72–78; Bate, *From Classic to Romantic*, pp. 46–48.

4. *Spectator* 160.

5. Dennis, *Works*, I, 363.

6. Francis Bacon, *The Advancement of Learning* (1605), bk. 2, ch. 12, pt. i.

7. *Spectators* 411, 412, 416, 421, 279.

8. *Spectator* 416, 418, 419.

9. *Spectator* 411, 412.

10. *Spectator* 409, 412.

11. *Spectator* 411, 412, 420, 421.

12. *Spectator* 412.

13. Joseph Spence, *Anecdotes* (1898), p. 172.

14. A tribute to the comprehensiveness of Akenside's poem in the variety of sources and traditions with which it is connected. As early as 1795, Anne Laetitia Barbauld's *Essay on Akenside's Poem* viewed it as a poetic account of Addison's, and indirectly Locke's, psychology. Martin Kallich stresses the poem's relation to the doctrine of association of ideas, with "no original contribution," in *MLN* 62 (1947): 170. Margaret Sherwood emphasizes the neo-Platonic element by way of Shaftesbury, in *Undercurrents of Influences in English Romantic Poetry* (1934), pp. 77–82. A. O. Aldridge emphasizes Akenside's eclecticism and his attempt to reconcile the empirical and neo-Platonic traditions, in *SP* 42 (1945): 769–770; *Journal of the History of Ideas* 5 (1949): 292–314; *MLQ* 8 (1947): 75–77. For a balanced discussion of the problem, especially the relation to Addison, see Robert Marsh, *MP* 59 (1961): 36–48.

15. *Pleasures*, "The Design." See also bk. I, "The Argument."

16. Bk. I, ll. 372–376. See also bk. I, "The Argument."

17. Bk. II, 1. 338; bk. III, ll. 381–382.

18. "The Design"; cf. Addison on the same thought.

19. Bk. III, ll. 383–391; cf. Shakespeare, *MND*, V. i. 12–17.

20. See e.g. Bk. II, ll. 311–350; bk. III, ll. 410–427.

21. Bk. III, ll. 392–408.

22. See McFarland, *Coleridge and Pantheist Tradition*, pp. 36, 336n; Ernst Cassirer, *Individuum und Kosmos*, pp. 150–175.

23. Bk. III, ll, 279–286.

24. Bk. III, ll. 600–604, 624–625.

25. Bk. III, "The Argument."

26. See A. S. P. Woodhouse, "Collins and the Creative Imagination: A Study in the Critical Background of His Odes (1746)," in *Studies in English*, ed. M. W. Wallace (1931), pp. 59–130, esp. pp. 59–95.

27. Monboddo, James Burnett, Lord, *Of the Origin & Progress of Language* (1773–1779), I, 179n.

## 5. THE INNER STRUCTURE OF LIFE: HUME AND JOHNSON

1. David Hume, *Treatise of Human Nature*, ed. L. A. Selby-Bigge (1896, 1928 repr.), p. 265. The best general discussion of Hume on the imagination remains W. C. Gore, *The Imagination in Spinoza and Hume* (1902).

2. Hume, "Dissertation on the Passions," *Essays*, ed. T. H. Green and T. H. Grose (1898), II, 145.

3. Hume, *Treatise*, p. 265. On the associationist strains in Hume and his relation to Hutcheson in particular, see Kallich, "Association of Ideas," *ELH* 12 (1945): 290–315, cited in ch. IV, n. 1.

4. *Treatise*, pp. 344–347; "Dissertation on the Passions," p. 140; cf. Hume, *Philosophical Works* (1826), III, 26–31.

5. "Dissertation on the Passions," pp. 139–143.

6. "Dissertation on the Passions," pp. 164–165; *Treatise*, p. 198. Hume uses fancy and imagination synonymously. Cf. Joshua Reynolds, *Discourse* XIII.

7. See e.g. Burke, *Reflections on the Revolution in France*, on the character of the French National Assembly, which he detests: "If we were to know nothing of this assembly but by its title and function, no colors could paint to the imagination anything more venerable" (III, 3, a).

8. Gore, *Imagination in Spinoza and Hume* p. 71.

9. Hume, *Treatise*, pp. 265–268, 198; Hume, "Concerning Human Understanding," *Essays*, pp. 40–42.

10. *Treatise*, p. 427.

11. On the relation of Hume's concept of tragedy to his psychology, especially his view of the imagination, see Ralph Cohen, *PQ* 41 (1962): 450–464.

12. Hume, *Philosophical Works*, III, 26–28.

13. Samuel Johnson, *Lives of the Poets*, ed. G. B. Hill (1905), I, 2; III, 217; I, 194, 235.

14. James Boswell, *Tour to the Hebrides*, in *Life of Johnson*, ed. Hill and L. F. Powell (1934–1950), V, 34–35.

15. *Rambler* 41; *Rasselas*, chs. 30–32.

16. *Rambler* 45; *Rasselas*, ch. 22.

17. On the necessity of restraining the dangerous influence of imagination on conduct, see Richard Fiddes, *General Treatise of Morality* (1724), pp. 188–189; Nathan Drake's *Literary Hours* (1798) contains a chapter "On the Government of the Imagination," which is in the same vein as Fiddes.

18. W. J. Bate, *Achievement of Samuel Johnson* (1955), pp. 93–107.

19. *Anecdotes in Johnsonian Miscellanies*, ed. G. B. Hill (1897), I, 199.

20. *Rambler* 60.

## 6. NEW AESTHETICS AND CRITICISM: THE ASSOCIATIONISTS AND THE SCOTS

1. Aristotle, *De Memoria et Reminiscentia* II, 6–11 (451b seq.).

2. For a general history of associationism, see Howard C. Warren, *A History of the Association Psychology* (1921). An excellent history is still that which Coleridge drew on extensively in his discussion of associationism in the *Biographia*, chs. V–VI: J. G. E. Maass, "Beiträge zur Geschichte der Lehre von der Vergesellschaftung der Vorstellungen" in *Versuch über die Einbildungskraft* (1797), pp. 311–453. Recent discussions include Bate, *From Classic to Romantic*, ch. 4; W. J. Hipple, *The Beautiful . . . British Aesthetic History* (1957), pp. 67–302 *passim;* Gordon McKenzie, *Critical Responsiveness: A Study of the Psychological Current in Later Eighteenth-Century Criticism* (1949), chs. 5–6; Martin Kallich, *Association of Ideas and Critical Theory in Eighteenth-Century England* (1970); W. J. Ong, "Psyche and the Geometers," *MP* 49 (1951–1952): 16–27; Ralph Cohen, "Association of Ideas and Poetic Unity," *PQ* 36 (1957): 465–474; Kallich, "The Argument Against the Association of Ideas in Eighteenth-Century Aesthetics," *MLQ* 15 (1954): 125–136.

3. Cf. MacLean, *John Locke*, pp. 132–134.

4. Robert Dodsley, *The Preceptor* (1748), II, 346–347.

5. George Turnbull, *Principles of Moral Philosophy* (1740), I, 90.

6. Turnbull, *Principles*, I, 60.

7. See Samuel Monk, *The Sublime: A Study of Critical Theories in XVIII-Century England* (1960 repr); T. M. Moore, *The Background of Burke's Theory of the Sublime* (1930). On associationism in Burke's aesthetics, see esp. Kallich, *Association of Ideas*, pp. 135–149.

8. Burke, *Enquiry*, 6th ed. (1770), pp. 15–16, 210.

9. *Memoirs of the Literary and Philosophical Society of Manchester*, I, 391.

10. Burke, *Enquiry*, pp. 229, 245.

11. Kames, *Elements of Criticism* (1762), I, 33. See also Hipple, *The Beautiful*, pp. 99–121, and the discussion of Blair, pp. 122–148, and more for comprehensive background and content, Helen Randall, *The Critical Theory of Lord Kames* (1944).

12. See Kames, *Elements*, I, 104–127, "Emotions Caused by Fiction."

13. Priestley, *Hartley's Theory of the Human Mind* (1775), p. iii. Priestley omits the "vibrations" and the "anatomical disquisitions" of Hartley.

14. Priestley, *Lectures on Oratory and Criticism* (1777), pp. 150, 130, 129.

15. *Lectures*, pp. 94–98; *Hartley's Theory*, pp. xxiii, xxvii, xxxiv, xxxvi.

16. *Lectures*, pp. 80, 86, 101, 122, 102.

17. Cf. Coleridge, *Shakespearean Criticism*, ed. Thomas Raysor (1930), II, 174.

18. Priestley, *Lectures*, pp. 101, 88, 261.

19. *Lectures*, p. 90. "Assent," a forerunner of Coleridge's "willing suspension of disbelief," was also used by Hartley.

20. *Lectures*, p. 90, 92.

21. *Lectures*, pp. 109, 172, 126–127; *Hartley's Theory*, p.xli.

22. *Lectures*, pp. 151, 154, 155.

23. Alexander Gerard, *An Essay on Genius* (1774), pp. 163–164.

24. *Practical Education* (1798), II, 639–640.

25. In Spurgeon, see esp. pp. 195–199. Cf. E. L. Tuveson, "The Imagery of Shakespeare: Dr. Clemen and Walter Whiter," *TLS*, Sept. 5, 1936.

## 7. INVESTIGATORS OF GENIUS: GERARD AND DUFF

1. Cassirer, *Philosophy of the Enlightenment*, p. 275.

2. *"Epoche der Forcierten Talente"* (1812).

3. For further discussion, see Cassirer's introduction to *Philosophy of Enlightenment*.

4. See Marjorie Greene, "Gerard's *Essay on Taste*," *MP* 41 (1943); W. J. Hipple, Introduction to Alexander Gerard, *An Essay on Taste* (Gainesville, Fla., 1936); Bernhard Fabian, Introduction to Gerard, *An Essay on Genius*, ed. Fabian (Munich, 1966).

5. Gerard, *Essay on Taste* (1759), pp. 173–174.

6. See Hipple, Introduction to *Essay on Taste*, pp. vi–viii.

7. Gerard, *Essay on Genius* (1774), pp. 27, 8, 29–30, 37, 26, 41. See Fabian's Introduction to *Essay on Genius*, pp. xi–xvii.

8. *Essay on Genius*, pp. 42–43, 57, 67–68.

9. *Essay on Taste*, 3rd ed. (1780), p. 161; *Essay on Genius*, pp. 152, 170; see also p. 163.

10. *Essay on Genius*, pp. 163, 183, 357, 173.

11. *Essay on Genius,* pp. 169–173, 357, 150; *Essay on Taste* (1780), p. 161.

12. *Essay on Genius,* pp. 44, 231, 47.

13. *Essay on Genius,* pp. 240–241, 216, 232–233, 30, 191.

14. *Essay on Genius,* p. 284.

15. See John Mahoney, Introduction to William Duff, *An Essay on Original Genius,* ed. Mahoney (Gainesville, Fla., 1964).

16. Duff, *An Essay on Original Genius and Its Various Modes of Exertion in Philosophy and the Fine Arts, Particularly in Poetry* (1767), pp. 125–126, 272, 295.

17. Duff, *Essay,* pp. 6–29, 70–71.

18. *Essay,* pp. 7, 71, 41, 75, 281–282, 89.

19. *Essay ,* pp. 58–59.

20. *Essay,* p. 38. Quintilian's *Institutes,* II, iv, or Cicero's *De Oratione,* II, xii may be Duff's source.

21. Duff, *Essay,* pp. 124, 192–193n, 181, 186–187.

22. *Essay,* pp. 152–153, 76–77, 87–88, 66–67. The image of rays, perhaps imitating St. Augustine, may be compared with Coleridge's many similar images of light and the eye, especially concerning the operation of ideas and the imagination.

23. Duff, *Essay,* p. 272.

24. Cf. W. J. Bate, *The Burden of the Past and the English Poet* (1970), pp. 49–50. See also Alex Page, "The Origin of Language and Eighteenth-Century English Criticism," *JEGP* 71 (1972): 12–21; Page, "Eighteenth-Century Theories of Poetic Language," Ph.D. diss., Harvard University (1953); René Wellek, *The Rise of English Literary History* (1941), pp. 47–94.

25. Duff, *Essay,* pp. 102–106; cf. Priestley, *Lectures,* pp. 131–132.

26. Gerard, *Essay on Genius,* p. 378; Duff, *Essay ,* pp. 11–16, 33–36.

27. Gerard, *Essay on Genius,* pp. 431, 391–392.

28. Duff, *Essay,* pp. 11–16, 67; Gerard, *Essay on Genius,* p. 394.

29. Gerard, *Essay on Genius,* pp. 318–319, 392, 325, 399, 406.

30. Maass, *Versuch,* p. 369.

31. F. W. J. Schelling, *Sämmtliche Werke,* ed. K. F. A. Schelling (1856–1861), V, 362.

## 8. SHADOWS A CENTURY LONG

1. See René Wellek, *A History of Modern Criticism* (1955– ), I, chs. 8–11. On contrasts of German and British approaches to the imagination, see Furst, *Romanticism,* pp. 135, 151–152, 128–203 *passim.*

2. See Thomas Abt, *A. G. Baumgartens Leben und Character* (Halle, 1765); Ernst Bergmann, *Die Begründung der deutschen Ästhetik durch A. G. Baumgarten und G. F. Meier* (Leipzig, 1911); Herbert Sommer, *Die Poetische Lehre A. G. Baumgarten* (Munich, 1911).

3. Christian Wolff, *Psychologica Empirica* (1738), p. 97.

4. *Psychologica Empirica,* pp. 53–120. See also Wolff, *Psychologica Rationalis* (1740), pp. 141–285. Cf. S. T. Coleridge, *Notebooks,* ed. Kathleen Coburn (1957– ), I, 905.

5. J. K. Bodmer, *Von dem Wunderbaren* (1740), p. 165. See also Abrams, *The Mirror and the Lamp,* pp. 276–278, 382–383; Max Wehrli, *J. K. Bodmer*

*und die Geschichte der Literatur* (Frauenfeld, 1936); Wolfgang Bender, *J. K. Bodmer und J. J. Breitinger* (Stuttgart, 1973); G. de Reynold, *Bodmer et l'école suisse* (Lausanne, 1912).

6. George Santayana, *Character and Opinion in the United States* (1921), p. 28.

7. Coleridge, *Biographia*, I, 91.

8. Maass, *Versuch*, pp. 312, 313.

9. Michael Hissmann, *Geschichte* (1777), pp. 4, 48–49.

10. *Geschichte*, pp. 93–144, 128–129, 134, 136.

11. *Geschichte*, p. 144.

12. Ernst Platner, *Anthropologie* (1772), pp. 262–269.

13. *Anthropologie*, pp. 275–276.


## 9. THE NEW FOCUS OF LITERATURE AND MYTH

1. Leonhard Meister, *Ueber die Schwermerei* (1775–1777), I, 1–8, 30–32; II, 1–17, 90–92, 94–107.

2. *Schwermerei*, I, 7; II, 2, 16–17.

3. J. G. Sulzer, *Allgemeine Theorie*, 2nd ed. (1792–1799), II, 10, 11.

4. *Allgemeine Theorie*, II, 14.

5. *Allgemeine Theorie*, I, 684, 683.

6. *Allgemeine Theorie*, II, 11.

7. *Allgemeine Theorie*, I, 683; cf. Abrams, *The Mirror and the Lamp*, pp. 42–46.

8. As quoted by Blankenburg, *Litterarische Zusätze* (1796), I, 619.

9. Sulzer, *Theorie der Dichtkunst* (1788), pp. 87, 9–12, 46–47.

10. See Murray Roston, *Prophet and Poet: The Bible and the Growth of Romanticism* (1965); Christian H. Sachs, *Der Ursprung des Mythosbegriffes in der Modernen Bibelwissenschaft* (Tübingen, 1952).

11. See e.g. Coleridge on the wheels of Eziekiel, discussed below, ch. 21.

12. Christoph Meiners, *Grundriss der Theorie und Geschichte der schönen Wissenschaften* (1787), pp. 13–14.

13. Among numerous studies of Vico, see esp. Isaiah Berlin, *Vico and Herder* (1976), pp. 3–142.

14. Karl Philipp Moritz, *Götterlehre*, in *The Rise of Modern Mythology*, ed. B. Feldman and R. D. Richardson (1972), pp. 264–266.

15. On Herder, see esp. Wellek, *History of Modern Criticism*, I, 181–200; Robert J. Clark, *Herder* (1955); M. H. Dewey, *Herder's Relation to the Aesthetic Theory of His Time* (1920); Herbert Lindner, *Das Problem des Spinozismus im Schaffen Goethes und Herders* (Weimar, 1960); R. S. Mayo, *Herder and the Beginnings of Comparative Literature* (1969); Berlin, *Vico and Herder; The Rise of Modern Mythology*, pp. 224–228. Abrams, *The Mirror and the Lamp*, p. 219, describes Herder as "the founding father of historical organology."

16. Akenside's note MM to his *Hymn to the Naiads*.

17. Especially pertinent on the influence of Spinoza and the assimilation of him within Romantic contexts is the discussion in McFarland, *Coleridge and the Pantheist Tradition*, pp. 53–106.

18. Spinoza, *Ethics*, II, xvii, scholium.

19. *Chief Works of Benedict Spinoza* (1951), I, 25.
20. Schelling, *Sämmtliche Werke*, II, 20.

## 10. THE GREAT METAMORPHOSIS: TETENS AND KANT

1. Coleridge, *Notebooks*, ed. Kathleen Coburn, II, 2375.
2. J. N. Tetens, *Philosophische Versuche* (1776–1777), I, 24–26.
3. *Versuche*, I, 24.
4. Schelling, *SW*, III, 558–559.
5. Tetens, *Versuche*, I, 24.
6. *Versuche*, I, 116–117, 140, 106.
7. *Versuche*, I, 107; cf. I, 25: "*Die Schaffungskraft der Seele geht weiter. Sie kann Vorstellungen machen. . . . Sie kann . . . neue einfache Vorstellungen bilden.*" This recalls Locke's complex ideas.
8. *Versuche*, I, 136.
9. *Versuche*, I, 139, 160, 117 .
10. *Versuche*, I, 136; cf. p. 138. Tetens may be drawing on Buffon. See *Versuche*, I, 411. Buffon does not, however, discuss an artistically creative power. See also Thomas McFarland, "The Origin and Significance of Coleridge's Theory of Secondary Imagination," in *New Perspectives on Coleridge and Wordsworth* ed. Geoffrey H. Hartman (1972), esp. pp. 205–214; Engell, Introduction to the forthcoming *Collected Coleridge* ed. of the *Biographia*.
11. *Versuche*, I, 107, 119n.
12. *Anhang zu dem fünf und zwanzigsten bis sechs und dreyssigsten Bände, Zweyte Abteilung* (n.d.), p. 1091. I am indebted to Fabian's ed. of Gerard.
13. Tetens, *Versuche*, I, 154–160, 587–589, 115. The sense of all-encompassing reason in Tetens (I, 587–589), is echoed in Schelling and Coleridge.
14. *Versuche*, I, 159.
15. Cf. "*selbstbildende Dichtkraft*" and "*Selbstmachen bildlicher Vorstellungen*" in *Versuche*, I, 160, 115.
16. Gerard, *Essay on Genius*, pp. 84, 65–67, 59.
17. Schelling, *SW*, III, 633. Cf. Tetens on free play and self-drive in Herder's *Besonnenheit* (*Versuche*, I, 748–749), and on *Selbsthätigkeit* related to the whole mind, especially understanding and reason (I, 588–589). Cf. also Schelling, *SW*, V, 384: "Art rests on the identity of conscious and unconscious activity."
18. Coleridge, *Notebooks*, II, 2382.
19. Tetens, *Versuche*, I, 138.
20. Schelling, *SW*, V, 446.
21. Tetens, *Versuche*, I, 136–141, 126–127, 684.
22. *Versuche*, I, 139–40, 684–685.
23. *Versuche*, I, 134–135.
24. Coleridge, *Biographia*, I, ch. 10, pp. 124–126.
25. Tetens, *Versuche*, I, 106–108, 139–141.
26. *Versuche*, I, 128, 411–415, 530–541 *passim.*
27. Tetens lacked confidence that this split could be bridged: "*Zwischen dem Sinnlichen und dem Transcendenten, zwischen Metaphysik und Physik, und eben so zwischen Metaphysik und Psychologie ist eine Kluft, über welche gar nicht wegzukommen ist*" (*Versuche*, I, 128).

28. See e.g. H. J. deVleeschauwer, *La Déduction transcendental dans l'oeuvre de Kant* (1934), II, 315–329; de Vleeschauwer, *The Development of Kantian Thought*, trans. A. R. C. Duncan (1962), pp. 68–69, 84–87; Kant, *Critique of Pure Reason*, B103–104, 151–152.

29. A121–124.

30. B179.

31. See Norman Kemp Smith, *A Commentary to Kant's "Critique of Pure Reason,"* 2nd ed. (1923), esp. pp. 225–338; T. D. Weldon, *Kant's Critique of Pure Reason* (1958), pp. 130–134, 162–167, 266–306; Donald W. Crawford, *Kant's Aesthetic Theory* (1974), pp. 21–121; McFarland, "Origin and Significance of Coleridge's Theory."

32. A141.

33.Gerard, *Essay on Genius*, ed. Fabian, pp. xxxix, xlviii; Kant, *Menschenkunde oder philosophische Anthropologie*, ed. F. C. Starke (Leipzig, 1831), p. 233 .

34. Gerard, *Essay on Genius*, p. xxxix; cf. Kant, *Critique of Judgment*, sec. 47–49.

35. Kant, *Critique of Judgment*, trans. James Creed Meredith (1911), pp. 41–42.

36. Quoted in Gerard, *Essay on Genius*, p. xxxv (Kant's *Reflexionen zur Anthropologie* No. 942).

## 11.  THE PSYCHE REACHES OUT: SYMPATHY

1. For the first detailed study of the subject in eighteenth-century critical theory, see W. J. Bate, "The Sympathetic Imagination in Eighteenth-Century Criticism," *ELH 12* (1945): 144–164, distilled and revised in Bate, *From Classic to Romantic* ch. 5; John Radner," The Sympathetic Imagination: Concepts of Altruism in Eighteenth-Century British Thought," Ph.D. diss. Harvard Univ., 1966. For discussion of a general rather than historical character, see esp. Max Scheler, *Wesen und Formen der Sympathie* (Bonn, 1923).

2. Blair, *Lectures*, II, 371–372.

3. Cited by Scott Elledge, "Theories of Generality and Particularity," *PMLA* 62 (1947): 179. Cf. the analogous emphasis that metaphors should be short in order to have full impact. Alex Page, "Faculty Psychology and Metaphor in Eighteenth-Century Criticism," *MP* 66 (1969): 241–243.

4. Thomas Reid, *Works*, ed. Dugald Stewart (1814), II, 440.

5. John Gilbert Cooper, *Letters Concerning Taste*, 3rd ed. (1757), p. 17.

6. Shaftesbury, *Characteristics*, I, 129–130; see also pp. 131–136.

7. Zachary Mayne, *Two Dissertations Concerning Sense and the Imagination* (1728), p. 74.

8. Hume, *Treatise*, bk. III, pt. 2, sec. 2; bk. II, pt. 2 sec. 5.

9. See Hume, *An Inquiry Concerning the Principles of Morals*, sec. 6, pt. 1.

10. Burke, *Enquiry*, (6th ed., 1770), pp. 70, 249–250, 323–324; Jacob Spon, *Recherches* (Lyons, 1683), p. 358.

11. Burke, *Enquiry*, p. 332.

12. James Balfour, *A Delineation of the Nature and Obligation of Morality* (1753), p. 54; David Fordyce, *Elements of Moral Philosophy* (1754), pp.

169–171; James Burgh, *The Dignity of Human Nature* (1754), pp. 243–244; Francis Hutcheson, *A System of Moral Philosophy* (1755), I, 19–21.

13. Adam Smith, *Theory of Moral Sentiments*, 2nd ed. (1761), pp. 2–3.

14. Smith, *Theory*, p. 3.

15. Archibald Alison, *Essays on the Nature and Principles of Taste* (1790), p. 390.

16. James Beattie, *Essays on Poetry and Music*, 2nd ed. (1778), p. 194; cf. his *Elements of Moral Science* (1792), I, 98–100; *Dissertations Moral and Critical* (1783), pp. 166–190.

17. Maurice Morgann, *Essay* (1777), p. 167.

18. Gerard, *Essay on Genius*, pp. 152–154.

19. Gerard, *Essay on Genius*, pp. 46–47.

20. Blair, *Lectures*, II, 507–508, 524–525.

21. Margaret Cavendish, *CCXI Sociable Letters* (1664), No. 123, pp. 144–149.

22. Elizabeth Montagu, *Essay on the Writings and Genius of Shakespeare* (1769), p. 37.

23. William Richardson, *A Philosophical Analysis*, 2nd ed. (1774), pp. 38, 10, 40.

24. Morgann, *Essay.*, pp. 61n, 58n.

25. Stewart, *Elements*, p. 432.

26. John Ogilvie, *Philosophical & Critical Observations on the Nature, Characters, & Various Species of Composition* (1774), I, 178, 277, 282–283.

27. Gerard, *Essay on Taste* (1759), p. 86.

28. Beattie, *Essays*, p. 151.

29. Priestley, *Lectures*, pp. 126–127.

30. *Philosophy of Rhetoric* (1776), I, 320.

31. Aaron Hill, *Essay on the Art of Acting* (1779), pp. 9–10.

32. See Berlin, *Vico and Herder*, pp. xxii, 154–155, 171–174, 186–188.

33. Beattie, *Essays*, p. 277.

34. Kames, *Elements*, I, 29–30, 217.

35. Alison, *Principles*, pp. 236, 239–240.

36. Priestley, *Lectures*, p. 127.

37. On the development of the idea of *ut musica poesis*, especially in Germany, see Abrams, *The Mirror and the Lamp*, pp. 91–94; for English treatments, see esp. Lawrence Lipking, *The Ordering of the Arts in Eighteenth-Century England* (Princeton, 1970), pp. 211–323.

38. Webb, *Observations*, pp. 6–7, 153.

## 12. THE PSYCHE REACHES OUT: COALESCENCE AND
### THE CHEMISTRY OF THE MIND

1. See Sir Leslie Stephen, *History of English Thought in the Eighteenth Century*, 3rd ed. (1927 repr.), II, 109–121.

2. Abraham Tucker, *The Light of Nature Pursued* (1768–1777), I(1), 359, 351, 338; I(2), 26.

3. Tucker, *Light*, I(1), 234–235, 241, 246; I(2), 25–26; I(1), 270.

4. *Light*, I(1), 338, 226; I(2), 9; I(1), 221, 227.

5. *Light,* I(1), 233, 234, 251.

6. *Light,* I(1), 227, 271, 230. Gerard cites the letters of Locke and Molyneux on a similar point, pp. 233, 283.

7. *Light,* 217–229, 249; I(2), 38, 39, 42; I(1), 285.

8. *Light,* I(1), 280–281.

9. *Light,* I(1), 360, 353.

10. *Light,* I(1), 349; I(2), 41. Tucker suggests the involuntary "machinery" of imagination yields more activity than "volition."

11. *Light,* I(1), 253; I(2), 18, 33–34, 41.

12. *Light,* I(1), 328–329; II(2), 336; I(1), 315–316.

13. "The Vision" is remarkable in its range of learning, speculation, and good humor. Some passages have a prophetic and mythological tone suggestive of Blake. For Tucker's choice of Search as his *nom de plume* in his work, see *Light,* II(2), 139–142. The motto of II(2) is Romans 1:19–20, significant verses for considering divine imagination or creative force as a power mediating between the ideal or spiritual and material reality. "The Vision," II(2), 270–271, suggests a correspondence between man's ideas and those of God.

14. See Hipple, *The Beautiful;* Tuveson, *Imagination;* Martin Kallich, "The Meaning of Archibald Alison's *Essays on Taste,*" *PQ* 27 (1948): 314–324. Among fairly ample German commentary, see also Constantin Fideles, *Versuch über Alison's Ästhetik* (Munich, 1911); Willi Real, *Untersuchungen zu A. Alisons Theorie des Geschmacks* (Frankfurt, 1973).

15. Alison, *Principles,* pp. 53, 126, 413, 5, 127, 133, 37, 41. There is no physiological basis for association in the *Principles.* See Hipple, *The Beautiful,* p. 169.

16. Alison, *Principles,* p. 121.

17. *Principles,* pp. 411, 7–10, 14.

18. *Principles,* pp. 139, 142–143, 146. Alison cites the lines in Thomson's *Winter* beginning "Along the woods, along the moorish fens."

19. *Principles,* pp. 63, 24–25, 211, 319, 391, 54, 92; cf. Alexander Gerard, *An Essay on Taste,* 3rd ed. (1780), "Of the Standard of Taste," pp. 197–274.

20. Alison, *Principles,* p. 120. See also Hipple, *Aesthetic Theory,* p. 176. Alison and others of the Scottish School, such as Reid, touch on a general premise developed by Kant.

21. See Hipple, *The Beautiful,* pp. 247–283, concerned mainly with Knight and the "picturesque," as is J. P. Mayoux, *R. P. Knight* (Paris, 1932). Of general interest is F. Massermann's critical biography in "Studies in English Literature: The Hague," no. 89 (1974).

22. Brown's Lecture XL in *Philosophy of the Human Mind* (1820), II, 333, explains "Reasons for Preferring the Term Suggestion, to the Phrase Association of Ideas." See also Warren, *History of the Association Psychology,* p. 73.

23. Brown, *Philosophy,* II, 391–392 (for the working of imagination "in the common offices of life"), 395, 412.

24. *Philosophy,* II, 389–390, 399, 360, 372–373. See also II, 407, on the imagination proceeding "with the plan already conceived by us."

25. *Philosophy,* I, 156.

26. However, the "humble" sort nevertheless is more important because it pervades the daily thoughts and actions of every person. See Brown, *Philosophy,* II, 391, 400.

27. *Philosophy,* II, 398, 403, 339, 280. Cf. Alison, "Analogies with the life of

man"; Hobbes, *Leviathan*, part 1, ch. 3, which divides mental discourse into two categories, the first "unguided, without design and inconstant . . . the second regulated by some desire, and design." The second is "the faculty of invention."

28. Brown, *Philosophy*, II, 276–277, 231–232.

29. *Philosophy*, II, 228, 397; III, 278–282; see also II, 87–98; III, 473, 158–159. Cf. Coleridge's remark that the poet depicts nature *"ad hominem."* For Brown's similarity to Alison, who was by then popular, see II, 13; III, 179–188. Brown mentions Smith (e.g. III, 233–234) and parallels Hazlitt's view of the imagination (II, 391–392).

30. Brown, *Philosophy*, III, 291, 154–155, 285–293.

31. *Philosophy*, II, 413.

32. Hume's atheism and skepticism help explain his fascination for other thinkers. He acted, in Gerard's phrase, like an "adversary muscle." Since Hobbes, many associationists tried to disconnect a skeptical and harsh view of human nature from empirical philosophy. Smith succeeded somewhat, which accounts in part for his popularity. Hazlitt's *Principles of Human Action* (1805) seemed the best answer to Hobbes. For "upward progression," see e.g. Thomson, *Spring*, ll. 866–900; Milton, *Paradise Lost*, V, 469-488, which Coleridge uses in the *Biographia*, ch. 13.

33. Brown, *Philosophy*, II, 414.

34. Coleridge, *Biographia*, II, ch. 24, 218; see also Brown, *Philosophy*, III, 98.

35. Coleridge, "On Poesy or Art," in *Biographia*, II, 262; Brown, *Philosophy*, III, 25.

36. Abrams, *The Mirror and the Lamp*, pp. 156–183, 201–212; Morgann, *Essay*, p. 59n.

## 13. DISTINCTIONS BETWEEN FANCY AND IMAGINATION

1. See John Bullitt and W. J. Bate, "Distinctions Between Fancy and Imagination in Eighteenth-Century English Criticism," *MLN* 60 (1945): 8–15, where many of the examples cited, especially those from Shaftesbury, Duff, and Stewart, are discussed more fully. Wilma Kennedy, *The English Heritage of Coleridge of Bristol* (1947), notes only a few of the distinctions mentioned by Bullitt and Bate.

2. Hester Lynch Piozzi, *British Synonymy* (1794), pp. 133–145. "An intelligent stranger will observe too, that although we give sex very arbitrarily to personified qualities—yet he will commonly find FANCY feminine, IMAGINATION masculine, I scarce know why."

3. Beattie, *Dissertations Moral and Critical* (1783), p. 72.

4. Bundy, *Theory of Imagination*, p. 278.

5. Dryden, Preface to *Annus Mirabilis* (1667), in *Essays*, ed. W. P. Ker, I, 15.

6. *Spectator* 411.

7. Shaftesbury, *Characteristics*, ed. Robertson, II, 174–175, 277n–278n. For other distinctions in the first half of the century (Richard Blackmore, Arbuckle, Cooper), see also Bullitt and Bate, "Distinctions," p. 11.

8. Duff, *Essay on Original Genius*, pp. 6–7, 52, 70–71, 89.

9. Tucker, *Light*, I(1), 312.

10. Reid, *Works*, ed. Stewart, II, 436–447.

11. Stewart, *Elements*, pp. 284–285, 477, 305–309.

12. Scott, *Elements*, p. 181; cf. Coleridge, *Miscellaneous Criticism*, ed. T. M. Raysor (1936), p. 436.

13. Thomas Cogan, *Ethical Treatise on the Passions* (1807), I, 209, 212–213, 249. Cf. Richard and Maria Edgeworth, *Practical Education* (1798), II, 603, a book Coleridge read enthusiastically (*Letters*, I, 418, no. 254).

14. Brown, *Philosophy*, II, 397; see also III, 147; II, 408–409.

15. Sulzer, *Allgemeine Theorie*, II, 3.

16. Platner, *Philosophische Aphorismen*, pp. 168–169.

17. Platner, *Anthropologie*, pp. 159–167.

18. Platner, *Anthropologie*, pp. 262, 262–263, 276.

19. Cf. Coleridge, *Collected Letters*, ed E. L. Griggs (1965–1971), IV, 613.

20. Maass, *Versuch*, pp. 14, 6, 195, 2–3, 15.

21. *Versuch*, pp. 62–163, 163–170.

22. Kant, *Anthropologie in Pragmatischer Hinsicht* (1800), I *Buch*, para. 28–29, 34.

23. Schelling, *SW*, V, 393–396.

24. Schelling, *SW*, V, 395. Cf Coleridge, *Biographia*, II, ch. 18, p. 65. See also Ruskin's distinction in *Modern Painters* (1843).

25. Schelling, *SW*, IV, 115n.; cf. I, 431n1.

26. Tetens, *Philosophische Versuche*, I, 108–109.

## 14. A PLATEAU IN BRITAIN AND DEVELOPMENTS IN AMERICA

1. See Bate, *From Classic to Romantic*, pp. 79–92; Hipple, *The Beautiful*, pp. 133–148, 284–302; Hoyt Trowbridge, "Platonism and Sir Joshua Reynolds," *English Studies* 21 (1939): 1–7; W. J. Hipple, "The Aesthetics of Dugald Stewart," *Journal of Aesthetics and Art Criticism* 14 (1955): 77–96.

2. Reynolds, *Discourse XIII*.

3. *Discourses* VII and XIII.

4. XIII.

5. XIII.

6. XIII.

7. XIII.

8. As quoted by John Black, Preface to A. W. Schlegel, *Course of Lectures on Dramatic Art and Literature*, trans. Black (London, 1815), I, v.

9. Stewart, *Elements*, pp. 502, 521.

10. *Elements*, p. 497.

11. *Port-Folio*, 1, no. 25 (June 20, 1801).

12. *North American Review*, vol. 19, 30.

13. John Witherspoon, *Lectures on Moral Philosophy* (Princeton, 1912), pp. 16–17. Text is from the first ed. of 1800. Others followed in 1810 and 1822.

14. *Port-Folio* 3, no. 52 (Dec. 24, 1803).

15. *Port-Folio* 10–11, n.s. 5–6 (1808): 331.

16. *Port-Folio* 3, no. 12 (Mar. 19, 1803).

17. *Monthly Register* vol. 2, pp. 312–318, 311.

## 15. ORGANIC SENSIBILITY: HAZLITT

1. Commentary on Hazlitt's concept of the imagination is unusually rich. See John Bullitt, "Hazlitt and the Romantic Conception of the Imagination," *PQ* 24 (1945): 343–361; W. J. Bate, *Criticism: The Major Texts* (1952), pp 281–292; Heschel Baker, *William Hazlitt* (1962). For more specific focus on the imagination, see W. P. Albrecht, *Hazlitt and the Creative Imagination* (1961), esp. chs. 1, 3, 5; Roy Park, *Hazlitt and the Spirit of the Age* (1971), esp. chs. 1, 3, 8; John Kinnaird, *William Hazlitt: Critic of Power* (1978), esp. chs. 1–8; John L. Mahoney, *The Logic of Passion* (Salzburg, 1978), esp. chs. 4–7.

2. William Hazlitt, *Complete Works*, ed. P. P. Howe (1930–1933), XX, 237; VIII, 83.

3. *Works*, XX, 170; I, 26; XX, 174, 179, 376–386; I, 80–81, 23; XX, 376; I, 51, 67, 56, 78; XX, 80–81, 162, 170–171, 12, 16; IV, 250; II, 113–114.

4. VIII, 237; I, 8–9, 42; XX, 50; I, 28; XX, 173, 179.

5. I, 1, 2, 39; XX, 170; I, 14–15, 2, 21; XX, 185; I, 23; cf. VI, 8, 23; I, 20; V, 101.

6. XVI, 185; XX, 12–13, 17; II, 114–119.

7. XII, 257; XX, 10, 32–35; II, 283, 117; XX, 19–20; II, 191; I, 124.

8. II, 153; XX, 279; XII, 51; II, 153. In several metaphors Hazlitt compares the activity of imagination to a body of water (XX, 251, 197–198).

9. I, 27; V, 51; VIII, 263.

10. "Poetry and Imagination" in *Letters and Social Aims.*

11. VIII, 36–37, 70, 77; IV, 175; William Hazlitt, *Literary Remains*, ed. Buliver and Talfound, I, 243–246; Hazlitt, *Works*, VIII, 31.

12. Wellek, *Immanuel Kant in England*, pp. 168–169; Hazlitt, *Works*, XX, 30n; XX, 326; I, 12, 43; VIII, 33, 35.

13. XX, 30n; I, 23; XII, 251; VI, 109; XVI, 8; cf. VI, 327. For Hazlitt's use of Hobbes, see II, 135; IV, 176. For the common use of the magnet as an image of imaginative force, see ch. 16.

14. XII, 151.

15. See VIII, 32; IV, 196; XVI, 209; VIII, 38 (We feel "by the principle of association, which is subtle and sure in proportion as it is variable and indefinite"); IX, 173; VIII, 42; cf. I, 127; VIII, 31, 104; XX, 374; XII, 297; I, 21; XII, 297, 50, 47–48, 46.

16. V, 7, 213; XX, 45.

17. IV, 75; V, 379.

18. XX, 46; V, 296–297; XX, 209–210; IV, 77; VI, 322, 23.

19. I, 56; IV, 77. See also VIII, 258–259, where the senses are differentiated according to the strength they provide for the associative process.

20. IV, 79–80; V, 26–27. Hazlitt criticizes Sidney because he "cannot let his imagination . . . dwell for a moment on the beauty or power of the real object" (VI, 321).

21. IV, 79; VIII, 258–259; IV, 77–78; V, 210. Gusto may be felt in a character as well as in an object. Hazlitt speaks of "the deep internal working" of hypocrisy (V, 219–220).

22. IV, 68. Beauty results from a special union of intrinsic qualities in nature and of feelings in the mind (XX, 390; VIII, 171).

23. XIX, 78; XVIII, 158 (Hazlitt's extensive italics deleted); XVII, 57, 61.

24. V, 3; XII, 245; IV, 75; VIII, 82–83. Cf. Coleridge's view that art is "the power of humanizing nature, of infusing the thoughts and passions . . . into

every thing which is the object of his contemplation" ("On Poesy or Art," *Biographia*, II, 253); V, 3-4; XVI, 63; XIX, 75; XX, 388.

25. VIII, 83; V, 3; *Hamlet*, IV, vii; cf. Hazlitt, *Works* IV, 271; XII, 153; V, 10; XIX, 79.

26. I, 147; IV, 160; V, 7, 15n; XX, 211; V, 347-348, 48.

27. XII, 250; XVII, 47; V, 54-55, 48; VIII, 39; XVI, 86; V, 55.

28. Hazlitt shared with Coleridge a love for the plain language and images of *Pilgrim's Progress* (V, 43).

29. V, 5; XII, 341.

30. V, 9; IV, 161.

31. XI, 28-29; IV, 13, 163; XVII, 207.

32. IV, 114; XIX, 11; V, 163; IV, 114; V, 156. For Hazlitt on Wordsworth, see VIII, 44; IV, 112, 120; XIX, 15-16; V, 129-130; IV, 92. For Shelley, see XVI, 265. Shelley "became the creature of his own will."

33. Childe Harold "volunteers his own Pilgrimage,—appoints his own penance,—makes his own confession,—and all—for nothing" (XX, 35).

34. Jerome Buckley, *The Victorian Temper* (1951), pp. 41-65; VI, 305; V, 271; XII, 60; Jan. 29, 1826, trans. John Oxenford in *Conversations of Goethe* (1850).

35. V, 53, 153; VIII, 42; IV, 88-89; cf. XI, 80.

36. XVII, 273; cf. 93, 213; IV, 75; XIX, 20; V, 162. Hazlitt may be thinking of *Die Räuber* or plays such as J. M. R. Lenz's *Der Hofmeister* or *Die Soldaten*.

37. VIII, 219; VI, 305; XII, 55; XX, 369; V, 144.

38. XX, 42, 352; VI, 22-23, 322; XX, 251. Hazlitt adopts "a modern distinction" by speaking of the Elizabethan "poetry of imagination" and the "poetry of fancy in the time of Charles I" (V, 82).

39. XX, 41, 150; XVII, 336; XII, 328; XX, 216.

40. XX, 304-305; XII, 290; V, 204-205; XVIII, 305; V, 52; XII, 297.

41. XVIII, 305; IV, 200.

42. XX, 296; IV, 18-19, 34; XX, 61; V, 16-17.

43. VIII, 49; XX, 299; VIII, 42; IV, 239.

44. XVI, 91; V, 48-50; IV, 358.

45. V, 50; IV, 229.

46. V, 50-53; IV, 250, 226, 260; XX, 90; V, 51; IV, 184. Hazlitt says, "Milton's learning has the effect of intuition" (V, 58-59). See above, ch. 5.

47. IV, 23; V, 191, 185, 46; IV, 293, 347.

48. VI, 106-107; XII, 302; XVI, 63.

49. V, 69-70, 6.

## 16. THE NEW PHILOSOPHERS' STONE AND THE NEW PIERIAN SPRING

1. J. G. Herder, *Sämmtliche Werke*, ed. Bernhard Suphan (1877-1913), XXIII, 313 (in the 1801 ed. of *Adrastea*: II, 229). Herder, despite the vast literature on his thought generally, seems to have only one discussion that has much to say about his concept of imagination in particular: J. E. Fugate, *The Psychological Basis of Herder's Aesthetic* (Paris, 1966). For general commentary, see Wellek, *History*, I, ch. 9; R. T. Clark, *Herder: His Life and Thought* (1955);

Berlin, *Vico and Herder* (1976). For the general German context, in Herder and especially the Schlegels and Novalis, see Furst, *Romanticism*, esp. chs. 2–3.

2. This and other passages are from Schiller, *Aesthetic Education of Man*, trans. and ed. by Elizabeth M. Wilkinson and L. A. Willoughby (Oxford, 1967).

3. See Coleridge, *Notebooks*, III, 3744; Coleridge, *The Friend*, in *Collected Coleridge*, I, 493. Schelling uses the term *Bildungstrieb* and suggests a connection between it and *Bildungskraft* (*SW*, II, 526–532, 565–566).

4. Cf. Schiller, *Aesthetic Education*, letter IX, para. 4.

5. Herder, *Werke*, VI, 188–192.

6. *Werke*, VII, 322, 371; cf. XXXI, 249.

7. See *Werke*, VII, 314, 361; I, 28; XIX, 351; XXXI, 249.

8. Tetens, *Versuche*, I, 111; cf. Schelling *SW*, I, 346n; II, 431.

9. See Schiller, *Aesthetic Education*, pp. xxxiii–xxxiv.

10. Fichte, *Sämmtliche Werke*, ed. J. H. Fichte (1846), VIII, 273, 275. "*Über Geist und Buchstab in der Philosophie*" first appeared in *Phil. Journal* 9 (1798): 199–232, 292–305.

11. Herder, *Werke*, VIII, 191–192.

12. Berlin, *Vico and Herder*, p. xxvi.

13. J. G. Fichte, *Werke*, ed. Reinhard Lauth, Hans Jacob, *et al.* (1961– ), II(1), 308.

14. Fichte, *Werke*, I(4), 192, 202; I(3), 190.

15. *Werke*, I(2), 368–369; I(3), 213.

16. II(3), 310; I(2), 361, 350–355, 382–385.

17. I(2), 359–361.

18. II(3), 316, 334.

19. I(2), 414–415; II(3), 324–327.

20. I(3), 334; II(3), 325; II(3), 311, 316–317, 298–299.

21. I(4), 192n.

22. I(3), 108; II(3), 161.

23. II(3), 303.

24. Fichte probably wrote it in 1794, but Schiller then had already been several years in developing the ideas found in the *Aesthetic Education*.

25. See Schiller, *Aesthetic Education*, letter II, para. 3. See also Victor Basch, *La Poétique de Schiller*, 2nd ed. (Paris, 1911); Ernst Cassirer, "Schiller und Shaftesbury," *Publications, English Goethe Society*, XI (1935); S. S. Kerry, "The Artist's Intuition in Schiller's Aesthetic Philosophy," *Publications, English Goethe Society*, XXVIII (1959) Kerry, *Schiller's Writings on Aesthetics* (Manchester, 1961); A. Tenenbaum, *Kants Ästhetik und ihr Einfluss auf Schiller* (Berlin, 1933); A. O. Lovejoy, "Schiller and the Genesis of English Romanticism," *Essays in the History of Ideas* (Baltimore, 1948).

26. Schiller, *Aesthetic Education*, letter XIV.

27. *Aesthetic Education*, letter XXVI, para. 10; p. lxvi.

28. Herder, *Adrastea* (1801), II, 228–229.

29. Christoph Wieland, *Wielands Kleinere Prosäische Schriften* (1794 rpr.), I, 289.

30. Schiller, *Aesthetic Education*, letter XXVI, paras. 5, 9–11; letter XXIV, para. 5; letter XXVI, para. 14.

31. Schiller to Goethe, Jan. 7, 1795.

32. Furst, *Romanticism*, pp. 153–155. The quotation from Schleiermacher

is from *Über die Religion,* quoted by Furst. On Novalis, see Wellek, *History,* II, 82–88. For general background, see T. L. Haering, *Novalis als Philosoph* (Stuttgart, 1954); John Neubauer, *Bi-Focal Vision* (Chapel Hill, 1971).

33. Novalis, *Gesammelte Werke,* ed. Carl Seelig (Zürich, 1945), II, 221 (Nos. 473 and 475).

34. Cf. Furst, *Romanticism,* p. 155; Novalis, *Werke,* III, 308 (No. 1859).

35. Novalis, *Werke,* IV, 126 (No. 2281).

36. Cf. Furst, *Romanticism,* pp. 150–152. In Collins' *Ode to Fear,* "Fancy lifts the veil between" us and "the World unknown."

37. Novalis, *Werke,* I, 255; III, 141 (No. 1247).

38. *Werke,* I, 259; as quoted by Furst, *Romanticism,* p. 128; cf. pp. 177–179.

39. Novalis, *Werke,* III, 25 (No. 816).

40. *Werke,* IV, p. 15 (No. 1921); cf. II, 301 (No. 692); II, 124 (No. 278); III, 307 (No. 1849).

41. *Werke,* I, 321–322; II, 145 (No. 300).

42. *Werke,* III, 25 (Nos. 817–818).

43. *Werke,* I, 302; cf. Furst, *Romanticism,* p. 139.

44. Novalis, *Werke,* III, 25 (No. 818); II, 186 (No. 373).

## 17. THE PROPHETIC AND VISIONARY: BLAKE AND SHELLEY

1. William Blake, *Jerusalem* 69:25; *Vision of the Last Judgment* (1810). See also Northrop Frye, *Fearful Symmetry* (1947); the imagination could be described as indirectly a principal theme of most Blake commentary. Less familiar, but dealing explicitly if at times thinly with the concept of the imagination, are articles by M. R. Lowery, *Northwest Missouri State College Studies,* XIV (1950), 105–131; Max Plowman, *New Adelphi* n.s. 3 (1930): 177–183; J. S. Pryke, *New Church Life* 48 (1928): 137–151; E. Rixecker, *Blakes psychologisches Darstellung der Imagination* (Marburg, 1939). Other more important works are cited below.

2. Cf. "A Vision of the Last Judgment," *The Poetry and Prose of William Blake,* ed. David V. Erdman, comm. Harold Bloom (1965), pp. 544–545, 555; *Jerusalem* 70:19; *Milton* 3:3.

3. Morton D. Paley, *Energy and the Imagination: A Study of the Development of Blake's Thought* (1970), p. 233n; Blake to Rev. John Trusler, Aug. 23, 1799.

4. Blake, "Vision of the Last Judgment."

5. Blake, *Jerusalem* 98:31–32.

6. See also Blake, "The Mental Traveller."

7. Thomas Taylor, *The Philosophical and Mathematical Commentaries of Proclus on the First Book of Euclid's Elements* (1792), II, 262, quoted by Paley, *Energy,* p. 208.

8. Frye, *Fearful Symmetry,* p. 293.

9. Blake, *Poetry and Prose,* p. 637.

10. Blake, *Milton* 29:65. Cf. Abrams, *The Mirror and the Lamp,* p. 216, for polar opposites in Blake's thought.

11. Frye, *Fearful Symmetry,* pp. 230, 281, 48–49, 126.

12. Frye, *Fearful Symmetry,* pp. 52, 300.

13. Frye, *Fearful Symmetry,* p. 415; Blake, *Poetry and Prose,* p. 544.

14. Paley, *Energy*, pp. 233–236.

15. Coleridge, to Rev. H. F. Cary, Feb. 6, 1818, *Collected Letters*, IV, 834; cf. Furst, *Romanticism*, pp. 164, 185–186.

16. Frye, *Fearful Symmetry*, pp. 272–273; Harold Bloom, *Shelley's Myth-making* (1959), pp. 232–236.

17. Shelley, "On Life" (1812–14?). See also Anthony Durand, *Shelley on the Nature of Poetry* (1948), chs. 1–4; E. J. Schulze, *Shelley's Theory of Poetry* (The Hague, 1966), esp. pp. 77–91; Earl Wasserman, *Shelley: A Critical Reading* (1971), chs. 5, 7. The richest study of Platonic sources in still J. A. Noto-poulos, *Shelley's Platonism* (1950); cf. J. E. Baker, *Shelley's Platonic Answer to a Platonic Attack on Poetry* (1965).

18. Shelley, "On Love" (1814–1819, pub. 1829).

19. See Carlos Baker, *Shelley's Major Poetry: The Fabric of a Vision* (1948), pp. 227–228.

20. Shelley, "On Life"; Shelley, *The Complete Works*, ed. Roger Ingpen and Walter E. Peck (1965), VII, 65; Shelley, "On Life"; cf. *Hellas*, ll. 801–802.

21. Shelley, *Works*, VII, 59. "Laws" and "sensations" suggest the laws of associationism.

22. *Works*, VII, 59.

23. Fichte, *Werke*, I(2), 314–315.

24. See Milton Wilson, *Shelley's Later Poetry* (1959), pp. 152–154.

25. Shelley, *Defence of Poetry*.

26. Fichte, *Werke*, II(3), 303.

27. See Baker, *Shelley's Platonic Answer*, esp. pp. 27–29.

28. Edward John Trelawny, *Recollections of the Last Days of Shelley and Byron* (1858).

29. Shelley, "On Life"; *Defence*.

30. Wilson, *Shelley's Later Poetry* p. 301; see also Wasserman, *Shelley*, pp. 176–177; Shelley, *Defence*; Fichte, *Werke*, I(3), 362.

## 18. WORDSWORTH

1. Wordsworth *Prelude* (1805) I, 582–583. References, unless otherwise stated, are to this text. Discussions of Wordsworth on the imagination are so interwoven with discussions of his poetry that the bulk of serious Wordsworth criticism could be appropriately listed. Especially relevant are Arthur Beatty, *William Wordsworth: His Doctrine and Art in Their Historical Relations*, rev. ed. (1927), which deals with the influence of Hartley and the associationists and, though outdated, is still of value; Douglas Bush, *Mythology and the Romantic Tradition*, rev. ed (1969); D. J. James, *Scepticism and Poetry* (1977), esp. p. 164; R. D. Havens, *The Mind of a Poet* (1941); N. P. Stalknecht, *Strange Seas of Thought* (1945); W. J. B. Owen's ed. of Preface to the *Lyrical Ballads* (*Anglistica*, 1957); Stephen Parrish, "The Wordsworth-Coleridge Controversy," *PMLA* 73 (1958): 152–163; Herbert Lindenberger, *On Wordsworth's Prelude* (1963); David Perkins, *The Quest for Permanence* (1959); Perkins, *Wordsworth and the Poetry of Sincerity* (1964); J. A. W. Hefferman, *Wordsworth's Theory of Poetry* (1969); Mary Warnock, *Imagination* (1976) esp. pp. 72–130; Wellek, *History*, II, ch. 5; E. D. Hirsch, Jr.,

*Wordsworth and Schelling* (1960), esp., pp. 15–25, 101–112, 117–125, 129–146.

2. Wordsworth, *Prelude* II, 266, 272.

3. Wordsworth, *Prose Works*, ed. W. J. B. Owen and J. W. Smyser (1974), III, 35n.

4. *Prelude*, II, 245, 250, 271–276.

5. *Prelude*, II, 243–245.

6. *Prelude*, I, 582–585.

7. *Prelude*, I, 433–438.

8. "Tintern Abbey," ll. 95–99; *Prose Works*, I, 124.

9. *Prelude*, II, 382–393.

10. *Prelude*, II, 409–411.

11. "Tintern Abbey," ll. 109–111; cf. *Excursion*, I, ll. 673–674.

12. *Prelude*, III, 124–127.

13. A point particularly stressed in the *Essay Supplementary.*

14. Preface (1800), *Prose Works*, I, 126, italics added.

15. *Prose Works*, III, 30–32.

16. *Prose Works*, III, 33.

17. *Prose Works*, III, 33; *Prelude*, XIII, 82–95.

18. *Prelude*, VIII, 511–518, 584–586.

19. *Prelude*, VII, 533–541.

20. Wordsworth, *Prose Works*, III, 31; 33–34.

21. *Prose Works*, III, 36.

22. *Prose Works*, 34–35; cf. Hirsch, *Wordsworth and Schelling*, pp. 129–131.

23. *Prelude*, VI, 531–536, 568–571.

24. *Prelude*, XII, 371–379.

25. *Prelude*, XIII, 167–170; V, 38–40.

26. *Prelude*, XIV, 188–189 (1850 ed.); XII, 54–55.

27. *Prelude*, XIII, 185–188.

28. *Prelude*, VI, 592–593 (1850 ed.).


## 19. GOETHE AND KEATS

1. See also Hirsch, *Wordsworth and Schelling*, p. 7.

2. J. W. Goethe, *Werke, Briefe und Gespräche*, ed. Ernst Beutler (1948–1954), XIII, 1020; *Werke*, XXII, 324. In the commentary on Goethe as a critic ("surprisingly meager," as René Wellek says), little touches on his concept of imagination. For general background, see William Bode, *Goethes Aesthetik* (Berlin, 1901); Otto Stelzer, *Goethe und die bildende Kunst* (Braunschweig, 1949); Wellek, *History;* Otto Harnack, *Die Klassische Aesthetik der Deutscher* (Leipzig, 1892), II, ch. 10.

3. Trans. Hermann J. Wiegand in *Goethe: Wisdom and Experience* (1949), pp. 103–104.

4. *Werke*, X, 424.

5. XIII, 328.

6. XIII, 1020; XXI, 817.

7. Goethe, "Shakespeare und kein Ende."

8. *Werke*, XXII, 872; XXIII, 366.

9. XXI, 528–529, 578; XIV, 742; XIII, 1020.

10. Bate, *Keats*, pp. 33–34; John Keats, *Letters*, ed. Hyder Rollins (1958), I, 186. See also J. M. Murry, *Keats and Shakespeare* (1935); Clarence Thorpe, *The Mind of John Keats* (1964 repr.); Bush, *Mythology and the Romantic Tradition*; D. J. James, *The Romantic Comedy* (1948); Perkins, *The Quest for Permanence*; Bate, *Keats*; John Jones, *John Keats's Dream of Truth* (1969); Walter Evert, *Aesthetic and Myth in the Poetry of Keats* (1965); M. A. Goldberg, *The Poetics of Romanticism: Toward a Reading of John Keats* (1969).

11. Keats, *Letters*, I, 403; II, 18.

12. *Letters* I, 189, 192.

13. I, 387; II, 234.

14. I, 193.

15. I, 184.

16. I, 262.

17. II, 80–81, 139.

18. I, 184, 271, 279.

19. I, 242–243.

20. I, 184–185.

21. See Bate, *Keats*, pp. 245, 262.

22. Keats, *Letters*, I, 281.

## 20. SCHELLING

1. Schelling, *SW*, V, 267. Here Schelling does not mean the fine arts alone, but the art of dialectic thought (which is given concrete body by the fine arts). Commentary on Schelling is extensive, but only some of it deals with his concept of the imagination. See Jean Gibelin, *L'Esthétique de Schelling d'après la Philosophie de l'art* (Paris, 1934), esp. pt. 2. Gabriel Marcel, *Coleridge et Schelling* (Paris, 1971 repr.), despite its promising title, has little to say about the imagination.

2. Schelling, *SW*, V, 10, 129, 135.

3. Cf. Coleridge, *Biographia*, ch. 13.

4. Schelling, *SW*, VII, 147; IV, 115 and n.

5. VII, 202.

6. V, 386. Cf. Coleridge, *Collected Letters*, IV, 690.

7. Schelling, *SW*, VII, 141, 217; V, 267.

8. V, 422–423; IV, 417; cf. V, 282–283.

9. V, 282.

10. V, 219; III, 438–440; cf. Coleridge, *Biographia*, I, 198.

11. *SW*, III, 558–559; cf. above, ch. 10.

12. III, 624–628.

13. See e.g. III 350–351, 369–371, 426, 610–611, 626–627, 630–634.

14. III, 625, 626.

15. See e.g. VII, 230–231.

16. VII, 182. Passages like this revealed to Coleridge how Schelling had changed his idea of the nature of the Absolute. See Coleridge to J. H. Green, *Letters* (1959), IV, 873–876.

17. *SW*, VII, 438.

18. VII, 439.

19. V, 217; VII, 143, 171; IV, 129n; V, 378; IV, 129; VII, 358.

20. VII, 213, 202 and *passim;* V, 248; 283; II, 65.

21. II, 45, 48; trans. Michael Bullock, *The True Voice of Feeling: Studies in English Romantic Poetry*, ed. Herbert Read (1953), p. 325.

22. IV, 547–548; cf. Herder, *Die Schöpfung;* Schiller, *Die Künstler*, ch. 16 above.

23. II, 67; VII, 202–203, 213–214, 232.

24. II, 12–15, 45–48.

25. II, 20, 72.

26. II, 20–22, 35–37. Schelling cites Jacobi, who had also introduced him to the thought of Bruno. See VII, 441–445; II, 35.

27. II, 69–72; IV, 77. See also Shelling, *Über das Wesen der Menschlichen Freiheit.*

28. See Shaftesbury, *Characteristics*, pt. 3, sec. 1.

29. Schelling, *SW,* IV, 125; III, 18–19, 261, 273, 287–289.

30. VII, 217; V, 275; VII, 183; V, 289, 469.

31. II, 66–68; IV, 417; V, 280; IV, 107–108.

32. III, 271, 11, 20, 450–451.

33. III, 345; 581–583, 610–611; V, 460.

34. V, 459–460; VII, 174; III, 627–628; V, 327; VI, 56.

35. III, 606, 615; V, 135.

36. V, 628–632; III, 554, 612–614, 618–619, 630–631, 634; IV, 89; V, 411, 422; III, 628.

37. V, 278; III, 621–622; Schelling, *Concerning the Plastic Arts*, trans. Bullock in *The True Voice*, p. 337.

38. V, 616, 619, 623, 349.

39. V, 460, 459.

40. V, 270–272.

41. III, 629.

42. III, 351.

43. III, 351.

44. Cf. V, 282.

45. The *Ältestes Systemprogramm* is sometimes attributed to Hölderlin. See *Über das Wesen*, ed. Horst Fuhrman (1964), pp. 5–6.

46. V, 357n.

47. V, 480; III, 350–351.

48. III, 625–630; cf. V, 361, 364, 369, 284: *"Die wahre Objektivität der Philosophie in ihrer Totalität ist nur die Kunst."*

49. V, 350, 284, 368.

50. Goethe, "Epoche der forcierten Talente" (1812).

51. Schelling, *SW,* V, 361; cf. 348.

52. V, 267.

53. V, 348, 352.

54. IV, 240–243; V, 361; VII, 173; V, 383; III, 623–624; VII, 189.

55. III, 620–622.

56. IV, 226; V, 384, 279; cf. IV, 423 (*"Das Universum ist im Absoluten als das vollkommenste organische Wesen und als das vollkommenste Kunstwerk gebildet: für die Vernunft, die es in ihm erkennt, in absoluter Wahrheit, für die Einbildungskraft, die es in ihm darstellt, in absoluter Schönheit"*); V, 384–385, 480; VI, 57–58; V, 370.

57. V, 406, 345, 350; Schelling, *Concerning the Plastic Arts*, p. 331; *SW*, VIII, 279; cf. V, 298.

58. VII, 394–396, 405–406; V, 459; VII, 438–439; V, 292–293, 431, 455; VII, 390.

59. V, 237–238, 308–313; cf. V, 372; III, 601; V, 280. Kant had stressed the role of the race, an issue that was of current and heated discussion.

## 21. COLERIDGE

1. The commentary on Coleridge as a critic—almost all of it being concerned with the imagination—is so extensive that the reader can only be referred to the bibliography by René Wellek in *The English Romantic Poets: A Review of Research and Criticism*, ed. Frank Jordan, 3rd ed. rev. (1972), pp. 209–258. Works especially helpful in writing this chapter included, besides Kathleen Coburn's annotation and commentary in her edition of *Coleridge's Notebooks* (3 vols. to date, 1957–    ), Alice Snyder, *The Critical Principle of the Reconciliation of Opposites* (Ann Arbor, 1918); I. A. Richards, *Coleridge on Imagination*, 3rd ed. rev. (1962); Gordon McKenzie, *Organic Unity in Coleridge* (Berkeley, 1939); Clarence Thorpe, "The Imagination: Coleridge vs. Wordsworth," *PQ* 18 (1939): 1–18; Thorpe, "Coleridge as Aesthetician and Critic," *JHI* 1 (1944): 387–414; W. J. Bate, in *Perspectives of Criticism*, ed. Harry Levin (1950), pp. 125–160; James Benziger, "Organic Unity: Leibniz to Coleridge," *PMLA* 46 (1951): 24–48; James V. Baker, *The Sacred River: Coleridge's Theory of the Imagination* (Baton Rouge, La., 1957); Richard H. Fogle, *The Idea of Coleridge's Criticism* (1962); J. A. Appleyard, *Coleridge's Philosophy of Literature* (Cambridge, Mass., 1965); McFarland, *Coleridge*; Owen Barfield, *What Coleridge Thought* (1971); John Beer, *Coleridge's Poetic Intelligence* (1977); Mary Warnock, *Imagination* (1976); Kathleen Coburn, *Experience into Thought* (Toronto, 1979); Wellek, *History*, vol. II. On the *Biographia* in particular, see the Introduction to the *Collected Coleridge*, ed. James Engell and W. J. Bate (to appear 1982; collected ed. cited hereafter as *CC*). On the Germans and Coleridge, see René Wellek, *Kant in England* (Princeton, 1931); Wellek, *History*, vol. II; McFarland, *Coleridge*, esp. ch. 1; Pt. II of my Introduction to the *Biographia* as well as annotations in that edition to chapters 5–13 in particular.

2. See in general McFarland, *Coleridge*.

3. *Biographia Literaria* (1907), II, ch. 14, p. 12; ch. 12 (hereafter *BL*); *Friend* (*CC*), I, 467n. The thought is in Schelling but others as well. Hazlitt, for instance, says much the same thing in his "Prospectus of English Philosophy."

4. *Aids to Reflection* (1825), p. 218n (hereafter *AR*).

5. *Philosophical Lectures*, ed. Coburn (1949), p. 116 (hereafter *PL*).

6. *AR*, p. 171n; *BL*, I, 109. Tetens and others used the terms in Germany.

7. *PL*, p. 116; cf. pp. 87, 106–108.

8. *Friend* (*CC*), I, 513.

9. *Table Talk* (1884), p. 70 (hereafter *TT*); *Anima Poetae* (1895), pp. 261–262 (hereafter *AP*).

10. *Letters*, I, no. 210.

11. *Friend (CC)*, I, 500.
12. *BL*, I, ch. 12, p. 167.
13. *BL*, I, 83.
14. *TT*, p. 34 (Jan. 3, 1823).
15. *BL*, II, 186.
16. *BL*, I, 91.
17. Santayana, *Character and Opinion*, p. 28.
18. *Memoir of the Life and Writing of William Taylor*, ed. J. W. Robberds (1843), II, 216 (Southey to Taylor, July 11, 1808); Coleridge, *Miscellaneous Criticism*, ed. Thomas Raysor (1936), pp. 386–387; *BL*, I, 73, 83.
19. Coleridge, *Notebooks*, II, 2402; *AR*, pp. 243–244; cf. *Notebooks*, II, 2151 (hereafter *CN*); *PL*, p. 334.
20. *Friend (CC)*, I, 524.
21. *CN*, II, 3325.
22. *AP*, p. 15; *PL*, pp. 114, 116.
23. Cf. *BL*, I, ch. 5, p. 57.
24. Coleridge, *Malta Notebooks* (1805); *AP*, p. 120.
25. *TT*, p. 165.
26. *AP*, pp. 143, 294.
27. *Letters*, IV, no. 1033.
28. *AR*, p. 172n; *CN*, III, 4333.
29. *CN*, III, 4426; cf. 4432, 4436; *Friend*, I, 467n; *TT*, p. 136.
30. *PL*, p. 87.
31. *Friend (CC)*, I, 177n, 520.
32. *AR*, p. 216; *AP*, p. 12.
33. Coleridge, *Statesman's Manual*, ed. R. J. White, p. 28 (hereafter *SM*) in *CC*.
34. Cf. Coleridge, *Lectures* (1795), in *CC*, ed. Lewis Patton and Peter Mann, p. 92; *Letters*, I, 211–212.
35. *AR*, p. 226n.
36. *SM (CC)*, App. E, pp. 113–114.
37. *AR*, pp. 226, 216.
38. *SM (CC)*, p. 114.
39. *TT*, p. 81.
40. *SM (CC)*, App. C, p. 69.
41. *Friend (CC)*, I, 521; *AR*, pp. 227–228.
42. *AR*, p. 226n.
43. *CN*, III, 3325.
44. *AR*, p. 226n.
45. *CN*, III, 4398; cf. *AP*, p. 186.
46. *SM (CC)*, p. 29.
47. *TT*, p. 232 (Aug. 20, 1833).
48. *BL*, I, 189.
49. *BL*, I, 199–200. See Introduction to *BL* in *CC*.
50. *PL*, pp. 111–112, 107–108, 187.
51. Ralph Waldo Emerson, *Collected Works*, ed. Robert E. Spiller and Alfred E. Ferguson (Cambridge, Mass., 1971–    ), I, 55.
52. *Friend (CC)*, I, 460, 463, 462, 515n.
53. *AR*, p. 228; cf. *PL*, p. 108.
54. *Friend (CC)*, I, 463.

55. *BL*, II, 45; Coleridge, *Shakespearean Criticism*, ed. Raysor (1930), II, 61.

56. *PL*, p. 187.

57. *CN*, III 3746.

58. *Friend (CC)*, I, 520, 463; *BL*, II, 45; *AR*, pp. 26–27, 247.

59. *PL*, pp. 333–334.

60. *BL*, I, 164, 187–188; 73.

61. *BL*, II, 218; I, 202.

62. *CN*, III, 3295.

63. *Friend (CC)*, I, 440n.

64. *BL*, I, 86.

65. *BL*, I, 202; cf. II, 54–55.

66. *BL*, I, 193, 202.

67. *BL*, I, 86.

68. *BL*, I, 180; II, 124, 12.

69. *Shakespearean Criticism*, II, 239.

70. *BL*, I, 100.

71. *BL*, I, 174. See also Schelling, *SW*, III, 338–342.

72. *BL*, I, 167.

73. *CN*, I, 1619; cf. *AP*, p. 39.

74. *CN*, II, 2546.

75. Keats, *Letters*, II, 209.

76. Coleridge, "On Poesy or Art," *BL*, II, 253, 262.

77. *CN*, III, 3286.

78. *Shakespearean Criticism*, II, 58; I, 42.

79. "On Poesy," *BL*, II, 258.

80. *BL*, II, 19; cf. *CN*, II, 2784; *BL*, I, 20.

81. *CN*, II, 2086; cf. *CL*, II, 810.

82. *CN*, III, 3246; "On Poesy," *BL*, II, 262.

83. *CN*, II, 2274; cf. *AP*, p. 87.

84. *BL*, II, 58–59; I, 5; *Wallenstein*, pt. 2, II.iv, ll. 123–131.

85. *BL*, II, 13.

86. *BL*, II, 159, 13.

87. *BL*, II, 226, 95, 88.

88. *Shakespearean Criticism*, II, 325; *Letters*, III, 360.

89. *BL*, II, 13, 124.

90. *TT*, p. 93.

91. *BL*, II, 49–54.

92. *BL*, II, 103.

93. *Shakespearean Criticism*, II, 138.

94. *CN*, II, 2112.

95. *Shakespearean Criticism*, II, 174.

96. *CN*, II, 2112.

97. *BL*, I, 30–31n.

98. *Shakespearean Criticism*, I, 25.

99. *Friend (CC)*, I, 455; cf. pp. 456, 514.

100. *BL*, II, 186–191.

101. *Shakespearean Criticism*, I, 137.

102. *Coleridge on the Seventeenth Century*, ed. Roberta Florence Brinkley (1955), p. 639; cf. *Miscellaneous Criticism*, pp. 56–57.

103. *BL*, II, 124.
104. *Shakespearean Criticism*, I, 131–132, 5.
105. *BL*, II, 20.
106. *CN*, III, 3247.
107. *BL*, II, 20; *AP*, p. 87; *CN*, III, 3247.
108. "Principles of Genial Criticism" in *BL*, II, 221; also *BL*, II, 104.
109. "Principles" in *BL*, II, 242, 232, 239.
110. "On Poesy" in *BL*, II, 256.
111. "Principles" in *BL*, II, 243; *BL*, II, 65.
112. "On Poesy" in *BL*, II, 259, 257.
113. "On Poesy" in *BL*, 258; *BL*, II, 187, "Principles" in *BL*, II, 235; "On Poesy" in *BL*, II, 257–259, "Principles" in *BL*, II, 243; *Friend* (*CC*), I, 512, 514–515, 520.
114. "On Poesy" in *BL*, II, 257.
115. "On Poesy" in *BL*, II, 253; *BL*, I, 135, 80.
116. *TT*, p. 136.
117. *CN*, II, 2596.
118. *BL*, II, 210.
119. *Letters*, I, no. 65.
120. *BL*, I, 99; *AR*, p. 27.
121. *Friend* (*CC*), I, 524; *Letters*, II, no. 510.
122. *CN*, I, 182.
123. *BL*, I, 10.
124. *BL*, I, 167, 172–173, 99; *Friend* (*CC*), I, 463.
125. *Friend* (*CC*), I, 500, 516; *AR*, p. 27.
126. *AP*, p. 120; *Friend* (*CC*), I, 522–523; *PL*, pp. 333–334.
127. *AR*, p. 184.
128. *BL*, II, 212; cf. I, 173.
129. *AR*, pp. 87, 184.
130. *BL*, I, 98.
131. *CN*, III, 4449.
132. *Letters*, IV, nos. 1033, 1150, 1145.
133. *Letters*, IV, no. 1145.
134. *Friend* (*CC*), I, 522n.
135. *AR*, p. 72; cf. *AP*, p. 62.
136. *Friend* (*CC*), I, 514; *AR*, pp. 72, 226–227; *CN*, III, 3325.
137. *AR*, p. 72.
138. *CN*, III, 3649.
139. *AR*, p. 171n; *SM* (*CC*), p. 29.
140. *Shakespearean Criticism*, II, 147.
141. Brinkley, p. 380.
142. *CN*, III, 4427.
143. *CN*, III, 4427.
144. *BL*, II, 218; *Friend* (*CC*), I, 515n.
145. Brinkley, p. 380.
146. *BL*, I, 200; "Principles" in *BL*, II, 230; see also *SM* (*CC*), p. 114n; *Friend* (*CC*), I, 515n; *AR*, p. 25n.
147. *PL*, p. 257.
148. Bate, *Keats*, p. 695.

# INDEX

Italicized page references indicate primary discussion.